James Turner

MW01221704

MySQL and JSP Web Applications

SAMS

201 West 103rd Street, Indianapolis, Indiana 46290

MySQL and JSP Web Applications

International Standard Book Number: 0-672-32309-5

Library of Congress Catalog Card Number: 2001094773

Printed in the United States of America

First Printing: March 2002

05   04   03   02   4   3   2   1

Trademarks

All terms mentioned in this book that are known to be trademarks or service marks have been appropriately capitalized. Sams Publishing cannot attest to the accuracy of this information. Use of a term in this book should not be regarded as affecting the validity of any trademark or service mark.

Warning and Disclaimer

Every effort has been made to make this book as complete and as accurate as possible, but no warranty or fitness is implied. The information provided is on an "as is" basis. The authors and the publisher shall have neither liability nor responsibility to any person or entity with respect to any loss or damages arising from the information contained in this book.

Executive Editor
Michael Stephens

Development Editor
Christy A. Franklin

Managing Editor
Matt Purcell

Project Editor
Natalie Harris

Copy Editor
Krista Hansing

Indexer
Sandra Henselmeier

Proofreader
Andrea Dugan

Technical Editor
Ed Peters

Team Coordinator
Pamalee Nelson

Interior Designer
Dan Armstrong

Cover Designer
Alan Clements

Production
Brad Lenser

Contents at a Glance

Table of Contents

About the Authors

James Turner is the manager of Black Bear Software, LLC. He has more than 22 years of experience in the computer field and has worked for organizations that include MIT, Xerox, Solbourne Computer, BBN Planet, and Interleaf. He has spent the last seven years managing and implementing e-commerce Web sites for companies including CVS, The Christian Science Monitor, and Woolworths UK.

Mr. Turner is also a well-published freelance journalist and technology writer who has written for publications including *The Christian Science Monitor*, *WIRED*, and *Web Developers Journal*. He lives in Derry, New Hampshire, in a 200-year-old colonial farmhouse along with his wife and son.

Dedication

To my wife, Bonnie, and son, Daniel—you get Daddy back now.

Acknowledgments

Working with software that's still in beta, as Tomcat 4 was when the writing of this book began, can be a challenge. Luckily, I had the dedicated Tomcat development community to support me when things went wrong. I'd especially like to thank Craig McClanahan of Sun, who went out of his way to answer my questions and who also reviewed information for the Struts chapter. He was gracious, even when he disagreed with my take on a topic.

I'd also like to thank Kevin Bedell and Srinivas Vanga, who acted as sanity checkers when I found myself wading into areas that were unfamiliar. And a general nod to all the Viridien alumni who worked with me on MarketMax, Woolworths, SuperDrug, and CVS. Those projects were the crucible in which my JSP knowledge was forged. See, guys, 80-hour weeks can pay off in the end!

Tell Us What You Think!

As the reader of this book, *you* are our most important critic and commentator. We value your opinion and want to know what we're doing right, what we could do better, what areas you'd like to see us publish in, and any other words of wisdom you're willing to pass our way.

As an Executive Editor for Sams Publishing, I welcome your comments. You can fax, e-mail, or write me directly to let me know what you did or didn't like about this book—as well as what we can do to make our books stronger.

Please note that I cannot help you with technical problems related to the topic of this book, and that due to the high volume of mail I receive, I might not be able to reply to every message.

When you write, please be sure to include this book's title and author, as well as your name and phone or fax number. I will carefully review your comments and share them with the author and editors who worked on the book.

Fax: 317-581-4770

E-mail: feedback@samspublishing.com

Mail: Michael Stephens
          Executive Editor
          Sams Publishing
          201 West 103rd Street
          Indianapolis, IN 46290 USA

An Introduction to Developing E-Commerce Applications with JSP

Who Are You and Why Are You Reading This Book?

There are at least three good reasons you could be holding this book in your hands right now:

- You are a Java programmer who has worked largely on front-end systems, such as browser-based applets, and you would like to learn how to implement the delicate internal clockwork that makes a modern e-commerce site work.

- You are an established e-commerce developer moving from tools such as ASP and CGI programming into a JSP environment and looking for a complete walkthrough of a basic implementation.

- You are a student or entry-level programmer looking for a good introduction to object-oriented design.

It's my fond hope that no matter which of these three (or perhaps more) motivations compelled you to pick up this book, you'll put it down knowing all of them. If I've done my job well, you should walk away a proficient JSP e-commerce developer who uses object-oriented design methodologies.

This book grew out of my frustration as a college instructor teaching a course in designing e-commerce Web sites. Specifically, I found that although there were foot-thick books on JSP, SQL, and OO design, there really wasn't a text that tied them all together and led the reader through the entire design process to a finished product.

This book is not for an absolute newcomer to software development, however. I'm going to assume that you've already picked up a few specific skills, and you're going to get lost pretty quickly without them:

- You have a moderate proficiency in Java.

- You've had some exposure to SQL, although we'll be using fairly simple syntax and the JDBC interface is explained in some depth.

- You're comfortable with basic HTML design, including forms, and you understand, at a simple level, how a Web page is delivered to a browser.

If you have these in your utility belt, you should be all set to party. So, with that brief introduction out of the way, it's time to move on.

So What Is JSP All About?

If you meet the requirements mentioned, you should already have a pretty good idea what the answer to this question is. JSP is all about doing highly object-oriented Web sites that can leverage all the best practices of modern software engineering. These practices include things such as SQL databases and UML-based design.

This isn't to say that JSP is a cure-all and that using it will automatically make your Web site a paragon of engineering art. It's just as possible to design bad Web sites in JSP as with any other technology. That's why, as you go through the text, you will see how to incorporate the best practices and how to avoid the pitfalls of convenience when projects get stressful.

JSP itself is an evolutionary step along the path that started with the first static Web servers, moved through CGI-enabled servers, and finally the first generation of script-enabled servers. JSP is less a Web server with a Java component than it is a Java engine that understands the Web.

JSP grew out of Java servlets. Servlets allow the developer to handle the incoming Web requests using a Java program that has access to all the normal information that a Common Gateway Interface (CGI) program would. In addition, the servlet has access to session-persistent objects. These are Java objects that are associated with a specific user session and can be used to store state between requests.

Servlet programming was a major step forward in allowing developers to write well-structured modular Web applications using an object-oriented language. It also solved the problem of state persistence, allowing more information to reside on the server during a transaction and less to have to pass back and forth between the user and the server.

Servlets still suffered from one major problem. Because they eventually need to spit out HTML, the HTML coding had to be embedded in the servlet code. This led to code fragments like the one shown here:

```
// Output the HTML Header
Out.println("<HTML>\n<HEAD>\n<TITLE>Thank you for Registering</TITLE></HEAD>\n");
Out.println("<IMG SRC=\"thanks.jpg\" WIDTH=200 HEIGHT=100 ALIGN=\"LEFT\">");
```

This kind of embedding gets very old very fast when you have to code a lot of pages. In addition, having to escape all of the quotation marks can lead to a lot of confusing and hard-to-find errors if you leave out a backslash.

Eventually, a still-better idea emerged. Suppose that you could combine the best of static HTML pages and with the interactive capabilities of servlets. The result was JavaServer Pages (on the Microsoft side, the result was Active Server Pages). As Figure I.1 shows, JSP is a complicated beast. In the next chapter, you'll walk through this flow in detail, but for the moment, here are the major steps:

1. A request comes in from a browser using the normal HTTP request format.

2. The Web server hands off the request to JSP. JSP looks at the filename and finds the appropriate JSP file.

3. The .jsp file is converted into a .java file, containing Java code that will create a class whose name is derived from the .jsp filename.

4. JSP then compiles the .java file using javac to produce a .class file. Note that the two previous steps are skipped if a .class file already exists and is newer than the .jsp file.

5. An instance of the newly created class is instantiated and sent the _jspService message.

6. The new instance looks to see if there is already an instance of the stuff.User object called user existing in the session object space for the currently connected user. If not, one is instantiated.

7. As part of servicing stuff.jsp, the user instance is called with the getUserName() method.

8. If the JSP processing requires access to information in a database, it uses JDBC to make the connection and handle the SQL requests.

That is the way that JSP handles requests.

As you can see, a tremendous amount of power is available in the JSP world. Developers are free to write Web pages that look mostly like HTML, except where callouts to Java are required. But, at the same time, they are free to develop fully fleshed-out object-oriented applications using all the features that Java can bring to bear. They also get all the benefits of servlets, including session persistence.

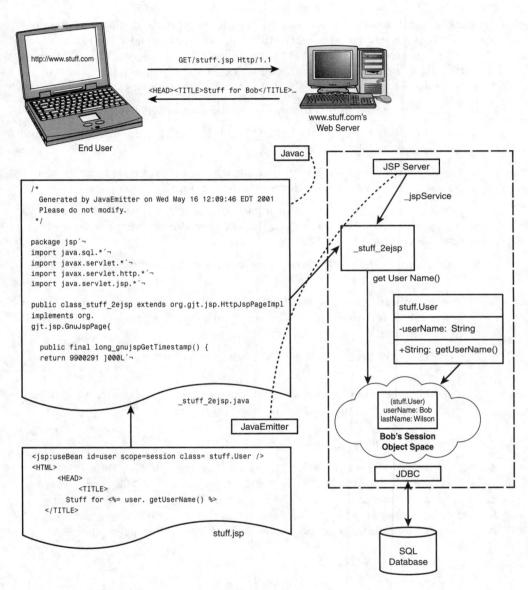

```
/*
   Generated by JavaEmitter on Wed May 16 12:09:46 EDT 2001
   Please do not modify.
*/

package jsp´¬
import java.sql.*´¬
import javax.servlet.*´¬
import javax.servlet.http.*´¬
import java.servlet.jsp.*´¬

public class_stuff_2ejsp extends org.gjt.jsp.HttpJspPageImpl
implements org.
gjt.jsp.GnuJspPage{

   public final long_gnujspGetTimestamp() {
   return 9900291 ]000L´¬
```

```
<jsp:useBean id=user scope=session class= stuff.User />
<HTML>
     <HEAD>
          <TITLE>
       Stuff for <%= user. getUserName() %>
     </TITLE>
```

FIGURE I.1   Looking at the JSP processing flow.

HOW IS JSP DIFFERENT FROM CGI?

Several differences exist, some superficial and some more important, between how CGI and JSP look at the world.

CGI is a transient beast. Every transaction with the user is a new day, started fresh with a blank slate. If you want to carry state forward from one click to the next, it needs to be carried along with the page, either as embedded hidden form tags, as some kind of a cookie placed in the query portion of the URL (leading to great URLs such as http://www.mysite.com/view.cgi?uid=234235435—not a real Web site), or as a session cookie delivered by the browser. And, any state that you do maintain resides externally, in either files or database tables, and must be reloaded on each request.

CGI also makes you turn the page inside out, putting your HTML inside print statements in whatever language you choose to write.

By comparison, JSP automatically carries along whatever state you want to preserve from request to request without any effort on your part. It lets you, as the developer, concentrate on business logic rather than figuring out the context of a request. It also lets you persist your state in object-oriented form, and it even lets two user sessions share objects between them.

The JSP page looks like HTML with some additional Java stuck in where programmatic output is needed, and it can be maintained by HTML designers, provided that they exercise some basic caution. It also allows the business logic to be separated from the presentation logic, which allows you to place the business rules in a well-defined set of classes away from the Web pages themselves.

An Overview of JSP Platforms

For a developer looking to deploy on JSP architecture, an abundance of platforms are available today, ranging from the cheap and simple to the outrageously expensive and complex. Depending on which platform you choose, different options and capabilities will be put in your tool belt to deploy your site. With that in mind, let's look at some of the current choices and what they bring to the table.

Tomcat

Tomcat is part of the Apache Software Foundation's Jakarta project, which also includes the Ant build tool, the Log4J logging tool, and the Struts application framework. It is an open-source initiative along the lines of Linux, allowing anyone to contribute to the final product if they want.

Tomcat is a no-frills "pure" implementation of the JSP and Java Servlet standards. Sites designed under Tomcat should work with no need to tweak them under any JSP-compliant server.

Just because it's free, don't discount it as some flimsy piece of software. Tomcat has had the benefit of many, many developers poring over it, and much as with other open-source projects, this has resulted in a very robust and efficient product.

Tomcat also has the advantage of running on just about anything with a modern Java development kit and a network connection, from low-end Windows boxes to multiprocessor Solaris servers. This holds to the Java "write once" philosophy. This allows you to scale your platform as the demand grows.

However, Tomcat falls short in the more advanced features needed by high-end Web sites, such as seamless failover. For that, you need to either write your own platform or go with one of the commercial (and much more expensive) platforms.

ATG Dynamo

Dynamo from Art Technology Group is part of a soup-to-nuts solution platform that also includes Dynamo Personalization Server and Dynamo Commerce Server. The first thing to know is that Dynamo is not cheap; it starts in the five figures and gets worse from there.

The main thing that Dynamo brings to the table is a lot of prefinished work if you want to implement certain kinds of e-commerce applications, especially ones involving shopping carts and member personalization. Even so, they are only templates; you'll still need to do extensive customization and extension to get them to work the way you want for your specific requirements.

Dynamo also has its own scripting language, which looks much like HTML, to use as an adjunct to JSP. The theory seems to be that it will make the people who work on the Web pages, but who are not developers, feel more comfortable if they don't see a lot of Java sprinkled in the middle of the HTML.

In reality, however, the tagging syntax is overly verbose and can end up making you use 20 lines to say what you could in 4 or 5 of pure JSP. I worked on one project in which we tried as hard as we could to do everything purely using the scripting language, at the customer's request, and we almost went insane from the effort.

iPlanet

iPlanet is the answer to the question, "What happens when you mate Netscape, Sun, and AOL?" In many ways, iPlanet is Tomcat on steroids. Sun lumps a lot of products, including an LDAP server, messaging server, and calendar server, under the iPlanet heading. However, we're going to talk about just the application server in this context.

iPlanet uses Sun's Java 2 Platform, Enterprise Edition (J2EE), as a base for JSP/EJB–based server. It is designed to be highly scalable, it offers support for high-reliability operations, and it can be integrated with many legacy applications through connectors.

For example, iPlanet can be configured easily to use IBM MQSeries messaging services or to talk to an SAP system. When you are deploying into a large existing customer with lots of big iron, these kinds of integration capabilities can be crucial timesavers.

At its heart, it's still a JSP server, though. And if you want to layer a lot of separate pieces onto Tomcat, you could make it look a lot like iPlanet, except perhaps for the intangible claims of Sun that it runs really fast and doesn't crash.

WebSphere

It wouldn't be a party unless IBM was invited, right? As part of the company's 180° turnaround from proprietary software to open source, IBM has come out with its own JSP server.

WebSphere is available in several editions, which span the range from a Tomcat-like JSP server to a full blown "do-everything" product, like iPlanet.

Again, like iPlanet, the major cards that IBM brings to the table are claims of high reliability and throughput, and easy integration with legacy applications—and it'll even shine your shoes.

WebLogic

Like IPlanet and WebSphere, WebLogic is a JSP platform layered with integration to back-end legacy systems, personalization, a portal server, and so on.

WebLogic claims that its application server is number 1 in the market, and it certainly seems to have a large and active customer base.

The choice between the big four commercial platforms will largely center on the feature set that you need and an evaluation of which platform best meets those needs.

If you're considering one of these platforms (especially iPlanet or WebSphere), it's probably for something really big and really complicated. They are 50-pound sledge hammers meant to address complex applications in large organizations. Thankfully, we won't be dealing with anything that massive in this book, so we will let them lie.

Why Do We Need Databases?

Well, one reason is so that Larry Ellison of Oracle can afford to keep himself on Prozac when he thinks about Bill Gates. A more serious answer is the same reason that drove man to first press a stick against a piece of wet mud: because it's good to write things down.

Web servers are marvelous creatures, but they're a bit like idiot savants. Ask them to serve a Web page or run a piece of Java, and they perform like a champ. But start asking them to remember what they did five minutes ago, and they develop amnesia faster than a character in a soap opera.

The first and most important reason that you use databases is that there's a lot in an e-commerce transaction that you need to remember and track:

- A user's name, address, credit card, and other information previously entered on a registration page
- What the user might have put into a shopping cart and left from a previous transaction
- What items are in stock, along with their price, description, and so on
- Orders that need to be fulfilled, orders that have been shipped, and items that have been backordered

Now, you could store all this information in a flat file on the server's hard disk, but there are other important properties that you want to have for this data:

- You want to be able to back out a transaction if part of it fails.
- You want to be able to locate the data somewhere more secure than the Web server, which could be in a DMZ or outside the firewall altogether.
- You want to be able to access data such as user data or products quickly, even if there are thousands or millions of them.

When you add these items to the shopping list, only a relational database will really do the job effectively.

Oracle

There's no question that Oracle is the heavyweight of the database business. Oracle is the dominant player, and for good reason. It offers a powerful, flexible, and reliable engine that is powering a good-sized piece of corporate America.

Unfortunately, Oracle's products are also rather expensive. Oracle licenses fall under the "if you have to ask, you can't afford it" category. But if you need it, you need it, regardless of the price.

Everyone Else

It might seem a bit flippant to stick Sybase, Ingres, IBM, and Microsoft into one lump. But the reality is, if you're not talking about Oracle, you're basically in the also-rans of market share. Microsoft has made a valiant effort to convince businesses that SQL Server is a viable alternative to Oracle, but it's an uphill battle and one that Microsoft doesn't seem to be winning.

To some extent, it doesn't really matter which database you use, and because the customer might already be using one, it's not a matter that you might have much control over. The important thing is, because all of the databases allow you to get to them via the Java Database Connectivity library (JDBC), as long as you don't write your SQL using proprietary syntax, you can move from one to another with ease.

MySQL

Once again, along came the little guys to save the day. Many sites don't need the battleship strength (and price tag) of Oracle. MySQL is an open-source SQL database available for anyone to use, with many (although not all) of the features of its big brothers, such as Oracle.

MySQL is available for just about any computer that has decent power—it is fairly lightweight on the processor and easy to install (10 minutes, as opposed to multiple hours for Oracle).

So, perhaps you are wondering, what's the catch? What are you not getting in MySQL that makes people turn to Oracle? Well, MySQL is a neat little package, but it is missing some things that would be nice to have in a perfect world.

A major feature that MySQL does not offer is database consistency checking. You can use foreign key tags in your schema, but MySQL cheerfully ignores them. A lot of DBAs I know would consider this a very bad thing.

A foreign key constraint prevents you from creating inconsistent data. For example, let's suppose that you had a scheme that looked like this:

```
CREATE TABLE USER (
      USERID INTEGER,
      FIRST_NAME    VARCHAR(80),
      LAST_NAME     VARCHAR(80));

CREATE TABLE PURCHASE (
      USERID FOREIGN KEY USER(USERID),
      ITEM INTEGER,
      QUANTITY INTEGER);
```

In a database such as Oracle's, if you created an entry in the PURCHASE table with a user ID of 3, there would have to already be a user ID of 3 in the USER table or an error would occur. Similarly, you couldn't delete user 3 from USER if it was referenced in PURCHASE.

The MySQL folks make a pretty impassioned argument in their documentation that depending on foreign keys for data integrity is a bad idea anyway, but convincing your DBA of this philosophy is likely to degrade into a religious debate.

In addition, some other features are missing, such as subselects and select into. But probably the other major piece that you will miss is the rollback/commit functionality. MySQL does implement rollback and commit for certain types of tables, but not all of them. Again, the MySQL folks offer their own spin on why this is okay, but being able to roll back transactions is (in my opinion) important enough to make sure that you have it available.

Rollback allows you to set a savepoint on the database before starting to do a series of transactions with it, and be able to either roll back to the original state or commit the changes at the end. For example, when recording a purchase, you need to record a debit against the user's account and enter a record into the shipping table so that you'll know later to ship the item. Let's say that the second part fails. You wouldn't want to charge the user but not ship the item. Thus, you'd want to roll back to the state before the transaction began.

So, MySQL isn't a full-blown production database—at least, not yet. It's still good enough for probably 90% of the e-commerce sites in the world, however. And version 4.0, which is in alpha as of this writing, addresses a number of these concerns, including row-level locking and transaction control.

Putting Tomcat and MySQL Together

Combining Tomcat and MySQL provides a powerful, reliable, and free platform that you can use to learn, develop, and deploy JSP applications. And, best of all, the code that you develop using this platform will run nicely using iPlanet and Oracle or WebSphere and SQL Server.

As a learning tool the two together are almost "reference implementations" of their respective protocols (JSP and SQL). As a result, you won't pick up any nasty vendor-proprietary bad habits while you're getting up to speed.

In addition, you can enjoy the knowledge that you are supporting the open-source software movement. Open-source software is code that is made freely available under one of several public licenses, frequently the GNU General Public License (GPL).

FACTS AND FICTION ABOUT THE GPL

The GNU General Public License is probably one of the most misunderstood documents in existence (with the exception of the "fan interference law" in baseball.) The basics break down to this:

1. If you place a piece of software under the GPL, anyone is free to make a copy of it in either source or executable form and give it to anyone else.

2. If you take a piece of software under the GPL and use it as a part of your product, you can't charge for that product beyond duplication costs.

Many people interpret this to mean that they can't use GPL software for commercial purposes. Nothing is farther from the truth. What you can't do is charge specifically for parts of your product that are partly or largely derived from GPL products.

You are free to use GPL code in the development of a Web site because you're not selling the site itself to a third party as a product. (Consulting companies fall into a weird quasi-space, but no one has gone after them for using GPL software to date.)

Why is it good to support this movement? There are two sides to this answer: one technical and one political. Technically, it's a good thing because open-source software tends to encourage the development of open standards such as JSP and JDBC, allowing you to choose your tools from among a larger group rather than being locked into one vendor's proprietary solution.

It's a positive thing politically because it keeps the large companies honest. WebLogic and iPlanet have to stay competitive and responsive because they know that there's a free solution out there if they aren't. And when you use open-source software, you are sending a message that your overriding concerns are features and reliability, not having a large company to sue if something goes wrong.

A Roadmap to E-Commerce Development

E-commerce developers have never had a larger suite of tools to use in deploying their magnum opuses than they do now. Many of us can remember our first Web site that had any kind of a back end, strung together with some C code or maybe a lot of Perl. Design consisted of flailing around until you ended up with something that you hoped resembled what the customer wanted. And you considered yourself lucky if the site did anything more than generate 404 and 501 error pages.

Today, of course, we have an entire arsenal of tools to assist us in putting together an impressive Web site. There are HTML development tools such as FrontPage, HotMetal, and Dreamweaver. Applications developers use Java in combination with integrated development tools (IDEs) such as TogetherJ. Data is stored in the latest versions of relational databases, which have been extended to support the Web. Believe me, you've never had it so good.

But with new toys come new challenges. More than ever, you need to start with a good understanding of the problem you're trying to solve, and a good process to ensure successful execution. In a while, we'll take a look at some of these best practices and how you'll be using them to build a working e-commerce Web site.

In case you're getting the idea that I'm some kind of standards addict, let me correct the impression right now. I have little patience for people who believe that the value of a project is equal to the weight of its documentation. In the fast-paced e-commerce world, you don't always have time to deforest a subcontinent before you begin actual work. At the same time, I've seen firsthand the perils of going off half-cocked before you have a thorough understanding of the problem.

The procedures that I recommend in this book are all designed around capturing and understanding the customer's needs. There is a minimum of paperwork designed solely to protect your job, and there's nothing that I haven't found essential through painful experience. For that reason, bypassing them is not recommended. You might be under intense pressure to start coding this instant, but if you start down a road before you know where you want to end up, you're likely to find yourself up the creek without a paddle (how's that for a contorted analogy?)

Before you can even begin designing, you need to understand what you're trying to do. This is the wonderful world of requirements gathering, and it will be spelled out in detail in Chapter 4, "The Sample Application Functional Requirements Document." Requirements gathering is the unglamorous paperwork-laden part of this business, but it is the single most important activity that you will undertake. The most wonderful Web site in the world won't earn you that holiday bonus if it doesn't do what your customer (internal or external) wants it to do.

More importantly, failure to comprehensively document the requirements early leads to two curses of this business: "feature creep" and last-minute redesign. Both will cause you to be rewriting your code late in the process when time is tight and tempers are frazzled. Doing it right the first time will save your sanity and your profit margins.

As part of this process, it can be very useful to develop a nonfunctional set of HTML pages as a mockup of the user's view of the site. One term for these pages I've heard used frequently is *wireframes*. They serve three purposes. First, they provide visual feedback to your customer so that you're both talking about the same thing. Second, they can uncover problems with site navigation and flow very early, when there's still ample time to fix it. Third, they can serve as templates for your JSP pages later in development.

THE FRONT END AND THE BACK END

Another pair of terms that you'll see a lot in this book is the front end and the back end. They form the division between what the user sees and the magic that goes on behind the scenes.

The front end consists of the presentation given to the user. Think of it as everything that the user can see and touch. In this environment, the JSP pages represent it.

The back end is all the grungy processing that occurs when the user makes a request (recording things in the database, sending email confirmations, and so on). It also includes integrations with other subsystems, such as an inventory system.

This book is almost entirely concerned with the back end and the interface between the front end and the back end. If you're looking for a tutorial on HTML design, this isn't the book for you.

At the end of the book, we'll look at the Struts development framework, which implements a particular type of front end/back end division called Model-View-Controller (MVC), and a more extreme division called Enterprise Java Beans (EJB).

The output of the requirements-gathering process is the functional requirements document (FRD). This is a contract between you and your customer: You're committing to a body of work, and your customer is committing to be satisfied with the results if they conform to the FRD. It is usually a detailed walkthrough of the entire site, describing what a visitor to the site can do at each stage and what must occur as a result of a user action. In addition, it must document things such as input validation (did the user enter the data right?) and any back-end processing that must occur.

The less specific you are in the FRD, the more "wiggle room" you've left the customer come development time. "You didn't say that the user couldn't enter the quantity in hexadecimal," says the customer, and you've suddenly bought yourself another man-day to add the feature. Again, it's a silly example, but bad things do happen if you don't resolve them early.

After you have gathered the requirements and turned them into some kind of FRD, you need to study the task and determine the underlying object models that you will be using for the project. Using an object-oriented language such as Java and relational databases such as MySQL forces you to think about problems in terms of objects first. You need to go through and identify your candidates using tools such as entity relationship diagrams (ERDs) and use cases.

You might have been exposed to Java classes and objects if you've written Java applets, perhaps using Swing. However, this only scratches the surface of what object-oriented programming is all about. A typical browser applet has one main class that does all the work and makes calls out to a few GUI classes. A fully developed e-commerce design can have dozens of classes, modeling everything from the customer to the products to a shopping cart, as you will soon see.

Next, you will get your underlying infrastructure in place. This means installing software that you'll need for the project, creating your database schema, and making sure that all the technology pieces talk to each other. Setting up your development platform can be one of the most frustrating experiences in the entire project. For example, I'm currently working on a project that requires six hours to set up the platform correctly. You'll be happy to hear that the setup and integration for the projects in this book will be easy. Only after you have completed all this will you be ready to start actually producing code.

The Next 17 Chapters

Okay, enough philosophy and political science. If you feel like you've been climbing up the roller coaster and are getting impatient for that first plunge, don't worry because the ground's about to fall out from under you.

In the next three chapters, we're going to provide a review of JSP and JDBC for those of you who have seen it, and a basic introduction for those who haven't. Then we're going to dive right in to our sample application and begin to apply the tools to a real-life problem.

First you will get your platform in place. Then you'll run a few tests to make sure that it works, and you'll get familiar with the building blocks that you'll be using. The building blocks are JSP, JDBC, and MySQL.

Next, you will go over the sample application using object-oriented design methodologies, including use cases and process flow diagrams. This ensures that by the time you actually get to the coding, you should already understand in your head what the site is supposed to look like.

Then you'll be ready to start coding. This book tends to lean toward a step-wise approach, getting one subsystem working and tested before moving forward to the next. This has the advantage of isolating problems to the most recently added code, and it also builds confidence by letting you see pieces of the site at work before the entire site is done.

You'll move through the site, starting with user login and registration and then moving to product display, purchase, shopping cart display, shipping and payment information capture, and finally checkout, fulfillment, and order history. Each section will be used to highlight different techniques and problem areas to watch out for. Most of these are culled from actual problems encountered during the development of real sites.

Even well-designed projects have a degree of trial and error, backtracking, and rethinking. This book attempts to capture as closely as possible the actual development process that you will go through while hammering out the sample application. When you've walked through the entire process, you should be well prepared to tackle your own JSP application, even if it's not a shopping-cart site.

PART I

JSP and JDBC

IN THIS PART

CHAPTER 1

A JSP/JDBC Review

If you already are a JSP guru, consider this chapter a quick refresher. If you are new to JSP, this should provide enough of a grounding to get you through the remainder of the book.

How Does JSP Work

To begin, let's look at the world's simplest JSP page, our version of the infamous "Hello World" program (see Listing 1.1).

LISTING 1.1   HelloWorld.jsp

```
<HTML>
 <HEAD><TITLE>Hello World!</TITLE></HEAD>
 <BODY>Hello World!</BODY>
</HTML>
```

Okay, I can hear the screams of protest already. "That isn't JSP—that's plain old HTML. What are you trying to pull? I want my money back!"

It might look like innocent HTML, and if you put it into a .html file on a Web server, it would be delivered as straight HTML. But look what happens to this innocent little snippet in Listing 1.2 if you put it into a .jsp file instead.

LISTING 1.2   HelloWorld as Java

```
package org.apache.jsp;

import javax.servlet.*;
import javax.servlet.http.*;
import javax.servlet.jsp.*;
import javax.servlet.jsp.tagext.*;
import org.apache.jasper.runtime.*;
```

LISTING 1.2   continued

```
public class _0002fjsp_0002fhello_0005fworld_jsp extends HttpJspBase {


    static {
    }
    public _0002fjsp_0002fhello_0005fworld_jsp( ) {
    }

    private static boolean _jspx_inited = false;

    public final void _jspx_init() throws org.apache.jasper.runtime.JspException {
    }

    public void _jspService(HttpServletRequest request, HttpServletResponse
response)
        throws java.io.IOException, ServletException {

        JspFactory _jspxFactory = null;
        PageContext pageContext = null;
        HttpSession session = null;
        ServletContext application = null;
        ServletConfig config = null;
        JspWriter out = null;
        Object page = this;
        String _value = null;
        try {

            if (_jspx_inited == false) {
                synchronized (this) {
                    if (_jspx_inited == false) {
                        _jspx_init();
                        _jspx_inited = true;
                    }
                }
            }
            _jspxFactory = JspFactory.getDefaultFactory();
            response.setContentType("text/html;charset=ISO-8859-1");
            pageContext = _jspxFactory.getPageContext(this, request, response,
                    "", true, 8192, true);

            application = pageContext.getServletContext();
            config = pageContext.getServletConfig();
            session = pageContext.getSession();
```

LISTING 1.2   continued

```
            out = pageContext.getOut();

            // HTML // begin [file="/jsp/hello_world.jsp";from=(0,0);to=(4,0)]
                out.write("<HTML>\r\n <HEAD><TITLE>Hello World!</TITLE></HEAD>\r\n
<BODY>Hello World!</BODY>\r\n</HTML>\r\n");

            // end

        } catch (Throwable t) {
            if (out != null && out.getBufferSize() != 0)
                out.clearBuffer();
            if (pageContext != null) pageContext.handlePageException(t);
        } finally {
            if (_jspxFactory != null) _jspxFactory.releasePageContext(pageContext);
        }
    }
}
```

Our simple HTML has been turned into Java code! However, if you look carefully, you'll see this line:

```
out.write("<HTML>\r\n <HEAD><TITLE>Hello World!</TITLE></HEAD>\r\n <BODY>Hello
➥World!</BODY>\r\n</HTML>\r\n");
```

The HTML is still living happily, embedded as a `write` statement inside the Java.

This example is important because it demonstrates the most important thing to remember about JSP. Even though you might think at the time that you're writing HTML with Java code embedded, you're really always writing Java code with HTML embedded.

Of course, if you used JSP only to output static HTML content, it would be a huge waste of resources and performance. JSP is great because programmatic functionality can be embedded into HTML. For example, let's look at a very simple JSP page in Listing 1.3.

LISTING 1.3   5loop.jsp

```
<HTML>
 <HEAD><TITLE>Hello World!</TITLE></HEAD>
 <BODY>
 <%
   int i = 0;
   while (i++ < 5) {
 %>
```

LISTING 1.3   continued

```
Hello World! Loop #
<% out.print(i); %>
<br>
<% } %>

</BODY>
</HTML>
```

We've suddenly corrupted the pure HTML file by placing Java code in the middle. The Java is delimited by the <% and %> characters. Now turn your thinking around 180°. We don't have an HTML file with a little Java embedded in it; we have a Java source with some HTML in it. Remember that all HTML in the source is going to turn into out.print statements in the intermediate .java file. So, when Java is placed in a JSP file, it is really escaping into the "real" world and out of the artificial HTML world. Just this once, we're going to look at a portion of the .java file in Listing 1.4 (leaving out most of the boilerplate from the "Hello World" example).

LISTING 1.4   A Java Fragment of JSP Code

```
        // HTML // begin [file="/jsp/5loop.jsp";from=(0,0);to=(3,1)]
            out.write("<HTML>\r\n <HEAD><TITLE>Hello World!</TITLE></HEAD>\r\n
<BODY>\r\n ");

        // end
        // begin [file="/jsp/5loop.jsp";from=(3,3);to=(6,1)]

                int i = 0;
                while (i++ < 5) {

        // end
        // HTML // begin [file="/jsp/5loop.jsp";from=(6,3);to=(8,2)]
            out.write(" \r\n  Hello World! Loop #\r\n  ");

        // end
        // begin [file="/jsp/5loop.jsp";from=(8,4);to=(8,19)]
              out.print(i);
        // end
        // HTML // begin [file="/jsp/5loop.jsp";from=(8,21);to=(10,1)]
            out.write("\r\n  <br>\r\n ");

        // end
        // begin [file="/jsp/5loop.jsp";from=(10,3);to=(10,6)]
                }
```

LISTING 1.4   continued

```
// end
// HTML // begin [file="/jsp/5loop.jsp";from=(10,8);to=(14,0)]
    out.write("\r\n\r\n</BODY>\r\n</HTML>\r\n");
```

As you can see, the Java code from the JSP file is included verbatim, while the HTML is put inside print statements. Although it might look strange to see HTML code wrapped inside a Java while loop in the .jsp file, it makes perfect sense when you see the resulting output file.

Running Tomcat

Before you can start playing with Tomcat for real, you'll need to set it up. Refer to Appendix A, "Getting and Installing JDK and Tomcat," for the appropriate walk-through for your operating system and setup for Tomcat.

Under Linux, you won't see much because the process is running in the background. Under Windows, you'll see the startup window shown in Figure 1.1.

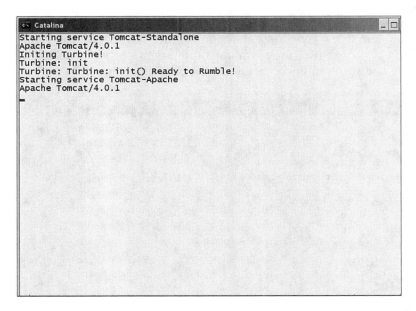

FIGURE 1.1   The Tomcat startup window.

By default, Tomcat listens on port 8080, so if you open up a browser and cruise to http://localhost:8080, you'll see the Tomcat splash page (shown in Figure 1.2).

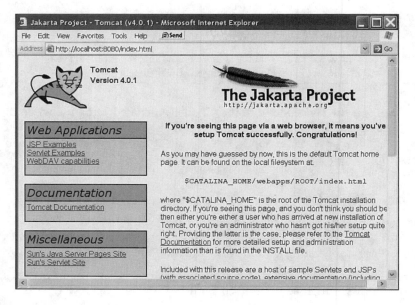

FIGURE 1.2   The Tomcat splash page.

Poking around in the JSP examples section is a nice way to see some sample JSP code, and to "smoke-test" the environment to make sure that it works. We'll click on examples and then run the numberguess program (see Figure 1.3).

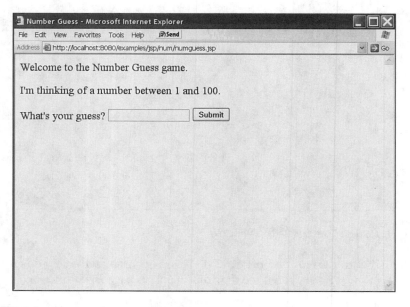

FIGURE 1.3   The numberguess program.

If the initial page displays correctly, Tomcat is set up correctly and you're ready to roll.

We could develop our JSP code under the ROOT Tomcat context (that's the one that displays the splash page), or even under the examples context. However, to keep things clean and, again, prevent lost work if we reinstall Tomcat, we'll set up a separate context to work in.

To do this, edit the server.xml file in the C:\Tomcat\Conf directory. This file looks complicated, but for these purposes, all we need to do is add a new context entry; it should go directly before the </Host> XML tag, which will lead to that portion of the file that looks like Listing 1.5. The new XML is highlighted.

LISTING 1.5   Changes to server.xml

```
    </Context>

    <! - Tomcat Book Context -->
    <Context path="/cartapp" docBase="c:\CARTAPP" debug="0"
             reloadable="true">
      <Logger className="org.apache.catalina.logger.FileLogger"
                prefix="localhost_cartapp_log." suffix=".txt"
             timestamp="true"/>
      <Environment name="maxExemptions" type="java.lang.Integer"
                   value="15"/>
      <Parameter name="context.param.name" value="context.param.value"
                   override="false"/>
      <Resource name="mail/session" auth="CONTAINER"
                type="javax.mail.Session"/>
      <ResourceParams name="mail/session">
        <parameter>
          <name>mail.smtp.host</name>
          <value>localhost</value>
        </parameter>
      </ResourceParams>
    </Context>

    </Host>
```

We are creating a context called /cartapp (which means that the URL of JSP served from this context will be http://localhost:8080/cartapp). Then we tell it to look for its files in the C:\CARTAPP directory.

After Tomcat is restarted, put a simple JSP file (such as the "Hello World" example) into C:\CARTAPP\jsp\hello_world.jsp and look at it by browsing to http://localhost:8080/cartapp/jsp/hello_world.jsp. If everything's set up right, you'll see the Hello World page.

Finding the Java Sources

As soon as you start developing JSP, you'll run into your first Java error (either a syntax error or an exception). Because JSP is executing Java code instead of the raw JSP source, it can be tricky to figure out exactly where the error occurred.

Let's look at both types of errors and see how to track them down. First, let's create a JSP file with a simple syntax error in Listing 1.6.

LISTING 1.6   fiveloop_syntax.jsp

```
<HTML>
 <HEAD><TITLE>Hello World!</TITLE></HEAD>
 <BODY>
 <%
   int i = 0;
   while (i++ < 5) {
%>
 Hello World! Loop #
 <% out.print(j); %>
 <br>
 <% } %>

</BODY>
</HTML>
```

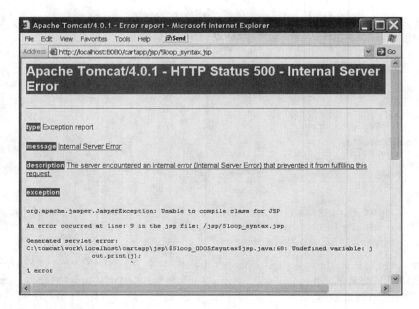

FIGURE 1.4   A syntax error

Luckily, syntax errors generate fairly easy-to-read error messages and even print out the offending line so that you can locate it in your sources as shown in Figure 1.4.

Less easy to deal with are runtime exceptions. Let's generate a divide-by-zero error in Listing 1.7.

LISTING 1.7   fiveloop_runtime.jsp

```
<HTML>
 <HEAD><TITLE>Hello World!</TITLE></HEAD>
 <BODY>
 <%
   int i = 0;
   while (i++ < 5) {
 %>
  Hello World! Loop #
 <%
     out.print(i/0);
 %>
  <br>
 <% } %>

</BODY>
</HTML>
```

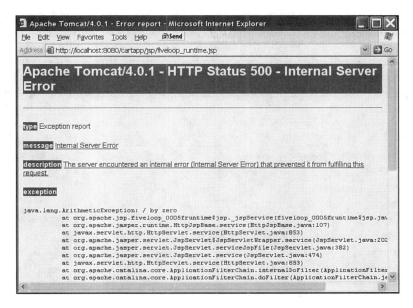

FIGURE 1.5   A runtime error.

In this case, the clues are more obscured, but it is still fairly simple to find the guilty party. You simply need to find the Java file that was generated from the JSP. Looking at the backtrace, as shown in Figure 1.5, you can see that the fiveloop_runtime.jsp source got turned into fiveloop_0005fruntime_jsp.java and that the error occurred on line 70 of that file. So now, all you need to do is to find out where Tomcat stashes the Java files and look at the source.

Underneath the base Tomcat directory is a directory called work. If you look there, you'll find another directory called localhost and, underneath there, a directory for every context that has been defined for Tomcat. If you look one level further, inside the cartapp directory, you'll find a jsp directory; inside that directory is the .java file. If you open it with an editor and look at line 70, you'll see this:

```
out.print(i/0);
```

Debugging a JSP program is basically the same process as debugging a normal Java program, except that you have to find the .java file first.

You can also look at the log to see an error, something that can be very useful if you are trying to look at a runtime error at a later date or if a third party tells you that there has been a problem on the site. The log filename is configurable in the context definition inside server.xml; the files are located in TOMCAT_HOME/logs (in our case, C:\TOMCAT\logs\localhost_cartapp_log.%date%.txt, where %date% is the current date).

A Quick Look at JDBC and MySQL

After completing the setup instructions in Appendix B, "Getting and Installing MySQL and JDBC," you should have a working MySQL and JDBC installation in place. Now let's create a small table in MySQL and try getting to it from JSP. Rather than create the table directly by typing to the command line, you'll put the commands in a file and run it so that you can fix things more easily if you make a typo. You'll put all of your SQL scripts in their own directory under CARTAPP to keep them organized. (See Listing 1.8.)

LISTING 1.8   employees.sql

```
drop table IF EXISTS employees;

create table employees (
        lname_txt        char(50),
        fname_txt        char(50),
        employee_num     integer primary key,
        address1_txt     char(120),
        address2_txt     char(120),
        city          char(50),
        state         char(2),
        zip           char(10),
        phone         char(14));
```

LISTING 1.8   continued

```
insert into employees values
        ('Jones', 'Bob', 1, '27 Mockingbird Lane', NULL,
         'Springfield', 'MA', '11223-4321', '1-617-555-1212');

insert into employees values
        ('Smith', 'John', 2, '55 Boring Street Name', 'Apt 1',
         'Roswell', 'NM', '65444-4556', '1-800-AMA-LIEN');
```

Now you can bring up the mysql interface and use the \. syntax to run commands from a file (see Figure 1.6). Be sure not to terminate a \. command with a ; like a normal SQL command; it confuses the mysql parser.

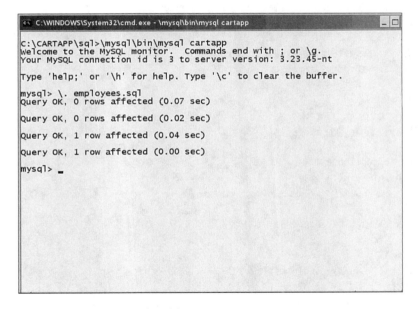

FIGURE 1.6   Creating a sample table.

To write a JSP page that talks to the database, you need to do several things. Listing 1.9 is a small sample program that walks through the bare minimum.

LISTING 1.9   employee_list.jsp

```
<HTML>
 <HEAD><TITLE>Employee List</TITLE></HEAD>
 <BODY>
<%@ page import="java.sql.*" %>
```

LISTING 1.9   continued

```
<TABLE BORDER=1 width="75%">
<TR><TH>Last Name</TH><TH>First Name</TH></TR>
<%
Connection conn = null;
Statement st = null;
ResultSet rs = null;

try {
    Class.forName("org.gjt.mm.mysql.Driver").newInstance();
    conn =
     DriverManager.getConnection("jdbc:mysql://localhost/cartapp");

    st = conn.createStatement();
    rs = st.executeQuery("select * from employees");
    while(rs.next()) {
%>
<TR><TD><%= rs.getString("lname_txt") %></TD>
<TD><%= rs.getString("fname_txt") %></TD></TR>
<%
    }
%>
</TABLE>
<%
} catch (Exception ex) {
    ex.printStackTrace();
    %>
</TABLE>
Ooops, something bad happened:
<%
    } finally {
    if (rs != null) rs.close();
    if (st != null) st.close();
    if (conn != null) conn.close();
    }
%>
</BODY>
</HTML>
```

The first thing you have to do is to make the java.sql.* classes available for use in
this file. In normal Java, you could just say import java.sql.*; and it would

happen. In a JSP page, however, imports have to be done with a special syntax, hence the `<%@ page import` line. We'll look at this and similar tags in more detail in the next chapter.

In JDBC, you deal primarily with three things: connections, statements, and result sets. Mainly to facilitate the `finally` clause that you see at the bottom of the page, you need to declare the variables to hold them and set them to null before you begin.

Any time you're dealing with SQL in Java, you need to expect and handle java.sql.SQLException, which can occur because of database errors. So, wrap all of your database code inside a `try` so that you can attempt to handle failures correctly.

The next line, instantiating an instance of the mm.mysql.Driver class, is required to register the DriverManager.

An instance of your JDBC driver needs to be registered with the DriverManager before your call to `getConnection()` can make the proper connection. Most JDBC drivers have a static initializer in the class, so as soon as the class is loaded, a new instance will be registered with the DriverManager. (Others force you to create a new instance, which is another line of code.)

Two other ways of doing this are to directly import your driver class (this limits your ability to use other drivers) or to specify the driver name in a system property so that Java automatically loads it.

The `createStatement` call does the work of actually making a connection to the MySQL database. The argument is a URL-style string, with the first two sections (`jdbc` and `mysql`) always the same. The third section (`localhost`) could also be the hostname of another machine, allowing you to run your server on one box and your database on another. The final portion (`cartapp`) is the name of the database to connect to. You could also specify a username and password for a database that required it.

When you have a connection, you can create a statement. Two types of statements exist: the plain type that you're using here and a `PreparedStatement`. You can then call `executeQuery` with the SQL code as the argument, which returns a `ResultSet` object.

When you have a `ResultSet`, you can iterate over it using `rs.next()`, which will return `true` until the rows of data that match the query are exhausted. Inside the `while` loop, you break back out to HTML to put in the tags for the TR and TD of the table you're building.

Rather than go back into JSP and use `out.write` to send the actual contents of each row to the browser, you can use a handy shortcut. The `<%=` tag causes whatever is the Java expression between the `<%=` and `%>` tags to be sent to the browser. Notice that you don't end the expression with a `;` because it's a value and not a true statement.

If an error occurs during the connection to or query of the database, execution gets thrown to the `catch` clause. If this occurs, first print a backtrace to the log and then close the table and print a user-friendly error message.

Assuming that there's no error, once all the rows have printed, you can close the table. Then, because it appears in a `finally` clause, you can attempt to close all the open database objects, regardless of whether an error occurred. Because an error might have occurred at any stage (trying to connect, to allocate a statement, and so on), you must make sure that there is an object to close before you try closing it. This is why you must check to make sure that the connection object is not null; it might have thrown an error during initial assignment.

At last, you can close up the last few open tags and you're finished. Figure 1.7 shows the resulting view from a browser.

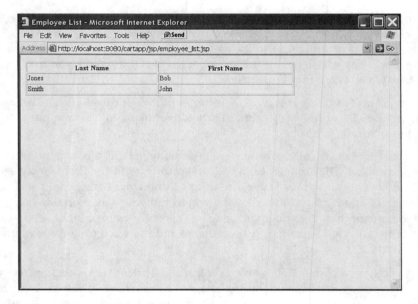

FIGURE 1.7   Creating a sample table.

Working with `ResultSets`

When you get a `ResultSet` back from a query, there are several ways to get at the data inside. You can refer to the columns positionally or by name. Let's look at a few code fragments to demonstrate the difference:

```
ResultSet rs = st.executeQuery("SELECT * FROM employees");

while (rs.next()) {
```

```
    String lname = rs.getString("lname_txt");
}
```

This example uses reference by name. You ask for column values by using the name of the column as an argument to the getX method:

```
ResultSet rs = st.executeQuery("SELECT lname_txt, fname_txt FROM employees");

while (rs.next()) {
    String lname = rs.getString(1);
}
```

This uses positional reference. The integer argument to getString refers to the position of the column in the list of columns specified in the query, starting with 1 for the first field.

In general, you shouldn't use positional notation with a * column list. You might think that you know the order that the columns will be returned in, but that could change if the scheme is rebuilt or moved to a different database. In fact, it is a good idea to always use a reference by name, even when explicitly listing the columns in the SQL statement. That is because it makes the code clearer—the getX call has the name of the column that it's fetching rather than an arbitrary index. This also means that if another column is added to the start of the select statement, the getX calls don't all need to be renumbered.

In general, it's a good idea to write your queries to explicitly list the fields that you want to get. You also might run into problems with using name-based reference with certain databases, and it could be a bit slower than using positional reference. However, the clarity and additional protection from changes in the query are often worth it.

In addition to getString, you can use getInt, getFloat, getDate, and getTimestamp (among others). JDBC tries to be smart about type conversions, so if you do a getString on an integer column, you'll get a string containing the printed representation of the column.

Using PreparedStatement

The ordinary Statement class is fine for running queries that don't have parameters, but as soon as you need to be able to add Java variables to SQL statements, they get clumsy. For example, let's say that you have a variable called findLast that is holding a string containing a last name. You want to find all the employees with that last name. To do it with a statement, it would have to look like this:

```
Statement st = conn.createStatement();
ResultSet rs = st.executeQuery("SELECT * FROM employees where lname_txt = '" +
➡findLast + "'");
```

That's an unattractive piece of code, especially because you have to remember to put single quotes around the string value. But worse, if there are "special characters such as ' that are meaningful to SQL in the string (for example, if the name were O'Donnell), the query will throw a SQL exception.

Thankfully, Java offers a way around this complication. Instead of using `Statement`, you can use `PreparedStatement`. Let's look at that code again, this time using `PreparedStatement`:

```
PreparedStatement st = conn.prepareStatement("SELECT * FROM employees where
➡lname_txt = ?");
st.setString(1, findLast);
ResultSet rs = st.executeQuery();
```

The `setString` call takes a positional first argument and replaces the nth ? in the prepared statement with its second argument. It automatically determines whether it needs to put quotes around the value or escape any special characters inside the value. There are equivalent versions of all the `getX` functions, `setString`, `setFloat`, `setDate`, and so on.

MORE BENEFITS OF PREPARED STATEMENTS

In addition to cleaning up your code by letting you drop positional values into SQL statements, there are other reasons to use `PreparedStatement`.

If you need to run a SQL statement repeatedly, you can use the same prepared statement with different arguments. The database has to parse and compile the SQL statement only once, which means that you gain a performance boost.

Also, if you want to insert binary data into a database, the only way to do it is with a `PreparedStatement`.

Inserting, Deleting, and Updating

Instead of using `executeQuery` on a `Statement` or `PreparedStatement`, you can use `executeUpdate`, which returns nothing. This method is used for any non-select SQL function. Here are a few examples showing what you can do with `executeUpdate`:

```
Statement st = conn.createStatement();
st.executeUpdate("delete from employees");

PreparedStatement pst =
```

```
    conn.prepareStatement("INSERT INTO employees (lname_txt, fname_txt,
employee_num) "+
                          "values (?, ?, ?)");
pst.setString(1, "Jones");
pst.setString(2, "Bob");
pst.setInt(3, 22);
pst.executeUpdate();
pst.close();

pst =   conn.prepareStatement("UPDATE employees set employee_num = ? where
lname_txt=? and fname_txt = ?"); pst.setString(1, "Jones");
pst.setString(2, "Bob");
pst.setInt(3, 23);
pst.executeUpdate();
pst.close();
```

The first example simply deletes all of the employee records. The second example adds a new employee record. Just as in a select, ? instances are replaced with the appropriate values using the setX methods. The second example also shows how a long SQL statement would be broken across several lines for readability. The final example shows how to update a row using parameters for both the where and set clauses.

Although it wasn't used in the previous code, executeUpdate returns a value, an integer that is the number of rows modified. This is useful, for example, if you want to either modify an existing record or create a new one. You can run an update statement and, if no rows are returned, you know to run an insert.

Using Cursors

Another way to update or delete data is to use a cursor. While looping through the results of a query, you can modify, delete, or add records, but only if you set up the statement the right way.

By default, when you execute a query, it's run in a kind of "read-only" mode. You can step through the values using the next() method on the record set, but that's it.

If the code hands an extra pair of arguments to createConnection or prepareStatement, you can create a ResultSet that can move back and forth inside the query, as well as update and append to.

Unfortunately, as of the current release of the MySQL JDBC driver, this is a not-ready-for-prime-time feature. Luckily, most of the time you are better off doing an explicit insert or update anyway because code that iterates through the rows with cursors is likely to be less efficient and harder to understand.

Summary

This chapter covered a lot of ground, including a quick overview of both JSP and JDBC. JSP files look like Java embedded in HTML, but they end up being turned into HTML embedded in Java. You can find the .java file that was produced from a JSP file in the work subdirectory of Tomcat; you can use these files to help debug errors. JDBC is the connection between JSP and a SQL database. You can use either `Statement` or `PreparedStatement` to run a query, depending on whether you will need to rerun it or pass in parameters to the query. Data is returned from a JDBC query in a `ResultSet`.

You also learned that you can get values from an individual row using the `getX` methods, that `executeUpdate` allows you to insert, modify, or delete rows from the database. Cursors allow you to modify records as you iterate over a `ResultSet`.

In Chapter 2, "Java Beans and JSP," we go into more depth about JSP, specifically how it can interact with Java Beans to create persistent session data.

CHAPTER 2

Java Beans and JSP

Java Beans are fundamental to the operation of JSP. They are the nuggets of information that persist between requests, that are filled in by forms, and that otherwise provide the glue to make your Web site work.

Beans themselves are very simple. They are merely Java classes that obey a few simple conventions. More than likely, you've already written a few Beans, but we'll start off with a quick review of them before talking about how JSP uses Beans.

Bean Basics

A Bean is an encapsulated unit of data with accessor methods to set and get properties, and action methods to do things with the data. As a simple example, a user Bean might have properties such as lastName, firstName, city, state, and zipCode. It might also have action methods such as validateZipCode or saveToDatabase.

The only real requirement for a Bean is that it implements a get and set method of each property that it contains. The methods must start with get or set. That's the basic definition of a Bean.

Let's look at a simple Bean that implements user data in Listing 2.1.

LISTING 2.1   User.java

```
package com.cartapp.user;

public class User {
    protected String lastName;
    protected String firstName;

    public String getLastName() {
      return lastName;
    }
```

LISTING 2.1 Continued

```
    public void setLastName(String lname) {
      lastName = lname;
    }

    public String getFirstName() {
      return firstName;
    }

    public void setFirstName(String fname) {
      firstName = fname;
    }
}
```

Obviously, a real user object would store a lot more information, as you'll see later in the chapter. However, this example lets you see how to access data in a Bean. You should always make the actual class variables holding the data protected because good encapsulation methodology indicates that all outside access should be through the methods.

Bean Persistence

Now that you have this simple Bean, you can start to play with it using JSP. JSP uses a persistence model that lets you maintain a Java object for the scope of the current page, the current request, the current user session, or the entire time that the server is running. These four types of persistence are referred to as page scope, request scope, session scope, and application scope.

- An object with page scope is available during the evaluation of this JSP only. This means that if the request is forwarded to another page in the same application, the object will not be preserved.

- An object stored with request scope is available during the entire processing of the current request from a client. This object will be preserved if the request is forwarded to another page.

- Session-scoped objects are associated with a user session, which is created when a user first encounters the server and persists until it is explicitly destroyed or the session times out. Objects with session scope can be accessed at any point during the session.

- Application-scoped objects are available to any page of any user session, for the life of the application. They are akin to global variables.

HOW DOES JSP MAKE PERSISTENCE WORK?

Web requests are theoretically stateless. All that a Web server knows about an incoming request is the IP address of the requester (which actually might be a proxy server), the URL, perhaps some posted data, and miscellaneous information about the client browser. So how does JSP maintain the illusion of a persistent session across multiple requests?

As you might already know, the answer is cookies. Two types of cookies exist in the world, the "evil" ones that stay around forever (or some long period of time) and those that identify you or things about you to a Web server during a single browser session. These cookies use the `expire=date` feature of the HTTP cookie specification. However, if you don't specify an expiration date, the cookie automatically disappears as soon as the user closes the browser.

These more benign cookies are ideal for uniquely identifying a user session while someone is visiting your Web site. JSP automatically assigns you a temporary cookie when you first come to the site and then uses it to keep your objects associated with you.

This can lead to an interesting problem seen mainly in testing. If you have two browser windows open, one for testing and one looking at the admin interface, for example, you can end up changing your session ID by logging in on the second window, which can make the first one "lose track" of where it is because it loses all of its associated session data.

Because of the paranoia over cookies, some users turn them off altogether. In that case, JSP uses URL rewriting, which means placing a parameter in all the links and form submits from a Web page that identifies the session. This leads to URLs like:

```
http://www.mysite.com/hithere.jsp?sessionid=345234523454325565
```

A big problem with URL rewriting is that if the user bookmarks the page, it will include the session ID in the bookmark, which can lead to later confusion for the Web server if the user tries to return to the page.

Permanent cookies can also be very useful in Web design. We'll talk about them and why they aren't as terrible as some make them out to be in Chapter 8, "Retrieving, Storing, and Verifying User Input."

Using useBean

Listings 2.2 and 2.3 show a pair of pages that use a Bean to pass data from one to the other inside the same session.

LISTING 2.2   handoff1.jsp

```
<jsp:useBean id="handoff" scope="session" class="com.cartapp.user.User" />
<HTML>
<BODY>
This is the setting page!
<%
    handoff.setFirstName("George");
%>
</BODY>
</HTML>
```

LISTING 2.3   handoff2.jsp

```
<jsp:useBean id="handoff" scope="session" class="com.cartapp.user.User" />
<HTML>
<BODY>
<H1>This is the getting page!<br>handoff=
<%= handoff.getFirstName() %></H1>
</BODY>
</HTML>
```

If you request handoff1.jsp and then handoff2.jsp, you'll get the Web page shown in Figure 2.1.

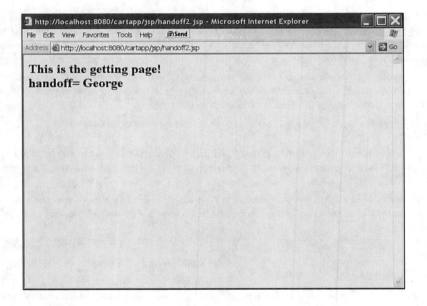

FIGURE 2.1   Handing off a value between Web pages.

The most interesting thing to look at here is the useBean tag at the top of the files. This tag tells JSP to persist a Bean with the ID specified for the scope requested—in this case, one named handoff—for the life of the session.

When a Bean has been instantiated with a given ID, any other page that requests that ID, as long as it's inside the specified scope, will get the same object. This allows the JSP application to carry a set of objects as it processes requests associated with the same user, for example.

ONE NAME, MULTIPLE CLASS, JSP GO BOOM!

One of the more irritating bugs to track down in JSP can occur if you inadvertently use the same ID name with two different classes. To understand why this breaks JSP, let's look at some code snippets and the underlying Java that they produce. Listing 2.4 shows a slightly different version of handoff2.jsp.

LISTING 2.4 handoff_broke.jsp

```
<jsp:useBean id="handoff" scope="session" class="com.cartapp.user.DifferentUser" />
<HTML>
<BODY>
<H1>This is the getting page!<br>handoff=
<%= handoff.getFirstName() %></H1>
</BODY>
</HTML>
```

DifferentUser is just a copy of the User class under a different name. When you request handoff_broke.jsp from Tomcat (after running handoff1.jsp), you get the error page shown in Figure 2.2.

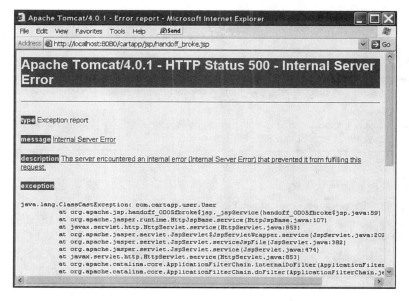

FIGURE 2.2 A broken handoff.

Here's why: The useBean tag in handoff1.jsp turns into this Java:

```
com.cartapp.user.User handoff = null;
boolean _jspx_specialhandoff  = false;
 synchronized (session) {
    handoff= (com.cartapp.user.User)
            pageContext.getAttribute("handoff",PageContext.SESSION_SCOPE);
```

LISTING 2.4   Continued

```
if ( handoff == null ) {
  _jspx_specialhandoff = true;
    try {
       handoff = (com.cartapp.user.User)
                 java.beans.Beans.instantiate(this.getClass().getClassLoader(),
                                 "com.cartapp.user.User");
```

In contrast, handoff_broke.jsp has the following:

```
com.cartapp.user.DifferentUser handoff = null;
boolean _jspx_specialhandoff  = false;
 synchronized (session) {
   handoff= (com.cartapp.user.DifferentUser)
           pageContext.getAttribute("handoff",PageContext.SESSION_SCOPE);
   if ( handoff == null ) {
      _jspx_specialhandoff = true;
      try {
          handoff = (com.cartapp.user.DifferentUser)
                   java.beans.Beans.instantiate(this.getClass().getClassLoader(),
                                   "com.cartapp.user.DifferentUser");
```

When handoff_broke.jsp is run, it calls pageContext.getAttribute to get the object called handoff. It then tries to cast it to the DifferentUser class. Unfortunately, when handoff1 is run, it creates an object of type User; when the cast tries to coerce it to DifferentUser, it fails.

Thus, it's very important to keep your persistent object names straight and not to use the same name for objects of two different types.

The setProperty **Tag**

Along with the useBean tag, other JSP tags talk to Java Beans. The most useful is the jsp:setProperty tag. It allows you to fill in a Bean's values from form data coming in from a submit.

Here's a demonstration of how setProperty can work. First, let's add a simple validation to User.java:

```
public boolean isValidUserData() {
  return ((firstName != null) && (firstName.length() > 0) &&
         (lastName != null) && (lastName.length() > 0));
}
```

Now let's create a new user form (see Listing 2.4) and a handler page for the form (see Listing 2.5).

LISTING 2.4   new_user_form.jsp

```
<jsp:useBean id="user" scope="session" class="com.cartapp.user.User" />
<BODY>
<H1>Enter New User Data</H1>
<FORM ACTION="create_user.jsp" METHOD="POST">
Last Name: <INPUT TYPE="TEXT" NAME="lastName"><BR>
First Name: <INPUT TYPE="TEXT" NAME="firstName"><BR>
<INPUT TYPE="SUBMIT">
</FORM>
</BODY>
```

LISTING 2.5   create_user.jsp

```
<jsp:useBean id="user" scope="session" class="com.cartapp.user.User" />
<jsp:setProperty name="user" property="*" />
<BODY>
<H1>Validating New User Data</H1>
<%
    if (user.isValidUserData()) {
%>
<H2>User Data Validated</H2>
<% } else { %>
<H2>Missing Either Last or First Name</H2>
    <% } %>
</BODY>
```

You should stop and restart Tomcat to make sure that you get the new version of the class file.

When you submit the form with no data in the fields, you get the screen shown in Figure 2.3.

In comparison, when both fields are filled out correctly, you get the screen shown in Figure 2.4.

Later in the book, we'll look at form validation in much more detail. For the moment, let's concentrate on what the setProperty tag does.

For every form field that is handed to the JSP page in the request, JSP checks to see if the setProperty tag is specifying a Bean with an equivalent property. For example, there's a field called lastName in the form, and a setLastName accessor in the user Bean. JSP tries to coerce the data in the field into the type of the accessor's argument, and then call the accessor to set the property.

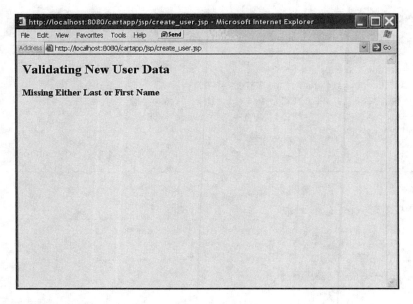

FIGURE 2.3   Missing data.

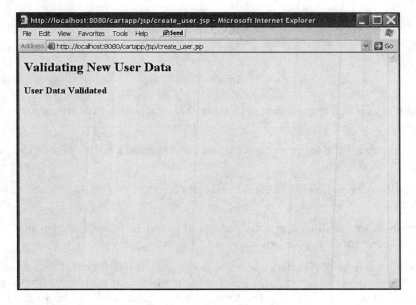

FIGURE 2.4   Everything is there.

WHO GETS THE DATA?

Let's suppose that you have two user objects instantiated under different IDs (which is perfectly legal). Let's further suppose that you use a setProperty tag on both of them. Which one will get the data from the form submit?

The answer is, both. As each setProperty is encountered, it runs over the same list of request variables from the form and tries to find matches in the Bean specified. This means that you need to be careful when setting several Beans from one form. For example, if you are setting the credit card and user data from a single form, and both credit card and user have a property called name, both setName methods will be called if there is a name field in the form and you use setProperty with the * option. To avoid this problem, you can use setProperty with an explicit third argument stating which property you want to set. However, this can get cumbersome when you have several dozen properties to set. A better solution is to use userName and creditCardName as property names instead so that they are unique.

Getting Beans to See Each Other

Sooner or later, you're going to want to let two Beans see each other. For example, if you have a globally persistent phone directory object and a session-persistent user object, you might want the user object to be capable of referencing the phone directory object.

```
<jsp:useBean id="user" scope="session" class="com.cartapp.user.User" />
<jsp:useBean id="directory" scope="application" class="com.cartapp.directory.Direc-
tory" />
<BODY>
<H1>My Phone Number</H1>
My phone number is <%= user.getMyPhoneNumber(directory) %>
</BODY>
```

Of course, you could also write it as follows:

```
My phone number is <%= directory.getUserPhoneNumber(user) %>
```

This works a lot of the time, especially if you need to reference the other object only once, but it doesn't work in all cases. Consider the following code:

```
<jsp:useBean id="user" scope="session" class="com.cartapp.user.User" />
<jsp:useBean id="directory" scope="application" class="com.cartapp.directory.Direc-
tory" />
<jsp:setProperty name="user" property="*" />
```

Let's further suppose that the form that calls this JSP page has a field called phoneNumber, and you want to validate the phone number against the phone directory. In the setPhoneNumber method of user, you need a handle on the directory object. In this case, there's no way to hand it in via an argument. Here's one workaround:

```
<jsp:useBean id="user" scope="session" class="com.cartapp.user.User" />
<jsp:useBean id="directory" scope="application" class="com.cartapp.directory.Direc-
tory" />
<% user.setSystemDirectory(directory); %>
<jsp:setProperty name="user" property="*" />
```

You need to provide a new property on the user object called `systemDirectory` of type `com.cartapp.directory.Directory`, which gets set right before you do the `setProperty`. Then the `setPhoneNumber` method can use the local object's reference to the `directory` object.

A final way to get access is to access it in the Bean via the request object, which we'll talk about in Chapter 3, "Using Servlet Functionality with JSP."

Application-Scoped Object and Singleton Classes

As you design your application, you're going to find that most of the Beans that you use are session-scoped. You might find the occasional use for a request-scoped Bean, one that stays around only as long as the current request, but they're usually few and far between.

If you find yourself using application-scoped Beans, you might want to consider using a singleton class to map the object into the local session. A singleton has the advantage that only one copy can ever exist in a virtual machine, even if you accidentally throw away the reference to it. In contrast, you can create multiple instances of a class at the application level if you inadvertently use different ID names for the useBean. Singletons or application-level Beans are best for objects that are needed to share a common data set among many sessions or to provide a common computational function across many sessions.

A CASE STUDY WITH SINGLETONS

One example of using a singleton class is to have a separate class to do totals and subtotals on a shopping cart rather than put those methods in the cart themselves, which is a technique that I've used on an e-commerce project. I implemented an interface for a generic shopping cart and wrote a calculation engine that had a number of methods to do various subtotals, all of which took that interface as an argument. Then I had the folks developing the actual shopping cart class implement the interface for their class.

By doing this, we ended up with a calculation engine that was independent of the implementation of the cart itself. This meant that, theoretically, we could reuse the calculation engine in other projects, even if they implemented a different shopping cart.

Because we needed only one calculation engine for the application, we implemented it as a singleton class that could be called at will to get the one instance. We never had to worry about leaving copies lying around somewhere in memory or be careful the overhead of creating a new instance each time we needed it because only one was ever created; all subsequent calls to the factory simply returned the same object.

The only caution with this approach is that it is not thread-safe. In the case of the calculation engine, no state is associated with the object, so there is no danger that two threads could change some attribute of the single object at the same time. However, this might not always be the case. If there is the potential for mayhem if two threads are changing state in the class at the same time, you must either define the methods as synchronized or use multiple instances.

Wrapping Up Beans

It wouldn't be an overstatement to say that Java Beans are the key to making JSP work. They're the difference between a simple scripting language that lets you put programmatic content on a Web page and a programming environment that lets you leverage all the power of object-oriented design for your application.

Java Beans contain state, which is accessed using get and set methods on the Bean. They also have scope in JSP—either page, request, session, or application. Different scopes allow the bean to persist for different amounts of time. jsp:useBean is used to associate a Bean with a name and a scope on a JSP page. jsp:setProperty is used to apply form values to a Bean. Singleton classes can be used to avoid creating multiple instances of an application-level Bean.

In the next chapter, which is the last chapter of pure JSP review, you'll look at servlets along with the request and response objects, which allow you to interact with the page servicing process at a microscopic level. Then you'll be ready to move on to the sample application.

3

Using Servlet Functionality with JSP

Servlets are the objects that make things happen in a JSP application. As you've seen, even a plain JSP is really a servlet in disguise (or, rather, it is turned into a servlet by the JSP engine). In this chapter, you'll learn how to access the functionality of servlets from your JSP code and Beans.

Moving from CGI to Servlets

Servlets represented the second step that Java-enabled Web servers took away from the old CGI paradigm. In CGI-based Web programming, the CGI program was an external program run by the server. It took input from environment variables and the standard input stream, and it sent its response back via standard output.

CGI-based designs worked well for quite a long time, but they had a number of problems. For one thing, a significant processing cost was associated with spawning a new process each time a CGI request came in. In addition, it was extremely difficult to carry persistent data around because each process started fresh.

The first step was to allow designers to link their own libraries into the running server binary (under Netscape, this was called NSAPI, for example). This not only drastically increased performance, but it also allowed the code to gain access to internal server functionality.

Java servlets were developed to provide the best of both worlds. Because the Java servlet runtime was persistent and lived close to the Web server, it could interact with Web requests at a detailed level. But because it was Java, it was easy to firewall potential crashes off the server itself by catching exceptions at the top level of the servlet loop.

Also, because the servlet classes are standard, servlet code will run without modification (usually) on any Java-enabled Web server.

Looking at an Example Servlet

Servlets are conceptually simple. You configure your Web server to map a certain URL path to a Java class (different servers do this differently). The Java class needs to extend HttpServlet and handle one of several methods: doGet, doPost, doPut, or doDelete. (doGet or doPost are used most commonly.)

These messages reflect the various ways that servlets are invoked by a GET, POST, PUT, or DELETE HTTP request from a client (although DELETE is rare). The servlet is responsible for setting the mime type, error code, cookies, and other status information about the request, as well as returning the content.

Let's say that the path /baseballstats has been mapped to the class BaseBallStatServlet. This is a class that knows about the current batting averages of major league baseball players. To use it, you send a URL like this:

http://www.baseballstats.com/baseballstats?player=Nomar Garciapara

Listing 3.1 is a simple implementation of that servlet.

LISTING 3.1   BaseBallStatServlet.ava

```
import javax.servlet.*;
import javax.servlet.http.*;

public class BaseBallStatServlet extends HttpServlet {
    protected void doGet(HttpServletRequest req, HttpServletResponse resp)
    throws java.io.IOException {
    resp.setContentType("text/html");
    java.io.PrintWriter html = resp.getWriter();

    String player = (String) req.getParameter("player");

    html.println("<HTML><HEAD><TITLE>MLB Player Stats</TITLE></HEAD>");
    html.println("<BODY>");

    if ((player == null) || (player.length() == 0)) {
        html.println("<H1>No Player Requested</H1>");
    } else {
        if (player.equals("Nomar Garciapara")) {
        html.println("<H1>Nomar is batting .932</H1>");
        } else {
```

LISTING 3.1   Continued

```
        html.println("<H1>" + player + " is batting .234</H1>");
        }
    }
    html.println("</BODY></HTML>");
    }
}
```

Ignoring for the moment the bias toward a certain Boston slugger, you can see that all the basic elements of a servlet are in place.

The doGet method is handed the request and response objects. The request has all the parameters handed in to the Web request, including cookies, form submissions, and header data. The response is used to formulate a reply to request.

To create the reply, the first thing you need to do is to set the content type of the reply. In most cases, that will be text/html, although you might be generating other types of replies, such as XML.

Next, you need to get a handle on the output stream so that you can start generating HTML. In cases in which you are writing text data (as opposed to binary data, such as if you were programmatically generating a JPG file), you want to get a PrintWriter, which you can find by calling getWriter on the response object.

Next you use getParameter on the request to get the form or URL submitted player name. You need to make sure to check for blank or null values for this parameter, or an exception might occur later.

Output the boilerplate HTML header for the document, then compare the name of the player against your primitive database, close the HTML forms, and you're finished with the request.

JSP: Servlets, Only Better!

Although we'll spend the rest of the chapter discussing the servlet objects because JSP uses them heavily, I'm going to say right here and now that using servlets themselves is not something I'd recommend.

This is because they obscure the functionality of the site and require ugly embedding of HTML inside Java. One of the features of JSP is that the formatting (HTML) has been largely segregated from the coding (Java). When you start using pure servlets, you have to put HTML code right in the middle of the Java.

As a result, you need to recompile the class every time you change a minor page format feature. This gets very exhausting very quickly during development, and it is worse in a deployed site.

Also, because of the indirection between the URL and the class name, you can have a difficult time trying to find the actual code behind a servlet request. It usually involves looking at the server configuration file, which can be confusing.

More to the point, everything that a servlet does can be done with a JSP page. Listings 3.2 and 3.3 show a JSP page and a Bean that do the same thing. Notice how much more clearly JSP does it in Listing 3.2.

LISTING 3.2   BaseBallStats.jsp

```
<jsp:useBean id="statEngine" scope="session" class="com.mlb.stats.statBean" />
<HTML><HEAD><TITLE>MLB Player Stats</TITLE></HEAD>
<BODY>
<H1><%= statEngine.processRequest(request, response) %> </H1>
</BODY>
</HTML>
```

LISTING 3.3   statBean.java

```
package com.mlb.stats;

import javax.servlet.*;
import javax.servlet.http.*;

public class statBean {
    public String processRequest(HttpServletRequest req,
                 HttpServletResponse resp) {

    String player = (String) req.getParameter("player");
    if ((player == null) || (player.length() == 0)) {
        return("No Player Requested");
    } else {
        if (player.equals("Nomar Garciapara")) {
        return("Nomar is batting .932");
        } else {
        return(player + " is batting .234");
        }
    }
    }
}
```

This is a much more desirable division of labor, with the JSP handling the HTML formatting and the back-end Java Bean handling the business logic. A third way (and the official JSP way) to write this is using jsp:setProperties to handle the form submit instead of letting the Bean decode the form arguments.

Servlet Functionality Inside JSP

If servlet programming is yesterday's news, why is a chapter devoted to it? The reason is that there's a lot of useful functionality in the Servlet API to take advantage of.

The previous code highlights one example—sometimes you want to explicitly handle a form submission rather than use the Bean property-setting mechanisms. This might be because you want to do a certain type of error checking (more on this in Chapter 8, "Retrieving, Storing, and Verifying User Input") or because you want to set values in a manner that's more complicated than the useProperty mechanism allows.

Beyond the getParameter functionality, there are a lot of other things that the various servlet classes can tell you. Let's break them down class by class.

HttpServletRequest

The HttpServletRequest object, which is available as request in a JSP page, contains all the information that is passed from the browser to the server during a Web transaction. The following code highlights a few of the things that can be extracted.

First, you'll extend the user object with another property:

```
protected String userName;

public String getUserName() {
return userName;
}

public void setUserName(String uname) {
userName = uname;
}
```

Listing 3.4 gives the actual JSP code.

LISTING 3.4   HttpObjectDemo.jsp

```
<jsp:useBean id="user" scope="session" class="com.cartapp.user.User" />
<jsp:setProperty name="user" property="*" />
<HTML>
<HEAD>
<TITLE>HttpRequest/HttpResponse Demo</TITLE>
</HEAD>
<BODY>
    <%
Cookie [] cookies = request.getCookies();
boolean found_cookie = false;

if (cookies != null) {
```

LISTING 3.4   Continued

```
        for (int i = 0; i < cookies.length; i++) {
        if (cookies[i].getName().equals("cartAppUserName")) {
            user.setUserName(cookies[i].getValue());
            found_cookie = true;
        }
        }
}
if (!found_cookie) {
    if (user.getUserName() != null) {
    Cookie setCookie = new Cookie("cartAppUserName", user.getUserName());
    setCookie.setMaxAge(3600 * 24 * 265);   // Expire in one year
    response.addCookie(setCookie);
    found_cookie = true;
    }
}
if (!found_cookie) {
    %>
<FORM METHOD="POST">
Please Enter Your User Name: <INPUT TYPE="TEXT" NAME="userName"><BR>
<INPUT TYPE="SUBMIT">
</FORM>
<% } else { %>
<H1>Hello <%= user.getUserName() %></H1>
    <%
    if (request.getAuthType() != null) {
    %> You don't need to use a secure connection.<p> <%
    }
    %>
    For your information, your session id is <%= request.getRequestedSessionId()
%><p>
    You accessed this page using a <%= request.getMethod() %><p>

    <%
    if (request.isRequestedSessionIdFromURL()) { %>
        You know, using URL rewriting is ugly, turn on cookie support.<p>
    <% } else { %>
        Good, you support cookies, nice choice.<p>
    <% }
 } %>
</BODY>
</HTML>
```

The first time you run this code, you'll see the page shown in Figure 3.1

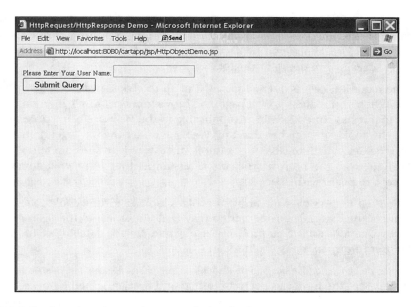

FIGURE 3.1   Running the servlet example for the first time.

If you fill in a value for the username and hit submit, you'll see the page shown in Figure 3.2

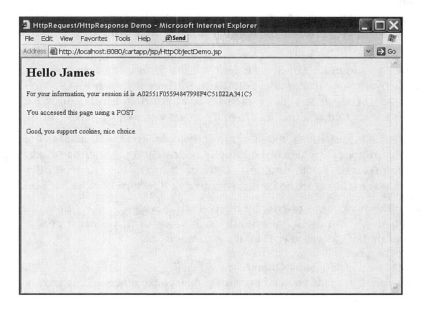

FIGURE 3.2   Running the servlet example for the second time.

Let's go through the code and see what's going on. The first two lines of JSP should look familiar. They do the same importation and property setting of the User class as you've done before. When you first access the page, there are no parameters passed in, so the setProperty does nothing.

Next, the request object is queried for a list of all the cookies handed in with the request. When you request a Web page, the browser checks to see if any of the cookies that it has stored locally are applicable to the Web site being accessed. Usually, the cookie is stored so that any Web site under the top-level domain will be sent the cookie—which means, for example, that www1.mysite.com and www2.mysite.com can both see the cookie (assuming that you own a domain called mysite.com to begin with).

The code then iterates over the array of cookies looking for the cookie that holds the username of the user. If the code finds a match, it writes it into the Bean and sets a flag. In a real application, you probably also would make a database call to load all sorts of user information, as you'll see in Chapter 8.

If the code didn't find the cookie, it checks to see if the Bean's username is set. If it is, it means that the form has been submitted and that a username now resides inside the user object. If that is the case, the code adds a new cookie to the response object to set the username cookie to the submitted value with a one-year expiration.

If the cookie wasn't found, and it wasn't being written for the first time because of a form submit, it displays a form to let the user input one from a form. When the user hits Submit, he is brought back around to this page, but now setProperty places the submitted username into the user Bean. This means that when the code comes along that checks if there's a username present in the Bean, it will be true and the cookie will be set.

If a cookie was found, a check is made to see if a secure SSL request was used, which would be overkill for this application. Next, the user is shown his session ID, which is a unique ID code generated for each session to distinguish incoming requests. Then the user is told whether a GET, POST, or PUT was used to access this page.

The session ID is usually stored as a transient cookie (one with a MaxAge of -1, which means that it goes away when the browser is closed). If the user has disabled cookies, the session ID is passed around using URL rewriting. If that's happening, the user is sent a message telling him to be less paranoid and to turn cookies back on.

What you've just seen is essentially the code that every site that implements "remembering" your username goes through. Consider it your first peek at the process of making a customer-friendly Web site work.

The HttpServletResponse Object

You saw one thing that you can do with the response object in the last section—use it to set a cookie.

Listing 3.5 is a simple JSP page that demonstrates a number of neat things that you can do with the response object.

LISTING 3.5   HttpResponseDemo.jsp

```
<%
String arg = "default";
if (request.getParameter("arg") != null) {
    arg = request.getParameter("arg");
}


if (arg.equals("redirect")) {
    response.sendRedirect("http://www.cnn.com/");
} else if (arg.equals("xml")) {
    response.setContentType("text/xml");
%>
<Vegetable>
  <Name>Carrot</Name>
  <Color>Orange</Color>
  <Consumer>Bugs Bunny</Consumer>
</Vegetable>
<%
    } else {
    response.sendError(HttpServletResponse.SC_NOT_FOUND,
            "There's No Such Page!");
    }
%>
```

If you request the page with no arguments in the URL, you get an error message (see Figure 3.3).

This is an example of using the sendError method of the response object, which lets you generate an arbitrary status response for the request. In this case, we're generating a 404, file not found, although with a customized message rather than the generic Tomcat error message for a 404.

If you pass in arg=redirect on the URL, you get redirected to the CNN Web page. There are some specific restrictions on using redirect. The main restriction is that you have to make sure that the redirect is requested before any content is sent to the browser; otherwise, the redirect string shows up as text in the Web page.

If you use arg=xml, you're sent back some XML content. This demonstrates an important point—JSP and Java servlets can return more than just HTML content. By using the setContentType message, you can generate a response of any content type you want. For example, you could generate a JPG image using one of the Java image-manipulation libraries and send it back by setting the content type to image/jpeg (see Figure 3.4).

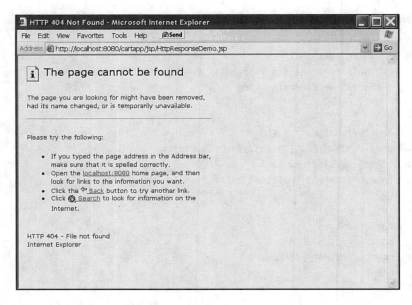

FIGURE 3.3   Using the `sendError` method.

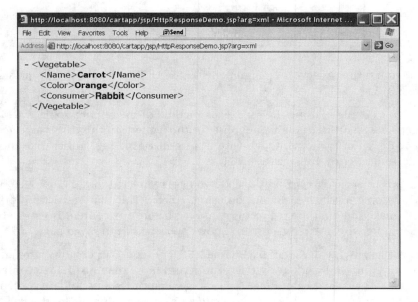

FIGURE 3.4   Sending XML by setting the content type.

The End of the Beginning

This concludes the overview of JSP, JDBC, and servlet technology. We haven't covered everything in the standards, by any means, but we'll pick up the rest as we go through developing the sample application.

This chapter discussed servlets as they represent an evolution away from CGI toward more persistent and developer-friendly technologies. However, even with all of a servlet's functionality, it is JSP that allows you to produce HTML with greater ease than developing pure servlet-based applications.

And because you use the same servlet objects in JSP pages, it's important to understand how servlets work. The servlet objects also can be used to get cookies and other user state information and to redirect or generate errors.

From this point on, things focus a lot more on how to do specific things and a lot less on general technology. But before we dive into the how-to, we're going to spend a little time talking about the what-to—the things you need to have in place before you begin, such as object design, the database schema, and a good understanding of the user requirements.

In Chapter 4, "The Sample Application Functional Requirements Document," you'll be introduced to the Books for Geeks company. We're going to look at their preliminary design for an e-commerce Web site, decide what questions to ask, and create a functional requirements documents (FRD). One of the things that I've learned through painful experience is that if you don't thoroughly understand what the customer needs and expects, you're heading toward disaster before you even begin to code.

> **NOTE**
>
> If you're going to become a proficient JSP developer, you'll need a more in-depth knowledge of JSP and servlets than has been presented here. A good place to start is with the JSP and servlet JavaDoc and specifications, which are included with the code on the Web site (www.samspublishing.com). You will see a lot more of this technology later in the book, but it will be solely the pieces needed to code the application.

PART II

Sample Application: Functional Requirements

IN THIS PART

4

The Sample Application Functional Requirements Document

Functional requirements documents (FRDs) are to projects what DNA is to an organism. If done right, everything needed to bring the project to a successful conclusion should be a logical result of the information contained in the FRD.

But FRDs don't just happen by themselves. They're a product of a careful collaboration between the development team and the client. The client, as stakeholder, is the only entity that understands what is really needed. And you, as the developer, have the responsibility to translate that set of requirements into an end product that meets those needs. The FRD represents those needs outlined on paper.

To illustrate how to create an FRD, you'll be taken through the process of developing one for the hypothetical Books for Geeks (BFG) site. Not only is it a useful exercise in its own right, but this is also the blueprint for the code that will be written in the remainder of the book.

FRDS: A CAUTIONARY TALE

If you don't get the details right the first time, you can end up paying the price at the end, as I once found out.

Working on a $2 million documentation project, we were in the final days before signoff and final delivery. Suddenly, the customer informed us that at page 100 in a document, the standard being used required that page to be printed as page 99-1 instead. Unfortunately, the page autonumbering code that we had been using for the previous two years in the code didn't support this kind of sequence. And, of course, the requirements document didn't say a thing about page numbering one way or the other. We had to rip it all out and write our own, at the cost of an extra two to three man weeks.

The moral of the tale? If you don't ask for the details up front, you might make assumptions in your coding that don't meet the customer's expectations.

Welcome to Books for Geeks

It's a bright, beautiful Monday morning, and you're having your initial meeting with the CTO of Books for Geeks and her staff. You've landed the contract to implement the e-commerce Web site that's going to make the company the leader in online sales of technical books.

Having already won the business, you should know a fair amount about the application you'll be designing. In fact, in most cases, you'll already have seen an FRD of some kind. After all, how can you bid on a piece of work if you don't know what the work entails?

Unfortunately, having an FRD available during the proposal stage can be more the exception than the rule when doing development. Often the FRD is as basic as "We want a Web site to sell stuff." It's your job as developer to review whatever specifications do exist and to clarify as early as possible any uncertainties before they turn into problems.

The FRD is a description of how a site should work from the perspective of a user (either end user or administrative). It also should describe any legacy systems that will need to interface with the application. In addition, it might specify certain platforms or technologies that are required, such as LDAP or J2EE.

Developers often find themselves locked into a technology because someone in a position of power heard that it was cool or was "the next big thing." Part of the requirements process might involve explaining the impacts of using a specific piece of software, both on the schedule and on reliability.

In some cases, the client might not have any idea about how he wants the application to work. In that case, it's your job to act as a knowledge engineer, helping to refine the FRD toward something that you can code from.

The FRD is used to generate the use cases that, in turn, drive the object model and database design. As you review each piece of functionality with the client, ask yourself these questions:

- What are all the possible paths that lead to this piece of functionality?

- What state must be preserved through the action?

- What are all the possible exits from this action?

- What errors can occur during the processing of this action?

- Are there access restrictions on this action?

- What other systems is the action dependent on?

You also need to listen for key phrases that will clue you in to the objects that will need to be modeled, such as user, product, cart, order, history, and so on.

A High-Level View

The Books for Geeks team has already developed a set of wireframes for the proposed Web site. Often the wireframes are produced by the HTML design team (either the client's team or an in-house team working with your group). These people are usually somewhat savvy about usability issues and the limitations of the Web, so you, as developer, stand a pretty good chance of being able to use the design as is.

Occasionally, however, you get handed something that's totally unusable. Either the site flow is awkward, it requires the technology to do something that just isn't possible, or it opens up security holes. You could end up going through several iterations with the design team to get an acceptable set of wireframes.

With these principles in mind, you can look at the requirements for Books for Geeks (BFG). To begin, take a look at Figure 4.1, which shows an overview of the site flow based on the wireframes we've been given.

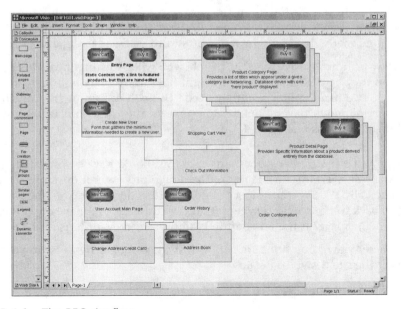

FIGURE 4.1   The BFG site flow.

In this site, all roads hopefully lead to a purchase. Customers enter the site, navigate to products that they want to buy, eventually check out with their shopping cart by giving payment and shipping information, and leave as happy shoppers.

In addition, the site should have some functionality to allow customers to maintain lists of addresses and credit cards so that they don't have to type in this information every time they visit.

Usually, you'll have a slew of questions for the client before you even begin to look at specifics, and building this site is no exception.

In the case of the BFG site, you'd want to know some things simply based on previous experience using or developing e-commerce sites:

- Is the customer allowed to purchase items before logging into the site? For that matter, do you require customers to have a registered account on the site before completing a purchase? In the BFG example site (as in most modern sites) the customer may register before buying, register as a part of the first purchase, or choose not to register and purchase the items as a one-shot transaction. As a result, you will need to handle all of these possibilities in the code.

- Where should the Buy button take the user? On some sites, the Buy button is actually coded as a targeted form or HREF, which brings up an invisible target page that then adds the item to the cart without disturbing the main page. This can be very useful for allowing the customer to purchase many items from a page without having to hit the Back button. Other sites bring the customer to the cart view with each purchase. In the BFG case, the client wants to use the second method, adding the items by stealth using a target page.

- How technically savvy are the people who will be maintaining this content? Can they be trusted to create the right links for the Buy buttons? How much technical handholding will they need? This will determine how much automation you might have to build into even a "static" page to make sure that the functionality is maintained.

These are just a few of many questions that you should have investigated up front because the answers inform the rest of the design process. For example, if the Buy button actually takes the customer to another page, do you need to have a way to navigate back to the previous page so that the customer can make other purchases from the same page? If the Buy button is an off-screen event, this isn't a factor.

When these type of questions are out of the way, you're ready to begin your examination of the site design in detail.

The Entry Page

A typical user experience starts with the entry page. Figure 4.2 shows a wireframe of the entry page. The entry page is statically maintained by the customer's creative department; it will be used to highlight one or more featured books, will offer navigational links into product categories, and will offer access to the customer's profile.

When we say that the page is maintained statically, this means that the content on the page is placed there by HTML designers explicitly. In contrast, some of the pages deeper into the site are created almost purely by JSP operating against database data.

If you've visited many e-commerce sites, this will be familiar. The entry page is often highly stylized with many complicated design elements whose purpose is to entice the customer to purchase specific products. As you navigate down into product categories, the pages begin to look more like lists and less like a designed advertisement.

Sites are organized this way because it's very person-intensive to design pages by hand; this treatment is usually reserved for the top strata of the site. The more specific sections don't need to sell product as much because if you're on one of these pages, you presumably have an interest in the product already. Thus, the complex design is saved for the very few pages that serve as a first introduction to the products available.

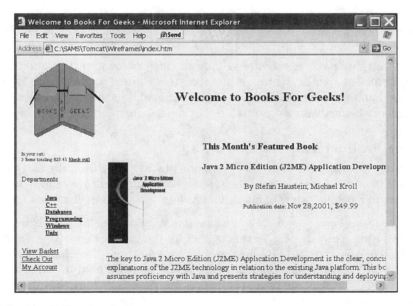

FIGURE 4.2   The BFG entry page.

This page includes a mini-cart, as do most of the pages on the site. The mini-cart gives a synoptic view of the current shopping cart contents, which is typically the number of items in the cart and the total price. Whenever you have content that will be replicated throughout multiple pages of the site, you want to immediately think about using server-side includes to isolate the content on functionality into a single file for maintainability.

You also need to think about the likelihood of mishaps when you have a page that has both complex JSP content and HTML content that will be frequently updated by nondevelopers. It's a very easy thing for an HTML designer to mistype an edit and break programmatic functionality embedded in JSP. That's why it's good practice to clearly demark JSP sections of the pages. Luckily, more people in the creative side of the business are familiar with JSP and know how to avoid breaking it.

Because there are individual products on the entry page, it is possible for a customer to click on the Buy button and directly add an item to the cart. In fact, the customer will be able to purchase items on any number of pages, so the buy functionality is another good candidate for a server-side include.

The Category View

Assuming that the customer doesn't want to purchase the featured item on the front page, several paths can be taken. The first path is to navigate down into one of the product categories, via either the drop-down menu or the sidebar. The sidebar, by the way, is another piece of reused content that should be considered for an include.

The category pages (see Figure 4.3) are an amalgam of static text and template-driven content. The item at the top of the page (the featured or "hero" product) is HTML copy hand-generated by the creative department, but the full listing of books in the category being displayed is produced by a database query.

The Product View

Along with the same "buy now" functionality available from the entry page, customers can navigate from the category page (or featured products on the entry page) to a detailed view of a specific product, as shown in Figure 4.4.

The page in Figure 4.4 is really just an extension of the "JSP page as a database-publishing template" model that is used for the catalog detail page. In other words, it's a JSP page that can be edited for look and feel but that actually gets the content from the database. As has already been mentioned, doing things this way means that you design most of the pages only once, for the master copy, and the actual pages are displayed by populating the master with the specific details of each product. In a site with a few thousand products, this is the only way that you can realistically get the site up.

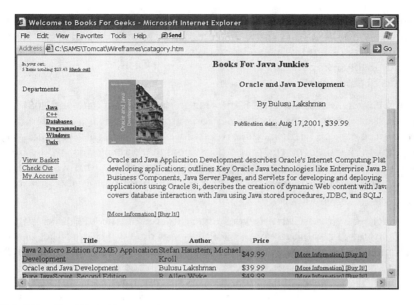

FIGURE 4.3   The BFG category view.

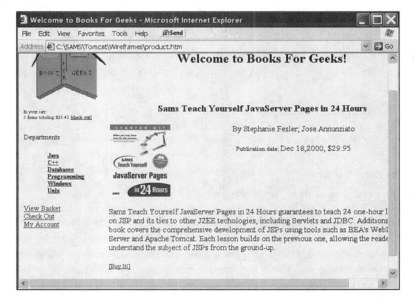

FIGURE 4.4   The BFG product view.

An issue that needs to be addressed with the customer at this point is that of saved URLs in browsers. Will you expose the category or product IDs in the URL of the specific category or product pages? If not, you're looking at a totally different architecture (probably using the MVC model that you'll see in Chapter 16, "The Struts Application Framework").

Typically, JSP pages pass all of their information using form data and POST methods, as well as state information saved in session variables (for example, I'm currently looking at the catalog.) This method results in a single URL for the entire site, which has the advantage that the customers don't bookmark a page that would break if it was the first one encountered during a session. For example, this would be an issue if a customer bookmarked a page for editing account information and then tried to access it before he had logged in.

The countering argument about exposing arguments on the URL links is that sometimes it's useful to be able to save a URL that goes directly to a product or category. For example, if one customer wants to be able to pass on a pointer to a specific product to a friend, there's no way to do it when all the navigational cues are hidden from the URL. So, clearly, there are trade-offs in both directions. In the case of the BFG site, the client wants the category and product navigation to be exposed and wants the rest of the site (especially the account editing) to use POST methods, to try to get the best of both worlds.

The Shopping Cart View

After the customer has filled his basket with a load of goodies, he may either go directly to checkout or review his cart on the full-blown order review page (see Figure 4.5).

Unlike the mini-cart that appears on each page, the shopping cart view lets the customer see the full details of the order, including promotional discounts, and gives the customer the ability to make changes in quantity or remove items altogether.

TODAY ONLY, 10% OFF!

Promotional discounts are an interesting part of an e-commerce Web site. I recently completed work on a site that had seven separate classes of promotions that could run in any combination, from BOGOs (buy one, get one free) to percentage discounts on categories of items.

Promotions can be a real challenge to implement. The site in question also wanted to be able to implement things such as "buy two items from a given manufacturer, get one free," which made the design of the rules engine quite complicated. In the Books for Geeks sample site, the client has asked for a relatively simple promotion model involving fixed-amount discounts on specific items. This is just enough to show the details of how promotions look and feel and how they can be implemented. In this case, a promotional value is shown by a cross-out on the normal price, and the promotional price is shown in red below it (as can be seen in Figure 4.5).

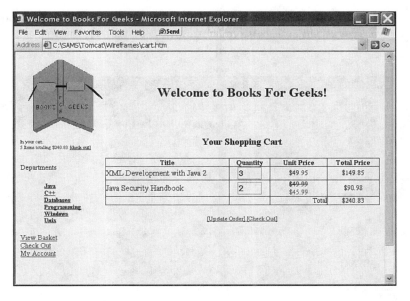

FIGURE 4.5   The BFG shopping cart view.

Here's another important point, one that clients often forget to think about: If you are going to have things like promotions on products and categories, this data presumably will be stored and implemented from a database. How does the client enter the data?

Administrative support can turn into as large-scale of a programming effort as the main consumer site itself. Many a project can be sunk by having these last-minute considerations appear as an "oh, by the way" item at the 11th hour.

In the case of the BFG site, the client has a savvy DBA who will manually maintain all the tables needed to keep the site happy. Trust me that there is basically nothing to be learned from actually showing the implementation of an administrative interface; it is basically a subset of the tricks that you use to deploy the main site.

The Checkout Page

After the customer approves the order or goes directly to the checkout page (see Figure 4.6) from the main site, he will need to fill in his customer order information, such as billing and shipping addresses, shipping details, and payment information. The customer order information is by far the most complicated part of most sites, including this one. There are a few different reasons for this:

- This page contains a lot of validation of data and error checking, and it might require the customer to return to the same page several times to fix bad entries.

- It must integrate with another part of the application—the address book. This allows a logged-in and registered customer to avoid retyping the same information every time he makes a purchase.

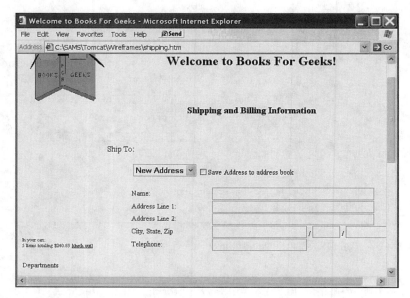

FIGURE 4.6   The BFG checkout view.

When the customer has successfully filled out the checkout page, the application does a number of things behind the scenes. First, it uses a tax calculation application (which is stubbed out in the sample) to compute the proper tax. Next, it uses a third-party shipping application to calculate the shipping charges.

Third-party applications such as tax, shipping, and credit card validation can often remain undecided upon for the first few weeks of a project, as you and the client investigate different products for compatibility and price. The reason that no one in their right mind does them in-house is that they are incredibly complicated in anything but the simplest cases, and good (if sometimes expensive) third-party solutions already exist for them. This is another important reason to provide a good API between the rest of the code and these applications. I've worked on projects in which the tax application was changed three times during the course of the project.

The Order Confirmation Page

When the purchase information is filled out, the customer is taken to the order confirmation page (see Figure 4.7) to verify the order and shipping information one last time. Then the customer presumably will proceed to place the order, although a surprising number of customers "bail out" of an order at the last moment.

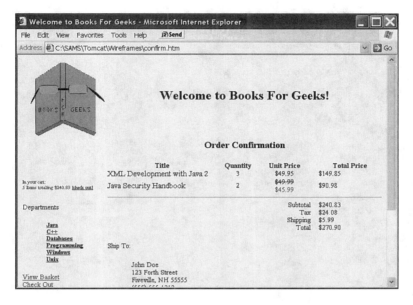

FIGURE 4.7   The BFG order confirmation view.

The Order Receipt

If the order is confirmed, many things occur between that page and the order receipt page (see Figure 4.8), specifically these:

- The application calls a third-party credit card authorization package (stubbed out here) to validate and charge for the order.

- The order details are written into the database.

- If the customer entered a new credit card or address and requested that this information be saved into his profile (assuming that this customer has created an account), this information spills back into those tables.

If, by some miracle, all of this goes as planed, the customer is given a printable receipt. But suppose that it doesn't. Something could go wrong in so many places in the order pipeline just described, from a failure in a third-party application to a full database failure. You will need to work out with the client exactly how these failure notices should be displayed to the customer and what steps the customer can use to retry the operation.

In this sample BFG application, all roads of failure lead to a general "ooopsie" page that makes no attempt to return the customer to the road of virtue. A customer's only recourse is to hit the Back button and try again.

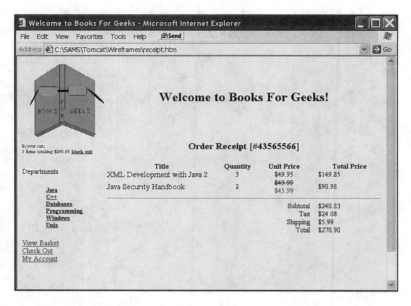

FIGURE 4.8   The BFG order receipt view.

Account Maintenance

Another section of the site is devoted entirely to allowing the creation and maintenance of customer accounts. It begins on the main customer account page (see Figure 4.9).

This page is basically an informational and navigational tool. From here, the customer can do the following:

- Edit and create new shipping addresses (so that he can add a list of friends to buy gifts for).

- Edit a list of credit cards, each of which has an associated billing address.

- View his order history. This brings the customer to the order receipt page for specific orders. For the convenience of nonregistered customers, this page can also be reached from another form that lets the user enter an order number.

A NOTE ON SECURITY

The last item on the previous list, letting the customer view the order by entering an order number, is essentially a security hole, especially if order numbers are sequential.

It doesn't take a super-hacker to figure out that if someone can enter his own order number, he can enter others just as easily. For this reason, the order receipt page certainly doesn't want to display the credit card information—at least, not more that something of the "**** **** **** 1234" variety. But even displaying the name, address, and books ordered allows anyone to invade the privacy of someone who thought that a private order was being placed. Even if you blank out the shipping information, a competitor could use a script to sequentially view every order on your site and know exactly what you're selling.

In these kinds of situations, you have explicitly exposed the method of your potential destruction, but a clever hacker could do this behind your back in lots of ways. For example, if you support a hidden form field value to pass the order number from the confirmation page to the receipt page, a hacker could save the confirmation page to disk, edit the order number to be one higher or lower, and then resubmit the form. If you don't write things just right, that hacker could view the order receipt. Worse, if you are a little bit too clever, the site might recognize that the hacker's order has already been placed and kick the hacker back around to the checkout page with the real customer's credit card information displayed.

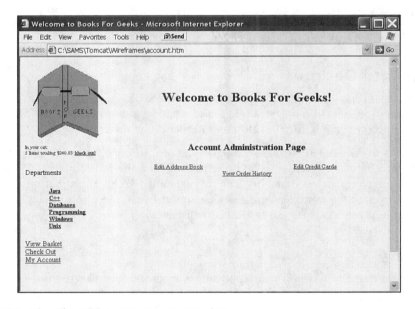

FIGURE 4.9   The BFG customer account view.

Additional Questions

Just as you might want to know a number of things before you begin to examine the site, a number of questions might not be apparent until after you've completed a first walkthrough of the design:

- If the customer is not registered and checks off the appropriate box on the checkout page, is a new user account created for him? Yes, in the case of this site, even though this adds more complexity to the final order checkout process.

- We haven't talked about how registered users are identified. Usernames are complicated. Either you end up having the site generate names that no customer can remember (I'm JTurner234234 on www.geekbooks.com and JTurner435545 on www.nerdbooks.com), or you let the customer chose and then go through the cycle of selecting different names until he finds an unused one. In the BFG example, this username problem was avoided by using e-mail accounts as customer usernames. This can cause users in a household with multiple people but a single e-mail address to share an account, but those are a rarity and this doesn't pose much of an issue.

- The client might not have mentioned that e-mails go out when an order has completed successfully, when changes are made to the account, or when a user requests that his password be mailed (the infamous lost password page).

- Some pages (such as the lost password page) weren't included in the wireframes shown here. We'll do them on the fly during the development process.

Diving into Design

Now that you have a basic understanding of the site design, let's move on to developing use cases, creating object models, and creating a database schema. This will be covered next in Chapter 5, "Developing ERDs and Use Cases."

The Books for Geeks FRD was on the light side of the continuum, made up of several wireframes and a high-level description of the site functionality. FRDs can be much more complicated than this. The more detailed an FRD is, the more secure you can be in your time estimates and risk assessment of a project because less during the development process is left for last-minute discovery.

Summary

Before you begin to develop your application, it's important to work out exactly what the application needs to do. This is the purpose of an FRD. It documents the way that users will encounter the application and the functionalities that will be available to them. An FRD also provides a framework for determining issues that must be resolved before development begins. It is the contract between you and the client regarding what must be delivered. An FRD can be developed based on a series of conversations with the client, mockups (sometimes called wireframes), or both.

Some overall issues must be addressed before you can begin to design an FRD, and others will crop up during the thought and design process.

When you've completed the FRD and received approval, you'll be ready to move on to the next phase (design), with a good understanding of the overall needs of the client and how the applications flow will work as a whole.

5

Developing ERDs and Use Cases

Between the FRD and the actual development of the application, there's the all-important architectural work. In a small application, this could be negligible or might even be rolled into the development as you go along.

In larger projects, however, you need to keep everyone dancing to the same tune. This means, among other things, that you've thought out how you're going to represent the various objects that make up the application, and you've made a list of all the functionality that needs to be implemented so that none of the details fall through the cracks. This is where entity relationship diagrams (ERDs) and use cases come in.

The Entity Relation Diagram

If you've had any exposure to object-oriented programming, you're sure to have encountered entity relation diagrams (ERD) at some point. At its core, the ERD is a snapshot of all the players that make up an application and how those players relate to each other.

JAVA AND OOP

By its nature, there's no way you can program in Java without developing objects. After all, every Java program is really a class. But, as with any other tool, it can be used in a right way and a wrong way.

Most Java texts try to teach the basics of good object-oriented design, but if you come from a background of mainly developing applets, you might never have worked with more than one or two classes, or even objects. When you begin to develop large applications based on Java, you need to apply object-oriented methodologies to the project, or you'll end up with a mess.

This book tries to introduce and demonstrate good OO design techniques, but there's no replacement for a strong grounding in the technologies. I encourage anyone who is approaching this type of development without a background in OO to pick up a good book on the topic.

An ERD doesn't say anything about how an application works—that is left to use cases. The ERD is concerned with only the units of information that make up the application and how they connect.

After you've developed the use cases and thought about how you want to implement the application, you transform the ERD into a static class diagram, which is similar to an ERD. In addition to documenting the contents of the objects, however, a static class diagram also documents what the objects do (or at least what methods they implement).

SPEAKING OO

A note about terminology use: In the industry, terms such as *ERD*, *class diagram*, and *use case* have very specific definitions with rules about how to draw the box and lines, what a dotted line means, and such. People make a lot of money writing books about how to make these beautiful diagrams. Specifically, the Unified Modeling Language (UML), which is really just a codification of a collection of tools for representing object-oriented design, has become an industry unto itself.

In my opinion, some people have begun to mistake the model for the thing that the model is supposed to represent. They get so hung up on doing a perfect UML design that they never really get going on the actual application until late in the game. The antithesis of this approach is the extreme programming model, which relies more on short development cycles with frequent customer feedback.

Tools such as UML do have their place. They have several advantages in large projects. For example, tools such as TogetherJ can automatically move between UML designs and actual code/database schemas. You can also be more confident that everyone is looking at the design in the same way.

Personally, I've never bothered a great deal with that degree of formalism; it strikes me as an exercise in getting good at something that's not really about getting the job done. When you see a diagram in this book and it doesn't look like the ones you see in the more formal books, just squint a bit and go for the meaning.

Before we begin an ERD for the Books for Geeks Web site, let's look at a simple ERD for a hypothetical object model of a car with people in it (see Figure 5.1).

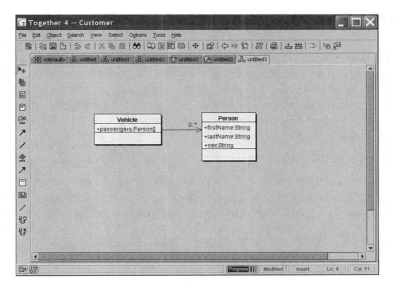

FIGURE 5.1   A very simple ERD.

This rather basic example has two classes, Vehicle and Person. The Vehicle class has a single attribute, an array of Person objects called passengers. The Person class, in turn, has the person's last name, first name, and sex as attributes. The ERD lets you see graphically that the Vehicle class references the Person class through the Passenger attribute. These diagrams were developed using TogetherJ, one of the more popular Java OO tools. While TogetherJ will create Java skeletons and database schemas for you based on your designs, it was used in these examples only to draw diagrams. I'm still of the old school, and I like to do my design work in Emacs.

ERDs are a good way to begin to understand where the information in an application is stored and grouped. It also serves as a template for your database schema because objects usually map nearly one to one into database tables.

Mining High-Level Use Cases Descriptions for Objects

The traditional wisdom is that you develop your list of objects by detailing all the use cases and then extracting all the nouns. I find that you can get to the same place much faster by describing the application at a high level (as kind of a mission statement for an application) and isolating the nouns from that description.

Here is the mission statement for the BFG Web site:

A user enters the site. There the user is presented with a list of products organized into categories. He can place products into his shopping cart, select a shipping address from his address book or enter it manually, specify an existing credit card from his wallet or enter the card number manually, and approve the order. The credit card is then validated and an order is generated. The price of products could be affected by promotions that are currently running on the site. The user can also add, edit, and delete entries from his address book and wallet.

Now let's take another look at it, with the potential objects in italics:

A *user* enters the site. There the user is presented with a list of *products* organized into *categories*. He can place *products* into his *shopping cart*, select a shipping *address* from his *address book* or enter it manually, specify an existing *credit card* from his *wallet* or enter the card number manually, and approve the *order*. The *credit card* is then validated and an *order* is generated. The price of *products* might be affected by *promotions* that are currently running on the site. The user can also add, edit, and delete entries from his *address book* and *wallet*.

Note that it is a good idea to be judicious in your selection of nouns. Some books advocate literally grabbing every noun (which would have included words such as *site*, *entries*, and *list*), but it is preferable to filter out the nouns that don't really translate into real objects as you look over the description.

At this point, it becomes a matter of personal style regarding how you proceed. I usually like to sketch out the class diagram before proceeding to use cases. Some might argue that this is backward, that you need to have your use cases fully realized before you design your objects. I disagree, for two reasons:

- Even before you dive into use cases, you normally have a pretty good idea what the application needs to do. Thus, you can take a first cut at the attributes that each class will make use of before you dive into details.

- For me, at least, doing use cases isn't an exercise in isolation. I'm also starting to think about implementation as I detail the cases. Knowing what my palette of objects is before I start helps that process.

The case against this approach is that you can end up refactoring your objects a lot as you gain more detailed knowledge of the application. While this might be an issue once you begin coding, it isn't often a real problem when refactoring is still in the paper-and-pencil stage. Clearly, you want to understand the entire application through a detailed set of use cases before you begin to create a database schema, but this shouldn't prevent you from drawing out a few rough ideas of table layouts before you start.

The User Class

Let's begin by looking at the User class because the user/customer is usually the center of the application's purpose. What do you need to know about a user?

Obviously, the client will have information that he wants you to capture about the user—things that aren't directly related to making the application work but that are important to the business model. For example, the fact that the customer's phone number is required doesn't really change the way the site works much in terms of design, but it can be critical for the business users from an operational standpoint. For example, they might want to call a customer if there is a problem with an order.

In addition to the client's requirements, you'll find the need for housekeeping attributes and other implementation-specific information that the client neither knows nor cares about. As the application development progresses, you will also find that you're discovering new attributes to add. That's okay; an ERD should be a living document until the code freezes before deployment. You always discover things you hadn't thought about when you start coding.

In an e-commerce site, you usually know what you need to capture about the user: name, address, telephone number, e-mail address, and billing information. This represents the bare minimum. This case would seem to lead naturally to the ERD shown in Figure 5.2

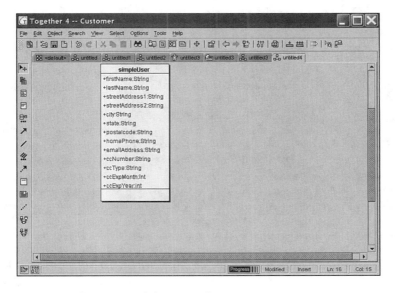

FIGURE 5.2   A simplistic view of the User class.

WHEN THINGS GET COMPLEX

The bare-minimum user schema is just that—the bare minimum. I've worked on pharmacy sites that had to capture significant amounts of medical information about the customer. Everything from the physician's name to drug allergies and current prescriptions needed to be captured, in multipage forms with all sorts of validations and cross-checks.

I've also done insurance sites with more than 300 pieces of information being captured on a single, compact enrollment form. In this case, things were a bit easier because I had the paper form to use for comparison. In fact, it was a requirement that the online form match the paper version as closely as possible.

It's critical that you get the data set correct the first time. It's somewhere between difficult and impossible to get a piece of data after the customer has already been to the site and gone. A good set of use cases should include this information.

The data set that you need to capture for a customer, however, is a bit more complicated than it might seem. For one thing, most e-commerce sites (including this one) allow you to ship a purchase to one address and bill it to another address. This would require the class to look more like Figure 5.3.

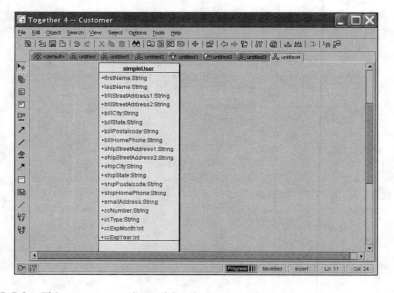

FIGURE 5.3 Things get complicated for the User class.

Not only is the User object quickly filling with attributes (and you haven't even begun to add those that will be needed for application housekeeping), but even this design for the User object won't handle your needs because you allow multiple shipping addresses to be stored with the user in an address book, and multiple billing addresses to be stored with the user in his wallet of credit cards (each credit card has an associated address.)

To make multiple addresses work, you need to break addresses as well as credit cards into their own object classes. Credit cards, in turn, point to address objects as well. This leads to the ERD shown in Figure 5.4.

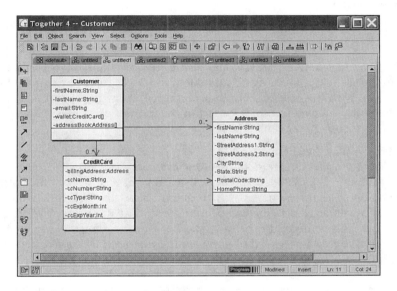

FIGURE 5.4   The User class and associates.

The Customer class has been reduced to the bare essentials: last and first name of the customer, e-mail address, and arrays of addresses and credit cards. Credit cards also use the address object, but because this object stores only last name and first name for an address and some credit cards require a middle name or initial, the name on the credit card is stored explicitly rather than using the name fields of the address.

It should be noted that this design will work only for customers in the United States. For international use, you would need to add fields such as Country and make sure that you allowed enough space for non–U.S. telephone numbers and postal codes. Frankly, very few e-commerce sites are prepared for the numerous headaches associated with international business anyway; details such as shipping, tariffs, and taxation get very complicated in international cases.

You might also consider using more internationalized names for variables, such as givenName rather than firstName. This can be confusing for developers, however, and I'll wager that many U.S. developers couldn't tell you what a "given name" was, but they'd all know what a first name was. If you're going to be mapping to LDAP (see Chapter 15, " Using LDAP with JNDI"), you're going to end up having to use terms such as `givenName` anyway because those are the names used in the standard LDAP schema.

Still a lot of details are left to explore at this point, especially in regard to how this data will actually be stored in the database. This gives you enough information to continue, though.

The `Product` Class

Now that you have customers, it would be nice if they could buy something. For that, you need the products. Again, the Books for Geeks folks have no doubt supplied you with the product data: title, author(s), ISBN, price, and descriptive text. But there is also hierarchical information in the form of categories that you need to model. This is shown in Figure 5.5.

One question that the client has not yet been asked and that now needs to be posed is this: Can a product live in more than one category? The answer, in this case, is yes. For example, a book like this that deals with Java, Web sites, and databases might end up in all three categories. This doesn't affect the ERD much, but it does mean that the database schema will be more complicated. This type of after-the-fact need for details is common in the early stage of a project; you will rarely remember to ask everything that you need to know on the first pass. Of course, the danger lies in details that you haven't asked about by the time the project ends.

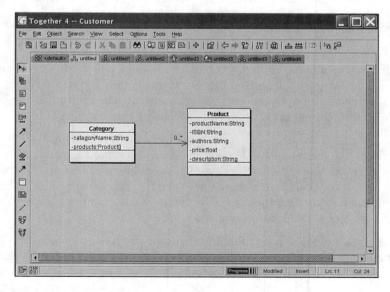

FIGURE 5.5 Products and categories.

The Shopping Cart and Order Classes

Looking back on the initial list of classes captured from the mission statement, it looks like everything with the exception of three classes has been modeled—the shopping cart, the order, and promotions. Let's hold off on promotions until the detailed use cases are done, but let's consider the shopping cart and order classes now.

A shopping cart is a list of products that the customer has placed into his basket, whereas the order is the shopping cart once the customer has decided to actually purchase the items. In some ways, they're very different. A shopping cart is temporary, meaning that it might not persist beyond the current session. An order is forever, and it needs to be stored and available at any point in the future for fulfillment and auditing.

In other ways, they are similar. Both store lists of products and quantities, both need to do calculations to figure out the current balance, and so on. In fact, they are so similar that you can use the same classes to store information for both purposes. So, although there will be an order object that stores information specific to orders, it will use the same shopping cart object to store the actual contents of the order.

At this point, an interesting subtlety occurs. Orders need to be snapshots of the information in place at the time the order was taken. This means that, as much as you might like to have the order point to the address and credit card objects that were used to place the order, they might be edited or removed by the customer after the date of purchase. As a result, you need to actually duplicate that data in the database for explicit storage. You'll do this by creating new address and credit card objects to hold the values as they were at the time the order was placed (see Figure 5.6).

The same goes for products—the price might change, as might the product description. The order object needs to hold the user's ordered products as they were the day they were ordered. How are you going to do this? The practical answer is to reuse the product objects to store the unique products that a customer purchased, but then to store them in a different table in the database. This might sound a bit confusing, but it will be clearer once you start coding.

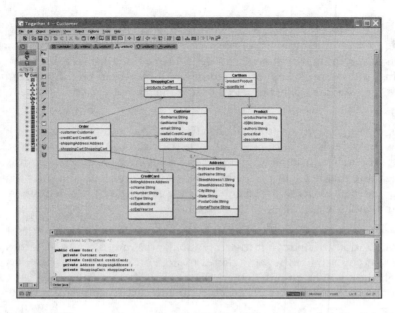

FIGURE 5.6   New address and credit card objects hold the values when an order is placed.

Use Cases

Use cases are both a blessing and a curse. On one hand, they are the absolute Bible of what you need to do to make the application work. Without a well-defined set of use cases, you're at the mercy of the client, who can then add new functionality on a whim and claim that it's inside the scope of the project.

On the other hand, use cases are often the dullest, least interesting, most tedious (did I mention boring?) part of the software-development process. They represent a methodical walk through every single way someone can possibly use the application and every possible outcome. It's somewhat like a brute-force computational approach to software design. In any event, it must be done, so it's best to just get started.

An important thing to remember is that, during the process of capturing use cases, you should concentrate on gathering the requirements rather than trying to figure out how to implement them, although you may find yourself flagging certain items as important to remember during implementation. Use-case development is supposed to be about brainstorming, not nitpicking the details.

Use Case: A New User Enters the Site

Start with a new user approaching the site. There are formalized diagrams for use-case analysis, but they can be a bit clumsy, so let's stick to a textual description.

Users are presented with a standard entry page, as was already described. However, in place of the normal "Hello John" message that a registered user with a cookie would receive, the new user gets a "Would you like to register?" prompt and a "Registered users log in here" link.

At this point, you might protest that neither of those elements appeared on the wireframes. This is an example of a feature that the client's business users (the people who understand the business needs of the site) wanted but the graphic designers didn't know about. So, we'll assume two things for the moment:

- Such elements will be designed by the time development begins.

- You need to keep a cookie around with the user ID (which is an e-mail address in the BFG example) to recognize and greet users when they log in.

On the entry page, users can immediately purchase the featured item(s) on the page. This means that both registered and unregistered users can place items in the cart. They can also navigate to a category, click the Login button, or click the Register button. A new user, however, should not be given access to the My Account pages because new users don't have them yet.

Use Case: An Existing User Enters the Site

This is essentially the same as the new user case, except that the personal greeting replaces the registration section. You also need to add a "Not John? Click here to log in as another user or register" button, which will then need to lead to another page for login and registration.

In addition, the My Account links will be active for existing users. Also, if the user had previously placed items in a basket and his session timed out, those items need to spill back into the cart. Notice that you now have a new requirement to create a persistent shopping cart based on this use case.

Use Case: A User Clicks a Category Page

When a user clicks one of the category links, the page is populated from a template. The top portion of the template shows the "hero" product. (In business jargon, this is the product that should be specially featured on a piece of advertising.) The identity of the hero product for a category is flagged in the database. When you hear this, you should immediately make a note to yourself that the category class will need a new attribute—a pointer to the product that is the featured product for the category.

As you saw in the wireframe in the previous chapter, on the Web page the product list is a table that lists the title, author, and price of each product in the category with Buy and More Info links. The Buy button should refresh the current page so that the mini-cart total will update.

One thing that should raise a red flag at this point and that has not yet been addressed are the number of items to display per page. Suppose that there are 250 products in a category. Do you display them all on a single page? Do you display the first 10 and have Back and Next buttons to let users navigate? And what order do you need to display these products in? By author? By title?

In this case, the client requests that all the appropriate titles be listed on the same page, that the default be to list by title, but that the user should be able to reorder the list by clicking the headings of the table. In the back of your mind, remember that the object you use to model the user session will need to store that data.

Use Case: User Clicks Buy from Any Page

Clicking the Buy button does several things. It adds the item to the cart, combining it with any existing items of the same type in the cart (one book A becomes two book A's rather than two entries for the same book). Then the server redisplays the same page with the updated mini-cart information.

Use Case: User Clicks More Info from Any Page

Clicking the More Info button brings the user to the product detail page. Again, this page is generated from a template with database calls. The only button on the page (other than the normal navigational tools) is a By button with a quantity box next to it.

Use Case: User Clicks View Cart from Any Page

The View Cart button takes the user to the view cart page, as described in the FRD. At this point, any promotional values are displayed (although the price in the mini-cart also reflects any promotions applied to the order).

Promotion Use Cases

Also at this point, you should have the details on the promotion design. Although some sites have hideously complex promotion requirements (I have worked on sites with as many as seven different types of promotions), the BFG site has only two. The

Buy One, Get One Free (BOGOF) promotion allows a customer to get a gift if he buys certain promoted items. The Percent Off (%OFF) promotion specifies a certain percentage discount to be applied to targeted books.

And, as is sometimes the case, only one of these promotions will be live at the time the Web site is launched—the BOGOF promotion. Thus, although the schema should support both types, you'll need only code one right now.

Buy One, Get One Free

The BOGOF promotion works as follows: The BOGOF can apply either to a single book title or to a category of books. If the customer qualifies for a BOGOF based on a purchase of a certain threshold number of items, a gift item is placed in the cart with a zero price.

This leads to several interesting scenarios. For example, suppose that the gift item is already in the cart. Is that item made a free item, or is another copy of the item added to the cart? And if qualifying items are removed from the cart, does the gift item get removed, or is it simply made a nonfree item?

In the BFG example case, the client has indicated that the gift items are not normally sold. For example, a customer might get a leatherette Palm Pilot case if he purchases J2ME books. Because the gifts will not appear in the normal category listings, the customer has no way to add them manually.

If items are removed, bringing the total in the cart below the threshold, the gift is also to be removed.

%OFF

The %OFF promo is much more straightforward. Again, the promotion can apply to a specific book or a category of books. In this case, the promotion requires that the specified discount be taken off the cover price.

If two %OFF promotions happen to apply to the same item, the discount is not compounded. The customer gets the highest of the discounts.

All discounts are indicated by a red line of text under the item in the cart, specifying what discount was received.

The end result of the promotion use cases is this: You'll need to be able to store two different kinds of items in the shopping cart—items that are promotional and regular items. This can be done with two different object classes or with a common class with a flag to indicate the promotional state of the item.

You'll also need objects to model the promotions themselves, objects that will iterate over the cart and modify the cart as appropriate for the individual promotions.

Use Case: User Clicks Checkout from Any Page

The Checkout button takes the customer to the billing and shipping (or checkout) page. At this point, the customer either can choose from a pre-existing shipping address and payment method (if he is a registered customer) or can fill in the form manually. A check box at the bottom of the page allows the customer to register as a new user, but this box is present only if the customer is not already logged in.

A list of shipping methods is also presented as radio buttons with shipping costs. This information is stored in the database; you'll need to add some new objects to model it.

Use Case: User Clicks Submit from Checkout Page

After the customer presses the Submit order button on the checkout page, the following validations and calculations need to occur:

- Check that first and last names are not blank
- Check that the shipping address line is not blank
- Check that the shipping city is not blank
- Check that the shipping state is selected on the pull-down menu
- Check that the shipping postal code is not blank and either is *NNNNN* or *NNNNN-NNNN* (where *N* is a digit)
- Check that the e-mail address is not blank and is of the form XXXXXX@TTTTTT.ZZZZZZ
- Check that the credit card number is not blank
- Check that the credit card prefix is valid for the credit card type
- Check that the credit card passes checksum validation
- Check that the credit card name and address pass validation checks for shipping name and address
- Check that the shipping method is selected

A failure of any of the validation checks causes the application to redisplay the page with all the data filled in and a red error message indicating the problem directly above the field in question.

If all the validations are successful, the order-confirmation page is displayed. This page includes the cost for the selected shipping method and any tax calculated (this is the first time you could calculate tax for an order because you previously didn't know where it was being shipped.)

Use Case: User Clicks Buy It on Order-Confirmation Page

When the customer confirms the order, the credit card number that was given is authorized for the charge, the order is written into the database, a confirmation e-mail is sent to the customer, and the customer is brought to the order-receipt page. If the credit card authorization fails, the customer is brought back to the shipping and billing page, with an error message at the top indicating that there was a problem with the credit card.

In addition, if a new address or credit card was used and the Save to Address Book or Save to Wallet box was checked, that data is spilled back to the appropriate database table. If the Register Me check box was checked, a new user is created on the fly.

Use Case: Registered User Clicks My Account from Any Page

Clicking on the My Account button (which is available only to registered users who have logged in) will present a user with the account page, which is basically a navigational tool to the three things that a user can do with an account.

Use Case: User Clicks the My Order History Button from the My Account Page

Clicking the My Order History button causes a list of all the orders placed during the last 30 days to appear in table form with the order number, date, and order total price displayed. Clicking an order number brings up the order receipt.

Use Case: User Clicks the My Address Book Button from the My Account Page

Clicking the address book brings up a list of all of a user's stored shipping addresses in table form, along with an Add New button. Clicking an address allows the user to edit the entry, which is validated as if it were being used in an order. Clicking Add New also brings up a blank form, which is validated in the same manner.

Use Case: User Clicks the My Wallet Button from the My Account Page

Clicking the My Wallet button brings up a list of stored credit cards. The user can edit or add to the list in the same manner as the address book, with the same validations that are done for a credit card in an order.

Use Case: User Clicks Create New User Button

This presents the customer with a form with the basic user information (e-mail address and password with password confirmation). Although a lot more information is required to actually place an order, the site will not gather address book details or credit card information at this point because that much information might be a barrier to entry, making the customer fill in a lot of information before he actually needs to.

Moving Ahead

Now that you understand the application, you need to put in place the database schema that will underpin it. That's the mission of the next chapter. When you have data in place, you'll be ready to start coding, beginning with the user registration portion of the application.

In a real project, you would go back after the use cases were complete and refine the ERD to reflect any new discoveries that you made during additional discussions with the client. In this case, the ERD that you started with is good enough to take you into database design. There are also aspects of the object model that would be much more complex in a live e-commerce site. For example, you haven't done anything about representing shipping methods.

As with any large application, the ERD and use cases presented here will have to evolve as the actual application comes together. Some things have been forgotten or overlooked, and other things will turn out to be clumsy or impractical in practice. That's the purpose of change control—to allow both the client and the implementers to make course corrections midstream without anyone panicking. Most major projects have a person at the management level whose main purpose is to handle change control and "scope creep."

CHANGE ISN'T ALWAYS GOOD

As used in software engineering, *scope* refers to the set of features or functionalities that are required to be present in the finished product. Items are either in scope or out of scope. It is usually the job of the project manager to work with the client, handling change control to the FRD.

For example, if you were developing software for an automated teller machine, it would probably be in scope for the machine to be capable of giving the correct amount of money on a withdrawal (at least, one hopes that it would be in scope...).

However, the client might suddenly decide that the bank customer should be allowed to specify how the withdrawal should be paid out (in five $10 bills rather than two $20s and a $10, for example). Unless that had been mentioned up front during requirement gathering, it would probably be considered out of scope by the development team.

At this point, the project manager would contact the client, indicate that the request was out of scope, and look for direction from the client. On a time and materials project, in which the client pays by the hour, the project manager would present an estimate for the cost of the new requirement. On a fixed-price contract, the client would need to increase the cost of the project, remove another requirement, or drop the request.

It's common in large projects to see requirements bargaining, in which new requirements are traded for less important ones already in the FRD. When the client manages to sneak in new requirements because the FRD was vague or because he has the clout to push them through, developers complain about scope creep.

Summary

ERDs and use cases are the concrete representation of what an application is required to do and what kind of information you need to maintain to do it.

ERDs can be thought of as the nouns of the application; use cases are the verbs. You can get an initial idea of the ERDs and use cases by developing a mission statement for the application, a short summary of the requirements from a very high level.

You can develop a simple ERD before you gather the specific use cases; it will be refined afterward in light of the specific requirements.

6

Creating the Database Schema and Populating Data

At this point, you should have a good idea of how an application will be represented in Java objects—you're halfway there. But Java objects by themselves have no permanence, so you'll need to back up some of them with database records to hold their data for long-term retrieval.

In this chapter, you'll learn how to design and populate a database schema that can interact with JSP. As you'll see, sometimes a single Java object maps to a single table, and sometimes it maps to several. In addition, you'll see how MySQL handles sequences and you'll learn the special requirements that this imposes on design.

The Fading Role of the DBA

In the early years of e-commerce, the database administrator   (DBA) was someone whose sole responsibility was the care and feeding of the database. In those days, setting up (for example) an Oracle instance was a monumental effort, and having someone who knew all the pitfalls to do it for you was a real benefit.

Well, those days are over. Modern databases are much more simple to set up and maintain, and the developer doesn't have the luxury of leaving all the database maintenance to another person anymore. Modern applications coexist with their database back ends like conjoined twins, so the developer needs to be an integral part of the database design.

That said, there's still a place for dedicated database professionals. When you start dealing with the very high end of the database spectrum (multiple redundant servers, geographically distributed databases, or highly tuned schemas), you still might need to call in these database specialists.

Building a Database Schema

Now that you're ready to build your schema and populate it with data, it's worth talking about how to manage your database.

In the BFG example, MySQL is the database that was chosen. Accordingly, a database instance, called BFG, was created to use with it. Although you can do schema and database maintenance on the fly during development, it's important to capture all that information into scripts that can be run repeatedly, each time re-creating a perfect beginning state for your database.

WHY USE MYSQL?

When choosing a database for a JSP project, a number of considerations come into play. MySQL certainly has one overwhelming characteristic that places it at the head of the class: It's free.

If price were the only factor, that would be the end of the story. However, MySQL does have its problems. Although each release offers a huge leap from the previous one in functionality, MySQL still lags behind the commercial products.

When choosing a database, you need to consider not only your needs today, but also your anticipated growth. This is because, unlike application platforms that can be interchanged without a lot of difficulty, it's an extremely involved proposition to swap out databases midstream.

You need to consider both the size of your data and how complex the queries are that you'll be running on it. For example, when you start to introduce a lot of inner joins into your queries, you can really bog down database performance.

There's no doubt that, as of today, the commercial databases such as Oracle and Sybase offer better high-end performance. So, if you're looking at an application that's going to do hundreds or thousands of transactions an hour, you might need to move up to one of these packages, although it won't be cheap.

For the purposes of these examples, though, and for most small to midsize Web applications, MySQL will do just as well as the larger packages.

To begin, you need a script to create the database itself. This can be done directly from the MySQL GUI, but, again, you want it to be easily and automatically reproducible, even by untrained personnel. Listing 6.1 shows the script version for Windows (you'd need a different version for Linux, although the SQL scripts themselves would remain the same):

LISTING 6.1   database_create.bat

```
REM Script to create the Books For Geeks database instance

if NOT DEFINED MYSQL_HOME SET MYSQL_HOME=C:\MYSQL

%MYSQL_HOME%\bin\mysqladmin drop BFG
%MYSQL_HOME%\bin\mysqladmin create BFG
%MYSQL_HOME%\bin\mysqladmin reload

%MYSQL_HOME%\bin\mysql -e="\. bfg_init.sql" BFG
```

This script assumes either that the environment variable MYSQL_HOME has been created or that MYSQL lives in C:\MYSQL. If you've followed the instructions in Appendix B, "Getting and Installing MySQL and JDBC," this is where it will be installed. Otherwise, you'll need to create an environment variable called MYSQL_HOME with the correct path. First, the script drops the current BFG database (if it exists), re-creates it, and reloads the database privileges tables, just in case (Appendix B goes into more detail about MySQL's access control system.) Then it goes on to execute an init script.

Similarly, the bfg_init file (shown in Listing 6.2) is just a list of further initializations to run. You might notice that SQL (like UNIX shell scripts) uses the # character for comments.

LISTING 6.2   bfg_init.sql

```
# Initialization scripts for the BFG website

\. init_customer.sql
\. init_products.sql
\. init_order.sql
\. init_promotions.sql
\. init_misc.sql
\. init_data.sql
```

The Customer Tables

It's not until you get into the first of these subscripts (init_customer, Listing 6.3) that you finally start to write some real SQL.

LISTING 6.3   init_customer.sql

```
# Schema creation for customer-related tables

drop table if exists CUSTOMER;

create table CUSTOMER (
      CUSTOMER_ID    int not null auto_increment,
      EMAIL_ADDRESS  char(50) not null unique,
      PASSWORD             char(20) not null,
      primary key(CUSTOMER_ID),
      index(EMAIL_ADDRESS));

drop table if exists ADDRESS;
create table ADDRESS (
      ADDRESS_ID     int not null auto_increment,
      FIRST_NAME     char(30) not null,
      LAST_NAME      char(40) not null,
      STREET_1           char(128) not null,
      STREET_2           char(128),
      CITY         char(50) not null,
      STATE        char(2) not null,
      POSTAL_CODE    char(10) not null,
      primary key(ADDRESS_ID));

drop table if exists ADDRESS_BOOK;
create table ADDRESS_BOOK (
      CUSTOMER_KEY     int references CUSTOMER,
      ADDRESS_KEY      int references ADDRESS);

drop table if exists CREDIT_CARD;
create table CREDIT_CARD (
      CUSTOMER_KEY     int references CUSTOMER,
      CARD_TYPE        char(5) not null,
      CARD_NUMBER      char(25) not null,
      CARD_OWNERNAME   char(50) not null,
      CARD_EXPMONTH    int not null,
      CARD_EXPYEAR     int not null,
      ADDRESS_KEY      int references ADDRESS);
```

As discussed, the customer table itself is pretty sparse: All it holds is a unique ID for the customer, the customer's e-mail address (which is the visible key to the customer), and the password for the account.

Because MySQL doesn't have sequences like Oracle's sequences, you have to use an autoincrementing int field instead. The basic mistake that developers make in this situation is to assume that they can do an insert into this table, read back MAX(CUSTOMER_KEY), and learn the value for the newly created customer. This would work in a single-threaded application, but not in one in which several sessions might try to create a user at the same time. Thankfully, MySQL has the capability to read back the value of an autoincrementing column when an insert is executed, so you'll be able to use this method instead. The only other alternative is to put a lock on the table just before doing the insert, immediately read back the value, and then unlock the table again (you don't want to lock it too long because others might need to use it.)

If you used the ADDRESS table only to store the addresses in the address book, you could just embed CUSTOMER_KEY as a foreign key in the ADDRESS table itself. But because you also reference ADDRESS in the credit card table, you need to make a cross-reference table called ADDRESS_BOOK to hold the one-to-many relationship between CUSTOMER and ADDRESS.

Because only one address is associated with a given credit card, you can embed the ADDRESS ID directly in the CREDIT_CARD table. The CARD_NUMBER field is made larger than most card numbers actually are (16 digits) because some newer European cards are 20 digits, and who knows what the future may hold. It's better to waste a few bytes per record now than have to modify the entire schema later.

Another interesting question to consider at this point is whether to store the credit card expiration date as a date field or as separate integer fields. By storing it as a date, you can easily check for credit card currency with the Date.before and Date.after methods, but you'd have to construct and deconstruct the dates from the fields in the forms. Because the comparisons are simple (basically, is the expiration year greater than the current year, or is the year equal and the month greater?), you are better off storing the date as discrete fields instead, as this example does.

The Product Tables

Now you're ready to look at the product and category tables. In the application in Listing 6.4, you're dealing with a simple one-layer hierarchy of products, so the schema is relatively simple.

LISTING 6.4   init_product.sql

```
# Schema creation for product-related tables

drop table if exists PRODUCT;

create table PRODUCT (
```

LISTING 6.4   Continued

```
        ISBN        char(20) not null,
        TITLE       varchar(128) not null,
        PRICE       float not null,
        PUB_DATE            date not null,
        DESCRIPTION  blob,
        primary key(ISBN));

drop table if exists AUTHOR;

create table AUTHOR (
        AUTHOR_ID    int not null unique,
        AUTHOR_NAME  char(128) not null,
        primary key(AUTHOR_ID));

drop table if exists PRODUCT_AUTHOR_XREF;

create table PRODUCT_AUTHOR_XREF (
        PRODUCT_ISBN  char(20) references PRODUCT,
        AUTHOR_ID     int references AUTHOR);

drop table if exists CATEGORY;

create table CATEGORY (
        CATEGORY_ID    int not null,
        CATEGORY_NAME  char(30) not null,
        FEATURED_PRODUCT        char(20) references PRODUCT,
        primary key(CATEGORY_ID));

drop table if exists CATEGORY_PRODUCT_XREF;

create table CATEGORY_PRODUCT_XREF (
        CATEGORY_ID   int references CATEGORY,
        PRODUCT_ISBN  char(20) references PRODUCT);
```

The product table itself holds the basic information captured about a book: the price, title, and so on. Because the descriptions can be longer than 255 characters, which is the limit for MySQL char strings, use a blob instead. Blobs are used in SQL to hold large chunks of data (such as images), but they can be used for large text blocks as well.

You embed attributes (such as ISBN) that are uniquely associated with this product, but not the authors. The author is not directly embedded in the product for two reasons. First, there is frequently more than one author of a book. Second, making this a separate joined table, it will be easier to add search functionalities such as "show me all books by author X."

The author table is joined with a simple cross-reference. No autoincrementing field is used for the author ID because this data will come from a static file, not from dynamic creation of new records during the application's execution. In other words, these records are prepopulated and the author ID can be hardwired into the file used to fill the table. You need to know the value of the ID so that you can use it to prepopulate other tables that depend on it (such as promotions).

Categories are also a simple table with a cross-reference to the products that live in the category. The only item of note here is the featured product field, which is used to indicate which product should be displayed at the top of the category page.

The Order Tables

The order contains pointers to credit card and shipping address records stored in the CREDIT_CARD and ADDRESS tables. In addition, it contains specific information about the order total price and subtotals for shipping and tax. By the way, the table is called ORDERS rather than ORDER because ORDER is a reserved word in many SQL dialects.

You need to be able to look at an order as it was on the day that the customer placed it. The ORDER_ITEM table stores just enough information to be able to display a product on an order history page or generate a bill of lading for the shipping department to fulfill the order.

LISTING 6.5   init_order.sql

```
# Schema creation for order-related tables

drop table if exists ORDERS;

create table ORDERS (
      ORDER_ID           int not null auto_increment,
      EMAIL_ADDRESS char(50),
      ADDRESS_KEY   int references ADDRESS,
      CARD_KEY           int references CREDIT_CARD,
      ORDER_DATE         date,
      ORDER_SUBTOTAL  float,
      ORDER_TAX          float,
      ORDER_SHIPPING  float,
```

LISTING 6.5   Continued

```
        ORDER_TOTAL        float,
        primary key(ORDER_ID));
drop table if exists ORDER_ITEM;

create table ORDER_ITEM (
        ORDER_ID                   int references ORDERS,
        PRODUCT_ISBN          char(20) not null,
        PRODUCT_TITLE         varchar(128) not null,
        QUANTITY                   int not null,
        UNIT_PRICE            float not null,
        TOTAL_PRICE           float not null);
```

Again, this is not difficult—it has everything that the site needs to capture for the client during an order. You record the various totals in the database rather than having the application compute them on the fly later because you don't want the application to display a different total if you change the totaling logic so that a difference occurs because of rounding.

The Promotion Table

The promotions table defines the two promotions defined (the BOGOF and %OFF promotions). The supporting table is very simple, as Listing 6.6 shows.

LISTING 6.6   init_promotions.sql

```
# Schema creation for product-related tables

drop table if exists PROMOTION;

create table PROMOTION (
        PROMO_ID              int not null unique,
        PROMO_NAME      char(30) not null,
        PROD_OR_CAT     char(1) not null,
        CATEGORY_ID     int references CATEGORY,
        PRODUCT_ISBN    char(20) references PRODUCT,
        PROMO_TYPE      char(1) not null,
        DISCOUNT_QUANT  int not null);
```

Again, the promotional ID is just a unique canned ID number specified in the initialization data. The promotional name is used for display purposes, such as to show the customer what promotion he has received. The PROD_OR_CAT field is either a P for a product-specific promotion or a C for a category-specific promotion. Depending on whether it is a product or a category promotion, the CATEGORY_ID or the PRODUCT_ISBN will be filled out. The promotional type is either % or B (for percent off or BOGOF). The quantity field stores the discount (either an integer percentage value such as 20 for 20%, or the number of books that it takes to qualify for the BOGOF— 3 for "buy 3, get 1 free," for example).

You might be tempted to make PROD_OR_CAT or PROMO_TYPE Boolean fields (for example, IS_BOGOF). The peril with this approach is that it leaves no room for expansion. You're assuming that promotions are either BOGOFs or they're not. If you add a third type of promotion later, you'd have to change your database schema to incorporate the addition.

NOTE

If you write SQL queries using the % character, you might get into trouble if you use a like qualifier because % is the wildcard operator in like. There's little danger of that in this case because PROMO_TYPE is a single-character field, so you'd be unlikely to use like. Try to use values that are easily recognized whenever possible, but you also could use P for percent instead.

Populating Data

The init_misc script is for miscellaneous tables. Because you don't have any that you know of yet, this script is left empty. The init_data script (see Listing 6.7) is a large one; it contains all the initialization data for the application and is basically just a file full of insert statements. You begin with a series of delete statements:

LISTING 6.7   init_data.sql

```
# Data population

delete from CATEGORY_PRODUCT_XREF;
delete from CATEGORY;
delete from PRODUCT;
delete from PROMOTION;

insert into PRODUCT (TITLE, PUB_DATE, ISBN, DESCRIPTION, PRICE) values
      ('Java 2 Micro Edition (J2ME) Application Development',
       '2001-11-28','672320959','The key to Java 2 Micro Edition (J2ME)
➥Application Development is the clear, concise explanations of the
➥J2ME technology in relation to the existing Java platform. This
➥book assumes proficiency with Java and presents strategies for
➥understanding and deploying J2ME applications. The book presents
```

LISTING 6.7   Continued

```
➥numerous real-world examples, including health care and financial
➥sector examples from the authors\' professional experience.', 49.99);

insert into PRODUCT (TITLE, PUB_DATE, ISBN, DESCRIPTION, PRICE) values
        ('Oracle and Java Development',
         '2001-08-17','672321173','Oracle and Java Application Development
➥describes Oracle\'s Internet Computing Platform for developing
➥applications; outlines Key Oracle Java technologies like Enterprise
➥Java Beans, Business Components, Java Server Pages, and Servlets
➥for developing and deploying applications using Oracle 8i;.describes
➥the creation of dynamic Web content with Java.; and covers database
➥interaction with Java using Java stored procedures, JDBC, and
➥SQLJ.', 39.99);

insert into PRODUCT (TITLE, PUB_DATE, ISBN, DESCRIPTION, PRICE) values
        ('Sams Teach Yourself Wireless Java with J2ME in 21 Days',
         '2001-06-27','672321424','Sams Teach Yourself Wireless Java
➥with J2ME in 21 Days begins by establishing the basic parameters
➥of J2ME development and its uses in building wireless applications.
➥The tutorial chapters introduce both text and graphical application
➥development for typical wireless devices. Finally, the book presents
➥the major types of applications that the wireless developer will
➥build-information management, communications, games, etc. The
➥book also introduces the basic concepts of networking wireless
➥devices through Java. ', 39.99);

insert into PRODUCT (TITLE, PUB_DATE, ISBN, DESCRIPTION, PRICE) values
        ('Wireless Java Programming with Java 2 Micro Edition',
         '2001-05-24','672321351','Wireless Device Programming with Java
➥2 Micro Edition assumes readers are motivated to build the next
➥generation wireless application by leveraging the J2ME technology.
➥The book provides commercial-quality code and examples primarily
➥based on the industry-leading Motorola phone emulator.', 49.99);

insert into PRODUCT (TITLE, PUB_DATE, ISBN, DESCRIPTION, PRICE) values
        ('"Developing Java Servlets, Second Edition"',
         '2001-05-21','672321076','Developing Java Servlets, Second Edition,
➥is a comprehensive, code-intensive book for professional Java
➥developers. It explains the Java Servlet API architecture and
➥client/server development concepts and contains detailed,
➥professional programming techniques for building sophisticated
```

LISTING 6.7   Continued

```
➥e-commerce and database servlet applications. New topics covered
➥in the updated edition are: JavaMail; Servlets with XML, JSP,
➥and EJB; Pluggable web applications; Wireless servlets with
➥WML/WMLScripts. ', 39.99);

insert into PRODUCT (TITLE, PUB_DATE, ISBN, DESCRIPTION, PRICE) values
     ('"Sams Teach Yourself Java 2 in 21 Days, Professional
➥Reference Edition, Second Edition"',
       '2001-05-21','672320614','Sams Teach Yourself Java in 21 Days
➥continues to be one of the most popular, best-selling Java
➥tutorials on the market. It has been acclaimed for its clear
➥and personable writing, for its extensive use of examples,
➥and for its logical and complete organization. The Professional
➥Reference Edition of the book includes an extra seven chapters
➥covering advanced topics like object serialization, remote
➥method invocation, accessibility, security, JavaBeans, JDBC,
➥and advanced data structures - as well as a 200-page reference
➥section detailing the most commonly used aspects of the Java
➥language. This edition of the book has been updated and revised
➥to cover version 1.3 of the Java 2 Standard Edition SDK, and
➥the book\'s CD-ROM includes a fully functional Java compiler,
➥as well as the book\'s source code and a collection of third-
➥party Java development tools and utilities. ', 49.99);

insert into PRODUCT (TITLE, PUB_DATE, ISBN, DESCRIPTION, PRICE) values
     ('Sams Teach Yourself JavaServer Pages in 24 Hours',
       '2000-12-18','672320231','Sams Teach Yourself JavaServer Pages
➥in 24 Hours guarantees to teach 24 one-hour lessons on JSP and
➥its ties to other J2EE technologies, including Servlets and
➥JDBC. Additionally, this book covers the comprehensive
➥development of JSPs using tools such as BEA\'s WebLogic Server
➥and Apache Tomcat. Each lesson builds on the previous one,
➥allowing the reader to understand the subject of JSPs from
➥the ground-up.', 29.95);

insert into PRODUCT (TITLE, PUB_DATE, ISBN, DESCRIPTION, PRICE) values
     ('Sams Teach Yourself Java 2 in 24 Hours, Second Edition',
       '2000-11-17','672320363','Revised and updated edition of the
➥leading Java tutorial for beginners with no previous programming
➥experience. The book\'s short, simple one-hour chapters are
➥easy to understand and they carefully step the reader through
```

LISTING 6.7   Continued

```
➥the fundamentals of Java programming. This edition has been
➥updated to cover the new Java SDK version 1.3. Readers love
➥this book -- they say it explains Java better than any other
➥book they\'ve seen, and that it\'s very clear, well-written,
➥and interesting to read. They even appreciate the author\'s
➥somewhat unique sense of humor.', 24.99);

insert into PRODUCT (TITLE, PUB_DATE, ISBN, DESCRIPTION, PRICE) values
        ('XML Development with Java 2',
          '2000-10-18','672316536','XML Development with Java 2 provides
➥the information and techniques a Java developer will need to
➥integrate XML into Java-based applications. This book presents
➥a fast-paced introduction to XML and moves quickly into the
➥areas where XML has the biggest impact on Java Development.
➥The book covers crucial topics such as the XML Document Object
➥Model (DOM), Using Java and XSL to transform and format XML
➥data, Integrating XML into JavaBeans and EJB development, and
➥using XML with Java Servlets. The authors also cover the impact
➥XML has on Java database access and the way XML works with
➥the Swing classes.', 49.99);

insert into PRODUCT (TITLE, PUB_DATE, ISBN, DESCRIPTION, PRICE) values
        ('"Sams Teach Yourself JavaScript in 24 Hours, Second Edition"',
          '2000-10-9','672320258','Second edition updates the current
➥best-selling book to cover the latest version,
➥JavaScript 1.5', 24.99);

insert into PRODUCT (TITLE, PUB_DATE, ISBN, DESCRIPTION, PRICE) values
        ('Java Security Handbook',
          '2000-09-21','672316021','This book is a comprehensive guide
➥to Java security issues. It assumes you are an experienced
➥Java programmer, but have little experience with creating
➥secure applications. This book covers formulating and enacting
➥a network security policy to protect end-users, building
➥e-commerce and database applications that can safely exchange
➥secure information over networks and the Internet, cryptography,
➥digital signatures, key management, and distributed computing:
➥CORBA, RMI, and servlets.', 49.99);

insert into PRODUCT (TITLE, PUB_DATE, ISBN, DESCRIPTION, PRICE) values
        ('"Sams Teach Yourself Java 2 in 21 Days, Second Edition"',
          '2000-09-20','672319586','Sams Teach Yourself Java in 21 Days,
```

LISTING 6.7   Continued

```
➥Second Edition is known for its clear and personable writing,
➥its extensive use of examples, and its logical step-by-step
➥organization. This new edition maintains and improves upon
➥all these qualities, while updating and revising the material
➥to cover the latest developments in Java and the way the
➥language is used today.', 29.99);

insert into PRODUCT (TITLE, PUB_DATE, ISBN, DESCRIPTION, PRICE) values
        ('"JavaScript Unleashed, Third Edition"',
         '2000-06-23','067231763X','JavaScript Unleashed, Third Edition
➥serves as a reference to the JavaScript language for the high-
➥end programmer as well as a guide for developing JavaScript
➥applications from the ground up. The topics most important
➥to the intermediate to advanced JavaScript programmer are
➥covered, including Web security, integrating JavaScript with
➥Java, and forms and data validation. Other topics include
➥creating special effects with JavaScript, controlling layers
➥with JavaScript, DHTML and Cascading Style Sheets, and using
➥lookup tables in JavaScript. Some of the new topics covered
➥are Internet Explorer 5, Active Server Pages, Netscape Plug-in
➥autoinstalls and applets digital signature verification, and
➥content layering.', 49.99);

insert into PRODUCT (TITLE, PUB_DATE, ISBN, DESCRIPTION, PRICE) values
        ('Pure JSP: Java Server Pages',
         '2000-06-8','672319020','Pure JSP gives a very concise conceptual
➥overview of the JavaServer Pages technology and its related
➥components. Once you have a firm foundation with the JSP
➥technology, related topics such as JavaBeans, JDBC and Servlets
➥are covered at a very high level. The book moves on to explain
➥a large number of JSP techniques, which were determined by
➥studying problems faced by JSP users in the professional world.
➥The final section covers the more technical aspects of the JSP
➥technology. Topics include related API\'s, server configuration,
➥and charts and diagrams related to developing JSP applications.',
➥34.99);

insert into PRODUCT (TITLE, PUB_DATE, ISBN, DESCRIPTION, PRICE) values
        ('Building Java Enterprise Systems with J2EE',
         '2000-06-7','672317958','The practical angle of Building Java
➥Enterprise Systems with J2EE provides the conceptual background
➥and wealth of code examples needed to actually assemble systems
```

LISTING 6.7   Continued

```
➥in a useful manner with the J2EE technologies. Furthermore, this
➥book demonstrates how the technologies complement and build on
➥top of one another via evolution of a cohesive and real sample
➥application. You can use this book to learn, develop, and design
➥your custom applications immediately.', 59.99);

insert into PRODUCT (TITLE, PUB_DATE, ISBN, DESCRIPTION, PRICE) values
        ('JavaBeans Unleashed',
        '1999-12-22','067231424X','JavaBeans Unleashed is a practical,
➥professional, and comprehensive guide to JavaBeans. It assumes
➥you are an experienced Java programmer but have little experience
➥developing network and client/server applications. This book
➥also contains an introduction to Enterprise JavaBeans, a new
➥Java specification from Sun. JavaBeans works with the most
➥popular distributed object protocols, so CORBA (the distributed
➥object leading protocol from the Object Management Group), Java
➥IDL (Interface Definition Language allows Java apps access to
➥CORBA), and JNDI (Java Naming and Directory Interface which
➥allows Java applications to access files on any network server)
➥are also covered.', 49.99);

insert into PRODUCT (TITLE, PUB_DATE, ISBN, DESCRIPTION, PRICE) values
        ('Pure Java 2',
        '1999-12-22','672316544','Pure Java 2 is a substantial and
➥focused reference for professional Java programmers. This
➥book begins with an accelerated introduction to Java 2 so
➥that you can quickly understand the new concepts and begin
➥developing your own applications. Professional programmers
➥prefer to learn by examining code, so Pure Java 2 also contains
➥hundreds of programming techniques, complete with well-commented
➥code examples that you can immediately use in your own Java
➥programs.', 24.99);

insert into PRODUCT (TITLE, PUB_DATE, ISBN, DESCRIPTION, PRICE) values
        ('Sams Teach Yourself Java 2 Online in Web Time',
        '1999-09-1','672316684','Sams Teach Yourself Java 2 Online in
➥Web Time helps the first-time programmer or the programmer new
➥to Java to learn Java and its APIs. Written in a warm and familiar
➥style, Teach Yourself Java in WebTime requires no previous
➥programming experience. It incorporates the proven instructional
➥techniques of the Teach Yourself series, including end-of-section
```

LISTING 6.7 Continued

```
➥quizzes and programming exercises that allow you to review and
➥expand upon the concepts and skills presented in that chapter.
➥The learning experience is further enhanced with an instructional
➥Web site.', 49.99);

insert into PRODUCT (TITLE, PUB_DATE, ISBN, DESCRIPTION, PRICE) values
        ('Java GUI Development',
        '1999-08-25','672315467','Java GUI Development covers the Java
➥2 AWT, JFC, and Swing Toolkit technologies for GUI programming.
➥It provides professional developers and software engineers with
➥1) a clear understanding of the conceptual framework behind Java
➥2 GUI tools, 2) descriptions of Java GUI idioms, and 3) practical
➥programming techniques proven to work with these tools. This
➥approach enables developers to solve difficult GUI programming
➥tasks faster, write tighter and faster code, and implement more
➥sophisticated GUI designs. ', 34.99);

insert into PRODUCT (TITLE, PUB_DATE, ISBN, DESCRIPTION, PRICE) values
        ('Java Thread Programming',
        '1999-08-20','672315858','Java Thread Programming shows you how
➥to take full advantage of Java\'s thread facilities: when to use
➥threads to increase your program\'s efficiency, how to use them
➥effectively, and how to avoid common mistakes. There is thorough
➥coverage of the Thread API, ThreadGroup classes, the Runnable
➥interface, and the synchronized operator. Extensive, complete,
➥code examples show programmers the details of creating and
➥managing threads in real-world applications.', 34.99);

insert into PRODUCT (TITLE, PUB_DATE, ISBN, DESCRIPTION, PRICE) values
        ('Pure JavaScript',
        '1999-08-19','672315475','Pure JavaScript is a substantial and
➥focused reference for experienced Web developers. This book
➥begins with an accelerated introduction to the newest features
➥of JavaScript so that experienced Web developers can quickly
➥understand the concepts of JavaScript and begin developing
➥their own JavaScript solutions immediately. Pure JavaScript
➥also contains insightful programming techniques, complete
➥with well-commented code examples that you can immediately
➥use in your own JavaScripts. This book contains the most complete,
➥easily accessible JavaScript object reference with syntax,
➥definitions, and examples of well-commented code for each
➥entry.', 34.99);
```

LISTING 6.7   Continued

```
insert into PRODUCT (TITLE, PUB_DATE, ISBN, DESCRIPTION, PRICE) values
        ('Developing Java Servlets',
         '1999-06-21','672316005','Developing Java Servlets is a
➥comprehensive, code-intensive book for professional Java
➥developers. It explains the Java Servlet API architecture
➥and client-server development concepts, and contains detailed,
➥professional programming techniques for building sophisticated
➥e-commerce and database servlet applications. This book explains
➥HTTP, MIME, server-side includes, and other web-based client-
➥server technologies that developers need to understand to build
➥any servlet application. In addition, the book covers JDBC, RMI,
➥CORBA, and other object technologies to the degree are needed
➥to build sophisticated Java servlets.', 29.99);

insert into PRODUCT (TITLE, PUB_DATE, ISBN, DESCRIPTION, PRICE) values
        ('Java 2 for Professional Developers',
         '1999-06-18','672316978','Java 2 for Professional Developers
➥is a practical, code-intensive approach for readers who need
➥to use Java for professional software development. This book
➥teaches Java programming concepts and techniques within the
➥context of professional, object- oriented, software analysis
➥and design. Apply these concepts, idioms, and real-world
➥applications to your own programs to become a more efficient
➥and successful Java developer. In addition to the basic Java
➥language, this book covers JFC, AWT, security, threads, sockets,
➥JARs, JavaBeans, developing packages, and testing and
➥debugging.', 34.99);

insert into PRODUCT (TITLE, PUB_DATE, ISBN, DESCRIPTION, PRICE) values
        ('Java 2 Platform Unleashed',
         '1999-04-9','672316315','Java 2 Platform Unleashed is completely
➥revised for Java 2. This complete reference covers all the core
➥APIs of the Java 2 platform as well as higher-level topics that
➥experienced Java programmers need to know. The book includes
➥thousands of lines of code to demonstrate the sophisticated
➥programming techniques that experienced Java programmers demand.
➥Written for experienced Java programmers.', 49.99);

insert into PRODUCT (TITLE, PUB_DATE, ISBN, DESCRIPTION, PRICE) values
        ('Sams Teach Yourself Java 2 in 21 Days',
```

LISTING 6.7   Continued

```
        '1999-03-23','672316382','Sams Teach Yourself Java in 21 Days
➥continues to be the most popular, best-selling Java tutorial
➥on the market. It has been acclaimed for its clear and personable
➥writing, for its extensive use of examples, and for its logical
➥and complete organization. The third edition of the book maintains
➥and improves upon all these qualities while updating the material
➥to cover the latest developments in the Java language - such as
➥using Java Foundation Classes, Java 2D Classes, and
➥JavaBeans.', 29.99);

insert into PRODUCT (TITLE, PUB_DATE, ISBN, DESCRIPTION, PRICE) values
        ('The Official VisiBroker for Java Handbook',
        '1999-03-23','672314517','The Official VisiBroker for Java
➥Handbook provides a comprehensive guide to learning how to
➥effectively program with the VisiBroker for Java (VBJ)
➥development tool. This book focuses exclusively on how to
➥use the tool and all of its features and APIs, as well as
➥how to execute both routine and sophisticated tasks. It serves
➥as the most comprehensive collection of VBJ code samples available
➥today and a hands-on reference tool that starts with the VisiBroker
➥for Java basics and concludes by showing you how to make the most
➥difficult features easy to use. High-level issues are discussed,
➥but only in the context of how the tool should be deployed or
➥implemented.', 39.99);

insert into PRODUCT (TITLE, PUB_DATE, ISBN, DESCRIPTION, PRICE) values
        ('Java Distributed Objects',
        '1998-12-22','672315378','This book is a comprehensive guide
➥to Java distributed computing. It assumes the reader is an
➥experienced Java programming, but has little experience with
➥network programming and distributed objects. This book covers
➥networking, distributed computing architectures, advanced Java
➥facilities, security, data management, and specific distributed
➥computing techniques including sockets, Remote Method Invocation
➥ (RMI), Java servlets, Microsoft\'s Distributed Component Model
➥ (DCOM), and the Common Object Request Broker Architecture (CORBA).
➥This book covers all these protocols, gives advice on when to use
➥each protocol, and demonstrates how they work (or don\'t work)
➥together.', 49.99);

insert into PRODUCT (TITLE, PUB_DATE, ISBN, DESCRIPTION, PRICE) values
```

LISTING 6.7   Continued

```
      ('Genuine Nagahyde PDA Carrying Case',
       '1998-12-22','PALMCASE','A genuine Nagahyde Palm-compatible PDA
➥case, just the thing to keep your precious PDA safe from the elements.
➥Made from the skin of the rare endangered Naga, this case is sure
➥to make you a hit at your next trade show.', 25.00);

insert into PRODUCT (TITLE, PUB_DATE, ISBN, DESCRIPTION, PRICE) values
      ('Jamaican Coffee',
       '1998-12-22','COFFEECAN','When a late night of engineering has
➥your eyes defocused and you just can\'t grind out that last
➥method, grind some of these imported Jamaican Blue Mountain
➥coffee beans instead.  The caffeine will be just the thing to
➥keep you going.', 12.00);

insert into AUTHOR (AUTHOR_ID, AUTHOR_NAME)
      values (1, 'Ben Forta');
insert into AUTHOR (AUTHOR_ID, AUTHOR_NAME)
      values (2, 'Bill Mccarty');
insert into AUTHOR (AUTHOR_ID, AUTHOR_NAME)
      values (3, 'Bulusu Lakshman');
insert into AUTHOR (AUTHOR_ID, AUTHOR_NAME)
      values (4, 'Charlton Ting');
insert into AUTHOR (AUTHOR_ID, AUTHOR_NAME)
      values (5, 'Donald Doherty');
insert into AUTHOR (AUTHOR_ID, AUTHOR_NAME)
      values (6, 'James Goodwill');
insert into AUTHOR (AUTHOR_ID, AUTHOR_NAME)
      values (7, 'Jamie Jaworski');
insert into AUTHOR (AUTHOR_ID, AUTHOR_NAME)
      values (8, 'Jason Gilliam');
insert into AUTHOR (AUTHOR_ID, AUTHOR_NAME)
      values (9, 'Jose Annunziato');
insert into AUTHOR (AUTHOR_ID, AUTHOR_NAME)
      values (10, 'Kenneth Litwak');
insert into AUTHOR (AUTHOR_ID, AUTHOR_NAME)
      values (11, 'Laura Lemay');
insert into AUTHOR (AUTHOR_ID, AUTHOR_NAME)
      values (12, 'Michael Kroll');
insert into AUTHOR (AUTHOR_ID, AUTHOR_NAME)
      values (13, 'Michael McCaffery');
```

LISTING 6.7   Continued

```
insert into AUTHOR (AUTHOR_ID, AUTHOR_NAME)
      values (14, 'Michael Moncur');
insert into AUTHOR (AUTHOR_ID, AUTHOR_NAME)
      values (15, 'Michael Morrison');
insert into AUTHOR (AUTHOR_ID, AUTHOR_NAME)
      values (16, 'Mike Morgan');
insert into AUTHOR (AUTHOR_ID, AUTHOR_NAME)
      values (17, 'Paul Hyde');
insert into AUTHOR (AUTHOR_ID, AUTHOR_NAME)
      values (18, 'Paul Perrone');
insert into AUTHOR (AUTHOR_ID, AUTHOR_NAME)
      values (19, 'R. Allen Wyke');
insert into AUTHOR (AUTHOR_ID, AUTHOR_NAME)
      values (20, 'Rogers Cadenhead');
insert into AUTHOR (AUTHOR_ID, AUTHOR_NAME)
      values (21, 'Stefan Haustein');
insert into AUTHOR (AUTHOR_ID, AUTHOR_NAME)
      values (22, 'Stephanie Fesler');
insert into AUTHOR (AUTHOR_ID, AUTHOR_NAME)
      values (23, 'Stephen Gilbert');
insert into AUTHOR (AUTHOR_ID, AUTHOR_NAME)
      values (24, 'Vartan Piroumian');
insert into AUTHOR (AUTHOR_ID, AUTHOR_NAME)
      values (25, 'Yu Feng');

insert into PRODUCT_AUTHOR_XREF (PRODUCT_ISBN, AUTHOR_ID)
      select '672320959', author_id from author where
➥author_name='Stefan Haustein';

insert into PRODUCT_AUTHOR_XREF (PRODUCT_ISBN, AUTHOR_ID)
      select '672320959', author_id from author where
➥author_name='Michael Kroll';

insert into PRODUCT_AUTHOR_XREF (PRODUCT_ISBN, AUTHOR_ID)
      select '672321173', author_id from author where
➥author_name='Bulusu Lakshman';

insert into PRODUCT_AUTHOR_XREF (PRODUCT_ISBN, AUTHOR_ID)
      select '672321416', author_id from author where
➥author_name='R. Allen Wyke';
```

LISTING 6.7   Continued

```
insert into PRODUCT_AUTHOR_XREF (PRODUCT_ISBN, AUTHOR_ID)
      select '672321424', author_id from author where
►author_name='Michael Morrison';

insert into PRODUCT_AUTHOR_XREF (PRODUCT_ISBN, AUTHOR_ID)
      select '672321351', author_id from author where
►author_name='Yu Feng';

insert into PRODUCT_AUTHOR_XREF (PRODUCT_ISBN, AUTHOR_ID)
      select '672321076', author_id from author where
►author_name='James Goodwill';

insert into PRODUCT_AUTHOR_XREF (PRODUCT_ISBN, AUTHOR_ID)
      select '672320614', author_id from author where
►author_name='Laura Lemay';

insert into PRODUCT_AUTHOR_XREF (PRODUCT_ISBN, AUTHOR_ID)
      select '672320231', author_id from author where
►author_name='Stephanie Fesler';

insert into PRODUCT_AUTHOR_XREF (PRODUCT_ISBN, AUTHOR_ID)
      select '672320231', author_id from author where
►author_name='Jose Annunziato';

insert into PRODUCT_AUTHOR_XREF (PRODUCT_ISBN, AUTHOR_ID)
      select '672320363', author_id from author where
►author_name='Rogers Cadenhead';

insert into PRODUCT_AUTHOR_XREF (PRODUCT_ISBN, AUTHOR_ID)
      select '672316536', author_id from author where
►author_name='Michael Daconta';

insert into PRODUCT_AUTHOR_XREF (PRODUCT_ISBN, AUTHOR_ID)
      select '672320258', author_id from author where
►author_name='Michael Moncur';

insert into PRODUCT_AUTHOR_XREF (PRODUCT_ISBN, AUTHOR_ID)
      select '672316021', author_id from author where
►author_name='Jamie Jaworski';
```

LISTING 6.7   Continued

```
insert into PRODUCT_AUTHOR_XREF  (PRODUCT_ISBN, AUTHOR_ID)
     select '672319586', author_id from author where
➥author_name='Rogers Cadenhead';

insert into PRODUCT_AUTHOR_XREF (PRODUCT_ISBN, AUTHOR_ID)
     select '672319586', author_id from author where
➥author_name='Laura Lemay';

insert into PRODUCT_AUTHOR_XREF (PRODUCT_ISBN, AUTHOR_ID)
     select '067231763X', author_id from author where
➥author_name='R. Allen Wyke';

insert into PRODUCT_AUTHOR_XREF (PRODUCT_ISBN, AUTHOR_ID)
     select '672319020', author_id from author where
➥author_name='James Goodwill';

insert into PRODUCT_AUTHOR_XREF (PRODUCT_ISBN, AUTHOR_ID)
     select '672317958', author_id from author where
➥author_name='Paul Perrone';

insert into PRODUCT_AUTHOR_XREF (PRODUCT_ISBN, AUTHOR_ID)
     select '067231424X', author_id from author where
➥author_name='Donald Doherty';

insert into PRODUCT_AUTHOR_XREF (PRODUCT_ISBN, AUTHOR_ID)
     select '672316544', author_id from author where
➥author_name='Kenneth Litwak';

insert into PRODUCT_AUTHOR_XREF (PRODUCT_ISBN, AUTHOR_ID)
     select '672316684', author_id from author where
➥author_name='Bill Mccarty';

insert into PRODUCT_AUTHOR_XREF (PRODUCT_ISBN, AUTHOR_ID)
     select '672316684', author_id from author where
➥author_name='Stephen Gilbert';

insert into PRODUCT_AUTHOR_XREF (PRODUCT_ISBN, AUTHOR_ID)
     select '672315467', author_id from author where
➥author_name='Vartan Piroumian';
```

LISTING 6.7   Continued

```
insert into PRODUCT_AUTHOR_XREF (PRODUCT_ISBN, AUTHOR_ID)
        select '672315858', author_id from author where
➥author_name='Paul Hyde';

insert into PRODUCT_AUTHOR_XREF (PRODUCT_ISBN, AUTHOR_ID)
        select '672315475', author_id from author where
➥author_name='Charlton Ting';

insert into PRODUCT_AUTHOR_XREF (PRODUCT_ISBN, AUTHOR_ID)
        select '672315475', author_id from author where
➥author_name='Jason Gilliam';

insert into PRODUCT_AUTHOR_XREF (PRODUCT_ISBN, AUTHOR_ID)
        select '672315475', author_id from author where
➥author_name='R. Allen Wyke';

insert into PRODUCT_AUTHOR_XREF (PRODUCT_ISBN, AUTHOR_ID)
        select '672316005', author_id from author where
➥author_name='James Goodwill';

insert into PRODUCT_AUTHOR_XREF (PRODUCT_ISBN, AUTHOR_ID)
        select '672316978', author_id from author where
➥author_name='Mike Morgan';

insert into PRODUCT_AUTHOR_XREF (PRODUCT_ISBN, AUTHOR_ID)
        select '672316315', author_id from author where
➥author_name='Jamie Jaworski';

insert into PRODUCT_AUTHOR_XREF (PRODUCT_ISBN, AUTHOR_ID)
        select '672316382', author_id from author where
➥author_name='Laura Lemay';

insert into PRODUCT_AUTHOR_XREF (PRODUCT_ISBN, AUTHOR_ID)
        select '672314517', author_id from author where
➥author_name='Michael McCaffery';

insert into PRODUCT_AUTHOR_XREF (PRODUCT_ISBN, AUTHOR_ID)
        select '672315378', author_id from author where
➥author_name='Bill Mccarty';
```

LISTING 6.7   Continued

```
insert into CATEGORY (CATEGORY_ID, CATEGORY_NAME, FEATURED_PRODUCT)
      values (1, 'Java', '672321076');

insert into CATEGORY (CATEGORY_ID,  CATEGORY_NAME, FEATURED_PRODUCT)
      values (2, 'J2ME', '672321351');

insert into CATEGORY (CATEGORY_ID, CATEGORY_NAME, FEATURED_PRODUCT)
      values (3, 'J2EE', '672317958');

insert into CATEGORY (CATEGORY_ID, CATEGORY_NAME, FEATURED_PRODUCT)
      values (4, 'JDBC', '672321173');

insert into CATEGORY_PRODUCT_XREF (CATEGORY_ID, PRODUCT_ISBN)
      values (1, '672320959');

insert into CATEGORY_PRODUCT_XREF (CATEGORY_ID, PRODUCT_ISBN)
      values (1, '672321173');

insert into CATEGORY_PRODUCT_XREF (CATEGORY_ID, PRODUCT_ISBN)
      values (1, '672321424');

insert into CATEGORY_PRODUCT_XREF (CATEGORY_ID, PRODUCT_ISBN)
      values (1, '672321351');

insert into CATEGORY_PRODUCT_XREF (CATEGORY_ID, PRODUCT_ISBN)
      values (1, '672321076');

insert into CATEGORY_PRODUCT_XREF (CATEGORY_ID, PRODUCT_ISBN)
      values (1, '672320614');

insert into CATEGORY_PRODUCT_XREF (CATEGORY_ID, PRODUCT_ISBN)
      values (1, '672320231');

insert into CATEGORY_PRODUCT_XREF (CATEGORY_ID, PRODUCT_ISBN)
      values (1, '672320363');

insert into CATEGORY_PRODUCT_XREF (CATEGORY_ID, PRODUCT_ISBN)
      values (1, '672316536');

insert into CATEGORY_PRODUCT_XREF (CATEGORY_ID, PRODUCT_ISBN)
      values (1, '672320258');
```

LISTING 6.7   Continued

```
insert into CATEGORY_PRODUCT_XREF (CATEGORY_ID, PRODUCT_ISBN)
     values (1, '672316021');

insert into CATEGORY_PRODUCT_XREF (CATEGORY_ID, PRODUCT_ISBN)
     values (1, '672319586');

insert into CATEGORY_PRODUCT_XREF (CATEGORY_ID, PRODUCT_ISBN)
     values (1, '067231763X');

insert into CATEGORY_PRODUCT_XREF  (CATEGORY_ID, PRODUCT_ISBN)
     values (1, '672319020');

insert into CATEGORY_PRODUCT_XREF (CATEGORY_ID, PRODUCT_ISBN)
     values (1, '672317958');

insert into CATEGORY_PRODUCT_XREF (CATEGORY_ID, PRODUCT_ISBN)
     values (1, '067231424X');

insert into CATEGORY_PRODUCT_XREF (CATEGORY_ID, PRODUCT_ISBN)
     values (1, '672316544');

insert into CATEGORY_PRODUCT_XREF (CATEGORY_ID, PRODUCT_ISBN)
     values (1, '672316684');

insert into CATEGORY_PRODUCT_XREF (CATEGORY_ID, PRODUCT_ISBN)
     values (1, '672315467');

insert into CATEGORY_PRODUCT_XREF  (CATEGORY_ID, PRODUCT_ISBN)
     values (1, '672315858');

insert into CATEGORY_PRODUCT_XREF (CATEGORY_ID, PRODUCT_ISBN)
     values (1, '672315475');

insert into CATEGORY_PRODUCT_XREF (CATEGORY_ID, PRODUCT_ISBN)
     values (1, '672316005');

insert into CATEGORY_PRODUCT_XREF (CATEGORY_ID, PRODUCT_ISBN)
     values (1, '672316978');

insert into CATEGORY_PRODUCT_XREF (CATEGORY_ID, PRODUCT_ISBN)
     values (1, '672316315');
```

LISTING 6.7   Continued

```
insert into CATEGORY_PRODUCT_XREF (CATEGORY_ID, PRODUCT_ISBN)
      values (1, '672316382');

insert into CATEGORY_PRODUCT_XREF (CATEGORY_ID, PRODUCT_ISBN)
      values (1, '672314517');

insert into CATEGORY_PRODUCT_XREF (CATEGORY_ID, PRODUCT_ISBN)
      values (1, '672315378');

insert into CATEGORY_PRODUCT_XREF (CATEGORY_ID, PRODUCT_ISBN)
      values (2, '672320959');

insert into CATEGORY_PRODUCT_XREF (CATEGORY_ID, PRODUCT_ISBN)
      values (2, '672321424');

insert into CATEGORY_PRODUCT_XREF (CATEGORY_ID, PRODUCT_ISBN)
      values (2, '672321351');

insert into CATEGORY_PRODUCT_XREF (CATEGORY_ID, PRODUCT_ISBN)
      values (3, '672320231');

insert into CATEGORY_PRODUCT_XREF (CATEGORY_ID, PRODUCT_ISBN)
      values (3, '672317958');

insert into CATEGORY_PRODUCT_XREF (CATEGORY_ID, PRODUCT_ISBN)
      values (4, '672321173');

insert into CATEGORY_PRODUCT_XREF (CATEGORY_ID, PRODUCT_ISBN)
      values (4, '672320614');

insert into CATEGORY_PRODUCT_XREF (CATEGORY_ID, PRODUCT_ISBN)
      values (4, '672320231');

insert into CATEGORY_PRODUCT_XREF (CATEGORY_ID, PRODUCT_ISBN)
      values (4, '672319020');

insert into CATEGORY_PRODUCT_XREF (CATEGORY_ID, PRODUCT_ISBN)
      values (4, '672316005');
```

Even though the init_bfg script re-creates all the tables, it begins by deleting all the data in the tables so that the script can be run separately to repopulate the product and promotion tables without losing customer and order data (an important thing on a live site).

The ordering of these statements is important because of cross-table dependencies. If you tried to drop products before you dropped the category cross-reference or the category table, some databases (although not MySQL) would complain that some foreign key constraints were being broken. You could also solve this by using a cascading delete, on databases such as Oracle that support it.

Next, you populate the product table. Again, ordering is important. You need to populate the products before you refer to the products in any cross-references or foreign keys.

Other than having to quote any single-quote characters in the description with a backslash, the product table is about as straightforward as life gets. Equally so is the author table—it simply contains the data for each author.

For the product-author cross-reference, things get a little fancier because the data that was imported into MySQL was from a tab-delimited spreadsheet file. Instead of hand-translating the author names into author IDs, a lookup was used on the newly created author table.

Next you come to the category list and the category cross-reference. The category table, like the author and product tables, simply describes each category. The table entries also reference a product, which are highlighted in the category display page under JSP.

Currently, there are no promotions to populate; they'll be added in Chapter 12, "Handling Complex Business Rules and Third-Party Integration."

The Database from 20,000 Feet

With the entire schema in place, you can use a tool such as Together to get an overall view of our database with an ERD. Together is a commercially available integrated development tool (IDE) that can also be used to model and create Java and EJB architectures. Although I'm from the older school that does everything using the emacs editor, a lot of developers swear by the visual design approach that tools such as Together employ.

You can immediately see that the data falls into three separate islands: the customer group, the product group, and the order group. As you go along, you're certain to add more to this schema, especially with regard to cart persistence using cookies, but this gives you enough to get going.

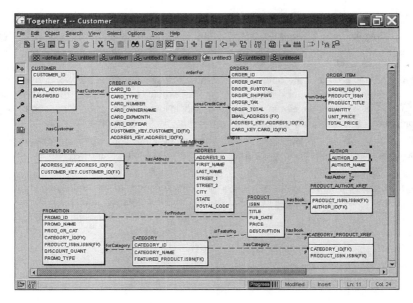

FIGURE 6.1   The ERD for the Books for Geeks scheme.

Summary

The SQL schema is the persistent embodiment of your Java classes. Although there might not be a one-to-one relationship between Java classes and SQL tables, any data that you want to have persist between sessions must live in a SQL database.

MySQL is a good database for small to moderately sized applications, with a reasonable feature set and zero cost. However, if you will deal with large amounts of data, you might want to consider a commercial database such as Oracle.

Because MySQL doesn't use sequences, you need to use the capability of MySQL to read back the value of the last inserted autoincrement column.

Now that you have all the scutwork out of the way and you have some data to play with, you're ready to start developing your application. In the next chapter, you'll begin by setting up the infrastructure that you'll need for the site.

MY PHILOSOPHY OF DEVELOPMENT

Old habits die hard. I began my career coding in LISP, a language that encourages the developer to write little pieces of code, test them, and put them together into larger finished products. That's still the way I code today.

Throughout the rest of the book, you'll see me get a section of the site working as a stand-alone piece, then test it, and integrate it with the whole. This nicely meshes with the current "en vogue" styles of development, which usually involve a lot of people working on separate pieces and then integrating them. EJB is all about this, for example.

I find that working this way gives me confidence in the reliability of the subsections so that when everything gets hooked together, there's less uncertainty about where new problems might be coming from.

Also, if you've got unit tests in place, you can make changes to the underlying code at a later date and know that you're still in good shape if the unit tests still run.

PART III

Sample Application: Implementation

IN THIS PART

7

Setting Up an Application's Infrastructure

So here you are, ready to start deploying the application. But before you do, you need to get some tools in place to make sure you do things right. Sometimes the tools that you use to build something can make as much difference in the quality of the finished product as your skill in using them, so it pays to pick the right tools to begin with. Just as beautiful houses are built on strong foundations, a well-functioning application depends on a strong infrastructure to support it.

It might seem like we're spending a lot of time setting up an infrastructure instead of working on the problem. There's a good reason for this, as anyone who has worked on a large project with multiple developers can attest.

If you don't set out standard coding practices early, you can spend half your time getting all the code in shape at the end of the project. For example, if everyone simply does their own database connection management, you can end up with too many connections open at once, or one group of developers might be sloppy and leave connections open.

This can be especially critical because connection leaks (and other types of resource leaks in general) are an insidious type of bug. They don't tend to show up during initial testing because a developer probably runs the application only for a few minutes, verifies that it works, and then shuts it down again.

It's not until later, during stress testing (or, worse, in live deployment), that you might find your application mysteriously dying after it has run for a while because some critical resource, such as the database connections, has been exhausted.

Similarly, if everyone does their own logging, it can become difficult to consolidate formats so that automated tools can monitor the logs for problems. You might find that you need to standardize not only the logging tools, but the syntax of the log messages themselves.

Another good candidate for standardization is internationalization of message strings. Essentially, anything that needs to be used site-wide should be standardized.

That said, you can leverage existing technologies for a number of subsystems or tasks. Specifically, they are build management, database connection pooling, and logging.

Build Management

You're going to be rebuilding and deploying the application frequently during the development of this application, so it behooves you to make that process as easy as possible.

Before you do, you should review the hierarchy of your various directories. On the source side, you have a top-level directory called bfg (Books for Geeks), which has the following structure:

```
bfg/ ->
  build.xml
  javadoc/ ->
  jsp/ ->
    index.jsp
  props/ ->
    com/ ->
      bfg/ ->
        customer/ ->
          SQLQueries.properties
  src/ ->
    bfg/ ->
      customer/ ->
        Customer.java
```

build.xml is the build script that you'll be editing. javadoc is a placeholder for the javadoc that you will eventually be producing. jsp holds (you guessed it) the jsp source. Props will store any property files that you create, and src holds the Java sources.

When you deploy the application, you want all the properties and Java class files to be jarred up into a single jar in the Tomcat lib directory. In fact, they should all reside in the lib directory in the application, which, in this case, is `C:\TOMCAT\WEBAPPS\BFG\WEB-INF\LIB`. When you followed the instructions to install the sample application (see Appendix C, "A Books for Geeks Quickstart"), you added this directory to the Tomcat configuration file.

Using Ant to do Automated Builds

A few years ago, an automated build process would have meant putting together a set of GNUmake scripts to compile and distribute the application, restart servers, and otherwise automate the tasks that you need to take care of. But, as anyone who has ever used gnumake can attest, it is more than a bit cryptic to work with. A misplaced space can break the entire makefile.

NOTE

GNUMake is the Free Software Foundation replacement for the standard UNIX make utility, which allows a skilled makefile author to compile, link, or install hundreds of files with a single command.

Fortunately, there is a new tool available that uses XML syntax to reduce the chance of errors, and it is even more powerful than make. That tool is ANT.

Detailed instructions for installing ANT and a brief tutorial can be found in Appendix A, "Getting and Installing JDK, Ant, and Tomcat"; however, the important points are reviewed here.

Ant uses an XML build.xml file to describe build tasks to be performed. As with make, you can describe different "targets," allowing yourself, for example, to have a compilation target, a distribution target, a javadoc target, and so on. The invocation syntax is straightforward in all cases:

```
ANT <targetname>
```

For example, you would use `ant dist` or `ant compile`.

Listing 7.1 is a very basic ANT script that you'll use to create and administer the BFG application.

LISTING 7.1   build.xml

```
<project name="BfgWebsite" default="dist" basedir=".">
  <property name="tomcatdir" value="/tomcat"/>
  <property name="appdir" value="${tomcatdir}/webapps/bfg"/>
  <property name="jarfile" value="bfgclasses.jar"/>

  <target name="init">
    <tstamp/>
  </target>

  <target name="compile" depends="init">
    <javac srcdir="src">
      <classpath>
        <pathelement path="${classpath}"/>
        <fileset dir="${tomcatdir}\lib">
          <include name="**/*.jar"/>
        </fileset>
      </classpath>
    </javac>
  </target>


  <target name="dist" depends="compile">
    <mkdir dir="${appdir}/WEB-INF/lib"/>
    <jar jarfile="${appdir}/WEB-INF/lib/${jarfile}">
        <fileset dir="src" includes="**/*.class"/>
        <fileset dir="props" includes="**/*.properties"/>
     </jar>
    <mkdir dir="${appdir}/jsp"/>
    <copy todir="${appdir}/jsp">
        <fileset dir="jsp"/>
    </copy>
  </target>

  <target name="javadoc">
    <mkdir dir="javadoc"/>
    <javadoc sourcepath="src" destdir="javadoc" author="true"
             version="true" use="true" packagenames="com.bfg.*">
      <classpath>
        <pathelement path="${classpath}"/>
        <fileset dir="${tomcatdir}\lib">
          <include name="**/*.jar"/>
```

LISTING 7.1   Continued

```
            </fileset>
          </classpath>
        </javadoc>
    </target>

    <target name="start">
        <exec dir="${tomcatdir}/bin" executable="startup.bat"
            os="Windows 2000" vmlauncher="false">
        </exec>
    </target>

    <target name="stop">
        <exec dir="${tomcatdir}/bin" executable="shutdown.bat"
            os="Windows 2000" vmlauncher="false">
        </exec>
    </target>

    <target name="restart" depends="stop,start">
    </target>

</project>
```

After initializing a few properties that you will use for the script (the location of Tomcat and the name of the jar file that you will be creating in the Tomcat library directory), you tell ant to create a timestamp whenever you ask for any target that depends on initialization (basically, compiling).

The javac directive tells Ant to compile any out-of-date Java source files that it finds under the directory specified in the srcdir portion of the directive (in this case, ., the current directory).

The dist target asks Ant to jar up any .class or .property files that it finds under the basedir and to place them where specified.

Finally, create a few targets to stop, start, and restart the Tomcat executable. This saves having to change directories every time you want to restart Tomcat.

As simple as this script is, it's all that is needed to manage the entire project. In a more complex project, you might include directives to check files automatically out of a source repository system such as CVS, to run automated regression testing, or to keep several servers synchronized when you deploy software to the master. ANT includes dozens of premade directives that will handle many of these tasks for you.

Logging and Database Connection Pooling

Another thing you're going to spend much of your time doing in this project is opening and closing database connections. If you were doing this using J2EE, you would have connection-pooling mechanisms available automatically. But because you are working in pure JSP, you have to manage the connections yourself.

Now, one way to handle this is to have each usage of the database open and close a connection explicitly. A number of problems are associated with this approach, however. For one thing, this would require every class that talked to the database to have enough information available to establish a connection. Also, opening and closing database connections are just about the most expensive thing an application can do, so you wouldn't want to do them lightly.

Another possibility to accomplish this task is to have a global database connection object hanging around as a session or application property. You could use that whenever you wanted to perform a database operation. This is getting closer to the "right" solution; however, it still requires every class that wants to use the connection to do a lookup on the session or application, which is also a bit computationally expensive. In addition, this solution requires you to monitor the connection because, if you leave it idle too long, it might time out. This also would force you to synchronize access to the database because having multiple threads using the same JDBC connection can cause some weird errors.

You could also write your own connection-pooling package, but, luckily, the good folks over at the Apache project have one already available as part of the Turbine project; you can just borrow theirs.

Turbine

Turbine is an application framework that allows developers to create secure Web applications. It has all the "glue" that developers find themselves looking for when they author complex applications, such as database connection pooling, job scheduling, parameter parsing, and so on. Turbine can be used as an all-in-one Web platform or as a series of discrete modules, as you will use it here.

Configuring Turbine

Instructions on where to get Turbine libraries and how to install them can be found in Appendix C. But before you can use the Turbine facilities themselves, you need to set up your application for Turbine. You also need to create a property file with some specific initialization values for the db pool in it, specifically for the application that you intend to build. Listing 7.2 is an example of what it looks like.

LISTING 7.2   /TomCat/webapps/bfg/TurbineResources.properties

```
# --------------------------------------------------------------------
#
#  S E R V I C E S
#
# --------------------------------------------------------------------
# Classes for Turbine Services should be defined here.
# Format: services.[name].classname=[implementing class]
#
# To specify properties of a service use the following syntax:
# service.[name].[property]=[value]

services.PoolBrokerService.classname=org.apache.turbine.services.db.TurbinePoolBro-
kerService
services.MapBrokerService.classname=org.apache.turbine.services.db.TurbineMapBroker
Service
```

The first few lines of the property file tells Turbine which classes to use for specific services (the db pooling and logging):

```
# --------------------------------------------------------------------
#
#  D A T A B A S E   S E T T I N G S
#
# --------------------------------------------------------------------
# These are your database settings.  Look in the
# org.apache.turbine.util.db.pool.* packages for more information.
# The default driver for Turbine is for MySQL.
#
# The parameters to connect to the default database.  You MUST
# configure these properly.
# --------------------------------------------------------------------

database.default.driver=org.gjt.mm.mysql.Driver
database.default.url=jdbc:mysql://localhost/BFG
database.default.username=bfguser
database.default.password=bfg
```

The first four lines of the database settings tell Turbine what database to connect to when allocating new entries in the pool:

```
# The number of database connections to cache per ConnectionPool
```

LISTING 7.2   Continued

```
# instance (specified per database).

database.default.maxConnections=50
```

The `maxConnections` setting is the maximum number of simultaneous connections to allow to the database. If a connection is requested beyond this limit, Turbine will wait for one to become available. You need to make sure that this is set high enough that, if a database query takes a few seconds, you don't run out of connections in the meantime.

```
# The amount of time (in milliseconds) that database connections will be
# cached (specified per database).
#
# Default: one hour = 60 * 60 * 1000

database.default.expiryTime=3600000
```

The `expiryTime` is how long an idle connection will be left in the pool before being closed.

```
# The amount of time (in milliseconds) a connection request will have to wait
# before a time out occurs and an error is thrown.
#
# Default: ten seconds = 10 * 1000

database.connectionWaitTimeout=10000
```

The `WaitTimeout` is how long a request for a connection can wait before an error is thrown. Again, set it high enough that you don't end up without enough time for a long query to finish when you're short on connections.

```
# The interval (in milliseconds) between which the PoolBrokerService logs
# the status of it's ConnectionPools.
#
# Default: No logging = 0 = 0 * 1000

database.logInterval=0
```

`logInterval` specifies how often the status of the connection pools should be sent to the log. Setting it to `0` means that the connection pools will never be sent.

```
# These are the supported JDBC drivers and their associated Turbine
# adaptor.  These properties are used by the DBFactory.  You can add
```

LISTING 7.2   Continued

```
# all the drivers you want here.

database.adaptor=DBMM
database.adaptor.DBMM=org.gjt.mm.mysql.Driver
```

The adaptor settings set Turbine up to use mysql as the database service to pool.

```
# Determines if the quantity column of the IDBroker's id_table should
# be increased automatically if requests for ids reaches a high
# volume.

database.idbroker.cleverquantity=true
```

The cleverquantity setting can be left unchanged from the value set in the example file provided with Turbine.

Before you can use the Turbine facilities for this application, you need to initialize Turbine by telling it where to find the configuration file that you just created. One way to do this is to have every piece of code that will use the database check to see if Turbine had been initialized, and to initialize Turbine if it has not. This not only involves a lot of unnecessary code, it also slows down the execution a great deal. Instead, you should take advantage of a feature of servlet engines (including Tomcat) that allows you to specify a servlet that will be initialized as part of application startup.

To specify the servlet, you create a class that extends the HttpServlet class. In Listing 7.3, the example is called TurbineInit, and it should reside in the com.bfg.services package.

LISTING 7.3   com/bfg/services/TurbineInit.java

```
TurbineInit.java
package com.bfg.services;

import javax.servlet.http.HttpServlet;
import javax.servlet.http.HttpServletRequest;
import javax.servlet.http.HttpServletResponse;
import java.io.PrintWriter;
import java.io.IOException;
import org.apache.turbine.util.TurbineConfig;

public class TurbineInit extends HttpServlet {

  public
```

LISTING 7.3   Continued

```
void init() {
    String prefix =  getServletContext().getRealPath("/");
    String dir = getInitParameter("turbine-resource-directory");
    TurbineConfig tc = new TurbineConfig(dir, "TurbineResources.properties");
    tc.init();
  }
public
void doGet(HttpServletRequest req, HttpServletResponse res) {
}
}
```

The class overloads two methods. One, the doGet method, is basically a noop but is required by HttpServlet. The init method is called during startup, and it's here that you put the code that initializes Turbine. Upon initialization, you run the call that tells Turbine where to find its configuration file. The path is relative to where Catalina was started, which is the TOMCAT_HOME/bin directory.

Now all you have to do is instruct Tomcat to use this servlet as part of the BFG application. To do this, place a simple web.xml file in the BFG web-inf directory, as shown in Listing 7.4.

LISTING 7.4   web.xml

```
<?xml version="1.0" encoding="ISO-8859-1"?>

<!DOCTYPE web-app
    PUBLIC "-//Sun Microsystems, Inc.//DTD Web Application 2.3//EN"
    "http://java.sun.com/j2ee/dtds/web-app_2_3.dtd">

    <web-app>
  <servlet>
    <servlet-name>log4j-init</servlet-name>
    <servlet-class>com.bfg.services.Log4jInit</servlet-class>
```

LISTING 7.4   Continued

```
<servlet>
  <servlet-name>turbine-init</servlet-name>
  <servlet-class>com.bfg.services.TurbineInit</servlet-class>

  <init-param>
    <param-name>turbine-resource-directory</param-name>
    <param-value>c:/tomcat/webapps/bfg/WEB-INF</param-value>

  </init-param>

  <load-on-startup>1</load-on-startup>
  </servlet>
</web-app>
```

All that the code in Listing 7.4 does is register TurbineInit as a servlet. You'll need to change the path to the turbine-resource-directory to whatever the absolute bfg WEB-INF directory path is.

You should also add code to your Ant script to automatically copy the web.xml and the TurbineResources.properties files from the source hierarchy. It's always dangerous to have application-specific files that live only in the deployed server; they might be overwritten by a reinstall. Putting them in the source hierarchy and having Ant install them ensures that you don't lose them. The additional lines in the dist section of the script are shown in Listing 7.5.

LISTING 7.5   Additions to build.xml

```
    <mkdir dir="${appdir}/logs"/>
.


.


.

    <copy todir="${appdir}">
      <fileset dir="." includes="TurbineResources.properties"/>
    </copy>
    <copy todir="${appdir}/WEB-INF">
      <fileset dir="." includes="web.xml"/>
    </copy>
```

Using Turbine Connection Pooling

Using the connection-pooling code is a pretty simple affair, as shown by the sample program in Listing 7.6.

LISTING 7.6   DBPool.jsp

```
<%@ page import="org.apache.turbine.util.TurbineConfig" %>
<%@ page import="org.apache.turbine.services.db.TurbineDB" %>
<%@ page import="org.apache.turbine.util.db.pool.DBConnection" %>
<%@ page import="java.sql.*" %>
<%@ page import="org.apache.turbine.util.Log" %>
<HTML>
<HEAD>
<TITLE>A JDBC SmokeTest</TITLE>
</HEAD>
<BODY>
This is a smoketest

<%
DBConnection dbConn = TurbineDB.getConnection();
PreparedStatement pstmt = dbConn.prepareStatement("select * from Customer");
ResultSet rs = pstmt.executeQuery();
if (rs.next()) {
    out.print("Got a result set!");
} else {
    out.print("No result set found!!");
}
rs.close();
pstmt.close();
TurbineDB.releaseConnection(dbConn);
%>
</BODY>
</HTML>
```

When `Turbine.DB` is sent a `getConnection` message, it allocates a `DBConnection` object from the pool, if one is available. If no object is available and the pool size has not been exceeded, `Turbine.DB` creates a new one; otherwise, it waits for a connection to free up. It uses the database connection information specified in the TurbineResources.properties file, which is in your application's base directory in Tomcat.

The DBConnection object wraps the java.sql.Connection object, which allows you to use createStatement and prepareStatement with it. When you are finished with the connection, you use releaseConnection to return it to the pool. In production code, you should always wrap all the code after the getConnection in a try and have the catch do a releaseConnection, to avoid leaks.

Using Log4J

You will want to generate log messages, both for debugging and to report state during the operation of the Web site. You should standardize this, too; otherwise, everyone will end up placing System.out.printlns all over the code, and you'll have a nightmare of a time cleaning them up later. The Apache folks have a nifty little (actually, fairly robust) logging package called Log4J (that's log for Java, get it?)

Log4J is easy to use but a bit tricky to configure. In the examples throughout the book, you will be using it in a fairly simple fashion, but it's worth taking about its full capabilities.

After installing Log4J using the instructions in Appendix C, you need to configure it for your application, just as Turbine needed to be configured. This is accomplished with another HttpServlet class that will be invoked on startup (see Listing 7.7).

LISTING 7.7   Log4JInit.java

```
package com.bfg.services;

import org.apache.log4j.PropertyConfigurator;
import javax.servlet.http.HttpServlet;
import javax.servlet.http.HttpServletRequest;
import javax.servlet.http.HttpServletResponse;
import java.io.PrintWriter;
import java.io.IOException;

public class Log4jInit extends HttpServlet {

  public
  void init() {
    String prefix =  getServletContext().getRealPath("/");
    String file = getInitParameter("log4j-init-file");
    // if the log4j-init-file is not set, then no point in trying
    if(file != null) {
      PropertyConfigurator.configure(prefix+file);
```

LISTING 7.7   Continued

```
    }

  }

  public
  void doGet(HttpServletRequest req, HttpServletResponse res) {
  }
}
```

The Log4jInit class simply gets the path and name of the property file with the initialization data for the Log4J package and then calls the Log4J configurator class that is set up to read its data from a configuration file.

With this class in place, you need to add another servlet to the web.xml configuration file to request that the Log4J initialization be run at startup. This is shown in Listing 7.8.

LISTING 7.8   Addition to web.xml for Log4J

```
<servlet>
  <servlet-name>log4j-init</servlet-name>
  <servlet-class>com.bfg.services.Log4jInit</servlet-class>

  <init-param>
    <param-name>log4j-init-file</param-name>
    <param-value>WEB-INF/log4j.properties</param-value>
  </init-param>

  <load-on-startup>1</load-on-startup>
</servlet>
```

As with the Turbine configuration files, you should make sure that you add code to your Ant build script to copy over the property file. You should also make sure that the logs directory is present so that Ant will have a location to write the log files to. Listing 7.9 shows the additions made to the build.xml script.

LISTING 7.9   Additions to build.xml

```
    <mkdir dir="${appdir}/logs"/>
  .
  .
  .
```

LISTING 7.9 Continued

```
<copy todir="${appdir}/WEB-INF">
    <fileset dir="props" includes="log4j.properties"/>
</copy>
```

To use Log4J, each class that wants to log puts the following code snippet in the source:

```
import org.apache.log4j.Category;
.
.
.
public class MyClass {
    static Category cat = Category.getInstance(MyClass.class);
```

The name of the class specified in the `getInstance` call should match the name of the class in which it is being used. This is because the name of the class will be included in the log output. The class and package are used to determine the level of logging output that will be generated, as you'll see shortly.

After this log code is in place, you use a standard set of logging functions to generate log messages:

```
cat.debug(String message)
cat.debug(String message, Throwable t)
cat.info(String message)
cat.info(String message, Throwable t)
cat.warn(String message)
cat.warn(String message, Throwable t)
cat.error(String message)
cat.error(String message, Throwable t)
cat.fatal(String message)
cat.fatal(String message, Throwable t)
```

Basically, there are two versions at each level: one that just prints a message and one that also prints a stacktrace from an exception. If you have an exception available, it's always a good idea to include it in the log message by using the two-argument versions of the logging methods. But if you are logging something that isn't the result of an exception, you can still use the simpler version.

Listings 7.10 and 7.11 show a simple example of Log4J that illustrates some of the ways you can log using the package.

LISTING 7.10   Logger.java

```java
package com.bfg.demo;

import org.apache.log4j.Category;

public class Logger {
    static Category cat = Category.getInstance(Logger.class);

    public Logger() {
      try {
          String aString = null;
          aString.substring(5);
      } catch (Exception e) {
          cat.error("Got error during substring", e);
      }
      cat.debug("Hi mom!");
    }
}
```

LISTING 7.11   LoggerDemo.jsp

```jsp
<%@ page import="com.bfg.demo.Logger" %>
<HTML>
<HEAD>
<TITLE>A Logger Smoketest</TITLE>
</HEAD>
<BODY>
This is a smoketest

<%
    Logger l = new Logger();
%>
</BODY>
</HTML>
```

When LoggerDemo.jsp is run from a browser, the following output should be
displayed in the console output (in the Tomcat window under Windows, or in
catalina.out under Linux).

```
0     [HttpProcessor[8080][4]] ERROR com.bfg.demo.Logger   - Got error during sub-
string
java.lang.NullPointerException
```

LISTING 7.11   Continued

```
        at com.bfg.demo.Logger.<init>(Unknown Source)
        at
org.apache.jsp._0002fjsp_0002fLoggerDemo_jsp._jspService(_0002fjsp_0002fLog-
gerDemo_jsp.java:61)
        at org.apache.jasper.runtime.HttpJspBase.service(HttpJspBase.java:107)
        at javax.servlet.http.HttpServlet.service(HttpServlet.java:853)
        at
org.apache.jasper.servlet.JspServlet$JspServletWrapper.service(JspServlet.java:200)
        at org.apache.jasper.servlet.JspServlet.serviceJspFile(JspServlet.java:379)
        at org.apache.jasper.servlet.JspServlet.service(JspServlet.java:456)
        at javax.servlet.http.HttpServlet.service(HttpServlet.java:853)
        at org.apache.catalina.core.ApplicationFilterChain.internalDoFilter(Appli-
cationFilterChain.java:247)
        .
        .
        .

10    [HttpProcessor[8080][4]] DEBUG com.bfg.demo.Logger  - Hi mom!
```

As you can see, the log information is presented in a structured format that is easy for automated monitoring tools to parse. You will use the Log4J interface throughout the application to provide error and debugging information.

Customizing Log4J

Now that you've seen Log4J in action, you can examine some of the ways that it can be customized to offer you just the information that you need. Take a look at that mysterious log4j.properties file, shown in listing 7.12:

LISTING 7.12   log4j.properties

```
# Set root category priority to DEBUG and its only appender to A1.
log4j.rootCategory=DEBUG, A1

# A1 is set to be a ConsoleAppender.
log4j.appender.A1=org.apache.log4j.ConsoleAppender

# A1 uses PatternLayout.
log4j.appender.A1.layout=org.apache.log4j.PatternLayout
log4j.appender.A1.layout.ConversionPattern=%-4r [%t] %-5p %c %x - %m%n
```

Looking at the file contents, you can begin to see that Log4J is more than just a simple console logging library. Log4J organizes everything around two basic concepts: categories and appenders.

Categories

Categories are used to sort the various log messages into a hierarchy. In the code you've seen so far (Listing 7.8), and by normal convention, categories are equivalent to classes with their packages, but this is by no means a requirement. You can pass any string into the `Category.getInstance` call.

You can then define various levels of logging for various categories, which gives you a great deal of flexibility. For example, you might frequently find that you need to turn on debugging in one specific file or set of files, but you don't want to open up the floodgates by enabling every debugging statement in the application.

Listing 7.13 shows a version of the properties file that enables logging for the `com.bfg.demo` classes but that shows only warnings or above for the rest of the application.

LISTING 7.13   A Different log4j.properties

```
# Set root category priority to WARN and its only appender to A1.
log4j.rootCategory=WARN, A1

# A1 is set to be a ConsoleAppender.
log4j.appender.A1=org.apache.log4j.ConsoleAppender

# A1 uses PatternLayout.
log4j.appender.A1.layout=org.apache.log4j.PatternLayout
log4j.appender.A1.layout.ConversionPattern=%-4r [%t] %-5p %c %x - %m%n

# Print debug messages for package com.bfg.demo
log4j.category.com.bfg.demo=DEBUG
```

Appenders

The other half of the Log4J equation consists of appenders. The appender that you have been using is the console appender, which just sends its output to the console. But Log4J allows for much more interesting possibilities. For example, you can send log messages to the UNIX Syslog, and because many remote monitoring tools know how to read the syslog, you can use them to monitor your Tomcat application.

Other appenders exist for JMS, NT events, and remote sockets. You also can write your own appender, if you need to—for example, to interface to a custom monitoring application.

Getting Ready to Code

At this point, the application infrastructure that you'll need is in place. You have Ant to manage your build and deployment processes. You have Turbine to deal with connection pooling. And you have log4J to allow everyone to produce nice, clean, consistent logging.

With the infrastructure in place, you will be ready to start laying down code in the next chapter. The work that you have done here will pay off in simple, easy-to-maintain code and consistent application deployment.

The nice thing about a well-designed framework is that, after it's in place, you rarely, if ever, have to worry about it again. And in a multiple-developer environment, knowing that everyone is building and deploying the application in the same way eliminates a major source of spurious bugs (the infamous "But it works fine on my machine" syndrome).

LAZINESS AS A VIRTUE

An important role in any software-development effort is the "tools guru"—the person who keeps up with all the open-source and commercial tools and libraries while acting as an evangelist for those tools in the project. It's the job of the tools guru to keep the development team focused on solving the client's problems rather than reinventing the wheel by creating framework components that are already available from third parties.

Larry Wall of Perl fame says that one of the virtues of a programmer is laziness. A good programmer doesn't write a piece of code if he can liberate it from an existing application or better yet, find a prepackaged solution that someone else has already come up with.

In this chapter, you saw two examples of that in the Turbine connection-pooling module and the Log4J. But there are countless examples, from the Xerces XML package to Apache and MySQL themselves. Knowing what's already out there before you write it yourself can save you both time and frustration, and can let you concentrate on the business problems rather than the technology.

Summary

A good applications infrastructure takes time to set up in the beginning of a project, but it can save hours or days of grief at the end. Now that you have completed this chapter, you have Ant to manage your build and deployment processes, Turbine for connection pooling, and log4J for consistent logging.

Infrastructure is important because it makes sure that all the team members are using the same tools in the same way, and it prevents examples of code that runs on one developer's machine but not on the deployment environment.

8

Retrieving, Storing, and Verifying User Input

W ell, it has been a bit of a journey, but you're finally ready to start laying down some Java and JSP. Now you can start to have some fun.

One of the main jobs of a Web developer is to write code that takes information from a user and does something with it. Unfortunately, users are only human, and they make mistakes. So, after that information has been collected, you also need to make sure that your code checks for those mistakes and acts on them. This chapter is all about that process.

The Customer Class

Your first goal is to create a new customer registration page and customer login functionality. To do this, you're going to need some underlying beans to hold on to the user's information. Looking back at your class diagram, you know that the Customer, AddressBook, and CreditCard objects will have to be implemented. Start with the simplest of the beans, the Customer bean. As with all beans, you should begin with the local storage and accessor methods for the properties of the class, as shown in Listing 8.1.

LISTING 8.1 Customer.java

```
package com.bfg.customer;

import java.util.Vector;

public class Customer {
    private String last_name;
    private String first_name;
```

LISTING 8.1   continued

```
private String email;
private String password;
private Vector addresses = new Vector();;;
private Vector wallet = new Vector();

static Category cat = Category.getInstance(Customer.class);
private int customer_id;

public int getCustomerId() {
  return customer_id;
}

public void setCustomerId(int id) {
  customer_id = id;
}


public String getLastName() {
  return last_name;
}

public void setLastName(String ln) {
  last_name = ln;
}

public String getFirstName() {
  return first_name;
}

public void setFirstName(String fn) {
  first_name = fn;
}

public String getEmail() {
  return email;
}

public void setEmail(String em) {
  email = em;
}
```

LISTING 8.1   Continued

```
public String getPassword() {
  return password;
}

public void setPassword(String pw) {
  password = pw;
}

public Vector getWallet() {
  return wallet;
}

public Vector getAddressBook() {
  return addresses;
}
}
```

No big surprises here—it's the same boilerplate that anyone who has ever written a bean knows and loves. The only thing to notice is that, rather than implementing a separate class to hold the credit cards and addresses in aggregate, you merely use a vector to hold them.

Reading and Writing Customers from the Database

Now you're ready to add the code to find, add, and modify customers. This means reading and writing from the database, which means that you're going to have to create SQL statements to read and write the objects. However, embedding the SQL directly into Java source is both messy and unstable because it requires that you recompile the class every time the SQL statement needs to be changed.

Using Resource Bundles

The `ResourceBundle` class can be used (and will be used later in the book) to provide different messages depending on locale, but it can also be used for the more mundane purpose of reading value out of a property file. In this case, you'll create a property file called com.bfg.customer.SQLQueries to hold the specific queries for the class. It looks like the file shown in Listing 8.2.

LISTING 8.2   com.bfg.customer.SQLQueries.properties

```
findQuery=SELECT * FROM CUSTOMER WHERE EMAIL_ADDRESS = ?
updateQuery=UPDATE CUSTOMER SET EMAIL_ADDRESS=?, PASSWORD=? WHERE CUSTOMER_ID=?
createQuery=INSERT INTO CUSTOMER (EMAIL_ADDRESS,PASSWORD) VALUES (?, ?)
deleteQuery=DELETE FROM CUSTOMER WHERE CUSTOMER_ID=?
```

Executing Reads and Writes to the Database

Now that you have a convenient place to store the SQL statements, you need to write the methods that will use them (see Listing 8.3).

LISTING 8.3   Additions to Customer.java

```java
import org.apache.turbine.services.db.TurbineDB;
import org.apache.turbine.util.db.pool.DBConnection;
import org.apache.turbine.util.TurbineConfig;
import com.bfg.exceptions.CustomerActivityException;
import com.bfg.exceptions.DuplicateEmailAddressException;
import java.sql.*;
import java.util.ResourceBundle;
import org.apache.log4j.Category;
    .
    .

    private static ResourceBundle sql_bundle =
      ResourceBundle.getBundle("com.bfg.customer.SQLQueries");

    public static Customer findCustomer(String emailAddress)
      throws CustomerActivityException {
      DBConnection dbConn = null;
      Customer cust = null;
      try
          {
              dbConn = TurbineDB.getConnection();
              if (dbConn == null) {
                  cat.error("Can't get database connection");
                  throw new CustomerActivityException();
              }
              PreparedStatement pstmt =
                  dbConn.prepareStatement(sql_bundle.getString("findQuery"));
              pstmt.setString(1, emailAddress);
              ResultSet rs = pstmt.executeQuery();
```

LISTING 8.3   Continued

```
            if (rs.next()) {
                cust = new Customer();
                cust.setCustomerId(rs.getInt("CUSTOMER_ID"));
                cust.setEmail(rs.getString("EMAIL_ADDRESS"));
                cust.setPassword(rs.getString("PASSWORD"));
            }
            rs.close();
            pstmt.close();
        }
    catch (Exception e)
        {
            cat.error("Error during findCustomer", e);
            throw new CustomerActivityException();
        }
    finally
        {
            try
                {
                    TurbineDB.releaseConnection(dbConn);
                }
            catch (Exception e)
                {
                    cat.error("Error during releaseConnection", e);
                }
        }
    return cust;

}
```

A new Exception has been defined—CustomerActivityException. You'll use this signal to call code that some kind of failure occurred during the processing of the operation. The advantage of throwing an explicit exception rather than returning null, for example, is that it forces the caller to at least be aware of the possibility of failure: Java will require the calling function to either catch or pass the exception explicitly.

The first thing you should do is to try to get a database connection from the pool. It's good coding practice to put in checks on return values like this one and flag an error if you didn't get what you expected. Once you have it, grab the appropriate SQL query string from the resource bundle and prepare a statement using that string. Then set the parameter for the e-mail address to the argument that was passed in, execute the query, and create a new Customer object if a match was found.

Be careful to catch any exceptions, and make sure that you return the connection to the pool no matter what. Otherwise, you can end up leaking connections and eventually exhausting your open database connection limit. You might also try to close open statements in the `finally` clause, to avoid leaving stray database cursors open. However, you must make sure that the statement has been set before trying to do a `close` on it; otherwise, you could end up trying to close null.

Now that you can read from the database, you need to write the other three methods. They follow along the same lines, as shown in Listing 8.4.

LISTING 8.4   More Additions to Customer.java

```
public void createCustomer()
  throws CustomerActivityException, DuplicateEmailAddressException {
  if (findCustomer(getEmail()) != null) {
      throw new DuplicateEmailAddressException();
  }
  DBConnection dbConn = null;
  try
      {
          dbConn = TurbineDB.getConnection();
          if (dbConn == null) {
              cat.error("Can't get database connection");
              throw new CustomerActivityException();
          }
          PreparedStatement pstmt =
              dbConn.prepareStatement(sql_bundle.getString("createQuery"));
          pstmt.setString(1, getEmail());
          pstmt.setString(2, getPassword());
          pstmt.executeUpdate();
          pstmt.close();
          pstmt =
              dbConn.prepareStatement(sql_bundle.getString("findQuery"));
          pstmt.setString(1, getEmail());
          ResultSet rs = pstmt.executeQuery();
          if (rs.next()) {
              setCustomerId(rs.getInt("CUSTOMER_ID"));
          } else {
              cat.error("Couldn't find record for new Customer");
          }
          rs.close();
          pstmt.close();
      }
  catch (Exception e)
      {
```

LISTING 8.4   Continued

```
                cat.error("Error during createCustomer", e);
                throw new CustomerActivityException();
            }
        finally
            {
                try
                    {
                        TurbineDB.releaseConnection(dbConn);
                    }
                catch (Exception e)
                    {
                        cat.error("Error during release connection", e);
                    }
            }
    }

    public void updateCustomer() throws CustomerActivityException {
      DBConnection dbConn = null;
      try
            {
                dbConn = TurbineDB.getConnection();
                if (dbConn == null) {
                    cat.error("Can't get database connection");
                    throw new CustomerActivityException();
                }
                PreparedStatement pstmt =
                    dbConn.prepareStatement(sql_bundle.getString("updateQuery"));
                pstmt.setString(1, getEmail());
                pstmt.setString(2, getPassword());
                pstmt.setInt(3, getCustomerId());
                pstmt.executeUpdate();
                pstmt.close();
            }
        catch (Exception e)
            {
                cat.error("Error during updateCustomer", e);
                throw new CustomerActivityException();
            }
        finally
            {
                try
                    {
```

LISTING 8.4   Continued

```
                    TurbineDB.releaseConnection(dbConn);
            }
        catch (Exception e)
            {
                cat.error("Error during release connection", e);
            }
        }
    }

    public void deleteCustomer() throws CustomerActivityException {
      DBConnection dbConn = null;
      try
        {
            dbConn = TurbineDB.getConnection();
            if (dbConn == null) {
                cat.error("Can't get database connection");
                throw new CustomerActivityException();
            }
            PreparedStatement pstmt =
                dbConn.prepareStatement(sql_bundle.getString("deleteQuery"));
            pstmt.setInt(1, getCustomerId());
            pstmt.executeUpdate();
            pstmt.close();
        }
      catch (Exception e)
        {
            cat.error("Error during deleteCustomer", e);
            throw new CustomerActivityException();

        }
      finally
        {
            try
                {
                    TurbineDB.releaseConnection(dbConn);
                }
            catch (Exception e)
                {
                    cat.error("Error during release connection", e);
                }
        }
    }
```

Things to note: In the create method, you need to look up the customer ID after you create the new customer record. Remember that the ID is an autoincrementing field, so you don't know the ID that you're going to get when you insert the new row. Because each e-mail address is unique, you can use the address as the key to look up the newly inserted row.

However, you do have to consider what will happen if someone tries to create an account using an e-mail address that already exists. The insert statement will fail and throw an exception, which will be caught, causing the customer ID field of the object to remain null. Rather than let this happen, the application should check to see if there's already a customer with that e-mail address. It should throw an explicit exception in this case, which will have to be caught and dealt with by the calling code.

Cleaning Up the Code

The rest of the methods in Listing 8.4 are straightforward, almost cookie-cutter. Compiling the finished file generates no errors, so you're mostly done for now with Customer.java. However, you need to practice some due diligence to avoid difficulties down the road.

Javadoc

All public methods need to have Javadoc written for them. As has already been pointed out, writing Javadoc is outside the scope of the book and has been left out of the printed examples to keep the page count inside the realm of sanity. However, you'll find full Javadoc in the source files found on the Web site.

Unit Tests

Unit tests are standalone tests that thoroughly exercise one particular piece of functionality. They are useful because they allow developers to make sure that all of the functionalities of their subsystems are working properly, independent of the application as a whole.

You should also put in a unit test for the class, if at all possible. When you start to develop complicated applications, especially J2EE and EJB applications, it could take 15 or 20 minutes to start up the full server. If problems occur in newly written code, it can be nearly impossible to track them down. Writing unit tests that can be run from the command line lets you quickly determine whether your code does at all what you expected. This has come in handy several times when my code was thought to cause an error, and I was able to demonstrate that it passed the unit test.

In this case, you can write a unit test if you hard-wire in some values to simulate input from outside functions calling into the class and to do the initializations on the connection pool that otherwise would be handled by the server startup (see Listing 8.5).

LISTING 8.5   Yet More Additions to Customer.java

```java
public static void main(String[] args) {
  TurbineConfig tc = new TurbineConfig("com/bfg/props/",
                                        "TurbineResources.properties");
  tc.init();

  Customer c = new Customer();
  c.setLastName("NameThatShouldNeverBeUsed");
  c.setFirstName("Joe");
  c.setPassword("easilyguessed");
  c.setEmail("namethatshouldneverbeused@bogussite.com");
  try {
      c.createCustomer();
      System.out.println("Good Test: Create Customer");
  } catch (Exception e) {
      System.out.println("Failed Test: Create Customer");
      e.printStackTrace();
  }
  try {
      c.createCustomer();
      System.out.println("Failed Test: Create Duplicate Customer");
  } catch (DuplicateEmailAddressException e) {
      System.out.println("Good Test: Create Duplicate Customer");
  } catch (Exception e) {
      System.out.println("Failed Test: Create Duplicate Customer");
      e.printStackTrace();
  }
  try {
      Customer c1 =
          findCustomer("namethatshouldneverbeused@bogussite.com");
      if (c1 != null) {
          System.out.println("Good Test: Find Real Customer");
      } else {
          System.out.println("Failed Test: Find Real Customer");
      }
  } catch (Exception e) {
      System.out.println("Failed Test: Find Real Customer");
  }
  try {
      Customer c1 =
          findCustomer("othernamethatshouldneverbeused@bogussite.com");
      if (c1 != null) {
```

LISTING 8.5   Continued

```
            System.out.println("Failed Test: Find Fake Customer");
        } else {
            System.out.println("Good Test: Find Fake Customer");
        }
    } catch (Exception e) {
        System.out.println("Failed Test: Find Fake Customer");
    }
    try {
        c.deleteCustomer();
        Customer c1 =
            findCustomer("namethatshouldneverbeused@bogussite.com");
        if (c1 != null) {
            System.out.println("Failed Test: Delete Customer");
        } else {
            System.out.println("Good Test: Delete Customer");
        }
    } catch (Exception e) {
        System.out.println("Failed Test: Delete Customer");
    }
}
```

This does what a good unit test should do—it exercises all of the functionality of the class (at least, the parts that aren't boilerplate, such as get and set methods). It is also careful to leave the database in the same state that it was found so that it can be run repeatedly. You need to add the Turbine configuration calls at the top because this does not run through Tomcat, so it will not get the initializations during startup.

Getting the unit test to run is a bit tricky, however, because it depends on subsystems such as Turbine being properly configured. You conceivably could invoke it by hand, but that would be quite tricky because you'd need to set up configuration elements such as the classpath perfectly each time you wanted to invoke the test. Instead, put some more targets in your Ant script to let you automatically invoke all of your unit tests. This also will come in handy when regression testing starts. Here's some code to do just that, in Listing 8.6.

LISTING 8.6   Additions to build.xml

```
<target name="test" depends="dist">
  <java classname="com.bfg.customer.Customer" fork="yes">
    <classpath>
    <pathelement path="${java.class.path}"/>
      <fileset dir="c:\tomcat\lib">
```

LISTING 8.6 Continued

```
            <include name="**/*.jar"/>
        </fileset>
        <pathelement path="src"/>
      </classpath>
    </java>
  </target>
```

Because this code will run from the base directory, and because TurbineConfig looks for its property file relative to where the Java executable is started, you need to specify the path in the TurbineConfig call as com/bfg/props/ so that it can find the file successfully. You also should have the Ant script configure Java to add the src directory to the class path so that it finds the class files to test.

When you run the unit test with ant test, you get the desired result:

```
C:\CARTAPP\bfg>ant test
Buildfile: build.xml

init:

compile:

dist:

test:
     [java] Turbine: init
     [java] Turbine: Turbine: init() Ready to Rumble!
     [java] Good Test: Create Customer
     [java] Good Test: Create Duplicate Customer
     [java] Good Test: Find Real Customer
     [java] Good Test: Find Fake Customer
     [java] Good Test: Delete Customer

BUILD SUCCESSFUL

Total time: 1 second
C:\CARTAPP\bfg>
```

If you don't get this result, either your database is set up incorrectly, you're not connecting to it correctly, or your SQL statements are in error.

Accessing the Customer Class from JSP

Having created your underlying class, you can proceed to hook it up to some JSP pages to actually do something. For the moment, these sections walk you through some bare-bones pages that create and retrieve customers.

To begin, set up a customer-creation page. Before you do, you need to think out your JSP document strategy. You already know that some elements, such as the mini-cart and navigational bars, will appear on most pages. One strategic approach that you can take is to use a single JSP file to control access to all of the site functionality and then have the code dispatch to different subpages inside the main page to display different content depending on the session state. This way, if a user bookmarks the page, he always comes to the entry page (because there will be no session state when the user starts).

For certain types of sites this is an advantage. For example, a site that has a lot of stateful transactions (that is, multistage transactions) might not want a user to book-mark some arbitrary intermediate Web page during the transaction processing.

The disadvantage to this approach is that you can't bookmark a page for a specific product, for example. Sometimes it's actually good to expose state through the URL query string, specifically so that it can be saved or sent to a friend. Also, the all-in-one page approach can lead to a fairly awkward and bloated piece of JSP if you're not careful. Because all the control for the application rests in a single file, it can end up being full of conditional pieces of logic and can become difficult to understand. One alternative is to use an MVC package such as Struts (see Chapter 16, "The Struts Application Framework"), but this approach has its own complexities and perils.

For that reason, and for clarity of demonstration, you'll use a few different JSP files to handle the site functionality.

Beginners to JSP (or to CGI, for that matter) are always taught to do form presentation and handling in two steps: first to display the form and then to handle the submission. The problem with this approach is that when you start dealing with validation and error handling, you find that the second step might need to redisplay the form with error messages, so you end up duplicating the form twice.

The method generally preferred by experienced developers is to create a single page that submits to itself, as you will do throughout this application. One thing to keep in mind with this technique is that you need some kind of state variable that allows you to track whether this is the first display or a subsequent display of the form. You don't want the code to try to validate the submitted data before you have actually filled out the form because it will flag them all as errors: They'll be blank.

The other trick is that if you're populating the form fields with the values provided from the last form submission, these values will be null on the first pass because there are no values to set them to and because the Customer object defaults them to null. To avoid displaying the string null in the form the first time through, you need to set the values to the empty string explicitly.

Listing 8.7 is a simple first pass on a customer-creation page.

LISTING 8.7   NewCustomer.jsp

```
<%@ page import="com.bfg.customer.Customer" %>
<jsp:useBean id="newcust" class="com.bfg.customer.Customer" scope="request"/>
<jsp:setProperty name="newcust" property="*"/>

<%
if (request.getParameter("SUBMITTED") != null) {
    try {
      newcust.createCustomer();
      response.sendRedirect("NewSuccess.jsp");
    } catch (com.bfg.exceptions.DuplicateEmailAddressException e) {
    }
}
if (newcust.getEmail() == null) {
    newcust.setEmail("");
}
if (newcust.getPassword() == null) {
    newcust.setPassword("");
}
%>
<HEAD><TITLE>Create New Customer Account</TITLE></HEAD><BODY>

<FORM METHOD=POST ACTION="NewCustomer.jsp">
<INPUT TYPE="HIDDEN" NAME="SUBMITTED" VALUE="T">
e-Mail Address: <INPUT NAME="email" TYPE="TEXT" SIZE=50
        VALUE="<%= newcust.getEmail() %>"><BR>
Password: <INPUT NAME="password" TYPE="TEXT" SIZE=50
        VALUE="<%= newcust.getPassword() %>"><BR>
<INPUT TYPE=SUBMIT>
</FORM>
</BODY>
```

The code uses the hidden field SUBMITTED to track whether this is the first time through or whether you're processing a previously displayed form. If it's the first time through, the JSP blanks out the two form field variables; otherwise, it tries to create a new user and then redirect to the success page. Because a redirect needs to come before any text is sent to the page, you must put all of this control logic above the first HTML in the document.

If the new user creation results in a duplicate entry, the JSP catches the DuplicateEmailAddressException, which results in the redirect being skipped.

Field Validation

This code is still lacking a bit. First, if the customer enters a duplicate e-mail address, the page does not provide any helpful feedback to let him know that it occurred. Second, because you're not validating the fields, someone could put total garbage into them and still create a new customer. Form-field validation is one of the major components of Web site design. You need to thoroughly understand what values are allowed in certain fields and how fields could be interdependent—in other words, Field 1 might be required only if Field 2 is filled in.

Validating fields is generally straight-forward. Returning error messages from validation is more complex and requires some decisions to be made. Basically, error conditions can be returned from validation in three ways; we'll consider each in turn.

Returning Errors in a Simple Vector

The most basic way to return error conditions is to have a single Vector property on the object being validated, called something like validationErrors. You add strings describing each validation error as you encounter them. You then put into the form a piece of JSP that looks like this:

```
<%
    Iterator errors = newcust.getValidationErrors().iterator();
    while (errors.hasNext()) {
        %>
        Error: <%= errors.next() %><BR>
<%
    }
%>
```

This will cause all the errors discovered to display just above the form, one after another.

Unique Error Properties

Over time, experience has shown that users have an easier time if you display the errors near the field that caused them, especially in long forms. This leads to the second technique: tying a read-only validation error property to each field that get sets by the validation method. You would use it as follows:

```
e-Mail Address: <INPUT NAME="email" TYPE="TEXT" SIZE=50
        VALUE="<%= newcust.getEmail() %>">
        <FONT COLOR="#FF0000"><%= newcust.getEmailValidationError() %></FONT><BR>
```

This results in a red error message being displayed next to the field, if present. It's a bit clumsy to code, however, because it requires adding a separate validation error accessor for each field in the form, which can add quite a bit of bulk to your Java source. This method also requires you to manually clear each field.

Using a `HashMap` for Errors

A technique that might work better is to provide a single `HashMap` to hold the error messages with a single accessor function. Listing 8.8 has the additional source in the Java, and Listing 8.9 shows how it's used in the JSP.

LISTING 8.8   Additions to Customer.java

```java
import java.util.HashMap;
.
.
.
    private HashMap validationErrors = new HashMap();

    public String getFieldError(String fieldname) {
      return((String)validationErrors.get(fieldname));
    }

    public void addFieldError(String fieldname, String error) {
      validationErrors.put(fieldname, error);
    }

    public boolean validateCustomer() {
      validationErrors.clear();
      boolean valid = true;
      if ((email == null) ||
          (email.length() == 0)) {
          addFieldError("email", "e-Mail Address is required.");
```

LISTING 8.8   Continued

```
            valid = false;
        } else {
            if (email.indexOf("@") == -1) {
                addFieldError("email", "Please supply a valid address.");
                valid = false;
            }
        }
        if ((password == null) ||
            (password.length() == 0)) {
            addFieldError("password", "Password is required.");
            valid = false;
        }
        return valid;
    }
```

The interesting thing to note here is that, because only one error message per field is allowed under this scheme, you want to make sure that the validation code doesn't check for an "@" unless the e-mail address is not blank. Otherwise, it will always set the "valid address" error, even on a blank field.

LISTING 8.9   The revised NewCustomer.jsp

```
<%@ page import="com.bfg.customer.Customer" %>
<jsp:useBean id="newcust" class="com.bfg.customer.Customer" scope="request"/>
<jsp:setProperty name="newcust" property="*"/>

<%
if (request.getParameter("SUBMITTED") != null) {
    try {
        if (newcust.validateCustomer()) {
            newcust.createCustomer();
            response.sendRedirect("NewSuccess.jsp");
        }
    } catch (com.bfg.exceptions.DuplicateEmailAddressException e) {
        newcust.addFieldError("email",
                            "e-Mail address already in use. <BR>" +
                            "Click <A HREF=\"lostPassword.jsp\">here</A> "+
                            "if you have forgotten your password.");
    }
}
if (newcust.getEmail() == null) {
    newcust.setEmail("");
```

LISTING 8.9   Continued

```
}
if (newcust.getPassword() == null) {
    newcust.setPassword("");
}
%>
<HEAD><TITLE>Create New Customer Account</TITLE></HEAD><BODY>

<FORM METHOD=POST ACTION="NewCustomer.jsp">
<INPUT TYPE="HIDDEN" NAME="SUBMITTED" VALUE="T">

<% if (newcust.getFieldError("email") != null) { %>
<FONT COLOR="#FF0000"><%= newcust.getFieldError("email")%></FONT><BR>
<% } %>

e-Mail Address: <INPUT NAME="email" TYPE="TEXT" SIZE=50
        VALUE="<%= newcust.getEmail() %>"><BR>

<% if (newcust.getFieldError("password") != null) { %>
<FONT COLOR="#FF0000"><%= newcust.getFieldError("password")%></FONT><BR>
<% } %>

Password: <INPUT NAME="password" TYPE="TEXT" SIZE=50
        VALUE="<%= newcust.getPassword() %>"><BR>
<INPUT TYPE=SUBMIT>
</FORM>
</BODY>
```

The first change made is to add a call to `validateCustomer` and to conditionalize trying to call `createCustomer` by the success of the validation.

In a more clever solution, you can use the same error-reporting mechanism to display the error for a duplicate e-mail address, including a link to a page that handles reminders for lost passwords.

Now you can place a conditional display of the error message above each field, nicely highlighted in red. If you look at Figures 8.1 and 8.2, you can see the results of trying to submit a blank form and an error generated for a previously used address.

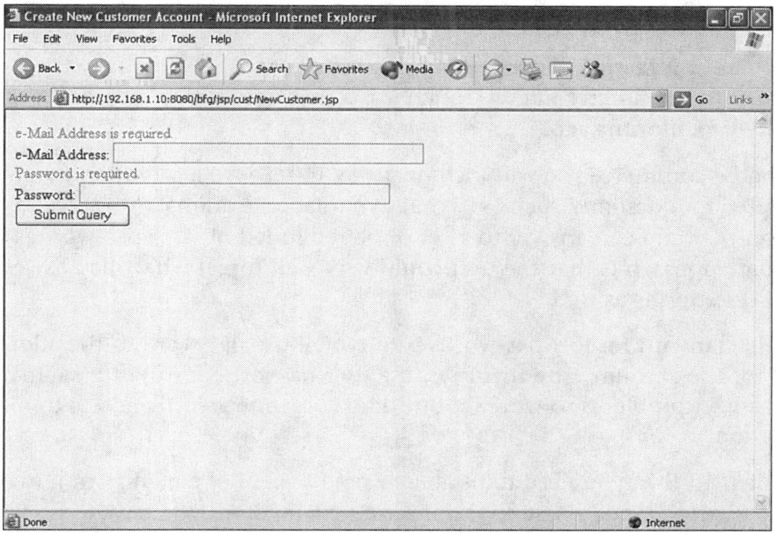

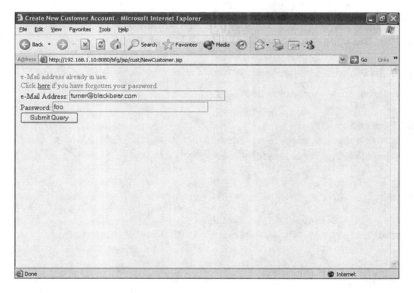

FIGURE 8.1   A blank form submission.

FIGURE 8.2   Trying a duplicate e-mail address.

Handling Forgotten Passwords

Humans are a forgetful species. Many of us consider ourselves lucky if we can remember our children's names, much less a password we selected for a site that we visited six months ago.

Any good e-commerce site will include a way to retrieve a forgotten password. Some have opted for questions, such as "What's your favorite animal?" to serve as a secondary question that you can answer to reset or be reminded of your password. The problem with that approach is that the user could very well forget what the answer to the second question is as well.

The gold standard for lost passwords is to e-mail the password to the address of record for the account. The theory is, if a user has lost control of his e-mail account, he has bigger problems to worry about than someone gaining access to his store registration.

To implement this, you need to be able to send a piece of e-mail from Java. Thankfully, Tomcat 4 includes built-in support for sending e-mail. All you have to do is configure it. Note that this requires the JavaMail and JavaBean Activation Framework libraries, both of which are available from Sun and are included in the extras directory in the zip file available on the Sams Web site.

To configure e-mail support, you need to add some text to the web.xml that you created for the bfg example application (see Listing 8.10).

LISTING 8.10   web.xml Revised

```
<?xml version="1.0" encoding="ISO-8859-1"?>

<!DOCTYPE web-app
    PUBLIC "-//Sun Microsystems, Inc.//DTD Web Application 2.3//EN"
    "http://java.sun.com/j2ee/dtds/web-app_2_3.dtd">

  <web-app>
 <servlet>
   <servlet-name>log4j-init</servlet-name>
   <servlet-class>com.bfg.services.Log4jInit</servlet-class>

   <init-param>
     <param-name>log4j-init-file</param-name>
     <param-value>WEB-INF/log4j.properties</param-value>
   </init-param>
```

LISTING 8.10   Continued

```
  <load-on-startup>1</load-on-startup>
</servlet>
<servlet>
  <servlet-name>turbine-init</servlet-name>
  <servlet-class>com.bfg.services.TurbineInit</servlet-class>

  <init-param>
    <param-name>turbine-resource-directory</param-name>
    <param-value>c:/tomcat/webapps/bfg/WEB-INF</param-value>

  </init-param>
  <load-on-startup>1</load-on-startup>
</servlet>
 <session-config>
  <session-timeout>5</session-timeout>
 </session-config>
 <resource-ref>
   <res-ref-name>mail/session</res-ref-name>
   <res-type>javax.mail.Session</res-type>
   <res-auth>Container</res-auth>
 </resource-ref>
```

The addition of the `resource-ref` lines is absolutely boilerplate; it doesn't change from application to application.

Next, you need to specify a valid SMTP host in your Tomcat server.xml file. When you first created the entry for the bfg application, you just copied the examples context entry that comes with Tomcat. That example sets the SMTP host to localhost, which works only if you're running an SMTP server on your local machine. This might be the case if you're using Linux, but it almost certainly is not the case on a Windows machine. Listing 8.12 shows a revised entry for your application in server.xml.

LISTING 8.12   The BFG Entry in server.xml

```
    <!-- BFG Context -->
    <Context path="/bfg" docBase="bfg" debug="0"
             reloadable="true">
      <Environment name="maxExemptions" type="java.lang.Integer"
                   value="15"/>
      <Parameter name="context.param.name" value="context.param.value"
                   override="false"/>
```

LISTING 8.12   Continued

```
        <Resource name="mail/session" auth="CONTAINER"
                type="javax.mail.Session"/>
        <ResourceParams name="mail/session">
          <parameter>
            <name>mail.smtp.host</name>
            <value>localhost</value>
          </parameter>
        </ResourceParams>
      </Context>
```

The relevant lines in the server.xml file are these:

```
        <name>mail.smtp.host</name>
        <value>localhost</value>
```

Under the bfg context, change localhost to the address of your SMTP server—either yours or the one that your ISP has you use.

Now that Java e-mail has been configured, you can add the appropriate functionality to the Customer class (see Listing 8.13).

LISTING 8.13   Additions to Customer.java for E-mail

```
import javax.naming.NamingException;
import javax.naming.Context;
import javax.naming.InitialContext;
import javax.naming.NamingEnumeration;
import javax.naming.directory.InitialDirContext;
import javax.mail.*;
import javax.mail.internet.InternetAddress;
import javax.mail.internet.MimeMessage;
import javax.mail.internet.AddressException;
    .
    .
    .

    private static ResourceBundle email_bundle =
      ResourceBundle.getBundle("com.bfg.emailProperties");
    .
    .
    .

    public void sendPasswordReminder()
      throws NamingException, AddressException, MessagingException {
```

LISTING 8.13   Continued

```
Context initCtx = new InitialContext();
Context envCtx = (Context) initCtx.lookup("java:comp/env");
Session session = (Session) envCtx.lookup("mail/session");

Message message = new MimeMessage(session);
message.setFrom(new InternetAddress(email_bundle.getString("fromAddr")));
InternetAddress to[] = new InternetAddress[1];
to[0] = new InternetAddress(email);
message.setRecipients(Message.RecipientType.TO, to);
message.setSubject(email_bundle.getString("lostSubj"));
message.setContent(email_bundle.getString("lostContent") + password,
                   "text/plain");
Transport.send(message);
}
```

After importing a number of new required classes needed for support of naming and e-mail, you define another resource bundle so that you can put things such as the sender's e-mail address and the text of the message into a property file rather than hard-wiring it in the Java code. This is the same philosophy that you adopted with the SQL query strings. Listing 8.14 shows the contents of this file.

LISTING 8.14   emailProperties.properties

```
#fromAddr=customerservice@bfgbooks.com
fromAddr=turner@blackbear.com
lostSubj=Lost Password Reminder
lostContent=Someone has sent a request for a password reminder using your\n\
e-Mail address.  If this person was not you, please contact us immediately\n\
so that we can address the situation.  If it was you, your password is\n\
included at the bottom of this message.\n\
\n\
Thank you,\n\
Books for Geeks Customer Service\n\
customerservice@bfgbooks.com\n\
\n\
PASSWORD=
```

Note that you probably won't be able to use the fake customer service address as the fromAddr field because most SMTP relay servers will bounce it as bogus. This is also true when developing a real application for which the domain name is not registered yet. For that reason, it has been commented out and a test address has been put in its place.

The Java Naming and Directory Interface (JNDI) is used to get a handle on the persistent mail session object that you defined for the application. The application gets a new MimeMessage; sets the addresses, subject, and content; and then sends the message.

With the back-end code written, all that's left is to write the JSP. An interesting security question to consider is this: Should you have a different message displayed if the user types in an e-mail address that isn't associated with a registered user? It can be argued that if you do this, it provides a way for a hacker to find out whether an e-mail address is valid so that he can try to guess the password; under that logic, you should display a generic "We'll send you your password if we find it" message, even if no such address really exists in your records.

The counter argument to that argument, in this case, is that the e-mail address is used as the customer's primary login key. All a hacker would need to do is to try to create a new account using that e-mail address and get the duplicate address message to know that the account was ripe for attack. In other words, there's no harm in letting a customer know that he didn't use the right address.

Listing 8.15 shows the JSP for implementing lost password.

LISTING 8.15   lostPassword.jsp

```
<%@ page import="com.bfg.customer.Customer" %>

<%
    String email = request.getParameter("email");
boolean not_found = false;
    if (email == null) {
      email = "";
    }
if (request.getParameter("SUBMITTED") != null) {
    Customer c = Customer.findCustomer(email);
    if (c != null) {
      c.sendPasswordReminder();
      response.sendRedirect("sendPassword.jsp");
    }
    not_found = true;
}
%>
<HEAD><TITLE>Lost Password Retrieval</TITLE></HEAD><BODY>
Please enter the e-Mail address you used to register your account.
```

LISTING 8.15   Continued

```
<FORM METHOD=POST ACTION="lostPassword.jsp">
<INPUT TYPE="HIDDEN" NAME="SUBMITTED" VALUE="T">

<% if (not_found) { %>
<FONT COLOR="#FF0000">Address not found in customer records.</FONT><BR>
<% } %>

e-Mail Address: <INPUT NAME="email" TYPE="TEXT" SIZE=50
        VALUE="<%= email %>"><BR>
<INPUT TYPE=SUBMIT>
</FORM>
</BODY>
```

Again, the "redirect on success" trick is used to keep the user on the same page if the e-mail address isn't found. The sendPassword.jsp page is a simple static page telling the user that the password has been sent. See Figures 8.3 and 8.4.

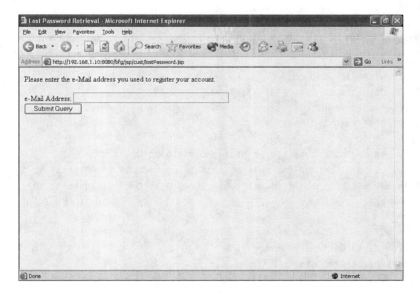

FIGURE 8.3   Lost password page.

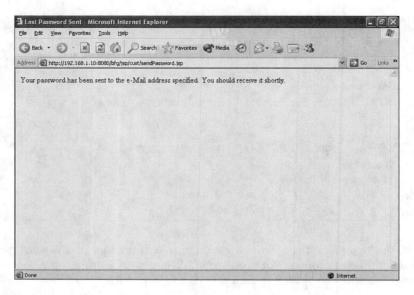

FIGURE 8.4   Lost password result.

If everything has been set up right and you specified an e-mail address that is actually your own, you will get a piece of e-mail that looks like this:

```
From: turner@blackbear.com
Sent: Sunday, October 14, 2001 11:59 AM
To: turner@blackbear.com
Subject: Lost Password Reminder

Someone has sent a request for a password reminder using your e-Mail
address.  If this person was not you, please contact us immediately so that we can
address the situation.  If it was you, your password is included at the bottom of
this message.

Thank you,
Books for Geeks Customer Service
customerservice@bfgbooks.com

PASSWORD=apassword
```

Using Cookies to Store Login

Many sites now use a permanent cookie to allow the customer to access the site without needing to log in. This has its good and bad points. The good side is that it reduces the barrier to entry that could discourage a customer from using your site. The bad side is that it potentially allows a hacker to gain unauthorized access to a user's account by either faking the cookie or gaining access to the user's PC. There's not much that you can do about the latter, but you can prevent the former from happening by taking a few basic precautions:

- Don't store just the username; store both the username and the password. That way, the hacker can't create the cookie by just knowing the username (in this case, the e-mail address) of the customer.

- Don't store the data in plain text in the cookie. Otherwise, it becomes too easy for someone gaining access to the computer to know what the information is simply by accessing the cookies file.

Look at how to implement automatic login using cookies on your site. To start, you will need to add some JSP to the login page to send a cookie back to the browser (see Listing 8.16).

LISTING 8.16   Login.jsp Revised

```
<%@ page import="com.bfg.customer.Customer" %>
<%@ page import="javax.servlet.http.Cookie" %>
<%@ page import="sun.misc.BASE64Encoder" %>

<jsp:useBean id="customer" class="com.bfg.customer.Customer" scope="session"/>

<%
String error = null;
if (request.getParameter("SUBMITTED") != null) {
    Customer c = Customer.findCustomer(request.getParameter("email"));
    if (c == null) {
      error = "No such e-Mail found, please try again.";
    } else {
      if (request.getParameter("password").equals(c.getPassword())) {
          customer = c;
          BASE64Encoder enc = new BASE64Encoder();
          Cookie cook = new Cookie("bfgUsername",
                                   enc.encode(c.getEmail().getBytes())));
          cook.setMaxAge(3600*24*365);
          response.addCookie(cook);
```

LISTING 8.16   Continued

```
        cook = new Cookie("bfgPassword",
                                 enc.encode(c.getPassword().getBytes())));
        cook.setMaxAge(3600*24*365);
        response.addCookie(cook);
        response.sendRedirect("LoggedIn.jsp");
    } else {
    error = "Invalid Password";
    }
  }
}
%>
<HEAD><TITLE>Please Log In</TITLE></HEAD><BODY>

<FORM METHOD=POST ACTION="Login.jsp">
<INPUT TYPE="HIDDEN" NAME="SUBMITTED" VALUE="T">

<% if (error != null) { %>
<FONT COLOR="#FF0000"><%= error %></FONT><BR>
<% } %>

e-Mail Address: <INPUT NAME="email" TYPE="TEXT" SIZE=50><BR>
Password: <INPUT NAME="password" TYPE="TEXT" SIZE=50><BR>
<INPUT TYPE=SUBMIT>
</FORM>
</BODY>
```

Yes, this is yet another form that submits to itself. When the user submits a username and password, the page looks up the customer to see if the e-mail address exists. If it does exist and the password matches the password in the database, two cookies are generated: one for the username and one for the password. The page encodes the data using Base64 encoding for two reasons. One reason is to provide some minimum protection of the data; the other reason is that certain symbols, such as "@," aren't legal in early implementations of cookies. Note that Base64 encoding is in no way a secure protocol for encryption. If you really want to protect the data, a secure method such as Pretty Good Encryption (PGP) or the government's Data Encryption Standard (DES) should be used.

Now that the user can log in, you need to write a JSP snippet to use throughout the site that checks for the cookie and logs in the user automatically if the cookie is available (see Listing 8.17).

LISTING 8.17   AutoLogin.jsp

```
<%@ page import="com.bfg.customer.Customer" %>
<%@ page import="javax.servlet.http.Cookie" %>
<%@ page import="sun.misc.BASE64Decoder" %>

<jsp:useBean id="customer" class="com.bfg.customer.Customer" scope="session"/>

<%
String email = null;
String password = null;
Cookie cook;

if (customer.getEmail() == null) {
    Cookie[] cookies = request.getCookies();
    BASE64Decoder dec = new BASE64Decoder();
    for (int i = 0; i < cookies.length; i++) {
      if (cookies[i].getName().equals("bfgUsername")) {
          email = new String(dec.decodeBuffer(cookies[i].getValue()));
      }
      if (cookies[i].getName().equals("bfgPassword")) {
          password = new String(dec.decodeBuffer(cookies[i].getValue()));
      }
    }
    if ((email != null) && (password != null)) {
      Customer c = Customer.findCustomer(email);
      if ((c != null) && (c.getPassword().equals(password))) {
          pageContext.setAttribute("customer",c, PageContext.SESSION_SCOPE);
      }
    }
}
%>
```

First you put in a check to see if the user already is logged in (if the session-scoped property customer has a non-null e-mail address). If the user isn't already logged in, you need to have the code run through all the request cookies looking for the user-name and password cookies and then decoding the cookies if they're found.

If a cookie is found, and if a user with that username and password exists, you can have the code set the session-scoped customer property to the customer that was just found. This means that the next time this code is run, it won't try to log in the user. Otherwise, the user will need to log in manually (or not at all, as the site permits).

Moving On

In this chapter, you've learned how to create a bean that interacts with JSP pages. To do this successfully, a bean class needs to provide accessors for all the properties of the object.

It also needs to provide methods to read and write these objects from the database if the object persists over time. This requires having some key that can be used to access a record uniquely.

Filling out forms requires form validation. Using a `HashMap` to store the validation errors lets you get at specific field errors without needing a separate property for each one. Tomcat supplies a convenient way to send e-mail from Java. You learned in this chapter how it can be used to implement a lost-password function.

Finally, you used cookies to store the username and password so that customers can be automatically logged in.

With the rudiments of user login and creation out of the way, it is time to move on to some product display. This is covered in the next chapter. However, don't think that you're finished with the `Customer` object just yet. You'll still have to tackle the address book and wallet before you're finished.

9

Publishing Data from Database Sources

One of the most powerful synergies of using a database together with JSP is that you can automatically generate Web content from database tables. In this chapter, you'll see how easy it is to do this.

Looking at the Default Document Structure

As you move on to the actual look and feel of the Web site, you have to start building the structure of your pages. Before this, you've been putting together test pages or rough drafts, but now you're going to need to write real pages that will evolve into finished products. Later, you can go back and polish the pages you've already written.

Looking back to the wireframes (see Figure 9.1), you can identify the various elements of the site. In the top left corner is a logo, and across the top is a welcome banner. Running down the left edge are the mini-cart and the department listing, followed by a couple of navigational links.

Some of this content, such as the banner, is static. The mini-cart reflects the current state of the order. The department listing is dynamically created from the list of departments.

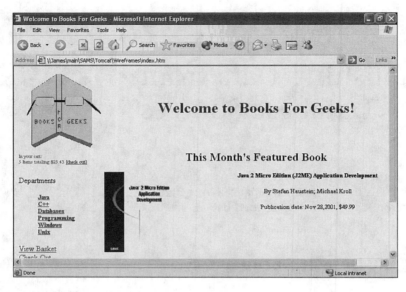

FIGURE 9.1   The BFG entry page.

You can use the wireframe HTML as a starting point for creating the real document. This is typically the way it works in a real project: You take the wireframes that have been created by the design folks and embed the real functionality in the site. This is because very few developers are competent designers, so they generally like to mess with all those layout features as little as possible.

Listing 9.1 shows the source for the wireframe of the entry page.

LISTING 9.1   index.jsp Wireframe Code

```
<html>

<head>
<title>Welcome to Books For Geeks</title>
</head>

<body>

<table border="0" cellpadding="0" cellspacing="0" width="100%">
  <tr>
    <td width="22%">
    <img border="0" src="../../../My%20Pictures/bfglogo.JPG" width="175"
height="168"></td>
```

LISTING 9.1   Continued

```
      <td width="78%">
      <h1 align="center"><font color="#0000FF">Welcome to Books For
Geeks!</font></h1>
      </td>
    </tr>
    <tr>
      <td width="22%">
      <table border="0" cellpadding="0" cellspacing="0" width="100%">
        <tr>
          <td width="50%" height="35"><font size="1">
          <font color="#008000">In your
          cart:<br>
          5 Items totaling $23.43</font>
          <a href="http://www.boston.com/sports/redsox">[check out]</a></font></td>
        </tr>
      </table>
      <p>Departments</p>
      <blockquote>
        <h5><a href="index.htm">Java</a><br>
        <a href="index.htm">C++</a><br>
        <a href="index.htm">Databases</a><br>
        <a href="index.htm">Programming</a><br>
        <a href="index.htm">Windows</a><br>
        <a href="index.htm">Unix</a></h5>
      </blockquote>
      <p><a href="index.htm">View Basket</a><br>
      <a href="index.htm">Check Out</a><br>
      <a href="index.htm">My Account</a></p>
      <p> </p>
      <p> </p>
      <p> </td>
      <td width="78%" valign="top">
      <h2 align="center">This Month's Featured Book</h2>
      <table border="0" cellpadding="0" cellspacing="0" width="639">
        <tr>
          <td>
          <img border="0" src="../0672320959.jpg" align="left" width="140"
height="173"></td>
          <td valign="top">
          <h3 align="center">
```

LISTING 9.1   Continued

```
      <span style="font-size: 10.0pt; font-family: Times New Roman">Java 2
      Micro Edition (J2ME) Application Development</span></h3>
      <p align="center">
      <span style="font-size: 10.0pt; font-family: Times New Roman">By Stefan
      Haustein; Michael Kroll</span></p>
      <p align="center"><font size="2" face="Times New Roman">Publication
      date: </font>
      <span style="font-size: 10.0pt; font-family: Times New Roman">Nov
      28,2001, $49.99</span></td>
    </tr>
  </table>
  <p><span style="font-size: 10.0pt">The key to Java 2 Micro Edition (J2ME)
  Application Development is the clear, concise explanations of the J2ME
  technology in relation to the existing Java platform. This book assumes
  proficiency with Java and presents strategies for understanding and
  deploying J2ME applications. The book presents numerous real-world examples,
  including health care and financial sector examples from the authors'
  professional experience.</span></p>
  <p><font size="2">[<a href="index.htm">More Information]</a>
  <a href="index.htm">[Buy It!]</a></font></p>
  <p align="center"> </td>
  </tr>
</table>

</body>

</html>
```

When you look at this source, you can quickly see that the changing content from page to page is going to live inside the <td> tag for the surrounding table. (In this example, that tag includes the table inside with the book information.)

You can approach this kind of document structure in basically two ways. The first is to make the surrounding content into included JSP files that the individual pages load. So, for example, this page would end up looking like Listing 9.2.

LISTING 9.2   One Approach to the Document Structure

```
<head>
<title>Welcome to Books For Geeks</title>
</head>

<%@ include file="bfgheader.jsp" %>

<h2 align="center">This Month's Featured Book</h2>
<table border="0" cellpadding="0" cellspacing="0" width="639">
 <tr>
  <td>
   <img border="0" src="../0672320959.jpg" align="left" width="140"
height="173"></td>
  <td valign="top">
    <h3 align="center">
    <span style="font-size: 10.0pt; font-family: Times New Roman">Java 2
     Micro Edition (J2ME) Application Development</span></h3>
     <p align="center">
    <span style="font-size: 10.0pt; font-family: Times New Roman">By Stefan
        Haustein; Michael Kroll</span></p>
        <p align="center"><font size="2" face="Times New Roman">Publication
        date: </font>
        <span style="font-size: 10.0pt; font-family: Times New Roman">Nov
        28,2001, $49.99</span></td>
      </tr>
    </table>
    <p><span style="font-size: 10.0pt">The key to Java 2 Micro Edition (J2ME)
    Application Development is the clear, concise explanations of the J2ME
    technology in relation to the existing Java platform. This book assumes
    proficiency with Java and presents strategies for understanding and
    deploying J2ME applications. The book presents numerous real-world examples,
    including health care and financial sector examples from the authors'
    professional experience.</span></p>
    <p><font size="2">[<a href="index.htm">More Information]</a>
    <a href="index.htm">[Buy It!]</a></font></p>
    <p align="center"> 

<%@ include file="bfgfooter.jsp" %>
```

You don't include the <head> in the header file because it differs from page to page. Notice that even though the site technically doesn't have a footer on the page, you need to include a footer document to close the tables from the header.

The alternative method is to invert the process. Instead of having a header and footer document, you would author a number of documents with the "guts" of the site that are wrapped by a master page that decides which subpage to include. In practice, it leads to a master page that looks like Listing 9.3.

LISTING 9.3   Turning the Approach Inside Out

```
<% String content = request.getParameter("content");
if (content == null) {
    content = "index";
}

String title = "";

if  (content.equals("index")) {
    title = "Welcome to Books For Geeks";
}
%>
<head>
<title><%= title %></title>
</head>

<body>

<table border="0" cellpadding="0" cellspacing="0" width="100%">
  <tr>
    <td width="22%">
    <img border="0" src="../../../My%20Pictures/bfglogo.JPG" width="175"
height="168"></td>
    <td width="78%">
    <h1 align="center"><font color="#0000FF">Welcome to Books For
Geeks!</font></h1>
    </td>
  </tr>
  <tr>
    <td width="22%">
    <table border="0" cellpadding="0" cellspacing="0" width="100%">
      <tr>
        <td width="50%" height="35"><font size="1">
```

LISTING 9.3   Continued

```
         <font color="#008000">In your
         cart:<br>
         5 Items totaling $23.43</font>
         <a href="http://www.boston.com/sports/redsox">[check out]</a></font></td>
       </tr>
     </table>
     <p>Departments</p>
     <blockquote>
       <h5><a href="index.htm">Java</a><br>
       <a href="index.htm">C++</a><br>
       <a href="index.htm">Databases</a><br>
       <a href="index.htm">Programming</a><br>
       <a href="index.htm">Windows</a><br>
       <a href="index.htm">Unix</a></h5>
     </blockquote>
     <p><a href="index.htm">View Basket</a><br>
     <a href="index.htm">Check Out</a><br>
     <a href="index.htm">My Account</a></p>
     <p> </p>
     <p> </p>
     <p> </td>
     <td width="78%" valign="top">
       <% if (content.equals("index")) { %>
           <%@ include file="bfgindexcontent.jsp" %>
         <% } %>
</td>
  </tr>
</table>

</body>
```

The major difference in this second document approach is in the way the site URLs will look. While the first approach would lead to "normal" URLs such as http://www.bfg.com/index.jsp, this method includes the content type as an argument to the URL, as in http://www.bfg.com/bfgmaster.jsp?content=index.

There's no convincing argument as to which is the better approach. The major benefit to the first approach is that you can add new pages to the site easily because you don't need to modify Java code inside a JSP to make it work. This is an important feature because it means that nontechnical people (such as the aforementioned designers) can create new content without having to come to the technical folks for help.

In some ways, the second approach is a more modern technique, representing the direction that the technology seems to be going in the industry, represented by frameworks such as Struts. It can be cumbersome to work with and difficult to justify except on dogmatic grounds in simple Web site designs; however, it has benefits in more complex applications (see Chapter 16, "The Struts Application Framework," for more details). In this example, you'll stick with the first approach, using separate pages for each functionality.

The Document Structure in Practice

To make this work, you'll create several subdirectories under the JSP parent directory. The overall structure will follow this form:

```
JSP ->
    index.jsp
    cust ->
      Login.jsp
    images ->
      bfglogo.jpg
      products ->
         34545656large.jpg
         34545656small.jpg
    includes ->
       bfgheader.jsp
       bfgfooter.jsp
```

To organize the file layout better, you'll create a number of directories to hold specific groups of pages (pages related to account maintenance under cust, product display pages under product, and so on). All the images will live under their own directory, with product images in a subdirectory by themselves. Finally, you will use a directory called include to hold the header and footer information.

When the organization has begun to take shape, you can move the pieces of the wireframe that you copied into the header, move the content and footer into the various appropriate subdirectories, and move the images where needed. When you do an ant dist and load up the Web page from Tomcat, you will see that it actually gets the same content that you've been looking at all along. Amazing!

One tweak that you will have to make is in the include directives. Here are what the modified include directives look like in the finished site:

```
<%@ include file="/jsp/includes/bfgheader.jsp" %>
<%@ include file="/jsp/includes/bfgfooter.jsp" %>
```

This might seem more than a little counterintuitive, especially because the image tag looks like this:

```
<img border="0" src="/bfg/jsp/images/products/0672320959.jpg" align="left"
width="140" height="173">
```

Why does the image tag's absolute path start at /bfg while the include tag starts at /jsp? It's because the image request is a normal HTTP transfer and is relative to the root of the Web server, whereas the include is relative to the application's root. This means that Tomcat is looking in the bfg directory already. By the way, this took a bit of research—and many JSP errors—to find out.

You should add one more thing to the header—a secondary include to the auto-login code that you wrote in Chapter 8, "Retrieving, Storing, and Verifying User Input." This will ensure that, no matter what page a user starts a session with, the site will try to extract the cookie and log in that user.

Listings 9.4 and 9.5 show the finished header and footer.

LISTING 9.4   bfgheader.jsp

```
<%@ page import="com.bfg.product.Category" %>
<%@ page import="java.util.Set" %>
<%@ page import="java.util.Iterator" %>
<body>

<table border="0" cellpadding="0" cellspacing="0" width="100%">
  <tr>
    <td width="22%">
    <img border="0" src="/bfg/jsp/images/bfglogo.jpg" width="175"
height="168"></td>
    <td width="78%">
    <h1 align="center"><font color="#0000FF">Welcome to Books For
Geeks!</font></h1>
    </td>
  </tr>
  <tr>
    <td width="22%">
    <table border="0" cellpadding="0" cellspacing="0" width="100%">
      <tr>
        <td width="50%" height="35"><font size="1">
        <font color="#008000">In your
        cart:<br>
        5 Items totaling $23.43</font>
```

LISTING 9.4   Continued

```
        <a href="http://www.boston.com/sports/redsox">[check out]</a></font></td>
      </tr>
    </table>
    <p>Departments</p>
    <blockquote>
      <h5><a href="index.htm">Java</a><br>
      <a href="index.htm">C++</a><br>
      <a href="index.htm">Databases</a><br>
      <a href="index.htm">Programming</a><br>
      <a href="index.htm">Windows</a><br>
      <a href="index.htm">Unix</a></h5>
    </blockquote>
    <p><a href="index.htm">View Basket</a><br>
    <a href="index.htm">Check Out</a><br>
    <a href="index.htm">My Account</a></p>
    <p> </p>
    <p> </p>
    <p> </td>
    <td width="78%" valign="top">
```

LISTING 9.5   bfgfooter.jsp

```
</td>
  </tr>
</table>

</body>
```

The Product and Category Classes

Before you can actually display the product and category pages, you need to create the underlying beans that the JSP pages depend on, much as you did with the Customer class in Chapter 8. These beans are a bit different, however, because they don't handle form input. Instead, they get their content by reading from the database (similar to the findCustomer method).

You can start with the product bean because the category bean will need to use it. You can find it in Listing 9.6.

LISTING 9.6   Product.java

```java
package com.bfg.product;

import java.util.Vector;
import java.util.HashMap;
import java.util.Iterator;
import java.text.SimpleDateFormat;
import java.text.NumberFormat;
import org.apache.turbine.services.db.TurbineDB;
import org.apache.turbine.util.db.pool.DBConnection;
import org.apache.turbine.util.TurbineConfig;
import com.bfg.exceptions.ProductActivityException;
import java.sql.*;
import java.util.ResourceBundle;
import org.apache.turbine.util.Log;

public class Product {
    private static ResourceBundle sql_bundle =
      ResourceBundle.getBundle("com.bfg.product.SQLQueries");


    protected String pISBN;
    protected String pTitle;
    protected Vector pAuthors = new Vector();
    protected float pPrice;
    protected java.sql.Date pPubDate;
    protected String pDescription;
    protected static HashMap products = new HashMap();

    public String getISBN() {
      return pISBN;
    }

    public String getTitle() {
      return pTitle;
    }

    public Vector getAuthors () {
        return pAuthors;
      }

    public String getAuthorString() {
```

LISTING 9.6   Continued

```
    Vector authors = getAuthors();
    if (authors.size() == 1) {
        return ((Author)authors.elementAt(0)).getName();
    }
    StringBuffer s = new StringBuffer();
    Iterator i = authors.iterator();

    while (i.hasNext()) {
        Author author = (Author) i.next();
        if (author == authors.firstElement()) {
            s.append(author.getName());
        } else {
            s.append("; " + author.getName());
        }
    }
    return(s.toString());
}

public float getPrice() {
  return pPrice;
}

public String getPriceString() {
  NumberFormat nf = NumberFormat.getCurrencyInstance();
  return nf.format(pPrice);
}

public java.sql.Date getPubDate() {
  return pPubDate;
}

public String getPubDateString() {
  SimpleDateFormat df = new SimpleDateFormat("MMM dd, yyyy");
  return(df.format(getPubDate()));
}

public String getDescription() {
  return pDescription;
}
public void setISBN(String ISBN) {
  pISBN = ISBN;
```

LISTING 9.6   Continued

```java
    }

    public void setTitle(String Title) {
      pTitle = Title;
    }

    public void setAuthors (Vector Authors) {
        pAuthors = Authors ;
     }

    public void setPrice(float Price) {
      pPrice = Price;
    }

    public void setPubDate(java.sql.Date PubDate) {
      pPubDate = PubDate;
    }

    public void setDescription(String Description) {
      pDescription = Description;
    }

    public static Product findProduct(String ISBN)
      throws ProductActivityException {
        if (products.get(ISBN) != null) {
            return (Product) products.get(ISBN);
        }
        DBConnection dbConn = null;
        Product prod = null;
        try
            {
                dbConn = TurbineDB.getConnection();
                if (dbConn == null) {
                    Log.error("jdbc", "Can't get database connection");
                    throw new ProductActivityException();
                }
                PreparedStatement pstmt =
                    dbConn.prepareStatement(sql_bundle.getString("findQuery"));
                pstmt.setString(1, ISBN);
                ResultSet rs = pstmt.executeQuery();
                if (rs.next()) {
```

LISTING 9.6   Continued

```
                    prod = new Product();
                    prod.setISBN(rs.getString("ISBN"));
                    prod.setTitle(rs.getString("TITLE"));
                    prod.setPrice(rs.getFloat("PRICE"));
                    prod.setPubDate(rs.getDate("PUB_DATE"));
                    prod.setDescription(rs.getString("DESCRIPTION"));
                }
                rs.close();
                pstmt.close();
                products.put(ISBN, prod);
                if (prod != null) {
                    pstmt =
                        dbConn.prepareStatement(sql_bundle.getString("author-
Query"));

                    pstmt.setString(1, ISBN);
                    rs = pstmt.executeQuery();
                    while (rs.next()) {
                        Author author =
                            Author.findAuthor(rs.getString("AUTHOR_NAME"));
                        prod.getAuthors().add(author);
                        author.getBooks().add(prod);
                    }
                    rs.close();
                    pstmt.close();
                }
            }
        catch (Exception e)
            {
            Log.error("jdbc", "Error during findProduct", e);
            e.printStackTrace();
            throw new ProductActivityException();
            }
        finally
            {
            try
                {
                    TurbineDB.releaseConnection(dbConn);
                }
            catch (Exception e)
                {
                    Log.error("jdbc", "Error during releaseConnection", e);
```

LISTING 9.6   Continued

```
                    }
            }
        return prod;
    }

    public static void main(String[] args) {
        TurbineConfig tc = new TurbineConfig("com/bfg/props/",
                                        "TurbineResources.properties");
        tc.init();

        try {
            Product p =
                findProduct("672320959");
            if (p != null) {
                System.out.println("Good Test: Find Real Product");
                System.out.println("Author string is: " +
                                    p.getAuthorString());
                System.out.println("Price is " + p.getPrice());
            } else {
                System.out.println("Failed Test: Find Real Product");
            }
        } catch (Exception e) {
            System.out.println("Failed Test: Find Real Product");
            e.printStackTrace();
        }
        try {
            Product p =
                findProduct("notanisbn");
            if (p != null) {
                System.out.println("Bad Test: Find Fake Product");
            } else {
                System.out.println("Good Test: Find Fake Product");
            }
        } catch (Exception e) {
            System.out.println("Failed Test: Find Fake Product");
            e.printStackTrace();
        }
    }}
```

The top of this file looks a lot like Customer.java—it contains all the accessors for the various bean properties that you need to get at. One difference is the HashMap called products. Unlike the Customer object, you don't want to read the product data from the database every time you need to look at it. The data rarely changes, and this is very costly in terms of performance. Instead, cache the data as you read it and use the cached value from that point forward.

One pitfall of taking this approach is that if you do change the product data and want to refresh things, you need to have a mechanism in place to accomplish this. With a vendor such as a book seller, whose inventory doesn't change every day, it's probably acceptable to just restart the server in the wee hours of the morning and let it reread everything. In a more dynamic retail environment, such as Wal-Mart, you would need to have some way of signaling the server to periodically update the caches. You would also need to build this kind of dynamic refreshing capability into the site if high availability was an issue.

The Author Object

The Product object makes use of the Author object because a product has a reference to the authors of the book. So, you need to implement the Author object now as well. The Author object, by the way, is extremely simple, as Listing 9.7 shows.

LISTING 9.7   Author.Java

```
package com.bfg.product;

import java.util.Vector;
import java.util.HashMap;

public class Author {
    protected static HashMap authors = new HashMap();

    protected Vector pBooks = new Vector();
    protected String pName;

    public Vector getBooks() {
      return pBooks;
    }

    public void setBooks(Vector Books) {
      pBooks = Books;
    }
```

LISTING 9.7   Continued

```
public String getName() {
  return pName;
}

public void setName(String Name) {
  pName = Name;
}

    public static Author findAuthor(String name) {
  if (authors.get(name) != null) {
      return ((Author) authors.get(name));
  }
  Author author = new Author();
  author.setName(name);
  authors.put(name, author);
  return author;
}
}
```

All that the class has is a property to store the author's name and another property that stores a list of the books that the author has written. This will come in useful if you add functionality that lets you click on an author's name and retrieve a list of books that the author has written. As with the products, you will have the class cache the authors.

The `getAuthorString` method is a JSP helper function. The authors of a book need to be displayed in a lot of places. Because they are stored as a vector of objects, it's easier to set up one place where the JSP can go to get a print-friendly version of the author list, rather than having to replicate the code in the JSP every time it is needed.

Similarly, `getPriceString` returns a formatted string with a dollar sign ($) and two decimal places on the right; otherwise, $49.90 would show up as 49.9 on the page. `getPubDateString` returns the publication date in the form that you want—just asking for the `Date` object gets you somewhere along the lines of `2001-10-02`.

`findProduct` works a lot like `findCustomer`, except that, because it is caching, it will need to check whether the book is in the cache first. If it is not, it must be read out of the database. The SQL queries from the SQLQueries.properties file are shown in Listing 9.8.

LISTING 9.8   SQLQueries.properties

```
findQuery=SELECT * FROM PRODUCT WHERE ISBN = ?
authorQuery=SELECT AUTHOR_NAME FROM AUTHOR,PRODUCT,PRODUCT_AUTHOR_XREF PAX \
                WHERE AUTHOR.AUTHOR_ID = PAX.AUTHOR_ID AND \
                PAX.PRODUCT_ISBN = PRODUCT.ISBN AND \
                PRODUCT.ISBN = ?
```

If the method finds a matching product, it looks for authors for that product. It goes through adding authors to the product and adding products to the authors. Finally, it releases the database connection and returns the product.

Now you can add a unit test for `Product` to the Ant script with the following additions to the test target (see Listing 9.9).

LISTING 9.9   Additions to build.xml

```
<java classname="com.bfg.product.Product" fork="yes">
  <classpath>
  <pathelement path="${java.class.path}"/>
    <fileset dir="c:\tomcat\lib">
      <include name="**/*.jar"/>
    </fileset>
    <pathelement path="src"/>
    <pathelement path="props"/>
  </classpath>
</java>
```

When you run the script, you can see that the unit test worked:

```
C:\CARTAPP\bfg>ant test
Buildfile: build.xml

init:

compile:
    [javac] Compiling 1 source file

dist:
      [jar] Building jar: C:\tomcat\webapps\bfg\WEB-INF\lib\bfgclasses.jar

test:
    [java] Turbine: init
    [java] Turbine: Turbine: init() Ready to Rumble!
```

LISTING 9.9   Continued

```
[java] Good Test: Create Customer
[java] Good Test: Create Duplicate Customer
[java] Good Test: Find Real Customer
[java] Good Test: Find Fake Customer
[java] Good Test: Delete Customer
[java] Turbine: init
[java] Turbine: Turbine: init() Ready to Rumble!
[java] Good Test: Find Real Product
[java] Author string is: Stefan Haustein; Michael Kroll

BUILD SUCCESSFUL

Total time: 3 seconds
```

Now you can write the JSP to display a product (see Listing 9.10) that is again based on the wireframe.

LISTING 9.10   Product.jsp

```
<%@ page import="com.bfg.product.Product" %>
<% Product prod = null;
if (((request.getParameter("ISBN") != null) &&
     (prod = Product.findProduct(request.getParameter("ISBN"))) != null)) {
%>
<head>
<title><%= prod.getTitle() %></title>
</head>

<%@ include file="/jsp/includes/bfgheader.jsp" %>

<h2 align="center"><span style="font-family: Times New Roman">
<%= prod.getTitle() %>
</span></h2>
<table border="0" cellpadding="0" cellspacing="0" style="border-collapse: collapse"
bordercolor="#111111" width="639" id="AutoNumber3">
 <tr>
   <td width="128">
    <img border="0" src="/bfg/jsp/images/products/<%= prod.getISBN() %>.jpg"
         align="left" width="125" height="155">
   </td>
   <td valign="top" width="511">
```

LISTING 9.10   Continued

```
    <p align="center">
    <span style="font-size: 10.0pt; font-family: Times New Roman">
       By <%= prod.getAuthorString() %>
    </span></p>
        <p align="center"><font size="2" face="Times New Roman">Publication
        date: </font>
        <span style="font-size: 10.0pt; font-family: Times New Roman">
         <%= prod.getPubDateString() %>, <%= prod.getPriceString() %></span></td>
   </tr>
</table>
<p><span style="font-size: 10.0pt"><%= prod.getDescription() %></span></p>
    <p><font size="2"><a href="buyit.jsp?ISBN=<%= prod.getISBN() %>">[Buy It!]
</a></font></p>
<p align="center"> </td>

<%@ include file="/jsp/includes/bfgfooter.jsp" %>
<% } else {%>

<head>
<title>ISBN Not Found</title>
</head>

<%@ include file="/jsp/includes/bfgheader.jsp" %>

<H1>The requested ISBN was not found.</H1>
If you believe you have reached this page in error, please contact
<A HREF="mailto: info@bfgbooks.com">info@bfgbooks.com</A>
<% } %>
```

The ISBN is passed in as a parameter, and the first thing that the JSP does—even before displaying the title—is to look up the ISBN. If it can't find the ISBN, you have it skip to the end and put up a helpful error message (see Figure 9.2).

On the other hand, if the customer requested a good ISBN, your beautiful product display page appears (see Figure 9.3).

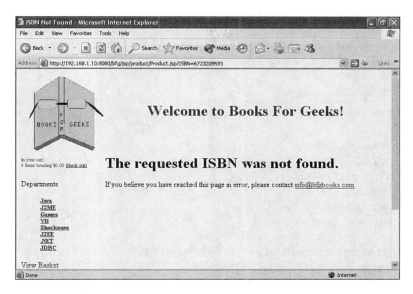

FIGURE 9.2   A bad ISBN.

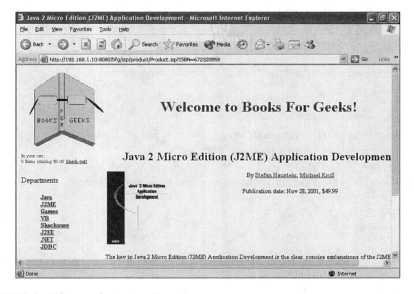

FIGURE 9.3   The product page in action.

As you can see, the code extracts various attributes of the book and puts them in place of the boilerplate text that the wireframe had used.

The Category Class

Now that you have products to put in it, you can create your Category object (see Listing 9.11). Again, most of it will look very familiar.

LISTING 9.11   The Category Class

```
package com.bfg.product;

import java.util.Vector;
import java.util.Set;
import java.util.HashMap;
import java.util.Iterator;
import java.text.NumberFormat;
import java.text.SimpleDateFormat;
import org.apache.turbine.services.db.TurbineDB;
import org.apache.turbine.util.db.pool.DBConnection;
import org.apache.turbine.util.TurbineConfig;
import com.bfg.exceptions.ProductActivityException;
import java.sql.*;
import java.util.ResourceBundle;
import org.apache.turbine.util.Log;

public class Category {
    private static ResourceBundle sql_bundle =
      ResourceBundle.getBundle("com.bfg.product.SQLQueries");


    protected int pID;
    protected Product pFeaturedProduct;
    protected Vector pProducts = new Vector();
    protected String pName;
    protected static HashMap categories = new HashMap();

    public int getID() {
      return pID;
    }

    public void setID(int ID) {
      pID = ID;
    }

    public String getName() {
```

LISTING 9.11   Continued

```
    return pName;
  }

  public void setName(String Name) {
   pName = Name;
  }

  public Product getFeaturedProduct() {
   return pFeaturedProduct;
  }

  public void setFeaturedProduct(Product Product) {
   pFeaturedProduct = Product;
  }

  public Vector getProducts() {
   return pProducts;
  }

  public void setProducts(Vector Products) {
   pProducts = Products;
  }

  public static Set getCategories() {
   return categories.keySet();
  }

  public static Category findCategory(String Name)
    throws ProductActivityException {
        if (categories.get(Name) != null) {
            return (Category) categories.get(Name);
        }
        DBConnection dbConn = null;
        Category cat = null;
        try
            {
                dbConn = TurbineDB.getConnection();
                if (dbConn == null) {
                    Log.error("jdbc", "Can't get database connection");
                    throw new ProductActivityException();
                }
```

LISTING 9.11   Continued

```
                    PreparedStatement pstmt =
                        dbConn.prepareStatement(sql_bundle.
➥getString("findCatQuery"));
                pstmt.setString(1, Name);
                ResultSet rs = pstmt.executeQuery();
                if (rs.next()) {
                    cat = new Category();
                    cat.setName(rs.getString("CATEGORY_NAME"));
                    cat.setID(rs.getInt("CATEGORY_ID"));
                    String feat = rs.getString("FEATURED_PRODUCT");
                    if (!rs.wasNull()) {
                        cat.setFeaturedProduct(Product.findProduct(feat));
                    }
                }
                rs.close();
                pstmt.close();
                if (cat != null) {
                    pstmt =

dbConn.prepareStatement(sql_bundle.[ic:ccc]getString("catProdQuery"));
                    pstmt.setInt(1, cat.getID());
                    rs = pstmt.executeQuery();
                    while (rs.next()) {
                        cat.getProducts().add(
➥Product.findProduct(rs.getString("PRODUCT_ISBN")));
                    }
                    rs.close();
                    pstmt.close();
                    categories.put(Name, cat);
                }


            }
        catch (Exception e)
            {
                Log.error("jdbc", "Error during findCategory", e);
                e.printStackTrace();
                throw new ProductActivityException();
            }
        finally
            {
                try
```

LISTING 9.11   Continued

```
                            {
                                TurbineDB.releaseConnection(dbConn);
                            }
                        catch (Exception e)
                            {
                                Log.error("jdbc", "Error during releaseConnection", e);
                            }
                    }
            return cat;
        }

static boolean allLoaded = false;

    public static void loadAllCategories()
      throws ProductActivityException {
      if (allLoaded) return;
      allLoaded = true;
      DBConnection dbConn = null;
      Category cat = null;
      try
          {
              dbConn = TurbineDB.getConnection();
              if (dbConn == null) {
                  lcat.error("Can't get database connection");
                  throw new ProductActivityException();
              }
              PreparedStatement pstmt =

dbConn.prepareStatement(sql_bundle.getString("findAllCats"));
              ResultSet rs = pstmt.executeQuery();
              while (rs.next()) {
                  findCategory(rs.getString("CATEGORY_NAME"));
              }
              rs.close();
              pstmt.close();
          }
        catch (Exception e)
            {
                lcat.error("Error during loadAllCategories", e);
                e.printStackTrace();
                throw new ProductActivityException();
```

LISTING 9.11   Continued

```
                }
            finally
                {
                    try
                        {
                            TurbineDB.releaseConnection(dbConn);
                        }
                    catch (Exception e)
                        {
                            lcat.error("Error during releaseConnection",
e);
                        }
                }
        }

    public static void main(String[] args) {
        TurbineConfig tc =
            new TurbineConfig("com/bfg/props/",
                            "TurbineResources.properties");
        tc.init();

        try {
            Category.loadAllCategories();
            Category c =
                findCategory("JDBC");
            if (c != null) {
                System.out.println("Good Test: Find Real Category");
            } else {
                System.out.println("Failed Test: Find Real Category");
            }
        } catch (Exception e) {
            System.out.println("Failed Test: Find Real Category");
            e.printStackTrace();
        }
        try {
            Category c =
                findCategory("notancat");
            if (c != null) {
                System.out.println("Bad Test: Find Fake Category");
            } else {
                System.out.println("Good Test: Find Fake Category");
```

LISTING 9.11 Continued

```
            }
        } catch (Exception e) {
            System.out.println("Failed Test: Find Fake Category");
            e.printStackTrace();
        }
    }
}
```

Among the highlights of Listing 9.11: When a category is loaded from the database, a subquery is run to find all the products and then load them because the category needs to have a pointer to all its products. You also must load the featured product.

As you can see, when you have objects that depend on other objects, you need to make sure that they're loaded in the right order. For example, if a category loads the featured product and the product has a pointer to the category (which isn't the case here), you would need to be sure to avoid an infinite recursion. To do this, you would need to make sure that the product and the category registered themselves in the appropriate cache before they tried to find the contained objects.

In the application as written, there are no such dependencies because everything is referenced from the top down, following this path:

```
Category -> Product -> Author
```

Because categories are at the top of the hierarchy, you need to have some way to get a list of them—for example, to present a sidebar menu. The loadAllCategories method loads all the categories in the database. After that, you can use getCategories to get the set and then iterate over it to get a list of categories. Listing 9.12 shows the modification to the bfgheader.jsp code to use this.

LISTING 9.12 Additions to bfgheader.jsp

```
<%@ page import="com.bfg.product.Category" %>
<%@ page import="java.util.Set" %>
<%@ page import="java.util.Iterator" %>
    .
    .
    .
    <p>Departments</p>
    <blockquote>
      <h5>
    <%
```

LISTING 9.12   Continued

```
Category.loadAllCategories();
Iterator it = Category.getCategories().iterator();
while (it.hasNext()) {
    String catName = (String) it.next();
%>
    <a href="/bfg/jsp/product/Category.jsp?category<%= catName %>"><%= catName
%></a><br>
        <%
        }
%>
    </h5>
    </blockquote>
```

The code gets the iterator of category names and creates HREFs for each one, calling Category.jsp with the category name as the argument.

So, now you should write Category.jsp. You can find it in Listing 9.13.

LISTING 9.13   Category.jsp

```
<%@ page import="com.bfg.product.Product" %>
<%@ page import="com.bfg.product.Category" %>
<%@ page import="java.util.Iterator" %>
<% Category cat = null;
if (((request.getParameter("category") != null) &&
     (cat = Category.findCategory(request.getParameter("category"))) != null)) {
%>
<head>
<title>Books About <%= cat.getName() %></title>
</head>

<%@ include file="/jsp/includes/bfgheader.jsp" %>


    <h2 align="center">Books About <%= cat.getName() %></h2>
        <%
if (cat.getFeaturedProduct() != null) {
    Product feat = cat.getFeaturedProduct();
%>
<table border="0" cellpadding="0" cellspacing="0" bordercolor="#111111"
width="639">
```

LISTING 9.13   Continued

```
     <tr>
       <td width="128">
       <img border="0" src="/bfg/jsp/images/products/<%= feat.getISBN() %>.jpg"
           align="left" width="113" height="140"></td>
       <td valign="top" width="511">
       <h3 align="center">
       <span style="font-size: 10.0pt; font-family: Times New Roman">
     <%= feat.getTitle() %>
     </span></h3>
       <p align="center">
       <span style="font-size: 10.0pt; font-family: Times New Roman">
     By <%= feat.getAuthorString() %>
     </span></p>
       <p align="center"><font size="2" face="Times New Roman">Publication
       date: </font>
       <span style="font-size: 10.0pt; font-family: Times New Roman">
     <%= feat.getPubDateString() %>, <%= feat.getPriceString() %>
     </span></td>
      </tr>
    </table>
    <p><span style="font-size: 10.0pt">
    <%= feat.getDescription() %>
    </span></p>
    <p><font size="2">
    <a href="index.htm">[Buy It!]</a></font></p>
    <p align="center"> </td>
  </tr>
</table>
    <% } %>
<table border="0" cellpadding="0" cellspacing="0"
       style="border-collapse: collapse" bordercolor="#111111"
       width="100%" id="AutoNumber4" height="253">
  <tr>
    <th width="38%" height="23" align="left">Title</th>
    <th width="23%" height="23" align="left">Author</th>
    <th width="11%" height="23" align="left">Price</th>
    <td width="28%" height="23" align="left"> </td>
  </tr>
    <%
    Iterator iter = cat.getProducts().iterator();
    while (iter.hasNext()) {
```

LISTING 9.13   Continued

```
      Product prod = (Product) iter.next();
%>
  <tr>
    <td width="38%" height="38" bgcolor="#00FFFF">
    <span style="font-size: 10.0pt; font-family: Times New Roman">
      <%= prod.getTitle() %>
    </span></td>
    <td width="23%" height="38" bgcolor="#00FFFF">
    <span style="font-size: 10.0pt; font-family: Times New Roman">
      <%= prod.getAuthorString() %>
    </span></td>
    <td width="11%" height="38" bgcolor="#00FFFF">
    <span style="font-size: 10.0pt; font-family: Times New Roman">
    <%= prod.getPriceString() %>
    </span></td>
    <td width="28%" height="38" bgcolor="#00FFFF">
    <p align="center"><font size="2">
      <a href="Product.jsp?ISBN=<%= prod.getISBN()%>">
      [More Information] </A>
    [Buy It!]</font></td>
  </tr>
      <% }
} else {
%>
<head>
<title>Category Not Found</title>
</head>

<%@ include file="/jsp/includes/bfgheader.jsp" %>

<H1>The requested Category was not found.</H1>
If you believe you have reached this page in error, please contact
<A HREF="mailto: info@bfgbooks.com">info@bfgbooks.com</A>
<% } %>
<%@ include file="/jsp/includes/bfgfooter.jsp" %>
```

Here you can really start mining the database for information. First, the code checks to see if it has been handed in a valid category name; otherwise, it splashes up the error page.

Assuming that it has a valid category name, the code generates a title based on the category name and checks whether there is a featured product for the category. If there is, the code creates a detailed product information listing with a link to the product information page.

After starting the table that will contain the list of books in the category, you can use an iterator over the vector of products and generate a line for each book. The More Information link is actually live; clicking on it takes the customer to the product detail page for that book. All this isn't bad for a day's work, as Figure 9.4 shows. But don't rest on your laurels just yet; you might as well go that last mile, so to speak, and implement the "list all books by an author" function.

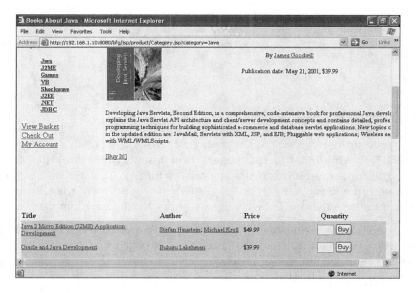

FIGURE 9.4   The finished category page.

Listing all the books by a particular author is actually simpler than it sounds. To start, change the getAuthorString method of Product (see Listing 9.14).

LISTING 9.14   Enhanced getAuthorString()

```
private String getAuthorHREF(Author author) {
  return "<A HREF=\"/bfg/jsp/product/ByAuthor.jsp?author=" +
     author.getName() + "\">" + author.getName() + "</A>";
}



public String getAuthorString() {
```

LISTING 9.14   Continued

```
    Vector authors = getAuthors();
    if (authors.size() == 1) {
        return (getAuthorHREF((Author)authors.elementAt(0)));
    }
    StringBuffer s = new StringBuffer();
    Iterator i = authors.iterator();

    while (i.hasNext()) {
        Author author = (Author) i.next();
        if (author == authors.firstElement()) {
            s.append(getAuthorHREF(author));
        } else {
            s.append("; " + getAuthorHREF(author));
        }
    }
    return(s.toString());
}
```

Basically, the string returned has simply been changed from a plain piece of text to a piece of HTML with links to a new page. Without modifying any of the JSP already written, you suddenly get this new functionality for free. To make things more general, you should probably place the absolute path portion of the URL in a resource bundle so that it can be changed without having to recompile the code.

Luckily, unlike some products such as Dynamo, you don't have to do anything special when you want to pass HTML back to a JSP page using <%=. JSP just sends whatever is returned out to the browser.

Now you can do a ByAuthor.jsp, which is nearly identical to Category.jsp (see Listing 9.15).

LISTING 9.15   ByAuthor.jsp

```
<%@ page import="com.bfg.product.Product" %>
<%@ page import="com.bfg.product.Author" %>
<%@ page import="java.util.Iterator" %>
<% Author author = null;
if (((request.getParameter("author") != null) &&
    (author = Author.findAuthor(request.getParameter("author"))) != null)) {
%>
<head>
<title>Books By <%= author.getName() %></title>
```

LISTING 9.15   Continued

```
</head>

<%@ include file="/jsp/includes/bfgheader.jsp" %>


    <h2 align="center">Books By <%= author.getName() %></h2>
<table border="0" cellpadding="5" cellspacing="0" style="border-collapse: collapse"
bordercolor="#111111" width="100%" id="AutoNumber4" height="253">
  <tr>
    <th width="38%" height="23" align="left">Title</th>
    <th width="23%" height="23" align="left">Author</th>
    <th width="11%" height="23" align="left">Price</th>
    <td width="28%" height="23" align="left"> </td>
  </tr>
    <%
    Iterator iter = author.getBooks().iterator();
    while (iter.hasNext()) {
      Product prod = (Product) iter.next();
%>
  <tr>
    <td width="38%" bgcolor="#00FFFF">
    <span style="font-size: 10.0pt; font-family: Times New Roman">
      <A HREF="Product.jsp?ISBN=<%= prod.getISBN() %>">
       <%= prod.getTitle() %></A>
    </span></td>
    <td width="23%" bgcolor="#00FFFF">
    <span style="font-size: 10.0pt; font-family: Times New Roman">
      <%= prod.getAuthorString() %>
    </span></td>
    <td width="11%" bgcolor="#00FFFF">
    <span style="font-size: 10.0pt; font-family: Times New Roman">
    <%= prod.getPriceString() %>
    </span></td>
    <td width="28%" bgcolor="#00FFFF">
    <p align="center"><font size="2"><a href="Product.jsp?ISBN=<%=
prod.getISBN()%>">
      [More Information] </A>
    [Buy It!]</font></td>
  </tr>
        <% }
} else {
```

LISTING 9.15   Continued

```
%>
<head>
<title>Author Not Found</title>
</head>

<%@ include file="/jsp/includes/bfgheader.jsp" %>

<H1>The requested Author was not found.</H1>
If you believe you have reached this page in error, please contact
<A HREF="mailto: info@bfgbooks.com">info@bfgbooks.com</A>
<% } %>
<%@ include file="/jsp/includes/bfgfooter.jsp" %>
```

Other than removing the featured product—which isn't applicable for authors—and doing the lookup for the iterator based on the author's books rather than the category's books, this is relatively much the same code as in Category.jsp. It produces the page shown in Figure 9.5.

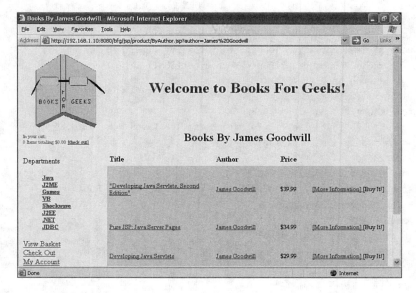

FIGURE 9.5   The ByAuthor page.

Cleaning Things Up

At this stage, the code is in good shape, for the most part, but you can still do a few things to make it better. For example, you have the same JSP in several different places. The code that produces the featured product is the same as the code for the product detail page. The code for the listing by author and by category are also the same. If you put them all into `includes`, it will reduce the size of the parent files and also reduce the number of places in the code that will need to be changed if you want to alter the files.

You should also think a little more carefully about what would happen if a `ProductActivityException` was thrown. You should be using a `try` to catch it and redirect to an error page.

And speaking of error pages, it is getting tiring putting the same error text at the bottom of each page with only slight variations. Perhaps it is time to rethink and standardize your error pages—something you can do in your spare time after reading the book.

One thing that you can be happy about is that, because of the way you designed the document hierarchy, people can bookmark or e-mail links to products, authors, and categories freely. This is a very important feature in an e-commerce site because it helps drive sales.

Summary

In this chapter, you've learned how to use JSP to automatically create content from the database. Each class that maps to a database row needs to have properties to represent all of the database data that will be used by the application.

Because objects may reference other objects that need to be loaded from the database, it's important to make sure that you don't implement an infinite loop by accident.

By driving content generation off the database, you can dynamically change the information presented on your site without having to change either classes or JSP.

The site is looking nice, but it's useless if you can't buy anything. In the next chapter, you will take a big step by actually implementing the Buy Me buttons that you've been putting all over the product pages.

You will also start to really use session objects. Right now you've only scratched the surface of what they can do, such as carrying over the contents of a shopping cart from page to page.

10

Session Persistence and Complex Form Handling

As you move on to implementing more complex functionality on the site, you'll begin to start depending more heavily on some features of Tomcat, specifically session-persistent objects.

You'll also be processing more complicated forms with less straightforward behaviors than the those you've dealt with to date. In this chapter, you'll see how the implementation of the shopping cart requires these features.

Implementing the Shopping Cart

With your products on display, you can start actually allowing people to buy them. To do this, you're going to need to implement a shopping cart. If you want, you can refer back to the design of the shopping cart in Chapter 4, "The Sample Application Functional Requirements Document."

A cart is essentially a container that you can put products into, with a few quirks. For example, putting a second copy of an item into a cart shouldn't make two entries; it should make a single item with a quantity of 2.

The cart has session persistence, like the customer. Unlike the customer object however, it doesn't get its contents from a database lookup. Eventually, when you get to filling and spilling content in Chapter 11, "Intersession Persistence," it will do this, but it doesn't for now. Instead, the cart has its contents modified by the actions of the customer during a shopping session.

The actual implementation of the cart is pretty simple, so the best approach is just to dive right into the code in Listings 10.1 and 10.2.

LISTING 10.1   Cart.java

```java
package com.bfg.cart;

import java.util.Vector;
import java.util.HashMap;
import java.util.Iterator;
import java.text.NumberFormat;
import org.apache.turbine.util.Log;
import com.bfg.product.Product;

public class Cart {
    protected HashMap contents = new HashMap();

    public Iterator getItems() {
      return contents.values().iterator();
    }

    public CartItem getItem(Product item) {
      return (CartItem)contents.get(item);
    }

    public void addItem(Product item, int quantity) {
      if (contents.get(item) != null) {
          ((CartItem)contents.get(item)).addQuantity(quantity);
      } else {
          CartItem citem = new CartItem();
          citem.setQuantity(quantity);
          citem.setProduct(item);
          contents.put(item, citem);
      }
    }

    public void removeItem(Product item) {
      contents.remove(item);
    }

    public int countItems() {
      return contents.size();
```

LISTING 10.1 Continued

```
    }

    public double getTotal() {
      double total = 0;
      Iterator it = contents.values().iterator();
      while (it.hasNext()) {
          total += ((CartItem)it.next()).getLineItemPrice();
      }
      return total;
    }

    public String getTotalString() {
      NumberFormat nf = NumberFormat.getCurrencyInstance();
      return nf.format(getTotal());
    }
}
```

LISTING 10.2 CartItem.java

```
package com.bfg.cart;

import java.text.NumberFormat;
import org.apache.turbine.util.Log;
import com.bfg.product.Product;

public class CartItem {
    private Product pProduct;
    private int pQuantity;
    private boolean isPromotionItem;

    public Product getProduct() {
      return pProduct;
    }

    public void setProduct(Product product) {
      pProduct = product;
    }

    public int getQuantity() {
      return pQuantity;
```

LISTING 10.2   Continued

```
    }

    public void setQuantity(int quantity) {
      pQuantity = quantity;
    }

    public void addQuantity(int quantity) {
      pQuantity += quantity;
    }

    public double getLineItemPrice() {
      return getQuantity() * getProduct().getPrice();
    }

    public String getLineItemPriceString() {
      NumberFormat nf = NumberFormat.getCurrencyInstance();
      return nf.format(getLineItemPrice());
    }
}
```

The cart is just a wrapper around a `HashMap` that holds the product and quantity of each item bought. If you add a couple of helper methods (such as `getTotal` in Listing 10.1), you can service the mini-cart efficiently (printed cost, number of items, and so on). Helper methods are ones that don't directly contribute to the functioning of the object but that provide a more convenient way to do something that's already implemented. `addItem` makes sure that it consolidates items if you add something already in the cart.

The `CartItem` is just a wrapper for the product and quantity; however, it has a flag to indicate that the item was placed in the cart by the successful execution of a promotion. This will become useful later when you implement promotions. Again, you also include a couple of helper functions.

With the cart written, you can implement the Buy button on your product pages (as shown in Listing 10.3).

LISTING 10.3   buyit.jsp

```
<%@ page import="com.bfg.product.Product" %>
<%@ page import="com.bfg.cart.Cart" %>

<jsp:useBean id="cart" class="com.bfg.cart.Cart" scope="session"/>

<%
```

LISTING 10.3   Continued

```
String ISBN = request.getParameter("ISBN");
Product prod = null;
if (ISBN != null) {
    prod = Product.findProduct(ISBN);
    if (prod != null) {
      cart.addItem(prod, 1);
    }
}
%>
You added <%= prod %> to your cart, new quantity <%= cart.countItems() %>
<SCRIPT>
if (window.opener && !window.opener.closed)
  window.opener.location.reload();
window.close();
</SCRIPT>
```

LISTING 10.4   Using the buyit Script

```
<a href="buyit.jsp?ISBN=<%= prod.getISBN() %>" TARGET="tempwindow">[Buy It!]
</a>
```

Basically, the link shown in Listing 10.4 opens a new temporary window that loads up the buyit.jsp page. buyit.jsp (shown in Listing 10.3) adds a product to the cart and then closes itself, usually before the customer even knows that it's open. Before it closes itself, however, the page tells the window that opened it to reload, which causes the mini-cart to refresh. Refinements to the Buy link would include opening a smaller window.

THE RESUBMIT PROBLEM

A problem that crops up consistently in this kind of page occurs when the user hits the Reload button. In a traditional design (and even the design you use for things such as new user creation), you submit back to the same page.

This means that if the user enters data and hits Submit, reloads the page, and answers Yes to the question "Do you want to resubmit the data?", the application executes the action twice. In the case of a shopping cart, this might mean putting twice as many items into the cart, for example.

By using a secondary window to do the actual cart adds and then closing it, you avoid this problem.

Speaking of the mini-cart, you can now implement it in bfgheader.jsp (see Listing 10.5).

LISTING 10.5   The Mini-cart in bfgheader.jsp

```
<tr>
   <td width="50%" height="35"><font size="1">
   <font color="#008000">In your
   cart:<br>
   <%= cart.countItems() %>
Item<%= (cart.countItems() == 1)?"":"s" %> totaling
<%= cart.getTotalString() %></font>
   <a href="http://www.boston.com/sports/redsox">[check out]</a></font></td>
</tr>
```

useBean is a great little construct that lets you associate an object with a degree of persistence. However, at least as implemented by Tomcat 4, it can cause you problems, too.

The main problem that you can run into occurs if you use it in an included file. For example, it would be nice to have a useBean in the bfgheader file to allow you to look at the cart bean and print the mini-cart values. Unfortunately, several files include bfgheader multiple times (to deal with success or failure). Tomcat can't process this because it tries to insert the useBean twice and gets a syntax error.

An alternative is to use curly-braces around a section of code that wants to reference a bean value and declare a local variable inside the brackets that uses getAttribute explicitly to get the bean value. Because the assignment is made inside the braces, it won't interfere with other code that needs to look at the same bean, even if the same variable name is used (see Listing 10.6 to see the revised bfgheader.jsp).

LISTING 10.6   bfgheader.jsp without useBean

```
<%@ page import="java.util.Iterator" %>
<%@ page import="com.bfg.cart.Cart" %>
<%@ page import="com.bfg.product.Category" %>
<%
{
Cart headercart = (Cart) pageContext.getAttribute("cart",
PageContext.SESSION_SCOPE);
%>

<body>
```

LISTING 10.6   Continued

```html
<table border="0" cellpadding="0" cellspacing="0" width="100%">
  <tr>
    <td width="22%">
    <img border="0" src="/bfg/jsp/images/bfglogo.jpg" width="175"
height="168"></td>
    <td width="78%">
    <h1 align="center"><font color="#0000FF">Welcome to Books For
Geeks!</font></h1>
    </td>
  </tr>
  <tr>
    <td width="22%">
    <table border="0" cellpadding="0" cellspacing="0" width="100%">
      <tr>
        <td width="50%" height="35"><font size="1">
        <font color="#008000">In your
        cart:<br>
    <%= headercart.countItems() %>
      Item<%= (headercart.countItems() == 1)?"":"s" %> totaling
      <%= headercart.getTotalString() %></font>
        <a href="http://www.boston.com/sports/redsox">[check
out]</a></font></td>
      </tr>
    </table>
    <p>Departments</p>
    <blockquote>
      <h5>
    <%
Category.loadAllCategories();
Iterator it = Category.getCategories().iterator();
while (it.hasNext()) {
    String catName = (String) it.next();
%>
    <a href="/bfg/jsp/product/Category.jsp?category=<%= catName %>"><%=
catName %></a><br>
      <%
      }
%>
    </h5>
    </blockquote>
```

LISTING 10.6   Continued

```
<p><a href="/bfg/jsp/shoppingcart.jsp">View Basket</a><br>
<a href="/bfg/jsp/checkout.jsp">Check Out</a><br>
<a href="/bfg/jsp/cust/MyAccount.jsp">My Account</a></p>
<p> </p>
<p> </p>
<p> </td>
<td width="78%" valign="top">
<% } %>
```

Use the ? operator to make sure that you choose the correct plural (0 items, 1 item, 2 items, and so on). The live version of the mini-cart is shown in Figure 10.1.

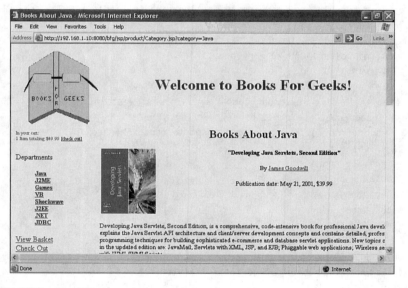

FIGURE 10.1   The Mini-cart in operation.

An interesting subject for debate rears its head at this point. When counting items, do two books of the same type count as one item or two items in the mini-cart? As implemented, they count as one, but you could do it the other way and be just as right. As always, what the customer wants is what the customer should get. In this case, the client wants the cart to count distinct product groups, not quantity.

WATCH OUT FOR `<%@ INCLUDE`!

If you don't watch yourself, you can get suckered by a quirk of Tomcat when you use included JSP files.

To understand why, remember how JSP works. The JSP files are converted into Java source and then are compiled. When the JSP changes, the Java is automatically recompiled to keep up.

Well, almost automatically. Included content isn't done dynamically at runtime; the Java source produced by Jasper (the JSP-to-Java translator) is done once and literally sticks the included JSP children right into the Java source that it produces. So, even though you might think of each file as its own little Java program, they're all really made into one big one.

When you change an included file (such as bfgheader.jsp), Jasper doesn't notice it, so it doesn't recompile the JSP files that include it. And because your Ant script copies only the JSP files that change, the parent JSP files won't be updated.

This can lead to interesting results. As you move from page to page, you might see one page with the changed content and the next page with the old content.

The only way to make sure that everything gets recompiled is to copy everything over every time you do an ant `dist`.

This behavior is not a part of the JSP specification, so you'll have to check for yourself to see if a non-Tomcat JSP platform has the same problem.

Buying More Than One Thing at Once

Buying a single item is relatively straightforward because you can handle it directly from the URL. But the client wants the customer to be able to purchase several items at the same time.

Listing 10.7 shows a section of Category.jsp rewritten to let the customer buy a quantity of multiple books. It replaces the current product display loop.

LISTING 10.7 Category.jsp Revisited

```
<FORM METHOD="POST" ACTION="buyit.jsp" TARGET="tempwindow">
<table border="0" cellpadding="0" cellspacing="0" style="border-collapse:
➥collapse" bordercolor="#111111" width="100%" id="AutoNumber4" height="253">  <tr>
    <th width="38%" height="23" align="left">Title</th>
    <th width="23%" height="23" align="left">Author</th>
    <th width="11%" height="23" align="left">Price</th>
    <th width="28%" height="23" align="center">Quantity</td>
  </tr>
    <%
    Iterator iter = cat.getProducts().iterator();
    while (iter.hasNext()) {
      Product prod = (Product) iter.next();
%>
  <tr>
    <td width="38%" height="38" bgcolor="#00FFFF">
```

LISTING 10.7   Continued

```
    <span style="font-size: 10.0pt; font-family: Times New Roman">
        <A HREF="Product.jsp?ISBN=<%= prod.getISBN() %>">
        <%= prod.getTitle() %></A>
    </span></td>
    <td width="23%" height="38" bgcolor="#00FFFF">
    <span style="font-size: 10.0pt; font-family: Times New Roman">
        <%= prod.getAuthorString() %>
    </span></td>
    <td width="11%" height="38" bgcolor="#00FFFF">
    <span style="font-size: 10.0pt; font-family: Times New Roman">
    <%= prod.getPriceString() %>
    </span></td>
    <td width="28%" height="38" bgcolor="#00FFFF">
    <p align="center"><font size="2">
    <INPUT NAME="ISBN<%= prod.getISBN() %>" TYPE="TEXT" SIZE=2>
    <INPUT TYPE="SUBMIT" VALUE="Buy">
    </font></td>      </tr>
</table>
</form>
```

The entire list of books has been wrapped in a table, a new heading called Quantity has been added to the table, and form fields have been placed beside each item to record the quantity. The Buy link has been changed to form Submit buttons (see Figure 10.2).

You might have noticed that the letters ISBN were added to the ISBN code for each book and that it was used as the form field name for each book. When you look at the revised buyit.jsp (see Listing 10.8), it becomes clear why.

LISTING 10.8   A Second Go at buyit.jsp

```
<%@ page import="com.bfg.product.Product" %>
<%@ page import="com.bfg.cart.Cart" %>
<%@ page import="java.util.Enumeration" %>
<%@ page import="java.text.NumberFormat" %>

<jsp:useBean id="cart" class="com.bfg.cart.Cart" scope="session"/>

<%
Enumeration names = request.getParameterNames();
NumberFormat nf = NumberFormat.getInstance();
while (names.hasMoreElements()) {
    String name = (String) names.nextElement();
    if (name.startsWith("ISBN")) {
```

LISTING 10.8 Continued

```
    String ISBN = name.substring(4);
    if ((request.getParameter(name) != null) &&
        (request.getParameter(name).length() > 0)) {
        try {
            int quantity = nf.parse(request.getParameter(name)).intValue();
            if (quantity > 0) {
                out.print("Looking for " + ISBN + "<BR>");
                Product prod = Product.findProduct(ISBN);
                if (prod != null) {
                    cart.addItem(prod, quantity);
                }
            }
        } catch (NumberFormatException e) {
        }
    }
}
%>
<SCRIPT>
if (window.opener && !window.opener.closed)
  window.opener.location.reload();
window.close();
</SCRIPT>
```

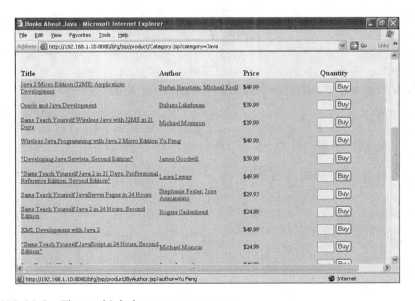

FIGURE 10.2 The multiple-buy category page.

You need to prepend ISBN to the field name because a number of other parameters might get handed to buyit, including the Submit buttons. To make it easier to pick the actual quantity fields out of the crowd, you put a distinct tag in front to make them stand out.

First, get a list of all the parameters. Iterate over them, looking for ones starting with ISBN. If the value is not blank, try parsing the value (if the customer types "garbage" into a field, it will throw a number format exception and skip over that field). Then, if the quantity is more than 0 (you wouldn't want someone entering "–80" and ending up with a credit of several thousand dollars!), add the quantity to the cart.

WHAT'S THE RIGHT THING TO DO?

Invariably, you'll come across vexing questions of functionality in the middle of the project. For example, the way the display pages have been implemented, 0 is shown for the quantity and whatever the customer types in is added and submitted to the existing order.

You could just as validly display the current quantity ordered in the boxes and alter the quantity when the customer submits it. This would let the customer remove items from an order without having to go to the shopping cart.

Which is the right way to go? Whichever way the client wants it to work! This kind of question underlines the need to stay in close communication with the stakeholder for the project during development.

Nothing strikes more fear in the heart of a developer than a client who says, "Oh, I don't care—do what you think is right." Nine times out of 10, what you decide to do will turn out to be *not* what the client wanted.

Extreme programming takes this point to its logical end, requiring the client to work directly with the developer through the entire project. You might not have this luxury in your project, but you should make sure that the guy or gal who has the final say isn't going on a month-long vacation to Tahiti right in the middle of your timeline.

Displaying and Editing the Shopping Cart

The mini-cart is nice for a quick heads-up on what you've bought, but the customer will also want to be able to view and edit a more detailed version of the cart. So, it's time to implement the shopping cart page, shown in Listing 10.9.

LISTING 10.9   shoppingcart.jsp

```
<%@ page import="com.bfg.product.Product" %>
<%@ page import="java.util.Iterator" %>
<%@ page import="com.bfg.cart.Cart" %>
<%@ page import="com.bfg.cart.CartItem" %>
```

LISTING 10.9   Continued

```
<jsp:useBean id="cart" class="com.bfg.cart.Cart" scope="session"/>

<head>
<title>Your Shopping Cart</title>
</head>

<%@ include file="/jsp/includes/bfgheader.jsp" %>


    <h2 align="center">Your Shopping Cart</h2>

<FORM METHOD="POST" ACTION="changeit.jsp" TARGET="tempwindow">
<table border="0" cellpadding="0" cellspacing="0" style="border-collapse: collapse"
bordercolor="#111111" width="100%">
  <tr>
    <th width="38%" height="23" align="left">Title</th>
    <th width="11%" height="23" align="left">Price</th>
    <th width="28%" height="23" align="center">Quantity</td>
    <th width="23%" height="23" align="left">Total</th>
  </tr>
    <%
    Iterator iter = cart.getItems();
    while (iter.hasNext()) {
      CartItem item = (CartItem) iter.next();
      Product prod = item.getProduct();
%>
  <tr>
    <td width="38%" bgcolor="#00FFFF">
    <font style="font-size: 10.0pt; font-family: Times New Roman">
        <A HREF="Product.jsp?ISBN=<%= prod.getISBN() %>">
        <%= prod.getTitle() %></A>
    </span><BR><BR></td>
    <td width="11%" bgcolor="#00FFFF">
    <span style="font-size: 10.0pt; font-family: Times New Roman">
    <%= prod.getPriceString() %>
    </span></td>
    <td width="28%" bgcolor="#00FFFF">
    <p align="center"><font size="2">
    <INPUT NAME="ISBN<%= prod.getISBN() %>" TYPE="TEXT" SIZE=2
    value=<%= item.getQuantity() %>>
    </font></td>
```

LISTING 10.9   Continued

```
   <td width="23%" bgcolor="#00FFFF">
   <span style="font-size: 10.0pt; font-family: Times New Roman">
   <%= item.getLineItemPriceString() %>
   </span></td>
  </tr>
     <% } %>
  <TR><TD COLSPAN=4><HR></TD></TR>
  <TR><TD> </TD>
  <TD> </TD>
  <TD ALIGN="center">
  <span style="font-size: 10.0pt; font-family: Times New Roman">
     Total*
  </span></TD>
    <TD>
  <span style="font-size: 10.0pt; font-family: Times New Roman">
   <%= cart.getTotalString()%>
  </span></TD></TR>
</TABLE>
<P>
<INPUT TYPE=SUBMIT NAME="update" VALUE="Update Order">
<INPUT TYPE=SUBMIT NAME="checkout" VALUE="Check Out"><P>
* - Total does not include shipping and/or taxes.
</FORM>

<%@ include file="/jsp/includes/bfgfooter.jsp" %>
```

Again, you are liberally using stolen code from another page: This page works a lot like the Catalog page, except that it iterates over the cart instead of over the catalog.

The Author column has been taken out and replaced at the end with a line-item total. A total at the bottom has also been added for the entire order, with a comment that it doesn't include taxes and the like. The results are shown in Figure 10.3.

The shopping cart sends its form data to another child window for processing, just as the catalog does. This child modifies and removes items instead of adding them, as you can see in Listing 10.10.

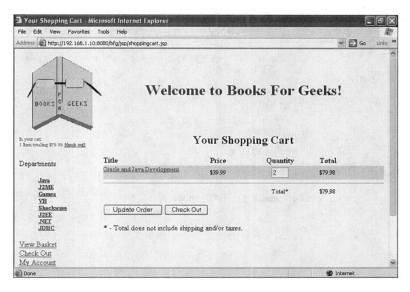

FIGURE 10.3   The shopping cart.

LISTING 10.10   changeit.jsp

```
<%@ page import="com.bfg.product.Product" %>
<%@ page import="com.bfg.cart.Cart" %>
<%@ page import="com.bfg.cart.CartItem" %>
<%@ page import="java.util.Enumeration" %>
<%@ page import="java.text.NumberFormat" %>

<jsp:useBean id="cart" class="com.bfg.cart.Cart" scope="session"/>
<%
Enumeration names = request.getParameterNames();
NumberFormat nf = NumberFormat.getInstance();
while (names.hasMoreElements()) {
    String name = (String) names.nextElement();
    if (name.startsWith("ISBN")) {
      String ISBN = name.substring(4);
      Product prod = Product.findProduct(ISBN);
      if (prod != null) {
            CartItem item = cart.getItem(prod);
          if (item != null) {
              if ((request.getParameter(name) != null) &&
                  (request.getParameter(name).length() > 0)) {
```

LISTING 10.10   Continued

```
                    try {
                        int quantity = nf.parse(request.getParameter(name)).
➥intValue();

                        out.print(quantity);
                        if (quantity > 0) {
                            item.setQuantity(quantity);
                        }
                        if (quantity == 0) {
                            cart.removeItem(prod);
                        }
                    } catch (NumberFormatException e) {
                    }
                }
            }
        }
    }
}
%>
<SCRIPT>
if (window.opener && !window.opener.closed)
<%
    if (request.getParameter("checkout") != null) {
%>
    window.opener.location = "/bfg/jsp/checkout.jsp";
<% } else { %>
    window.opener.location.reload();
<% } %>
window.close();
</SCRIPT>
```

You have the page run through the parameters just as in buyit, but this time you have it look for the matching item in the cart. If it's still there, you want it to check to see if the quantity is greater than 0. If it is, the page should modify the quantity of the cart item. If the quantity is 0, the page should remove the item from the cart altogether.

When the page is finished modifying the cart, it gets down to where it updates the parent window. You gave the Submit buttons names so that you can tell which one was pressed based on its presence in the parameter list. If the Checkout button was pressed, the code redirects the parent window to the as-yet-unwritten checkout page. Otherwise, you have it update the parent window to get the new contents.

CHECK, CHECK, AND CHECK AGAIN

It's just plain old good programming techniques. Never, ever, ever trust that you're going to get the value that you expect back from a method.

For example, in the `changeit` code, you have the code get the ISBN number from the parameter and then get the item with the corresponding code from the cart. But before the code does anything with the value, it checks to make sure that the value is not null.

How could it be null? After all, this page is called directly from the shopping cart page, and the only things that get passed as parameters are items known to be in the cart.

Well, suppose that someone zeroes out a quantity, removing the item from the cart. Then that customer hits the Back button, getting the previous version of the form with the item still in the cart ("Oops, I didn't want to remove that item."). Then the customer hits the Submit button again. Suddenly you've got the code looking for a match that isn't there. If you don't have the code check for null, it'll be throwing an exception and giving the customer an error page that will make them think much less of you as a developer.

Of course, if you really wanted to do the right thing, you should modify `changeit` to put new items in the cart if they aren't there.

Loose Ends

A lot of new functionality has been added, but it is a bit inconsistent in its application. You should do a fair amount of cleanup before moving on to the next piece of functionality:

- Attach the Buy buttons wherever there is a nonfunctional one now.

- Add quantity fields to the product display page and the "hero" item on top of the category page.

- Hook up the Buy and More Info buttons on the index page.

- Make the byAuthor.jsp page look like the category page.

It's important to take a minute every few days to step back and make sure that you haven't left any important details behind in the mad rush. Thoroughness can be the first casualty of a tight schedule, and few schedules aren't tight at some point. These changes should be made in the final source as found on the Web site, but they will not be discussed in detail here.

The Next Step: Filling and Spilling

Wow, this has been quite a bit of work for a few chapters. You now can have users register and look at products, and you can allow them to add and remove those products from the shopping cart.

In this chapter, you learned how you can do complicated form processing using the `Request` object directly. You also learned how to handle changing more than one value at the same time and how to generate forms programmatically.

In addition, you used a session object to carry state between form submissions (specifically, the contents of the shopping cart). You also learned how a child window can be used to do form processing without the perils of accidental resubmission.

If you take a quick look at your FRD, it is looking pretty good. You've got a big project coming up in checkout because it will have to deal with maintaining the address book and wallet, which have been totally ignored up to this point. Promotions have also been ignored, for the most part; you'll have to catch that up too.

Maintaining a customer's shopping cart when he ends a session without buying anything has not been covered. How do you suppose that will be done? That is another topic covered in the next chapter. Partial order fill and spill will be implemented there, as will the first stage of checkout (address and credit card capture). While you're at it, you'll also be implementing the address book and wallet-administration pages. It should be quite a ride!

11

Intersession Persistence

If Web sites had to deal with only the here and now, developing them would be a much easier undertaking. Alas, most sites need to also remember what has happened in the past and must be able to access that information in the future—that's persistence.

In this chapter, you'll see how to store data in the database so that it can be restored at a future time. This becomes critical when you want to be able to deal with a user session that times out, leaving unfinished business, but that is also at the core of other types of persistence, such as recording orders or updating user information.

Filling and Spilling

One of the requirements from the FRD was that if the user quits his session and has items in the cart that should be remembered the next time the user logs in. In e-commerce parlance, this is called "filling and spilling" the cart.

To accomplish this, you need to be able to detect when the user's session has gone away. The Servlet specification refers to this as "session invalidation" and (luckily) offers an easy way to watch for it.

When you give an object session persistence (with useBean or manually with pageContext.setAttribute), you can take advantage of an interface provided by Tomcat called HttpSessionBindingListener. If an object implements this interface and is bound into a session, it will be notified via this interface when it is first bound and when it is unbound.

Using this interface, you can watch for the unbinding of the Customer object and dump the current cart (if any) to the database when it happens.

First, you need somewhere to dump it to. Add a simple table to the schema (shown in Listing 11.1).

LISTING 11.1   init_cart.sql

```
# Schema creation for product-related tables

drop table if exists SAVED_CART;

create table SAVED_CART (
        ISBN          char(20) not null references PRODUCT,
        CUSTOMER_ID   int not null,
        QUANTITY               int not null);
```

SAVED_CART is simply a list of products and quantities that a given user has in his cart.

Now, extend Customer to dump to this table (see Listing 11.2).

LISTING 11.2   Additions to Customer.java

```
import javax.servlet.http.*;
.
.
.
public class Customer implements HttpSessionBindingListener {
    private Cart cart;

    public Cart getCart() {
      return cart;
    }

    public void setCart(Cart c) {
      cart = c;
    }
.
.
.

    public void valueBound(HttpSessionBindingEvent event) {
      cat.debug("User bound");
    }

    public void valueUnbound(HttpSessionBindingEvent event) {
      cat.debug("In unbound");
      DBConnection dbConn = null;
```

LISTING 11.2   Continued

```
Cart cart = getCart();
try
    {
        dbConn = TurbineDB.getConnection();
        if (dbConn == null) {
            cat.error("Can't get database connection");
        }
        PreparedStatement pstmt =
            dbConn.prepareStatement(sql_bundle.getString("cartClear"));
        pstmt.setInt(1, getCustomerId());
        pstmt.executeUpdate();
        pstmt.close();
        cat.debug("Deleted Cart");
        pstmt =
            dbConn.prepareStatement(sql_bundle.getString("cartAdd"));
        if (cart != null) {
            Iterator items = cart.getItems();
            while (items.hasNext()) {
                CartItem item = (CartItem) items.next();
                pstmt.setString(1, item.getProduct().getISBN());
                pstmt.setInt(2, item.getQuantity());
                pstmt.setInt(3, getCustomerId());
                pstmt.executeUpdate();
                cat.debug("Added item " + item.getProduct().getISBN());
            }
        } else {
                cat.debug("Cart is null");
        }
        pstmt.close();
    }
catch (Exception e)
    {
        cat.error("Error during valueUnbound", e);
    }
finally
    {
        try
            {
                TurbineDB.releaseConnection(dbConn);
            }
        catch (Exception e)
            {
```

LISTING 11.2   Continued

```
                         cat.error("Error during release connection", e);
                }
        }
}

public void fillCart() {
  DBConnection dbConn = null;
  Cart cart = getCart();
  try
      {
            dbConn = TurbineDB.getConnection();
            if (dbConn == null) {
                cat.error("Can't get database connection");
            }
            PreparedStatement pstmt =
                dbConn.prepareStatement(sql_bundle.getString("cartQuery"));
            pstmt.setInt(1, getCustomerId());
            ResultSet rs = pstmt.executeQuery();
            while (rs.next()) {
                Product p = Product.findProduct(rs.getString("ISBN"));
                if (p != null) {
                    cart.addItem(p, rs.getInt("QUANTITY"));
                }
            }
            rs.close();
            pstmt.close();
        }
    catch (Exception e)
        {
            cat.error("Error during fillCart", e);
        }
    finally
        {
            try
                {
                    TurbineDB.releaseConnection(dbConn);
                }
            catch (Exception e)
                {
                    cat.error("Error during release connection", e);
                }
        }
    }
```

The first thing you did is add `HttpSessionBindingListener` to the `Customer` class. You also added a property of the class called `cart` that will hold a pointer to the cart being used by the session.

Why do you need a pointer to the cart? Can't you just ask the session for it? Unfortunately, no. Consider what will happen upon session invalidation. Each session object will be unbound from the session. What happens if the cart is unbound before the customer is? When the customer asks for the cart, it will no longer be bound to the session. Therefore, you will have to keep a private pointer to the cart that will be available even if the session loses track of it. This will require some changes to the places on the site where you log in and create carts.

REFACTORING

Refactoring is that wonderful process by which you decide that you did things wrong the first time and then rewrite the code. There are two schools of thought regarding refactoring.

The "old school" (where "old" refers to the mid-1990s) says that refactoring means that you didn't do your requirements analysis in sufficient detail and, as a result, you're wasting time redoing work that you should have done the first time.

The "new school" (as represented by methodologies such as extreme programming) says that refactoring is an inevitable result of rapid prototyping, that requirements change over time, and that you need to be able to adapt your code to meet the changes.

As you might guess from the number of backtracks we've already taken during development, I tend to follow the new school. Most outstanding developers I've talked to say that they need to write code twice—once to understand the problem and once to perfect the solution. I've jokingly referred to this process as "programming by successive approximation."

My personal advice is this: If you're halfway through something and you suddenly realize that there's a better way to do something, don't be afraid to jump on it.

The first thing that the `valueUnbound` method of the class (which is the one called during invalidation) does is clear out any old cart values from the database. It does so by running the following statement from the `SQLProperties` file:

`cartClear=DELETE FROM SAVED_CART WHERE CUSTOMER_ID=?`

With the cart empty of any old values, take a look at the current cart and place a row into the database for each item in the cart using this line:

`cartAdd=INSERT INTO SAVED_CART (ISBN, QUANTITY, CUSTOMER_ID) VALUES (?, ?, ?)`

You will also add the `fillCart` method while you're in here. `fillCart` works in reverse, taking items out of the database with this line:

`cartQuery=SELECT ISBN, QUANTITY FROM SAVED_CART WHERE CUSTOMER_ID=?`

It then adds the products to the customer's current cart.

OF COOKIES AND COMBINING

When you use automatic login using cookies and cart fill and spill, you can run into some strange side effects. Consider the following scenario.

Joe User normally uses his home computer to log into BFG. As a result, his home system has his identity cookies on it, and he's always logged in when he's on the site.

Monday, Joe puts a copy of the book *The Applet and I* into his cart but never checks out. Eventually, the session times out and the book spills into his saved cart.

Tuesday, Joe is at work and realizes that he never bought the book. He goes to the BFG site. Now, because this is the first time he has used his work computer to surf BFG, there are no cookies there. Joe isn't forced to log in.

Joe placed a copy of *The Applet and I* into his cart and proceeds to the checkout pages. During checkout, he is given an opportunity to log in, and he takes it. Now the saved copy is filled into the cart.

What's the right thing to do? Realize that there's already a copy and not add it? Throw out the entire saved cart? Change the order to two copies?

In the application, the code is just going to mindlessly combine the existing cart and the new contents, but that's by no means the only solution—or the right one—for every application.

In short, as the developer, you need to keep in mind all the ways that a user's state can change during a session (reassociating a session with a specific user, logging out, performing automatic login with a cookie, and so on) and make sure that you've thought out all the ramifications.

Restoring State Upon Login

So, with this code in place, whenever a customer session is invalidated, the current cart will be spilled to the database. But what about getting the contents back?

Begin with AutoLogin.jsp, shown in Listing 11.3.

LISTING 11.3   AutoLogin.jsp Revised

```
<%@ page import="com.bfg.customer.Customer" %>
<%@ page import="com.bfg.cart.Cart" %>
<%@ page import="javax.servlet.http.Cookie" %>
<%@ page import="sun.misc.BASE64Decoder" %>


<%
{
  Cart cart = (Cart) pageContext.getAttribute("cart", PageContext.SESSION_SCOPE);
  if (cart == null) {
      cart = new Cart();
```

LISTING 11.3   Continued

```
        pageContext.setAttribute("cart", cart, PageContext.SESSION_SCOPE);
    }

    String email = null;
    String password = null;
    Cookie cook;

    Customer customer = (Customer)  pageContext.getAttribute("customer",PageCon
➥text.SESSION_SCOPE);
  if (customer == null) {
        Cookie[] cookies = request.getCookies();
        BASE64Decoder dec = new BASE64Decoder();
        for (int i = 0; i < cookies.length; i++) {
          if (cookies[i].getName().equals("bfgUsername")) {
              email = new String(dec.decodeBuffer(cookies[i].getValue()));
          }
          if (cookies[i].getName().equals("bfgPassword")) {
              password = new String(dec.decodeBuffer(cookies[i].getValue()));
          }
        }
        if ((email != null) && (password != null)) {
          Customer c = Customer.findCustomer(email);
          if ((c != null) && (c.getPassword().equals(password))) {
              c.setCart(cart);
              c.fillCart();
              pageContext.setAttribute("customer",c, PageContext.SESSION_SCOPE);
          }
        } else {
          Customer c = new Customer();
          c.setCart(cart);
          pageContext.setAttribute("customer", c, PageContext.SESSION_SCOPE);
        }
  }
}
%>
```

The first thing to notice is that all of the useBean tags have been taken out of here.
Also, everything is wrapped in a set of brackets, which means that it won't declare
any global variables that might interfere with variables declared in the main body of

the JSP that includes this file. The end result is to make this file totally transparent to any JSP file that includes it.

Instead of using useBean, use pageContext.getAttribute to look for session variables and then use setAttribute to set them. The first thing that the code does is look for a cart and establish one if it doesn't already exist. A cart will also need to be given to the Customer object soon.

Next, the code looks to see if there's a customer already associated with the session. If there is, the code deduces that the user must have already encountered this code, so it exits. This assumes that you're going to put this at the top of every JSP page, so that even if a customer goes directly to some obscure page in the middle of the site, the code can try to log in that customer.

If there is no customer for the session, the page looks for the cookies. If it finds them, it gets the customer information and then sets the existing cart to the cart that was made or found. In reality, since the cart is created at the same time this code runs, there should never be a time when no customer is associated with the session but a cart still exists.

Next, the code calls fillCart to read in any saved cart data, set the session cart object to the cart object that the page just created, and continue.

If the page doesn't find the customer or the cookie data, it just creates a new customer object, sets the cart, and continues.

While debugging this code, I discovered a fix that needs to be made to the code in the cookie-creation part of the login page. Because a path wasn't set for the cookies, they are returned to pages in the same directory as Login.jsp (the JSP cust subdirectory). This means that the autologin code would work only if the customer came to that page first. So, you need to add the following line to the two cookie creations in Login.jsp:

```
cook.setPath("/");
```

This causes it to return for any Web page on the site.

Now, how do you test this? Well, if you log in to make sure that you've got a cookie with the new path using Login.jsp, put some things in the cart, invalidate the session, and then come back to the index page, you should see that the cart still has your items in it.

But how do you invalidate the session? One solution is to wait for the session to time out. But how long will that take? Well, that turns out to be something that you can define in your web.xml file.

Listing 11.4 shows the web.xml file with a session timeout specified.

LISTING 11.4   web.xml with Session Timeout

```
<?xml version="1.0" encoding="ISO-8859-1"?>

<!DOCTYPE web-app
    PUBLIC "-//Sun Microsystems, Inc.//DTD Web Application 2.3//EN"
    "http://java.sun.com/j2ee/dtds/web-app_2_3.dtd">

    <web-app>
  <servlet>
    <servlet-name>log4j-init</servlet-name>
    <servlet-class>com.bfg.services.Log4jInit</servlet-class>

    <init-param>
      <param-name>log4j-init-file</param-name>
      <param-value>WEB-INF/log4j.properties</param-value>
    </init-param>

    <load-on-startup>1</load-on-startup>
  </servlet>
  <servlet>
    <servlet-name>turbine-init</servlet-name>
    <servlet-class>com.bfg.services.TurbineInit</servlet-class>

    <init-param>
      <param-name>turbine-resource-directory</param-name>
      <param-value>c:/tomcat/webapps/bfg/WEB-INF</param-value>

    </init-param>
    <load-on-startup>1</load-on-startup>
  </servlet>
   <session-config>
     <session-timeout>5</session-timeout>
   </session-config>
   <resource-ref>
     <res-ref-name>mail/session</res-ref-name>
     <res-type>javax.mail.Session</res-type>
     <res-auth>Container</res-auth>
   </resource-ref>
</web-app>
```

The line to look for is the one between the `<session-config>` tags. It specifies a session timeout of 5 minutes, which is good for testing but probably is a bit short for reality (30 minutes is a better choice).

```
<session-config>
  <session-timeout>5</session-timeout>
 </session-config>
```

The alternative to waiting for the session to time out is to manually invalidate the session. You can create a little JSP page to do this, shown in Listing 11.5.

LISTING 11.5   Logout.jsp

```
<% session.invalidate(); %>

<HEAD><TITLE>Session Invalidated</TITLE></HEAD><BODY>
<H1>Session Invalidated</H1>
</BODY>
```

If you go to this page after putting things in the cart, you'll force the session to invalidate. Then you can go back to the index page and automatically be logged back in.

Unfortunately, the only way to tell for sure that the fill and spill happened is to look at the debugging statements in the log:

```
2047848 [HttpProcessor[8080][4]] DEBUG com.bfg.customer.Customer  - User bound
2208361 [StandardManager[/bfg]] DEBUG com.bfg.customer.Customer  - In unbound
2208361 [StandardManager[/bfg]] DEBUG com.bfg.customer.Customer  - Deleted Cart
2208361 [StandardManager[/bfg]] DEBUG com.bfg.customer.Customer  - Added item 67
2320959
2208361 [StandardManager[/bfg]] DEBUG com.bfg.customer.Customer  - Added item 67
2321173
```

The Address Book

You need to get a couple of pieces of infrastructure in place before moving on to order checkout. One major piece of dangling functionality involves the wallet and the address book.

The wallet (the list of credit cards) will need to use addresses. As you recall way back in the ERD design, you used the `Address` object as a property of the credit card rather than recording address information separately in the credit card itself. As a result, you should get addresses working first.

To begin, you need several new queries in your properties file. To remind you, the schema for ADDRESS in the database is as follows:

```
create table ADDRESS (
        ADDRESS_ID      int not null auto_increment,
        FIRST_NAME      char(30) not null,
        LAST_NAME       char(40) not null,
        STREET_1            char(128) not null,
        STREET_2            char(128),
        CITY        char(50) not null,
        STATE       char(2) not null,
        POSTAL_CODE     char(10) not null,
        primary key(ADDRESS_ID));

create table ADDRESS_BOOK (
        CUSTOMER_KEY    int references CUSTOMER,
        ADDRESS_KEY     int references ADDRESS);
```

To create, modify, find, and delete from these tables, add the SQL shown in Listing 11.6.

LISTING 11.6   com.bfg.customer.SQLQueries.properties

```
addressQuery=SELECT * FROM ADDRESS WHERE ADDRESS_ID=?
addressDelete=DELETE FROM ADDRESS WHERE ADDRESS_ID=?
addressInsert=INSERT INTO ADDRESS (FIRST_NAME, LAST_NAME, STREET_1, \
            STREET_2, CITY, STATE, POSTAL_CODE) \
            VALUES (?, ?, ?, ?, ?, ?, ?)
addressUpdate=UPDATE ADDRESS SET FIRST_NAME=?, LAST_NAME=?, STREET_1=?, \
          STREET_2=?, CITY=?, STATE=?, POSTAL_CODE=? WHERE ADDRESS_ID=?
addressID=SELECT LAST_INSERT_ID()

getAddressBook=SELECT ADDRESS_KEY FROM ADDRESS_BOOK WHERE CUSTOMER_KEY=?
addAddress=INSERT INTO ADDRESS_BOOK (ADDRESS_KEY, CUSTOMER_KEY) VALUES (?, ?)
removeAddress=DELETE FROM ADDRESS_BOOK WHERE ADDRESS_KEY=? AND CUSTOMER_KEY=?
```

With these in place, you can write the Address bean (see Listing 11.7).

LISTING 11.7   Address.java

```
package com.bfg.customer;

import java.util.Vector;
import java.util.HashMap;
import java.util.Iterator;
import org.apache.turbine.services.db.TurbineDB;
import org.apache.turbine.util.db.pool.DBConnection;
import org.apache.turbine.util.TurbineConfig;
import com.bfg.exceptions.CustomerActivityException;
import java.sql.*;
import java.util.ResourceBundle;
import org.apache.log4j.Category;
import javax.naming.NamingException;
import javax.naming.Context;
import javax.naming.InitialContext;
import javax.naming.NamingEnumeration;
import javax.naming.directory.InitialDirContext;

public class Address {
    static Category cat = Category.getInstance(Address.class);

    private static ResourceBundle sql_bundle =
      ResourceBundle.getBundle("com.bfg.customer.SQLQueries");

    protected int addressID;
    protected String firstName;
    protected String lastName;
    protected String street1;
    protected String street2;
    protected String city;
    protected String state;
    protected String postalCode;

    public int getAddressID() {
      return addressID;
    }

    public void setAddressID(int id) {
      addressID = id;
    }
```

LISTING 11.7   Continued

```
public String getFirstName() {
  return firstName;
}

public void setFirstName(String name) {
  firstName = name;
}

public String getLastName() {
  return lastName;
}

public void setLastName(String name) {
  lastName = name;
}

public String getStreet1 () {
  return street1;
}

public void setStreet1(String street) {
  street1 = street;
}

public String getStreet2 () {
  return street2;
}

public void setStreet2(String street) {
  street2 = street;
}

public String getCity () {
  return city;
}

public void setCity(String c) {
  city = c;
}

public String getState () {
```

LISTING 11.7   Continued

```
      return state;
  }

  public void setState(String st) {
   state = st;
  }

  public String getPostalCode () {
   return postalCode;
  }

  public void setPostalCode(String pc) {
   postalCode = pc;
  }

  private HashMap validationErrors = new HashMap();

  public String getFieldError(String fieldname) {
   return((String)validationErrors.get(fieldname));
  }

  public void addFieldError(String fieldname, String error) {
   validationErrors.put(fieldname, error);
  }

  public boolean validateAddress() {
   validationErrors.clear();
   boolean valid = true;
   if ((lastName == null) ||
       (lastName.length() == 0)) {
       addFieldError("lastName", "Last Name is required.");
       valid = false;
   }
   if ((firstName == null) ||
       (firstName.length() == 0)) {
       addFieldError("firstName", "First Name is required.");
       valid = false;
   }
   if ((street1 == null) ||
       (street1.length() == 0)) {
       addFieldError("street1", "Street Address is required.");
```

LISTING 11.7   Continued

```
            valid = false;
        }
        if ((city == null) ||
            (city.length() == 0)) {
            addFieldError("city", "City is required.");
            valid = false;
        }
        if ((state == null) ||
            (state.length() == 0)) {
            addFieldError("state", "State is required.");
            valid = false;
        }
        if ((postalCode == null) ||
            (postalCode.length() == 0)) {
            addFieldError("postalCode", "Postal Code is required.");
            valid = false;
        }
        return valid;
    }

    public static Address findAddress(int ID)
      throws CustomerActivityException {
      Address addr = null;
        DBConnection dbConn = null;
        try
            {
                dbConn = TurbineDB.getConnection();
                if (dbConn == null) {
                    cat.error("Can't get database connection");
                    throw new CustomerActivityException();
                }
                PreparedStatement pstmt =
                    dbConn.prepareStatement(sql_bundle.getString("address
➥Query"));
                pstmt.setInt(1, ID);
                ResultSet rs = pstmt.executeQuery();
                if (rs.next()) {
                    addr = new Address();
                    addr.setFirstName(rs.getString("FIRST_NAME"));
                    addr.setLastName(rs.getString("LAST_NAME"));
                    addr.setStreet1(rs.getString("STREET_1"));
```

LISTING 11.7   Continued

```
                    addr.setStreet2(rs.getString("STREET_2"));
                    addr.setCity(rs.getString("CITY"));
                    addr.setState(rs.getString("STATE"));
                    addr.setPostalCode(rs.getString("POSTAL_CODE"));
                    addr.setAddressID(ID);
                } else {
                    cat.error("Couldn't find record for Address");
                }
                rs.close();
                pstmt.close();
            }
        catch (Exception e)
            {
                cat.error("Error during findAddress", e);
                throw new CustomerActivityException();
            }
        finally
            {
                try
                    {
                        TurbineDB.releaseConnection(dbConn);
                    }
                catch (Exception e)
                    {
                        cat.error("Error during release connection", e);
                    }
            }
        return addr;
    }

    public void createAddress()
      throws CustomerActivityException {
        DBConnection dbConn = null;
        try
            {
                dbConn = TurbineDB.getConnection();
                if (dbConn == null) {
                    cat.error("Can't get database connection");
                    throw new CustomerActivityException();
                }
                PreparedStatement pstmt =
```

LISTING 11.7   Continued

```
                        dbConn.prepareStatement(sql_bundle.getString("addressIn
➥sert"));
                pstmt.setString(1, getFirstName());
                pstmt.setString(2, getLastName());
                pstmt.setString(3, getStreet1());
                pstmt.setString(4, getStreet2());
                pstmt.setString(5, getCity());
                pstmt.setString(6, getState());
                pstmt.setString(7, getPostalCode());
                pstmt.executeUpdate();
                pstmt.close();
                pstmt =
                    dbConn.prepareStatement(sql_bundle.getString("addressID"));
                ResultSet rs = pstmt.executeQuery();
                if (rs.next()) {
                    addressID = rs.getInt(1);
                } else {
                    cat.error("Couldn't find record for new Address");
                }
                rs.close();
                pstmt.close();
            }
        catch (Exception e)
            {
                cat.error("Error during createAddress", e);
                throw new CustomerActivityException();
            }
        finally
            {
                try
                    {
                        TurbineDB.releaseConnection(dbConn);
                    }
                catch (Exception e)
                    {
                        cat.error("Error during release connection", e);
                    }
            }
    }

    public void updateAddress()
```

LISTING 11.7   Continued

```
    throws CustomerActivityException {
        DBConnection dbConn = null;
        try
            {
                dbConn = TurbineDB.getConnection();
                if (dbConn == null) {
                    cat.error("Can't get database connection");
                    throw new CustomerActivityException();
                }
                PreparedStatement pstmt =
                    dbConn.prepareStatement(sql_bundle.getString("addressUp
➥date"));
                pstmt.setString(1, getFirstName());
                pstmt.setString(2, getLastName());
                pstmt.setString(3, getStreet1());
                pstmt.setString(4, getStreet2());
                pstmt.setString(5, getCity());
                pstmt.setString(6, getState());
                pstmt.setString(7, getPostalCode());
                pstmt.setInt(8, getAddressID());
                pstmt.executeUpdate();
                pstmt.close();
            }
        catch (Exception e)
            {
                cat.error("Error during updateAddress", e);
                throw new CustomerActivityException();
            }
        finally
            {
                try
                    {
                        TurbineDB.releaseConnection(dbConn);
                    }
                catch (Exception e)
                    {
                        cat.error("Error during release connection", e);
                    }
            }
    }

    public void deleteAddress()
```

LISTING 11.7   Continued

```
        throws CustomerActivityException {
            DBConnection dbConn = null;
            try
                {
                    dbConn = TurbineDB.getConnection();
                    if (dbConn == null) {
                        cat.error("Can't get database connection");
                        throw new CustomerActivityException();
                    }
                    PreparedStatement pstmt =
                        dbConn.prepareStatement(sql_bundle.getString("address
➥Delete"));
                    pstmt.setInt(1, getAddressID());
                    pstmt.executeUpdate();
                    pstmt.close();
                }
            catch (Exception e)
                {
                    cat.error("Error during deleteAddress", e);
                    throw new CustomerActivityException();
                }
            finally
                {
                    try
                        {
                            TurbineDB.releaseConnection(dbConn);
                        }
                    catch (Exception e)
                        {
                            cat.error("Error during release connection", e);
                        }
                }
        }

}
```

You start with your normal collection of required libraries, set up for logging, and access to your SQL query resource bundle. Following that are the state variables for the object along with their accessors.

You need a validation hash map to store validation errors and a validation method that ensures that all the fields have been filled out.

The `find`, `create`, `modify`, and `delete` methods are almost identical to the code used in `Customer` (see Listing 8.1 in Chapter 8, "Retrieving, Storing, and Verifying User Input").

GAINING MOMENTUM: WHEN THE CODE STARTS FLOWING

There comes a point in every project (or in a major subcomponent of very large projects) when it seems that the volume of code starts to grow rapidly.

Where it once seemed to take a whole day to grind out a few hundred lines of Java, now you seem to be generating thousands. Major pieces of functionality start to appear like magic. What the heck is going on?

There are several reasons for this avalanche of code. For one thing, by that point in the project, you've probably ironed out all your infrastructure issues. Your code repository is working. You know how to log errors and get to the database from your code. So, instead of doing "science projects" all the time to discover how to get things done, you can concentrate on functionality.

You've also probably started to "wrap your mind" around the problem. I find that during the first couple of weeks on a new project, I'm just trying to learn the customer's terminology and requirements, understand any new platform technologies, learn the schema, and so on. Then one day I wake up and it all makes sense—I can see it from 30,000 feet and understand how everything fits together.

Finally, the nature of Java is that you end up doing a lot of cut-and-paste code reuse. When a bean needs to read in an instance from the database, it's going to be done pretty much the same way every time. So, you can copy and paste the code from the last object that did it. The more code you write, the more is borrowed code and the less new stuff you're writing.

The `createAddress` method lets you see a particular technique that you need to use with MySQL. Databases such as Oracle have objects called sequences that are set up to increment when read. Thus, if you do a `select` against it, you are sure to get the next number in sequence. You can then use that number as the index to a newly created row of a table.

MySQL does things a bit differently. If you indicate that a row is an autoincrementing index, you can get the value assigned to it with a `SELECT LAST_INSERT_ID()` SQL query after doing the `INSERT`. `LAST_INSERT_ID()` returns the value of the last autoincremented column created in this thread. Use it here to find the `ADDRESS_ID` of the address just created. You could have used this when you were inserting records into the Customer table, but in that case you could also use the unique e-mail address for a lookup.

To support your new address object, you need to add some things to the Customer object. Rather than use Vectors to hold the list of addresses and credit cards, change them to HashMaps so that they can be looked up by the database key, which will allow the Customer object to be used as a cache for its addresses and credit cards (see Listing 11.8).

You also need to add a couple of methods that will maintain the ADDRESS_BOOK record for a customer.

The Customer class should also automatically read in its address book when a customer is loaded. So, you need to add some code to findCustomer.

CACHING AND MULTIPLE LOGINS

In this application, you're caching objects such as the credit card and address lists. This allows greater performance and also lets you do a direct == comparison of objects rather than having to implement a .equals for them. This is because, by caching, you can be sure that a request for cardId 2345 always returns the same object.

This strategy is not without peril, however. Consider the following hypothetical situation.

Bob logs in from work to his account and changes the address for Mary Jones in his address book. Unfortunately, his wife, Susan, is also logged in at the same time from home. Because the address book is cached and first read in upon login, she has a version that precedes Bob's edit. If Susan tries to use the address book entry for Mary Jones, she'll get the old version.

If this is really an issue for your application, you can put code in place to enforce letting a user be logged in from only one location at a time. In most cases, the problems are mild and unlikely enough that this is not necessary.

LISTING 11.8   Changes to Customer.java

```
.
.
.
   private HashMap addresses = new HashMap();;
   private HashMap wallet = new HashMap();

   public HashMap getWallet() {
     return wallet;
   }

   public HashMap getAddressBook() {
     return addresses;
   }
.
.
.
```

LISTING 11.8   Continued

```
public static Customer findCustomer(String emailAddress)
    throws CustomerActivityException {
    DBConnection dbConn = null;
    Customer cust = null;
    try
        {
            dbConn = TurbineDB.getConnection();
            if (dbConn == null) {
                cat.error("Can't get database connection");
                throw new CustomerActivityException();
            }
            PreparedStatement pstmt =
                dbConn.prepareStatement(sql_bundle.getString("findQuery"));
            pstmt.setString(1, emailAddress);
            ResultSet rs = pstmt.executeQuery();
            if (rs.next()) {
                cust = new Customer();
                cust.setCustomerId(rs.getInt("CUSTOMER_ID"));
                cust.setEmail(rs.getString("EMAIL_ADDRESS"));
                cust.setPassword(rs.getString("PASSWORD"));
            } else {
                return null;
            }
            rs.close();
            pstmt.close();
            pstmt = dbConn.prepareStatement(sql_bundle.getString("getAddress
➥Book"));
            pstmt.setInt(1, cust.getCustomerId());
            rs = pstmt.executeQuery();
            while (rs.next()) {
                Address addr = Address.findAddress(rs.getInt(1));
                cust.addresses.put(new Integer(addr.getAddressID()),
                                    addr);
            }
            rs.close();
            pstmt.close();

        }
    catch (Exception e)
        {
            cat.error("Error during findCustomer", e);
```

LISTING 11.8 Continued

```
                        throw new CustomerActivityException();
                }
            finally
                {
                    try
                        {
                            TurbineDB.releaseConnection(dbConn);
                        }
                    catch (Exception e)
                        {
                            cat.error("Error during releaseConnection", e);
                        }
                }
            return cust;
    }

    public void addAddress(Address addr) throws CustomerActivityException {
        DBConnection dbConn = null;
        try
            {
                dbConn = TurbineDB.getConnection();
                if (dbConn == null) {
                    cat.error("Can't get database connection");
                    throw new CustomerActivityException();
                }
                PreparedStatement pstmt =
                    dbConn.prepareStatement(sql_bundle.getString("addAddress"));
                pstmt.setInt(1, addr.getAddressID());
                pstmt.setInt(2, getCustomerId());
                pstmt.executeUpdate();
                pstmt.close();
                getAddressBook().put(new Integer(addr.getAddressID()), addr);
            }
        catch (Exception e)
            {
                cat.error("Error during addAddress", e);
                throw new CustomerActivityException();

            }
        finally
            {
```

LISTING 11.8   Continued

```
                      try
                          {
                              TurbineDB.releaseConnection(dbConn);
                          }
                      catch (Exception e)
                          {
                              cat.error("Error during release connection", e);
                          }
                      }
           }


    public void deleteAddress(Address addr) throws CustomerActivityException {
         DBConnection dbConn = null;
         try
             {
                 dbConn = TurbineDB.getConnection();
                 if (dbConn == null) {
                     cat.error("Can't get database connection");
                     throw new CustomerActivityException();
                 }
                 PreparedStatement pstmt =
                     dbConn.prepareStatement(sql_bundle.getString("removeAd
➥dress"));
                 pstmt.setInt(1, addr.getAddressID());
                 pstmt.setInt(2, getCustomerId());
                 pstmt.executeUpdate();
                 pstmt.close();
             }
         catch (Exception e)
             {
                 cat.error("Error during addAddress", e);
                 throw new CustomerActivityException();

             }
         finally
             {
                 try
```

LISTING 11.8   Continued

```
                {
                    TurbineDB.releaseConnection(dbConn);
                }
            catch (Exception e)
                {
                    cat.error("Error during release connection", e);
                }
        }
    }
```

In this case, findAddress is used to get each address record instead of explicitly
doing a SQL query and building the addresses here or using a third class to explicitly
load and save the address book as a unit. The number of entries in the address book
is relatively small, so it was acceptable in this case to use a slightly less efficient technique rather than loading all the entries with a single query because it simplified the
code a bit. In the case of a query that might load a large number of rows, organizing
the code to do the loadup in a single call would be the preferred solution.

Now you need somewhere for the customer to make use of this new functionality.
Start with a top-level account maintenance page (see Listing 11.9).

LISTING 11.9   MyAccount.jsp

```
<%@ include file="/jsp/cust/AutoLogin.jsp" %>
<%@ page import="com.bfg.customer.Customer" %>
<%@ page import="com.bfg.customer.Address" %>
<%@ page import="java.util.Iterator" %>
<jsp:useBean id="customer" class="com.bfg.customer.Customer" scope="session"/>

<% if (customer.getEmail() == null) {
    response.sendRedirect("Login.jsp");
    return;
}
%>
<head>
<title>Account Maintainence</title>
</head>

<%@ include file="/jsp/includes/bfgheader.jsp" %>

<h2 align="center">Account Maintenance</h2>
```

LISTING 11.9   Continued

```
<center><h2>Address Book</h2></center>
<A HREF="NewAddress.jsp">Create New Address</A>
<% if (customer.getAddressBook().size() > 0) { %>
<TABLE WIDTH="100%">
  <TR><TH>Name</TH><TH>City</TH><TH>Edit</TH><TH>Delete</TH></TR>
<%
Iterator it = customer.getAddressBook().keySet().iterator();
while (it.hasNext()) {
    Address addr = (Address) customer.getAddressBook().get(it.next());
%>
      <TR><TD><%= addr.getFirstName() %> <%= addr.getLastName() %></TD>
          <TD><%= addr.getCity() %></TD>
          <TD><A HREF="NewAddress.jsp?operation=update&addressId=<%= addr.getAd-
dressID() %>">X</A></TD>
          <TD><A HREF="DeleteAddress.jsp?addressId=<%= addr.getAddressID() %>" TAR-
GET="tempwindow">X</A></TD></TR>
<% } %>
</TABLE>
<% } %>
<%@ include file="/jsp/includes/bfgfooter.jsp" %>
```

First, make sure that you've logged in from cookies, if you can. If the customer e-mail is still null, it means that you're not logged in and should be kicked over to the login page so that you can establish a cookie or create a new account.

Give the customer a link to create a new address, and then list all the addresses that already exist for the customer with edit and delete links. You'll notice that the edit and create links both go to the same JSP file—this is something that you learn to do after spending some time coding JSP form handlers.

Both `create` and `edit` are essentially the same operation. It turns out that you end up maintaining much less code if you combine the two and teach the handler the different actions to take.

Coding NewAddress.jsp (see Listing 11.10) involves a number of little tricks. Again, first make sure that you're logged in.

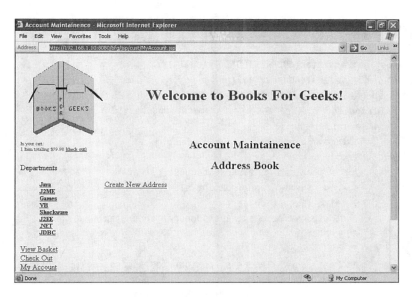

FIGURE 11.1 MyAccount.jsp with no addresses.

LISTING 11.10 NewAddress.jsp

```
<%@ include file="/jsp/cust/AutoLogin.jsp" %>
<%@ page import="com.bfg.customer.Customer" %>
<%@ page import="com.bfg.customer.Address" %>
<%@ page import="java.text.NumberFormat" %>
<jsp:useBean id="customer" class="com.bfg.customer.Customer" scope="session"/>
<jsp:useBean id="newaddr" class="com.bfg.customer.Address" scope="request"/>
<% if (customer.getEmail() == null) {
    response.sendRedirect("Login.jsp");
    return;
}
%>
<jsp:setProperty name="newaddr" property="*"/>
<%
NumberFormat nf = NumberFormat.getInstance();
String operation = request.getParameter("operation");
if (operation == null) {
    operation = "create";
```

LISTING 11.10   Continued

```
}
if (request.getParameter("SUBMITTED") != null) {
    if (newaddr.validateAddress()) {
      if (operation.equals("update")) {
          String addrId = request.getParameter("addressId");
          if (addrId != null) {
              Integer id = null;
              try {
                  Number num = nf.parse(request.getParameter("addressId"));
                  id = new Integer(num.intValue());
              } catch (Exception e) {
                  response.sendRedirect("general_error.jsp");
                  return;
              }
              Address addr = (Address) customer.getAddressBook().get(id);
              if (addr != null) {
                  newaddr.setAddressID(id.intValue());
                  newaddr.updateAddress();
                  customer.addAddress(newaddr);
                  response.sendRedirect("MyAccount.jsp");
                  return;
              } else {
                  response.sendRedirect("noaccess.jsp");
                  return;
              }
          } else {
              response.sendRedirect("general_error.jsp");
          }
      }
      else {
          newaddr.createAddress();
          customer.addAddress(newaddr);
          response.sendRedirect("MyAccount.jsp");
          return;
      }
    }
} else {
    if (operation.equals("update")) {
      String addrId = request.getParameter("addressId");
      if (addrId != null) {
          Integer id = null;
```

LISTING 11.10   Continued

```
            try {
                Number num = nf.parse(request.getParameter("addressId"));
                id = new Integer(num.intValue());
            } catch (Exception e) {
                response.sendRedirect("general_error.jsp");
                return;
            }
            Address addr = (Address) customer.getAddressBook().get(id);
            if (addr != null) {
                newaddr = addr;
            }
        }
    }
}
if (newaddr.getLastName() == null) {
    newaddr.setLastName("");
}
if (newaddr.getFirstName() == null) {
    newaddr.setFirstName("");
}
if (newaddr.getStreet1() == null) {
    newaddr.setStreet1("");
}
if (newaddr.getStreet2() == null) {
    newaddr.setStreet2("");
}
if (newaddr.getCity() == null) {
    newaddr.setCity("");
}
if  (newaddr.getState() == null) {
    newaddr.setState("");
}
if (newaddr.getPostalCode() == null) {
    newaddr.setPostalCode("");
}

%>
<% if (operation.equals("update")) { %>
<HEAD><TITLE>Edit Address</TITLE></HEAD><BODY>
<%      } else {%>
<HEAD><TITLE>Create New Address</TITLE></HEAD><BODY>
```

LISTING 11.10   Continued

```jsp
<% } %>
<%@ include file="/jsp/includes/bfgheader.jsp" %>
<% if (operation.equals("update")) { %>
<CENTER><H1>Edit Address</H1></CENTER>
<%      } else {%>
<CENTER><H1>Create New Address</H1></CENTER>
<% } %>
<FORM METHOD=POST ACTION="NewAddress.jsp">
<INPUT TYPE="HIDDEN" NAME="SUBMITTED" VALUE="T">
<INPUT TYPE="HIDDEN" NAME="operation" VALUE="<%= operation %>">
<INPUT TYPE="HIDDEN" NAME="addressId" VALUE="<%= request.getParameter("addressId")
%>">

<% if (newaddr.getFieldError("firstName") != null) { %>
<FONT COLOR="#FF0000"><%= newaddr.getFieldError("firstName")%></FONT><BR>
<% } %>

<% if (newaddr.getFieldError("lastName") != null) { %>
<FONT COLOR="#FF0000"><%= newaddr.getFieldError("lastName")%></FONT><BR>
<% } %>

First Name: <INPUT NAME="firstName" TYPE="TEXT" SIZE=30
      VALUE="<%= newaddr.getFirstName() %>">
Last Name: <INPUT NAME="lastName" TYPE="TEXT" SIZE=40
      VALUE="<%= newaddr.getLastName() %>"><BR>

<% if (newaddr.getFieldError("street1") != null) { %>
<FONT COLOR="#FF0000"><%= newaddr.getFieldError("street1")%></FONT><BR>
<% } %>

Street Addr 1: <INPUT NAME="street1" TYPE="TEXT" SIZE=80
      VALUE="<%= newaddr.getStreet1() %>"><BR>
Street Addr 2: <INPUT NAME="street2" TYPE="TEXT" SIZE=80
      VALUE="<%= newaddr.getStreet2() %>"><BR>

<% if (newaddr.getFieldError("city") != null) { %>
<FONT COLOR="#FF0000"><%= newaddr.getFieldError("city")%></FONT><BR>
<% } %>

<% if  (newaddr.getFieldError("state") != null) { %>
<FONT COLOR="#FF0000"><%= newaddr.getFieldError("state")%></FONT><BR>
```

LISTING 11.10   Continued

```
<% } %>

<% if (newaddr.getFieldError("postalCode") != null) { %>
<FONT COLOR="#FF0000"><%= newaddr.getFieldError("postalCode")%></FONT><BR>
<% } %>

City: <INPUT NAME="city" TYPE="TEXT" SIZE=50
        VALUE="<%= newaddr.getCity() %>">
State: <INPUT NAME="state" TYPE="TEXT" SIZE=2
        VALUE="<%= newaddr.getState() %>">
Postal Code: <INPUT NAME="postalCode" TYPE="TEXT" SIZE=10
        VALUE="<%= newaddr.getPostalCode() %>"><BR>

<INPUT TYPE=SUBMIT>
</FORM>
<%@ include file="/jsp/includes/bfgfooter.jsp" %>
```

The page first fills in the newaddr object with the values from the form. The first time through, there are no values, of course, but this is harmless in that case.

The parameter operation will be either create or update. If it's blank, the code defaults to create.

If the customer has already submitted the form, the page runs the address validation. If it succeeds, then it checks to see if the customer is updating. If so, it gets the addressId parameter, which is the ID of the address record to be updated. If it's null or it can't be parsed to an integer, it sends the user to a general error page. Note that whenever you do a response.sendRedirect, you should immediately follow it with a return. This will cause the servlet generated from the JSP code to return without processing the rest of the page.

If the page has a valid ID, it looks in the address book of the customer to see if it can find the ID. If so, the page sets the address of the temporary object holding the form values to equal the ID, calls updateAddress to write the new values to the database, and then tells the customer object to use the temporary address object as the new permanent one. Alternatively, the code could have copied all the fields from the temporary address to the address already in the address book, but that involves more code.

If that address ID was not found in the address book, something is wrong. It's possible that someone nasty is typing address book IDs in at random to try to steal information. So, the customer is sent to a "You Don't Have Permission to Look at That" page.

PROTECTING USER INFORMATION

The cardinal rule of e-commerce is this: "Thou shalt not disclose one user's information to another user."

This can take an awful lot of due diligence. You need to make sure that if you ever have to pass something such as an object ID to a form handler, the handler validates that the user has permission to view that data.

In other words, never assume that, just because a page is requesting a piece of information, the page should automatically be granted access to it. The nice thing about session objects is that the client browser has no way to directly change their state, so you can compare a requested operation (such as looking at a specific `create card` record) with the information stored in the session to determine whether the operation is legal.

In spite of your best efforts, your platform might still undo all your work. On one project I was involved with, a problem with the platform caused it to confuse which user was associated with which session, and it ended up writing address book (and credit card!) entries into the wrong user's account information.

It turned out to be especially pernicious to reproduce as well. It basically came down to, "Okay, Bob, you hit Submit and now hit Back. Now, Jane, hit Submit and now hit Back. Now both hit Submit at once—3, 2, 1, now!"

Luckily, this was caught during testing instead of production—yet another strong argument for thorough QA.

If the request is to create instead of update, a call is made to `createAddress`. Then the address object is added to the customer's address book and they are redirected to the account page.

If this is the customer's first time through the form and it's for updating, the page tries to find the address to be edited in the address book. If it finds it, it sets `newaddr` to the address, which makes the form fill in from the existing data rather than remain blank.

The next piece of code makes sure that blank entries are presented as `""` rather than as `null`. Then the page presents the appropriate page title and banner based on the operation.

The error flagging follows the model used in NewUser.jsp, in which error messages were displayed before each form field.

After the form has been used to create a few addresses, you can see them in the MyAccount page and edit them, if you want to.

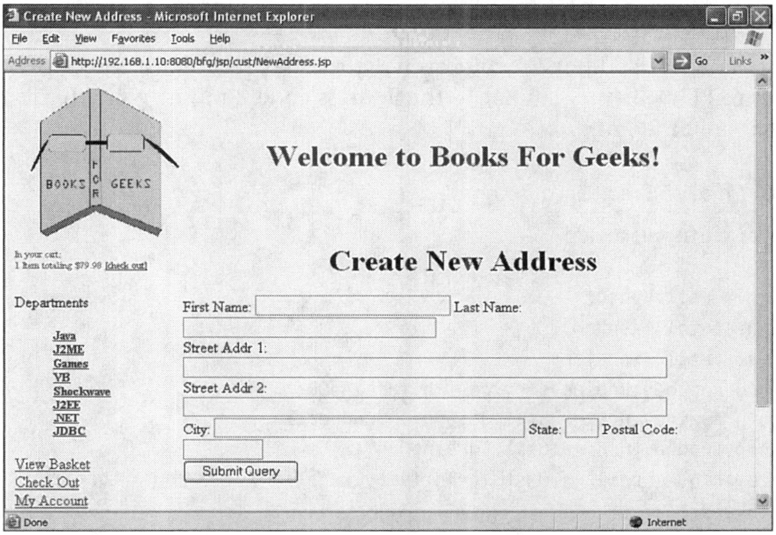

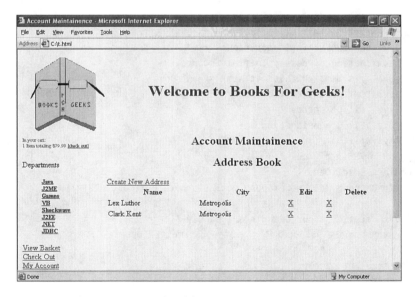

FIGURE 11.2   The NewAddress.jsp form.

FIGURE 11.3   MyAccount.jsp with addresses.

Credit Cards and the Wallet

Now that you have addresses, you can write the wallet. A lot of the credit card code (see Listing 11.11) is very similar to the address code. I'm just going to discuss the areas that are different.

LISTING 11.11   CreditCard.java

```
package com.bfg.customer;

import java.util.Vector;
import java.util.HashMap;
import java.util.Iterator;
import org.apache.turbine.services.db.TurbineDB;
import org.apache.turbine.util.db.pool.DBConnection;
import org.apache.turbine.util.TurbineConfig;
import com.bfg.exceptions.CustomerActivityException;
import java.sql.*;
import java.util.ResourceBundle;
import org.apache.log4j.Category;
import javax.naming.NamingException;
import javax.naming.Context;
import javax.naming.InitialContext;
import javax.naming.NamingEnumeration;
import javax.naming.directory.InitialDirContext;
import java.text.SimpleDateFormat;
import java.text.ParseException;
import java.util.Calendar;
import java.util.GregorianCalendar;
import java.util.Date;

public class CreditCard {
    static Category cat = Category.getInstance(CreditCard.class);

    private static ResourceBundle sql_bundle =
      ResourceBundle.getBundle("com.bfg.customer.SQLQueries");

    protected int cardID;
    protected Address address;
    protected Customer customer;
    protected String cardOwner;
    protected String cardType;
    protected String cardNumber;
```

LISTING 11.11   Continued

```
protected int expMonth;
protected int expYear;

public int getCardID() {
  return cardID;
}

public void setCardID(int id) {
  cardID = id;
}

public Address getAddress() {
  return address;
}

public void setAddress(Address addr) {
  address = addr;
}

public Customer getCustomer() {
  return customer;
}

public void setCustomer(Customer cust) {
  customer = cust;
}

public String getCardOwner() {
  return cardOwner;
}

public void setCardOwner(String name) {
  cardOwner = name;
}

public String getCardType() {
  return cardType;
}

public void setCardType(String name) {
  cardType = name;
```

LISTING 11.11   Continued

```
    }

    public String getCardNumber () {
      return cardNumber;
    }

    public String getObscuredNumber () {
      if ((cardNumber != null) &&
          (cardNumber.length() > 6)) {
          String digitsOnly = getDigitsOnly(cardNumber);
          String allStars = "*****************************************";
          return digitsOnly.substring(0,2) +
              allStars.substring(0, digitsOnly.length() - 6) +
              digitsOnly.substring(digitsOnly.length() - 4,
                                  digitsOnly.length());
      } else {
          return "";
      }
    }

    public void setCardNumber(String name) {
      cardNumber = name;
    }

    public int getExpMonth () {
      return expMonth;
    }

    public void setExpMonth(int month) {
      expMonth = month;
    }

    public int getExpYear () {
      return expYear;
    }

    public void setExpYear(int year) {
      expYear = year;
    }
    private HashMap validationErrors = new HashMap();
```

LISTING 11.11   Continued

```
public String getFieldError(String fieldname) {
  return((String)validationErrors.get(fieldname));
}

public void addFieldError(String fieldname, String error) {
  validationErrors.put(fieldname, error);
}

public boolean validateCCDate(int expMonth, int expYear) {
  SimpleDateFormat formatter = new SimpleDateFormat ("MM/yy");
  try {
      GregorianCalendar c =  new GregorianCalendar();
      c.setTime(formatter.parse(expMonth + "/" + expYear));
      c.roll(Calendar.MONTH, 1);
      c.set(Calendar.DATE, 1);
      c.set(Calendar.HOUR, 0);
      c.set(Calendar.MINUTE, 0);
      c.set(Calendar.SECOND, 0);
      Date now = new Date();
      return (now.compareTo(c.getTime()) < 0);
  } catch (ParseException ex) {};
  return false;
}
private String getDigitsOnly (String s) {
  StringBuffer digitsOnly = new StringBuffer ();
  char c;
  for (int i = 0; i < s.length (); i++) {
      c = s.charAt (i);
      if (Character.isDigit (c)) {
          digitsOnly.append (c);
      }
  }
  return digitsOnly.toString ();
}

public boolean validateCreditCardNumber (String cardNumber) {
  String digitsOnly = getDigitsOnly (cardNumber);
  int sum = 0;
  int digit = 0;
  int addend = 0;
  boolean timesTwo = false;
```

LISTING 11.11   Continued

```
int digitLength = digitsOnly.length();
boolean foundcard = false;

// MC
if (digitsOnly.startsWith("51") || digitsOnly.startsWith("52")
    || digitsOnly.startsWith("53") || digitsOnly.startsWith("54")) {
    if (digitLength != 16) return false;
    foundcard = true;
}
// VISA
if (digitsOnly.startsWith("4")) {
    if ((digitLength != 16) && (digitLength != 13)) return false;
    foundcard = true;
}
// AMEX
if (digitsOnly.startsWith("34") || digitsOnly.startsWith("37")) {
    if (digitLength != 15) return false;
    foundcard = true;
}
// DISC
if (digitsOnly.startsWith("6011")) {
    if (digitLength != 16) return false;
    foundcard = true;
}
if (!foundcard) return false;
for (int i = digitsOnly.length () - 1; i >= 0; i--) {
    digit = Integer.parseInt (digitsOnly.substring (i, i + 1));
    if (timesTwo) {
        addend = digit * 2;
        if (addend > 9) {
            addend -= 9;
        }
    }
    else {
        addend = digit;
    }
    sum += addend;
    timesTwo = !timesTwo;
}

int modulus = sum % 10;
```

LISTING 11.11 Continued

```
    return modulus == 0;

}

public boolean validateCreditCard() {
  validationErrors.clear();
  boolean valid = true;
  if ((cardType == null) ||
      (cardType.length() == 0)) {
      addFieldError("cardType", "Card Type is required.");
      valid = false;
  }
  if ((cardOwner == null) ||
      (cardOwner.length() == 0)) {
      addFieldError("cardOwner", "Cardholder Name is required.");
      valid = false;
  }
  if ((cardNumber == null) ||
      (cardNumber.length() == 0)) {
      addFieldError("cardNumber", "Card Number is required.");
      valid = false;
  } else {
      if (!validateCreditCardNumber(cardNumber)) {
          addFieldError("cardNumber", "Invalid Card Number");
          valid = false;
      }
  }
  if (expMonth == 0) {
      addFieldError("expMonth", "Expiration Month is required.");
      valid = false;
  }
  if (expYear == 0) {
      addFieldError("expYear", "Expiration Year is required.");
      valid = false;
  }
  if (!validateCCDate(expMonth, expYear)) {
      addFieldError("expYear", "Expired Card Date");
      valid = false;
  }
  return valid;
}
```

LISTING 11.11   Continued

```
public static CreditCard findCreditCard(int cardID)
  throws CustomerActivityException {
  CreditCard cc = null;
     DBConnection dbConn = null;
     try
         {
             dbConn = TurbineDB.getConnection();
             if (dbConn == null) {
                 cat.error("Can't get database connection");
                 throw new CustomerActivityException();
             }
             PreparedStatement pstmt =
                 dbConn.prepareStatement(sql_bundle.getString("creditQuery"));
             pstmt.setInt(1, cardID);
             ResultSet rs = pstmt.executeQuery();
             if (rs.next()) {
                 cc = new CreditCard();
                 cc.setCardType(rs.getString("CARD_TYPE"));
                 cc.setCardNumber(rs.getString("CARD_NUMBER"));
                 cc.setCardOwner(rs.getString("CARD_OWNERNAME"));
                 cc.setExpMonth(rs.getInt("CARD_EXPMONTH"));
                 cc.setExpYear(rs.getInt("CARD_EXPYEAR"));
                 cc.setAddress(Address.findAddress(rs.getInt("ADDRESS_KEY")));

cc.setCustomer(Customer.findCustomer(rs.getString("EMAIL_ADDRESS")));
             } else {
                 cat.error("Couldn't find record for Credit Card");
             }
             rs.close();
             pstmt.close();
         }
     catch (Exception e)
         {
             cat.error("Error during findCreditCard", e);
             throw new CustomerActivityException();
         }
     finally
         {
             try
                 {
                     TurbineDB.releaseConnection(dbConn);
```

LISTING 11.11   Continued

```
                                }
                        catch (Exception e)
                            {
                                cat.error("Error during release connection", e);
                            }
                    }
            return cc;
    }

    public void createCreditCard()
        throws CustomerActivityException {
            DBConnection dbConn = null;
            try
                {
                    dbConn = TurbineDB.getConnection();
                    if (dbConn == null) {
                        cat.error("Can't get database connection");
                        throw new CustomerActivityException();
                    }
                    PreparedStatement pstmt =
                        dbConn.prepareStatement(sql_bundle.getString("creditIn
➥sert"));
                    pstmt.setInt(1, getCustomer().getCustomerId());
                    pstmt.setString(2, getCardType());
                    pstmt.setString(3, getCardNumber());
                    pstmt.setString(4, getCardOwner());
                    pstmt.setInt(5, getExpMonth());
                    pstmt.setInt(6, getExpYear());
                    pstmt.setInt(7, getAddress().getAddressID());
                    pstmt.executeUpdate();
                    pstmt.close();
                    pstmt =
                        dbConn.prepareStatement(sql_bundle.getString("addressID"));
                    ResultSet rs = pstmt.executeQuery();
                    if (rs.next()) {
                        setCardID( rs.getInt(1));
                    } else {
                        cat.error("Couldn't find record for new Credit Card");
                    }
                    rs.close();
                    pstmt.close();
```

LISTING 11.11   Continued

```
                }
        catch (Exception e)
            {
                cat.error("Error during createCreditCard", e);
                throw new CustomerActivityException();
            }
        finally
            {
                try
                    {
                        TurbineDB.releaseConnection(dbConn);
                    }
                catch (Exception e)
                    {
                        cat.error("Error during release connection", e);
                    }
            }
    }

    public void updateCreditCard()
        throws CustomerActivityException {
            DBConnection dbConn = null;
            try
                {
                    dbConn = TurbineDB.getConnection();
                    if (dbConn == null) {
                        cat.error("Can't get database connection");
                        throw new CustomerActivityException();
                    }
                    PreparedStatement pstmt =
                        dbConn.prepareStatement(sql_bundle.getString("cardUpdate"));
                    pstmt.setInt(1, getCustomer().getCustomerId());
                    pstmt.setString(2, getCardType());
                    pstmt.setString(3, getCardNumber());
                    pstmt.setString(4, getCardOwner());
                    pstmt.setInt(5, getExpMonth());
                    pstmt.setInt(6, getExpYear());
                    pstmt.setInt(7, getAddress().getAddressID());
                    pstmt.setInt(8, getCardID());
                    pstmt.executeUpdate();
                    pstmt.close();
```

LISTING 11.11   Continued

```
            }
        catch (Exception e)
            {
                cat.error("Error during updateCreditCard", e);
                throw new CustomerActivityException();
            }
        finally
            {
                try
                    {
                        TurbineDB.releaseConnection(dbConn);
                    }
                catch (Exception e)
                    {
                        cat.error("Error during release connection", e);
                    }
            }
    }

    public void deleteCreditCard()
      throws CustomerActivityException {
        DBConnection dbConn = null;
        try
            {
                dbConn = TurbineDB.getConnection();
                if (dbConn == null) {
                    cat.error("Can't get database connection");
                    throw new CustomerActivityException();
                }
                getAddress().deleteAddress();
                PreparedStatement pstmt =
                    dbConn.prepareStatement(sql_bundle.getString("credit
➥Delete"));
                pstmt.setInt(1, getCardID());
                pstmt.executeUpdate();
                pstmt.close();
            }
        catch (Exception e)
            {
                cat.error("Error during deleteCreditCard", e);
                throw new CustomerActivityException();
```

LISTING 11.11   Continued

```
            }
        finally
          {
            try
              {
                  TurbineDB.releaseConnection(dbConn);
              }
            catch (Exception e)
              {
                  cat.error("Error during release connection", e);
              }
          }
      }

  }
```

The getObscuredNumber method is used to return the credit card number with everything but the first two and last four digits obscured.

At last, you have some interesting validations! First off, the code must make sure that it hasn't been handed an expired credit card. Working with dates in Java can seem a bit annoying at times because each of the various ways of representing time (Time, Date, and Calendar) has certain operations that it supports and certain ones that it doesn't. You might need to convert back and forth several times to get the final result. This code is one of several ways to find out whether a card is expired. It sets the calendar to the first second of the following month and checks whether today's date is greater than it—a card that expires on 10/02 really expires at midnight of 10/31/02.

If you wanted to internationalize the application, you would use resource bundles instead of the hard-wired error strings here so that locale-dependent messages can be returned.

You will also want to prevalidate the card number. This code will do a number of checks:

- Check to make sure that the prefix (the first one or two digits of the card) is valid.

- Check to make sure that the number of digits is appropriate for the card type.

- Use the industry checksum to make sure that the card is *likely* to be a valid one.

WHY PREVALIDATE?

Because you're eventually going to hand off the credit card to a third party for authorization, why prevalidate the card number?

First, card validation is a slow process involving a network transaction that can take from several seconds to a minute or more. So, it is much better to catch the simple errors that you can with a simple set of tests.

Second, authorization is the last thing that you do before recording the order. It will be difficult to navigate the user back to an editing screen to fix the number. So again, it's better to catch it early.

Interestingly, because you can determine the credit card type from the card number prefix, there's really no reason to request the card type explicitly, but consumers seem to expect it.

Because an ADDRESS record is being used to store the billing address for the credit card, the code needs to read in the Address object when it gets a credit card from the database.

Because the class needs the Address ID when it creates a new credit card, you'll need to have the code create the Address object first, set the credit card's Address field to it, and then call createCreditCard.

Adding Wallet Support to Customer

Now add the wallet support to Customer.java (see Listing 11.12), immediately following the code that you added to read in the address book in findCustomer. It's interesting to note that two different approaches were taken with addresses and credit cards. Because addresses are pointed to by both customers and credit cards, an xref table was used to associate them with customers. Because credit cards belong directly to customers, you could "hard-wire" the customer ID directly in the credit card record. That way Customer.java doesn't need a function to add and remove credit cards.

LISTING 11.12   More Changes to Customer.java

```
            pstmt = dbConn.prepareStatement(sql_bundle.getString("getWal
➥let"));
            pstmt.setInt(1, cust.getCustomerId());
            rs = pstmt.executeQuery();
            while (rs.next()) {
                CreditCard cc = CreditCard.findCreditCard(rs.getInt(1));
                cust.wallet.put(new Integer(cc.getCardID()), cc);
            }
            rs.close();
            pstmt.close();
```

Now it's time to write the JSP. The MyAccount code (in Listing 11.13) is a clone of the code for the address book (in Listing 11.9).

LISTING 11.13   Adding Credit Cards to MyAccount.jsp

```
<center><h2>Credit Cards</h2></center>
<A HREF="NewCreditCard.jsp">Add New Card</A>
<% if (customer.getWallet().size() > 0) { %>
<TABLE WIDTH="100%">
  <TR><TH>Cardholder</TH><TH>Card Number</TH><TH>Edit</TH><TH>Delete</TH></TR>
<%
Iterator it = customer.getWallet().keySet().iterator();
while (it.hasNext()) {
    CreditCard cc = (CreditCard) customer.getWallet().get(it.next());
%>
    <TR><TD><%= cc.getCardOwner() %> </TD>
        <TD><%= cc.getObscuredNumber() %></TD>
        <TD><A HREF="NewCreditCard.jsp?operation=update&cardId=<%= cc.getCardID()
%>">X</A></TD>
        <TD><A HREF="DeleteAddress.jsp?cardId=<%= cc.getCardID() %>" TARGET="tem
➥pwindow">X</A></TD></TR>
<% } %>
</TABLE>
<% } %>
```

The NewCreditCard.jsp (in Listing 11.14) code needs all the code that NewAddress.jsp had (because it needs to record the address), plus additional code to handle the credit card–specific data. It would be nice if you could somehow include the address code rather than duplicate it, but it is not worth the effort in this case—there's only a single reuse of the code, and making the address code general would involve some heavy rewrites.

LISTING 11.14   NewCreditCard.jsp

```
<%@ include file="/jsp/cust/AutoLogin.jsp" %>
<%@ page import="com.bfg.customer.Customer" %>
<%@ page import="com.bfg.customer.Address" %>
<%@ page import="com.bfg.customer.CreditCard" %>
<%@ page import="java.text.NumberFormat" %>
<jsp:useBean id="customer" class="com.bfg.customer.Customer" scope="session"/>
<jsp:useBean id="newaddr" class="com.bfg.customer.Address" scope="request"/>
<jsp:useBean id="newcredit" class="com.bfg.customer.CreditCard" scope="request"/>
<% if (customer.getEmail() == null) {
    response.sendRedirect("Login.jsp");
```

LISTING 11.14   Continued

```
    return;
}
%>
<jsp:setProperty name="newaddr" property="*"/>
<jsp:setProperty name="newcredit" property="*"/>

<%
NumberFormat nf = NumberFormat.getInstance();
String operation = request.getParameter("operation");
if (operation == null) {
    operation = "create";
}

String cardId = request.getParameter("cardId");
Integer id = null;
if (!operation.equals("update")) {
    newcredit.setCardNumber(request.getParameter("newCardNumber"));
} else {
    if ((cardId != null) && (cardId.length() > 0)) {
      try {
          Number num = nf.parse(request.getParameter("cardId"));
          id = new Integer(num.intValue());
      } catch (Exception e) {
          response.sendRedirect("general_error.jsp");
          return;
      }
    }

    CreditCard c = (CreditCard) customer.getWallet().get(id);
    if (c.getObscuredNumber().equals(request.getParameter("newCardNumber"))) {
      newcredit.setCardNumber(c.getCardNumber());
    } else {
    newcredit.setCardNumber(request.getParameter("newCardNumber"));
    }
}
if (request.getParameter("SUBMITTED") != null) {
    if (newcredit.validateCreditCard() && newaddr.validateAddress()) {
      if (operation.equals("update")) {
          CreditCard cc = (CreditCard) customer.getWallet().get(id);
          if (cc != null) {
              newcredit.setCustomer(customer);
              newcredit.setCardID(id.intValue());
```

LISTING 11.14   Continued

```
                newcredit.setAddress(newaddr);
                newcredit.setCustomer(customer);
                newaddr.setAddressID(cc.getAddress().getAddressID());
                newaddr.updateAddress();
                newcredit.updateCreditCard();
                customer.getWallet().put(id, newcredit);
                response.sendRedirect("MyAccount.jsp");
                return;
            } else {
                response.sendRedirect("noaccess.jsp");
                return;
            }
        }
        else {
            newaddr.createAddress();
            newcredit.setAddress(newaddr);
            newcredit.setCustomer(customer);
            newcredit.createCreditCard();
            customer.getWallet().put(new Integer(newcredit.getCardID()),
                              newcredit);
            response.sendRedirect("MyAccount.jsp");
            return;
        }
    }
} else {
    if (operation.equals("update")) {
      CreditCard card = (CreditCard) customer.getWallet().get(id);
      if (card != null) {
          newcredit = card;
          newaddr = card.getAddress();
      }
    }
}


if (newaddr.getLastName() == null) {
    newaddr.setLastName("");
}
if (newaddr.getFirstName() == null) {
    newaddr.setFirstName("");
}
if (newaddr.getStreet1() == null) {
```

LISTING 11.14   Continued

```
    newaddr.setStreet1("");
}
if (newaddr.getStreet2() == null) {
    newaddr.setStreet2("");
}
if (newaddr.getCity() == null) {
    newaddr.setCity("");
}
if (newaddr.getState() == null) {
    newaddr.setState("");
}
if (newaddr.getPostalCode() == null) {
    newaddr.setPostalCode("");
}

if (newcredit.getCardOwner() == null) {
    newcredit.setCardOwner("");
}

if (newcredit.getCardType() == null) {
    newcredit.setCardType("");
}

if (newcredit.getCardNumber() == null) {
    newcredit.setCardNumber("");
}

%>
<% if (operation.equals("update")) { %>
<HEAD><TITLE>Edit Credit Card</TITLE></HEAD><BODY>
<%    } else {%>
<HEAD><TITLE>Create Credit Card</TITLE></HEAD><BODY>
<% } %>
<%@ include file="/jsp/includes/bfgheader.jsp" %>
<% if (operation.equals("update")) { %>
<CENTER><H1>Edit Credit Card</H1></CENTER>
<%    } else {%>
<CENTER><H1>Create New Credit Card</H1></CENTER>
<% } %>
<FORM METHOD=POST ACTION="NewCreditCard.jsp">
<INPUT TYPE="HIDDEN" NAME="SUBMITTED" VALUE="T">
<INPUT TYPE="HIDDEN" NAME="operation" VALUE="<%= operation %>">
```

LISTING 11.14   Continued

```
<INPUT TYPE="HIDDEN" NAME="cardId" VALUE="<%= request.getParameter("cardId") %>">

<% if (newcredit.getFieldError("cardOwner") != null) { %>
<FONT COLOR="#FF0000"><%= newcredit.getFieldError("cardOwner")%></FONT><BR>
<% } %>

Name on Card: <INPUT NAME="cardOwner" TYPE="TEXT" SIZE=50
       VALUE="<%= newcredit.getCardOwner() %>"><BR>

<% if  (newcredit.getFieldError("cardType") != null) { %>
<FONT COLOR="#FF0000"><%= newcredit.getFieldError("cardType")%></FONT><BR>
<% } %>
Card Type: <SELECT NAME="cardType">
<OPTION VALUE="">---SELECT---
<OPTION VALUE="VISA"
    <%= (newcredit.getCardType().equals("VISA"))?" SELECTED":"" %>>Visa
<OPTION VALUE="MC"
    <%= (newcredit.getCardType().equals("MC"))?" SELECTED":"" %>>MasterCard
<OPTION VALUE="AMEX"
    <%= (newcredit.getCardType().equals("AMEX"))?" SELECTED":"" %>>American Express
<OPTION VALUE="DISC"
    <%= (newcredit.getCardType().equals("DISC"))?" SELECTED":"" %>>Discover
</SELECT><BR>

<% if (newcredit.getFieldError("cardNumber") != null) { %>
<FONT COLOR="#FF0000"><%= newcredit.getFieldError("cardNumber")%></FONT><BR>
<% } %>
<% if (newcredit.getFieldError("expMonth") != null) { %>
<FONT COLOR="#FF0000"><%= newcredit.getFieldError("expMonth")%></FONT><BR>
<% } %>

<% if  (newcredit.getFieldError("expYear") != null) { %>
<FONT COLOR="#FF0000"><%= newcredit.getFieldError("expYear")%></FONT><BR>
<% }
int expMonth = newcredit.getExpMonth();
int expYear = newcredit.getExpYear();
%>

Card Number: <INPUT NAME="newCardNumber" TYPE="TEXT" SIZE=25
       VALUE="<%=
operation.equals("update")?newcredit.getObscuredNumber():newcredit.getCardNumber()
```

LISTING 11.14   Continued

```
%>"><BR>

Expires: <SELECT NAME="expMonth">
  <OPTION VALUE="">SELECT
  <OPTION VALUE="1" <%= (expMonth == 1)?" SELECTED":"" %>>Jan
  <OPTION VALUE="2" <%= (expMonth == 2)?" SELECTED":"" %>>Feb
  <OPTION VALUE="3" <%= (expMonth == 3)?" SELECTED":"" %>>Mar
  <OPTION VALUE="4" <%= (expMonth == 4)?" SELECTED":"" %>>Apr
  <OPTION VALUE="5" <%= (expMonth == 5)?" SELECTED":"" %>>May
  <OPTION VALUE="6" <%= (expMonth == 6)?" SELECTED":"" %>>Jun
  <OPTION VALUE="7" <%= (expMonth == 7)?" SELECTED":"" %>>Jul
  <OPTION VALUE="8" <%= (expMonth == 8)?" SELECTED":"" %>>Aug
  <OPTION VALUE="9" <%= (expMonth == 9)?" SELECTED":"" %>>Sep
  <OPTION VALUE="10" <%= (expMonth == 10)?" SELECTED":"" %>>Oct
  <OPTION VALUE="11" <%= (expMonth == 11)?" SELECTED":"" %>>Nov
  <OPTION VALUE="12" <%= (expMonth == 12)?" SELECTED":"" %>>Dec
</SELECT> /

<SELECT NAME="expYear">
  <OPTION VALUE="">SELECT
  <OPTION VALUE="2002" <%= (expYear == 2002)?" SELECTED":"" %>>02
  <OPTION VALUE="2003" <%= (expYear == 2003)?" SELECTED":"" %>>03
  <OPTION VALUE="2004" <%= (expYear == 2004)?" SELECTED":"" %>>04
  <OPTION VALUE="2005" <%= (expYear == 2005)?" SELECTED":"" %>>05
  <OPTION VALUE="2006" <%= (expYear == 2006)?" SELECTED":"" %>>06
  <OPTION VALUE="2007" <%= (expYear == 2007)?" SELECTED":"" %>>07
  <OPTION VALUE="2008" <%= (expYear == 2008)?" SELECTED":"" %>>08
  <OPTION VALUE="2009" <%= (expYear == 2009)?" SELECTED":"" %>>09
  <OPTION VALUE="2010" <%= (expYear == 2010)?" SELECTED":"" %>>10
  <OPTION VALUE="2011" <%= (expYear == 2011)?" SELECTED":"" %>>11
  <OPTION VALUE="2012" <%= (expYear == 2012)?" SELECTED":"" %>>12<P>
</SELECT>

<H2>Billing Address</H2><P>

<% if (newaddr.getFieldError("firstName") != null) { %>
<FONT COLOR="#FF0000"><%= newaddr.getFieldError("firstName")%></FONT><BR>
<% } %>

<% if (newaddr.getFieldError("lastName") != null) { %>
<FONT COLOR="#FF0000"><%= newaddr.getFieldError("lastName")%></FONT><BR>
```

LISTING 11.14   Continued

```
<% } %>

First Name: <INPUT NAME="firstName" TYPE="TEXT" SIZE=30
      VALUE="<%= newaddr.getFirstName() %>">
Last Name: <INPUT NAME="lastName" TYPE="TEXT" SIZE=40
      VALUE="<%= newaddr.getLastName() %>"><BR>

<% if (newaddr.getFieldError("street1") != null) { %>
<FONT COLOR="#FF0000"><%= newaddr.getFieldError("street1")%></FONT><BR>
<% } %>

Street Addr 1: <INPUT NAME="street1" TYPE="TEXT" SIZE=80
      VALUE="<%= newaddr.getStreet1() %>"><BR>
Street Addr 2: <INPUT NAME="street2" TYPE="TEXT" SIZE=80
      VALUE="<%= newaddr.getStreet2() %>"><BR>

<% if (newaddr.getFieldError("city") != null) { %>
<FONT COLOR="#FF0000"><%= newaddr.getFieldError("city")%></FONT><BR>
<% } %>

<% if (newaddr.getFieldError("state") != null) { %>
<FONT COLOR="#FF0000"><%= newaddr.getFieldError("state")%></FONT><BR>
<% } %>

<% if  (newaddr.getFieldError("postalCode") != null) { %>
<FONT COLOR="#FF0000"><%= newaddr.getFieldError("postalCode")%></FONT><BR>
<% } %>

City: <INPUT NAME="city" TYPE="TEXT" SIZE=50
      VALUE="<%= newaddr.getCity() %>">
State: <INPUT NAME="state" TYPE="TEXT" SIZE=2
      VALUE="<%= newaddr.getState() %>">
Postal Code: <INPUT NAME="postalCode" TYPE="TEXT" SIZE=10
      VALUE="<%= newaddr.getPostalCode() %>"><BR>

<INPUT TYPE=SUBMIT>
</FORM>
<%@ include file="/jsp/includes/bfgfooter.jsp" %>
```

You'll be using some tricky code with the credit card number to avoid displaying it to the customer. This is so that if someone gains unauthorized access to the account, they can't view credit card numbers that already have been entered. Because of this, don't use `setProperties` to set the credit card from the form submit; hand it in as a property called `newCardNumber`.

If the page is not doing an update, the credit card number must be new. So, just set the bean's copy to the copy from the form submit. If the page is doing an update, it checks to see if the submitted card number is equal to the "obscured" version. If it is, the page gets the real card number and puts it in the `newcredit` bean.

Again, the code to update the database is basically the same as the code for addresses, but now it needs to write out both a new or modified address record *and* a new or modified credit card record.

If you have pull-down menus in your forms and you want them to come up with the previous value, you have to end up writing some cumbersome code to put a `SELECTED` tag on the appropriate value. I'm a fan of the `boolean?trueval:falseval` Java shorthand for these kinds of things.

You need to have the code hide the card information when it displays it in the form. If the page is in an update, it places the obscured version of the card number in the form. If the customer doesn't change it, the code will match it up when the customer submits it and will replace it with the real credit card number before writing it to the database. If the customer does change it, the page will take the value entered.

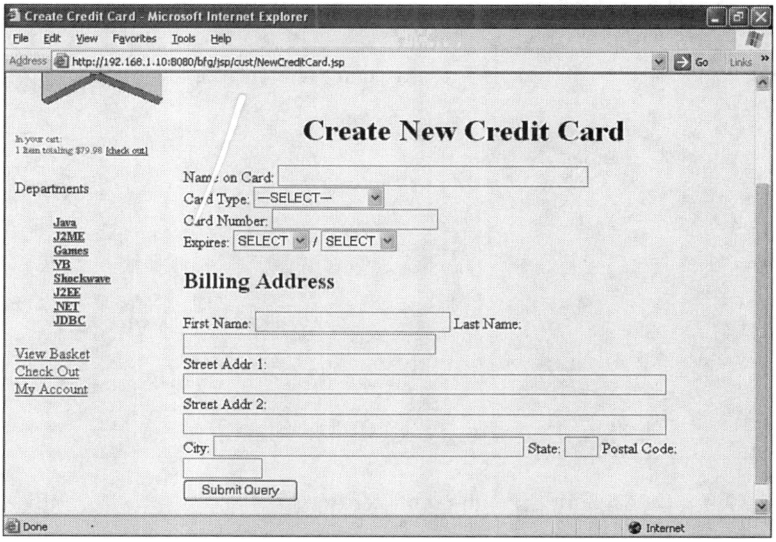

FIGURE 11.4 NewCreditCard.jsp

With credit card support in place, you can now create and edit your wallet to your heart's content.

TESTING CREDIT CARDS

Because you are prevalidating card numbers, you can't just type any value into the form and have it succeed. If you've done enough e-commerce work, you'll have memorized the valid test credit card numbers for each card issuer. These are numbers with the right numbers of digits and the right prefix—and numbers that pass the checksum algorithm. They are (as of this writing):

Visa: 4111 1111 1111 1111

MasterCard: 5500 0000 0000 0004

American Express: 340000000000009

Discover: 6011000000000004

Now, while these numbers will pass your primitive prevalidation routine, they're certain not to get by a real credit card authorization check, so don't get any ideas about picking up a Porsche using one of them!

We'll talk more about credit cards and authorization in Chapter 12, "Implementing Business Logic."

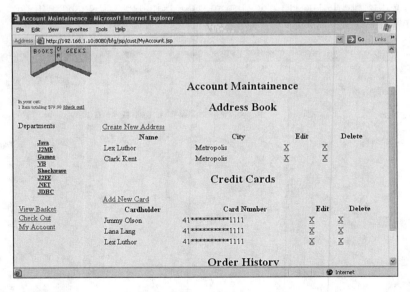

FIGURE 11.5   MyAccount.jsp with credit cards.

Time to Get Down to Business

In this chapter, you got a close look at how a combination of techniques can be used to retain customer information between sessions. Cookies can be used to store user login information so that you can have your application automatically identify the customer upon subsequent visits. `HttpSessionBindingListener` allows you to catch a session timeout and have your application spill data so that the current session isn't lost.

You also learned how to do more advanced form validations, including date and credit card number checks, and how to have one object automatically load in objects that it is related to.

That was certainly a chunk of code that you just went through. The next chapter gives you a break from database fill and spill. You will be looking at implementing business rules—specifically, simple promotions (such as buy one, get one free), taxation, and shipping charges.

You will also be implementing the major pieces of the checkout process. Luckily, with the address and credit card objects already in place, you're almost home free on that item. With that out of the way, all you'll have to do in Chapter 13, "Completing the Application," is charge the customer's card and record the order. Then you'll be open for business.

12

Implementing Business Logic

Another piece of functionality out of the FRD that hasn't been tackled yet is the promotions implementation. Promotions are an example of *business logic*; something that follows a specific, company-centric set of rules that might not be logical but that reflect the way things are done.

Another great example of business logic is shipping rules. A larger retailer might have a slew of complicated rules about when a customer should receive free shipping, which items qualify for overnight delivery, which items may be shipped only via ground transport, and so on.

You'll spend a lot of time coding business logic into an application. It's by far the most important thing to get right because it is what the clients know best and what will be noticed most quickly if it's not done the way they want.

Today Only! Buy One, Get One Free!

BFG promotions work as follows: If a customer buys over a threshold amount of a given book or books from a given category, that customer receives a free gift. As with most sites, the gifts themselves aren't "normal" merchandise; you won't find the gift items by searching the categories.

In this example, two promotions will be available at launch. Buy *Javabeans Unleashed* and get a can of coffee, and buy any two J2ME books and get a PDA cover.

First you have to enter the two promotional items and the two promotions (see Listing 12.1).

LISTING 12.1   Sample Data for the PROMOTION Table

```
insert into PRODUCT (TITLE, PUB_DATE, ISBN, DESCRIPTION, PRICE) values
      ('Genuine Nagahyde PDA Carrying Case',
       '1998-12-22','PALMCASE','A genuine Nagahyde Palm-compatible PDA case, \
just the thing to keep your precious PDA safe from the elements.  Made from the \
skin of the rare endangered Naga, this case is sure to make you a hit at your \
next trade show.', 25.00);


insert into PRODUCT (TITLE, PUB_DATE, ISBN, DESCRIPTION, PRICE) values
      ('Jamaican Coffee',
       '1998-12-22','COFFEECAN','When a late night of engineering has your eyes \
defocused and you just can\'t grind out that last method, grind some of these \
imported Jamaican Blue Mountain coffee beans instead.  The caffeine will be just \
the thing to keep you going.', 12.00);
   .
   .
   .
insert into PROMOTION (PROMO_ID, PROMO_NAME, PROD_OR_CAT,
                       CATEGORY_ID, PRODUCT_ISBN, PROMO_TYPE,
                       DISCOUNT_QUANT, GIFT_ID)
      values (1, 'Get a Palm Case with any 2 J2ME Books', 'C', 2,
             null, 'B', 2, 'PALMCASE');


insert into PROMOTION (PROMO_ID, PROMO_NAME, PROD_OR_CAT,
                       CATEGORY_ID, PRODUCT_ISBN, PROMO_TYPE,
                       DISCOUNT_QUANT, GIFT_ID)
      values (2, 'Buy Javabeans Unleashed, get a can of Jamaican Coffee',
             'P', null, '067231424X', 'B', 1, 'COFFEECAN');
```

The promotion code should review the contents of the cart, find any promotions whose qualifications have been met, and add the appropriate gift to the cart.

This is where the isPromotionItem property of the CartItem comes in. The shopping cart code needs to recalculate promotions every time the cart contents change. If the results of the last promotion calculation are not cleared first, more gifts will be added to the cart each time. Any promotional items need to be cleared out first, and the isPromotionItem flag lets you tell them apart.

Implementing Promotions

Now you're ready to write the promotion class itself (see Listing 12.2).

LISTING 12.2   Promotion.java

```java
package com.bfg.cart;

import java.util.Vector;
import java.util.HashMap;
import java.util.Iterator;
import java.text.NumberFormat;
import com.bfg.product.Product;
import com.bfg.product.Category;
import org.apache.turbine.services.db.TurbineDB;
import org.apache.turbine.util.db.pool.DBConnection;
import org.apache.turbine.util.TurbineConfig;
import com.bfg.exceptions.ProductActivityException;
import java.sql.*;
import java.util.ResourceBundle;

public class Promotion  {
    private static ResourceBundle sql_bundle =
      ResourceBundle.getBundle("com.bfg.cart.SQLQueries");

    static org.apache.log4j.Category cat =
org.apache.log4j.Category.getInstance(Promotion.class);

    static Vector promotions = new Vector();

    static boolean loaded = false;

    protected String promoName;

    protected Product targetItem;

    protected Category targetCategory;

    protected Product giftItem;

    protected int quantityRequired;

    protected boolean categoryPromotion = false;

    public String getPromoName() {
      return promoName;
```

LISTING 12.2   Continued

```
    }

    public boolean isCategoryPromotion() {
      return categoryPromotion;
    }

    public Product getTargetItem() {
      return targetItem;
    }

    public Category getTargetCategory() {
      return targetCategory;
    }

    public Product getGiftItem() {
      return giftItem;
    }

    public int getQuantityRequired() {
      return quantityRequired;
    }
    public static Vector getPromotions() {
      if (loaded) {
          return promotions;
      } else {
          loadPromotions();
          loaded = true;
          return promotions;
      }
    }
    public static void loadPromotions() {
      DBConnection dbConn = null;
      try
          {
              dbConn = TurbineDB.getConnection();
              if (dbConn == null) {
                  cat.error("Can't get database connection");
                  return;
              }
              PreparedStatement pstmt =
                  dbConn.prepareStatement(sql_bundle.getString("loadPromotions"));
```

LISTING 12.2   Continued

```
            ResultSet rs = pstmt.executeQuery();
            while (rs.next()) {
                Promotion promo = new Promotion();
                promo.giftItem = Product.findProduct(rs.getString("GIFT_ID"));
                promo.promoName = rs.getString("PROMO_NAME");
                promo.categoryPromotion =
                    (rs.getString("PROD_OR_CAT").equals("C"));
                if (promo.categoryPromotion) {
                    promo.targetCategory =
Category.findCategoryById(rs.getInt("CATEGORY_ID"));
                    if (promo.targetCategory == null) continue;
                } else {
                    promo.targetItem = Product.findProduct(rs.getString("PROD
➥UCT_ISBN"));
                    if (promo.targetItem == null) continue;
                }
                promo.quantityRequired = rs.getInt("DISCOUNT_QUANT");
                promotions.add(promo);
            }
            rs.close();
            pstmt.close();
        }
    catch (Exception e)
        {
            cat.error("Error during loadPromotions", e);
        }
    finally
        {
            try
                {
                    TurbineDB.releaseConnection(dbConn);
                }
            catch (Exception e)
                {
                    cat.error("Error during releaseConnection", e);
                }
        }
    }
    public static void runPromotions(Cart cart) {
      cart.removePromotionItems();
```

LISTING 12.2   Continued

```
        Iterator promos = getPromotions().iterator();

      while (promos.hasNext()) {
          Promotion promo = (Promotion) promos.next();
          promo.runPromotion(cart);
      }
    }
    public void runPromotion(Cart cart) {
      Iterator items = cart.getItems();

      int quant = 0;
      while (items.hasNext()) {
          CartItem item = (CartItem) items.next();
          if (isCategoryPromotion()) {
              if (targetCategory.getProducts().contains(item.getProduct())) {
                  quant += item.getQuantity();
              }
          } else {
              if (item.getProduct().equals(targetItem)) {
                  quant += item.getQuantity();
              }
          }
      }
      if (quant >= quantityRequired) {
          cart.addPromotionItem(giftItem, 1);
      }
    }
}
```

To create the promotion class, you start with your normal friends: logging initialization, getting your SQL statement bundle, and creating a bunch of bean properties.

getPromotions shows an alternative to the singleton pattern: It checks to see if it has already loaded the promotions. If not, it loads them before returning the vector.

Assuming that you need to load the promotions from the database, loadPromotions reads the entries from the database, finding either the product or the category, depending on the PROD_OR_CAT flag. If the product or category isn't found, it throws away the promotion.

OBJECTS THAT LOAD OTHER OBJECTS

You have to be rather careful when you have one object being loaded from the database that loads another object. For one thing, if the first loader hasn't closed its database connection before loading the child object (as is often the case when you're loading a number from one query), you'll consume two connections (or more, if that child loads other children). So, you need to make sure that you have enough connections available in your pool to avoid having to wait for a free one.

Another possibility that can occur is a circular reference. For example, suppose that you had products store their primary category. When you load the categories, the products would load, too, because categories load a list of their member products. When you load the product, it would try to load the category, which would try to load the products, and so on. This is a good way to exercise the stack of your JDK to failure.

One way around stack failure is the approach taken here. You use a findProduct and a findCategory that store previously found entries on a cache and update them back to the database upon update (called a "write-through" cache). When the product asks for its category, it is given the value from the cache (assuming that you're smart and had the code store it in the cache before it goes looking for children).

When you need to have promotions run over a cart, the promotion engine first clears out any existing promotional products. Then it gets a list of all the promotions and tries each one in turn to see if it matches the contents of the cart.

The promotion logic itself is fairly simple. It iterates over the cart items, looking for items either that are in the promotion target category (if it's a category promotion) or that are the target product (for a product promotion). If the total quantity in the cart is greater than the threshold, the engine moves the gift item into the cart with the promotionalItem flag set.

This is a fairly simple design for the promotion engine. In a more elaborate implementation (with seven different types of promotions) that I did for a major drug store chain, I implemented a base class for promotions and then had a number of specialized subclasses, one for each type of promotion. I also used a special loader class that knew how to read the promotions from the database and instantiated the correct specific class depending on the type of the promotion.

You need to modify the cart (see Listing 12.3) to run the promotion engine when items are added or removed from the cart. You also need a special addPromotionItem that doesn't run the promotion engine; otherwise, when the promotion engine adds a promotion item, the item would be called again recursively, leading to a stack overrun.

LISTING 12.3   Modifications to Cart.java

```java
public void addItem(Product item, int quantity) {
  if (contents.get(item) != null) {
      ((CartItem)contents.get(item)).addQuantity(quantity);
  } else {
      CartItem citem = new CartItem();
      citem.setQuantity(quantity);
      citem.setProduct(item);
      contents.put(item, citem);
  }
  Promotion.runPromotions(this);
}

public void addPromotionItem(Product item, int quantity) {
  CartItem citem = new CartItem();
  citem.setQuantity(quantity);
  citem.setProduct(item);
  citem.setPromotionItem(true);
  contents.put(item, citem);
}

public void removeItem(Product item) {
  contents.remove(item);
  Promotion.runPromotions(this);
}

public void removePromotionItems() {
  Vector removals = new Vector();
  Iterator items = getItems();

  while (items.hasNext()) {
      CartItem item = (CartItem) items.next();
      if (item.isPromotionItem()) {
          removals.add(item.getProduct());
      }
  }

  items = removals.iterator();
  while (items.hasNext()) {
      Product item = (Product) items.next();
      contents.remove(item);
  }
}
```

CartItem needs to be told that it shouldn't charge for promotional items and to return Free for the string version of the price. This is accomplished with the code in Listing 12.4.

LISTING 12.4   Additions to CartItem.java

```java
    private boolean isPromotionItem;
.
.
.

    public boolean isPromotionItem() {
      return isPromotionItem;
    }

    public void setPromotionItem(boolean isPromo) {
      isPromotionItem = isPromo;
    }

    public double getLineItemPrice() {
      if (isPromotionItem()) return 0D;
      return getQuantity() * getProduct().getPrice();
    }

    public String getLineItemPriceString() {
      if (isPromotionItem()) return "FREE!";
      NumberFormat nf = NumberFormat.getCurrencyInstance();
      return nf.format(getLineItemPrice());
    }
```

You also need to add some support in Category (see Listing 12.5) for finding categories by their ID; until now, you've only needed to search by name.

LISTING 12.5   Changes to Category.java

```java
    public static Category findCategoryById(int Id) throws ProductActivityException
{
        loadAllCategories();
        Iterator it = getCategories().iterator();

        while (it.hasNext()) {
            Category c = findCategory((String)it.next());
            if (c.getID() == Id) return c;
        }
        return null;
    }
```

Finally, make a small tweak to the shopping cart JSP code. The customer shouldn't be able to remove or change the quantity of free items (see Listing 12.6). Now the shopping cart will correctly compute and display promotions, as shown in Figure 12.1.

LISTING 12.6   Changes to ShoppingCart.jsp

```
<% if (item.isPromotionItem()) { %>
    <%= item.getQuantity() %>
<% } else { %>
    <INPUT NAME="ISBN<%= prod.getISBN() %>" TYPE="TEXT" SIZE=2
    value=<%= item.getQuantity() %>>
<% } %>
```

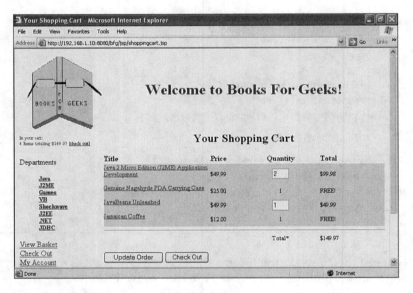

FIGURE 12.1   The shopping cart with promotions.

Stubbing Out Taxes and Shipping

As mentioned at the beginning of the chapter, shipping and taxes are two more tricky business logic subsystems.

In a real application, you would have to calculate taxes and shipping costs on your orders. This usually involves interfacing to third-party APIs that do the (sometimes complex) calculations, and return a value to be placed into the order. This is the same thing you will have to do with credit card authorization.

You usually won't be ready to actually integrate with the vendor's code (you might not even have chosen a vendor) when you write the code that requires that functionality. So, you'll need to stub something out for testing.

A good technique for any piece of code that's going to initially function in a test mode and later have the real API added is to put in a property that acts as a switch between the stub and the real functionality. This is helpful because you might work with developers who need to test the site but who won't have access to the real clients (for example, if the tax client runs on only Solaris).

With that in mind, you'll add some code to the cart to compute your taxes and shipping in Listing 12.7.

TAXING MATTERS

A brief prayer: Lord, give wisdom unto the many State Attorney Generals, and let them develop a comprehensive, simple, nationwide taxing structure sometime in the near future.

Integrating into a tax package is one of the most arduous experiences that a developer can encounter. That is because the current (circa fall 2001) taxing structure is so complicated. A purchase conceivably could fall under more than 9,000 different taxes, differing from state to city to county.

Not only are there way too many taxing authorities, but they all compute taxes differently. For example, groceries are exempt from taxes in Massachusetts. This means that not only do you need to know where your customer lives, but you also need to know what tax categories your products fall into.

It's not surprising that many companies take the legislatively provided way out of not charging tax. This won't work if you have "brick and mortar" stories in a lot of states, though (in other words, a physical as well as a virtual sales presence in that state), because you are often required to collect taxes for sales made in any state where you have a physical presence.

Disclaimer: I am not a tax attorney.

LISTING 12.7   Additions to Cart.java

```
import java.util.ResourceBundle;
import com.bfg.customer.Address;
.
.
.
    private static ResourceBundle property_bundle =
      ResourceBundle.getBundle("com.bfg.cart.Cart");
    public double getShipping(Address addr) {
      if ((property_bundle.getString("testShippingMode") != null) &&
          (property_bundle.getString("testShippingMode").equals("yes"))) {
        if ((addr.getState() != null) &&
```

LISTING 12.7   Continued

```
                (addr.getState().compareTo("MA") < 0)) {
                return countItems() * 1.25D;
            } else {
                return countItems() * 2.75D;
            }
        } else {
            cat.debug("No real shipping code in place yet");
            return 0D;
        }
    }

    public String getShippingString(Address addr) {
      NumberFormat nf = NumberFormat.getCurrencyInstance();
      return nf.format(getShipping(addr));
    }
    public double getTax(Address addr) {
      if ((property_bundle.getString("testTaxMode") != null) &&
          (property_bundle.getString("testTaxMode").equals("yes"))) {
            if ((addr.getState() != null) &&
                (addr.getState().compareTo("MA") < 0)) {
                return getTotal() * 0.05D;
            } else {
                return getTotal() * 0.10D;
            }
        } else {
            cat.debug("No real tax code in place yet");
            return 0D;
        }
    }

    public String getTaxString(Address addr) {
      NumberFormat nf = NumberFormat.getCurrencyInstance();
      return nf.format(getTax(addr));
    }
    public double getGrandTotal(Address addr) {
      return getTotal() + getShipping(addr) + getTax(addr);
    }

    public String getGrandTotalString(Address addr) {
      NumberFormat nf = NumberFormat.getCurrencyInstance();
      return nf.format(getGrandTotal(addr));
    }
```

For the stubbed-out tax code, you're employing this "complex" calculation: If the item is being sent to a state alphabetically before Massachusetts (MA), you charge that customer 5% tax; otherwise, the customer is charged 10% tax. Although this is certainly not accurate, it allows you to see whether different taxes are being computed based on location.

You can use the same technique for shipping, but in this case you'll use a fixed price per item in the cart. You also need to create the properties file that holds the test-mode flag values (see Listing 12.8).

You could just as easily do the computation of the display string for the prices in the JSP code that needs to display it, but it's always a good idea to hide your business logic (including totaling) in beans. Keeping the business logic in the beans also ensures that the calculation is always done right, lest someone forget to include taxes or shipping somewhere in the JSP.

LISTING 12.8   Cart.properties

```
testTaxMode=yes
testShippingMode=yes
```

Finalizing the Order

With the promotion, tax, and shipping building blocks in place, you can create a checkout page to capture the shipping address and credit card information and then display a final confirmation page that can include the shipping and tax. To begin, you need to create a JSP that combines the previously written address book and wallet functionality.

A good start in building this page is to see what the finished product will look like (see Figure 12.2). This will serve as a good roadmap to the underlying code.

Things are a bit trickier than with NewAddress or NewCreditCard because you need to capture two different addresses. This means that you can't use jsp:setProperty to set both of them—they would have to use the same field names in the form, which doesn't work.

Start with your normal JSP header boilerplate. Remember that the user is allowed to make purchases without logging in, so you can't assume that the customer has any valid values. You can use setProperty to fill in the shipping address and credit card information. You also need to set up a second address object called ccaddr. The page is shown in Listing 12.9.

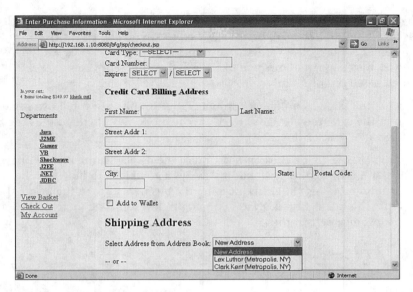

FIGURE 12.2   The order information page.

LISTING 12.9   Checkout.jsp

```
<%@ include file="/jsp/cust/AutoLogin.jsp" %>
<%@ page import="com.bfg.customer.Customer" %>
<%@ page import="com.bfg.customer.Address" %>
<%@ page import="com.bfg.customer.CreditCard" %>
<%@ page import="java.text.NumberFormat" %>
<jsp:useBean id="customer" class="com.bfg.customer.Customer" scope="session"/>
<jsp:useBean id="orderaddr" class="com.bfg.customer.Address" scope="session"/>
<jsp:useBean id="ordercredit" class="com.bfg.customer.CreditCard" scope="session"/>
<jsp:setProperty name="orderaddr" property="*"/>
<jsp:setProperty name="ordercredit" property="*"/>
<%
Address ccaddr = new Address();
NumberFormat nf = NumberFormat.getInstance();

boolean loggedInUser = (customer.getEmail() != null);
String selectedCCId = request.getParameter("selectedCCId");
String selectedAddrId = request.getParameter("selectedAddrId");
if (selectedCCId == null) {
    selectedCCId = "NEW";
```

LISTING 12.9   Continued

```
}

if (selectedAddrId == null) {
    selectedAddrId = "NEW";
}

if (request.getParameter("SUBMITTED") != null) {
    ccaddr.setFirstName(request.getParameter("ccFirstName"));
    ccaddr.setLastName(request.getParameter("ccLastName"));
    ccaddr.setStreet1(request.getParameter("ccStreet1"));
    ccaddr.setStreet2(request.getParameter("ccStreet2"));
    ccaddr.setCity(request.getParameter("ccCity"));
    ccaddr.setState(request.getParameter("ccState"));
    ccaddr.setPostalCode(request.getParameter("ccPostalCode"));

    Integer ccId;
    if (!selectedCCId.equals("NEW")) {
      try {
          Number num = nf.parse(selectedCCId);
          Integer CCId = new Integer(num.intValue());
          if (customer.getWallet().get(CCId) != null) {
              ordercredit = (CreditCard) customer.getWallet().get(CCId);
              ccaddr = ordercredit.getAddress();
              pageContext.setAttribute("ordercredit", ordercredit,
                                       PageContext.SESSION_SCOPE);
          }
      } catch (Exception e) {
          response.sendRedirect("general_error.jsp");
          return;
      }
    }

    if (!selectedAddrId.equals("NEW")) {
      try {
          Number num = nf.parse(selectedAddrId);
          Integer AddrId = new Integer(num.intValue());
          if (customer.getAddressBook().get(AddrId) != null) {
              orderaddr = (Address) customer.getAddressBook().get(AddrId);
              pageContext.setAttribute("orderaddr", orderaddr,
                                       PageContext.SESSION_SCOPE);
          }
```

LISTING 12.9   Continued

```
    } catch (Exception e) {
        response.sendRedirect("general_error.jsp");
        return;
    }
}

boolean goodAddress = orderaddr.validateAddress();
boolean goodCCAddress = ccaddr.validateAddress();
boolean goodCard = ordercredit.validateCreditCard();
if (goodAddress && goodCCAddress && goodCard) {
  if ((request.getParameter("createShip") != null) &&
      (request.getParameter("createShip").equals("yes"))) {
      orderaddr.createAddress();
      customer.addAddress(orderaddr);
  }
  if ((request.getParameter("createCC") != null) &&
      (request.getParameter("createCC").equals("yes"))) {
      ccaddr.createAddress();
      ordercredit.setAddress(ccaddr);
      ordercredit.setCustomer(customer);
      ordercredit.createCreditCard();
      customer.getWallet().put(new Integer(ordercredit.getCardID()),
                               ordercredit);
  }
  response.sendRedirect("finalConfirm.jsp");
  return;
}
} else {
    orderaddr = new Address();
    pageContext.setAttribute("orderaddr", orderaddr,
                         PageContext.SESSION_SCOPE);
    ordercredit = new CreditCard();
    pageContext.setAttribute("ordercredit", ordercredit,
                         PageContext.SESSION_SCOPE);
    ccaddr = new Address();
    pageContext.setAttribute("ccaddr", ccaddr,
                         PageContext.SESSION_SCOPE);
}

if (orderaddr.getLastName() == null) {
    orderaddr.setLastName("");
```

LISTING 12.9   Continued

```
}
if (orderaddr.getFirstName() == null) {
    orderaddr.setFirstName("");
}
if (orderaddr.getStreet1() == null) {
    orderaddr.setStreet1("");
}
if (orderaddr.getStreet2() == null) {
    orderaddr.setStreet2("");
}
if  (orderaddr.getCity() == null) {
    orderaddr.setCity("");
}

if (orderaddr.getState() == null) {
    orderaddr.setState("");
}

if (orderaddr.getPostalCode() == null) {
    orderaddr.setPostalCode("");
}

if (ccaddr.getLastName() == null) {
    ccaddr.setLastName("");
}

if (ccaddr.getFirstName() == null) {
    ccaddr.setFirstName("");
}

if (ccaddr.getStreet1() == null) {
    ccaddr.setStreet1("");
}

if (ccaddr.getStreet2() == null) {
    ccaddr.setStreet2("");
}

if  (ccaddr.getCity() == null) {
    ccaddr.setCity("");
```

LISTING 12.9   Continued

```
}

if (ccaddr.getState() == null) {
    ccaddr.setState("");
}

if (ccaddr.getPostalCode() == null) {
    ccaddr.setPostalCode("");
}

if (ordercredit.getCardOwner() == null) {
    ordercredit.setCardOwner("");
}

if (ordercredit.getCardType() == null) {
    ordercredit.setCardType("");
}

if (ordercredit.getCardNumber() == null) {
    ordercredit.setCardNumber("");
}

<HEAD><TITLE>Enter Purchase Information</TITLE></HEAD><BODY>
<%@ include file="/jsp/includes/bfgheader.jsp" %>
<CENTER><H1>Enter Purchase Information</H1></CENTER>
<FORM METHOD=POST ACTION="checkout.jsp">
<INPUT TYPE="HIDDEN" NAME="SUBMITTED" VALUE="T">
<H2>Credit Card</H2>
<% if (loggedInUser) {
    if (customer.getWallet().size() > 0) {
%>
if (ordercredit.getFieldError("cardOwner") != null) { %>
<FONT COLOR="#FF0000"><%= ordercredit.getFieldError("cardOwner")%></FONT><BR>
<% } %>

Name on Card: <INPUT NAME="cardOwner" TYPE="TEXT" SIZE=50
        VALUE="<%= ordercredit.getCardOwner() %>"><BR>

<% if (ordercredit.getFieldError("cardType") != null) { %>
<FONT COLOR="#FF0000"><%= ordercredit.getFieldError("cardType")%></FONT><BR>
```

LISTING 12.9   Continued

```
<% } %>

Card Type: <SELECT NAME="cardType">
<OPTION VALUE="">---SELECT---
<OPTION VALUE="VISA"
    <%= (ordercredit.getCardType().equals("VISA"))?" SELECTED":"" %>>Visa
<OPTION VALUE="MC"
    <%= (ordercredit.getCardType().equals("MC"))?" SELECTED":"" %>>MasterCard
<OPTION VALUE="AMEX"
    <%= (ordercredit.getCardType().equals("AMEX"))?" SELECTED":"" %>>American
Express
<OPTION VALUE="DISC"
    <%= (ordercredit.getCardType().equals("DISC"))?" SELECTED":"" %>>Discover
</SELECT><BR>

<% if (ordercredit.getFieldError("cardNumber") != null) { %>
<FONT COLOR="#FF0000"><%= ordercredit.getFieldError("cardNumber")%></FONT><BR>
<% } %>
<% if (ordercredit.getFieldError("expMonth") != null) { %>
<FONT COLOR="#FF0000"><%= ordercredit.getFieldError("expMonth")%></FONT><BR>
<% } %>

<% if (ordercredit.getFieldError("expYear") != null) { %>
<FONT COLOR="#FF0000"><%= ordercredit.getFieldError("expYear")%></FONT><BR>
<% }
int expMonth = ordercredit.getExpMonth();
int expYear = ordercredit.getExpYear();
%>


Card Number: <INPUT NAME="cardNumber" TYPE="TEXT" SIZE=25
      VALUE="<%= (!selectedCCId.equals("NEW"))?ordercredit.
➥getObscuredNumber():ordercredit.getCardNumber() %>"><BR>

Expires: <SELECT NAME="expMonth">
  <OPTION VALUE="">SELECT
  <OPTION VALUE="1" <%= (expMonth == 1)?" SELECTED":"" %>>Jan
  <OPTION VALUE="2" <%= (expMonth == 2)?" SELECTED":"" %>>Feb
  <OPTION VALUE="3" <%= (expMonth == 3)?" SELECTED":"" %>>Mar
  <OPTION VALUE="4" <%= (expMonth == 4)?" SELECTED":"" %>>Apr
  <OPTION VALUE="5" <%= (expMonth == 5)?" SELECTED":"" %>>May
```

LISTING 12.9   Continued

```
    <OPTION VALUE="6" <%= (expMonth == 6)?" SELECTED":"" %>>Jun
    <OPTION VALUE="7" <%= (expMonth == 7)?" SELECTED":"" %>>Jul
    <OPTION VALUE="8" <%= (expMonth == 8)?" SELECTED":"" %>>Aug
    <OPTION VALUE="9" <%= (expMonth == 9)?" SELECTED":"" %>>Sep
    <OPTION VALUE="10" <%= (expMonth == 10)?" SELECTED":"" %>>Oct
    <OPTION VALUE="11" <%= (expMonth == 11)?" SELECTED":"" %>>Nov
    <OPTION VALUE="12" <%= (expMonth == 12)?" SELECTED":"" %>>Dec
</SELECT> /

<SELECT NAME="expYear">
    <OPTION VALUE="">SELECT
    <OPTION VALUE="2002" <%= (expYear == 2002)?" SELECTED":"" %>>02
    <OPTION VALUE="2003" <%= (expYear == 2003)?" SELECTED":"" %>>03
    <OPTION VALUE="2004" <%= (expYear == 2004)?" SELECTED":"" %>>04
    <OPTION VALUE="2005" <%= (expYear == 2005)?" SELECTED":"" %>>05
    <OPTION VALUE="2006" <%= (expYear == 2006)?" SELECTED":"" %>>06
    <OPTION VALUE="2007" <%= (expYear == 2007)?" SELECTED":"" %>>07
    <OPTION VALUE="2008" <%= (expYear == 2008)?" SELECTED":"" %>>08
    <OPTION VALUE="2009" <%= (expYear == 2009)?" SELECTED":"" %>>09
    <OPTION VALUE="2010" <%= (expYear == 2010)?" SELECTED":"" %>>10
    <OPTION VALUE="2011" <%= (expYear == 2011)?" SELECTED":"" %>>11
    <OPTION VALUE="2012" <%= (expYear == 2012)?" SELECTED":"" %>>12<P>
</SELECT><P>
<H3>Credit Card Billing Address</H3><P>

<% if (ccaddr.getFieldError("firstName") != null) { %>
<FONT COLOR="#FF0000"><%= ccaddr.getFieldError("firstName")%></FONT><BR>
<% } %>

<% if (ccaddr.getFieldError("lastName") != null) { %>
<FONT COLOR="#FF0000"><%= ccaddr.getFieldError("lastName")%></FONT><BR>
<% } %>

First Name: <INPUT NAME="ccFirstName" TYPE="TEXT" SIZE=30
        VALUE="<%= ccaddr.getFirstName() %>">
Last Name: <INPUT NAME="ccLastName" TYPE="TEXT" SIZE=40
        VALUE="<%= ccaddr.getLastName() %>"><BR>

<% if (ccaddr.getFieldError("street1") != null) { %>
<FONT COLOR="#FF0000"><%= ccaddr.getFieldError("street1")%></FONT><BR>
```

LISTING 12.9   Continued

```
<% } %>


Street Addr 1: <INPUT NAME="ccStreet1" TYPE="TEXT" SIZE=80
        VALUE="<%= ccaddr.getStreet1() %>"><BR>
Street Addr 2: <INPUT NAME="ccStreet2" TYPE="TEXT" SIZE=80
        VALUE="<%= ccaddr.getStreet2() %>"><BR>


<% if (ccaddr.getFieldError("city") != null) { %>
<FONT COLOR="#FF0000"><%= ccaddr.getFieldError("city")%></FONT><BR>
<% } %>


<% if (ccaddr.getFieldError("state") != null) { %>
<FONT COLOR="#FF0000"><%= ccaddr.getFieldError("state")%></FONT><BR>
<% } %>


<% if (ccaddr.getFieldError("postalCode") != null) { %>
<FONT COLOR="#FF0000"><%= ccaddr.getFieldError("postalCode")%></FONT><BR>
<% } %>


City: <INPUT NAME="ccCity" TYPE="TEXT" SIZE=50
        VALUE="<%= ccaddr.getCity() %>">
State: <INPUT NAME="ccState" TYPE="TEXT" SIZE=2
        VALUE="<%= ccaddr.getState() %>">
Postal Code: <INPUT NAME="ccPostalCode" TYPE="TEXT" SIZE=10
        VALUE="<%= ccaddr.getPostalCode() %>"><P>
Select Card From Wallet: <SELECT NAME="selectedCCId">
<OPTION VALUE="NEW">New Card
<%
Iterator it = customer.getWallet().keySet().iterator();
while (it.hasNext()) {
    CreditCard cc = (CreditCard) customer.getWallet().get((Integer)it.next());
%>
    <OPTION VALUE="<%= cc.getCardID() %>"><%= cc.getCardType() %>:
➥<%= cc.getObscuredNumber() %>
<% } %>
</SELECT><P> -- or -- <P>
<% } else { %>
<INPUT TYPE="HIDDEN" NAME="selectedCCId" VALUE="NEW">
<% }
}
<% if (loggedInUser) { %>
```

LISTING 12.9   Continued

```
<INPUT TYPE="CHECKBOX" NAME="createCC" VALUE="yes"> Add to Wallet<P>
<% } %>
<H2>Shipping Address</H2>
<% if (loggedInUser) {
    if (customer.getAddressBook().size() > 0) {
%>
Select Address from Address Book: <SELECT NAME="selectedAddrId">
<OPTION VALUE="NEW">New Address
<%
Iterator it = customer.getAddressBook().keySet().iterator();
while (it.hasNext()) {
    Address ad = (Address) customer.getAddressBook().get((Integer)it.next());
%>
    <OPTION VALUE="<%= ad.getAddressID() %>"><%= ad.getFirstName() %>
              <%= ad.getLastName() %> (<%= ad.getCity() %>,
              <%= ad.getState() %>)
<% } %>
</SELECT><P> -- or -- <P>
<% } else { %>
<INPUT TYPE="HIDDEN" NAME="selectedAddrId" VALUE="NEW">
<% }
}

if (orderaddr.getFieldError("firstName") != null) { %>
<FONT COLOR="#FF0000"><%= orderaddr.getFieldError("firstName")%></FONT><BR>
<% } %>

<% if (orderaddr.getFieldError("lastName") != null) { %>
<FONT COLOR="#FF0000"><%= orderaddr.getFieldError("lastName")%></FONT><BR>
<% } %>

First Name: <INPUT NAME="firstName" TYPE="TEXT" SIZE=30
       VALUE="<%= orderaddr.getFirstName() %>">
Last Name: <INPUT NAME="lastName" TYPE="TEXT" SIZE=40
       VALUE="<%= orderaddr.getLastName() %>"><BR>

<% if (orderaddr.getFieldError("street1") != null) { %>
<FONT COLOR="#FF0000"><%= orderaddr.getFieldError("street1")%></FONT><BR>
<% } %>

Street Addr 1: <INPUT NAME="street1" TYPE="TEXT" SIZE=80
```

LISTING 12.9   Continued

```
        VALUE="<%= orderaddr.getStreet1() %>"><BR>
Street Addr 2: <INPUT NAME="street2" TYPE="TEXT" SIZE=80
        VALUE="<%= orderaddr.getStreet2() %>"><BR>

<% if (orderaddr.getFieldError("city") != null) { %>
<FONT COLOR="#FF0000"><%= orderaddr.getFieldError("city")%></FONT><BR>
<% } %>

<% if (orderaddr.getFieldError("state") != null) { %>
<FONT COLOR="#FF0000"><%= orderaddr.getFieldError("state")%></FONT><BR>
<% } %>

<% if (orderaddr.getFieldError("postalCode") != null) { %>
<FONT COLOR="#FF0000"><%= orderaddr.getFieldError("postalCode")%></FONT><BR>
<% } %>

City: <INPUT NAME="city" TYPE="TEXT" SIZE=50
        VALUE="<%= orderaddr.getCity() %>">
State: <INPUT NAME="state" TYPE="TEXT" SIZE=2
        VALUE="<%= orderaddr.getState() %>">
Postal Code: <INPUT NAME="postalCode" TYPE="TEXT" SIZE=10
        VALUE="<%= orderaddr.getPostalCode() %>"><P>
<% if (loggedInUser) { %>
<INPUT TYPE="CHECKBOX" NAME="createShip" VALUE="yes"> Add to Address Book<P>
<% } %>
<INPUT TYPE=SUBMIT>
</FORM>
<%@ include file="/jsp/includes/bfgfooter.jsp" %>
```

The page begins by getting a few useful values, such as whether the user is logged in and whether he has selected an existing credit card or address.

If the form has been submitted, the page needs to place the credit card address information in the associated values in ccaddr. This has the effect of doing a jsp:setProperty.

If you were passed a selected credit card ID, turn it from a String to an Integer and check to see whether that ID exists in the customer's wallet (of course, if the customer didn't log in, the wallet is empty). Because the code checks for the ID in the wallet, customers are prevented from specifying credit cards that they don't own. The same deal applies with the address. Note that you need to set the session-scoped variable to the new value, or it won't be updated on the next page.

If you just did `test1 && test2 && test3`, the second and third validations would not be run if the first one failed because of the way `&&` works. So, you should run the validations individually and then check the results.

If everything is okay with the validations, the page checks to see if it's supposed to create a new entry in the address book or wallet. If so, it creates the entries and inserts them. Finally, it moves the user to the final confirmation page with a redirect.

If this is the customer's first time in the form (not submitted), the code needs to clear out any old session-scoped order information so that it isn't displayed. And, ah yes, as usual, the page clears out the nulls so that they don't appear on the form.

The actual form starts at this point. Have the page check to see whether there are any entries in the wallet. If not, there's no sense in displaying the pull-down menu of choices.

If there is something in the wallet and you want the customer to have choices, have the page exhibit a pull-down menu with the default NEW item. The customer can fill in the form and choose from a list of existing credit cards (with numbers obscured, of course.)

Assuming that the customer isn't picking from an existing card in the wallet, he'll fill in the field for the credit card. Note that you have to name the fields with the names similar to `ccFirstName` so they don't conflict with the shipping address fields.

You also need to have the page to offer the customer a check box to save the credit card to his wallet. Now you need to write a similar code for the shipping address. See if the customer is logged in. If so, offer a list of addresses to choose from.

If the customer successfully fills in the checkout form, the page should give a final confirmation, as shown in Figure 12.3.

Final Confirmation

The code for the final conformation (given in Listing 12.10) itself is a duplicate of the shopping cart page, with the following changes:

- The quantity is always static rather than a fill-in value.

- Now that the application knows where it's being shipped to, you can have it add tax and shipping to the totals.

- The form submits to the credit card authorization page.

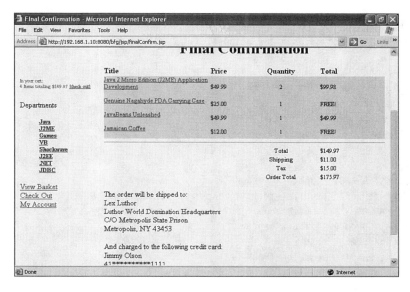

FIGURE 12.3   The final confirmation page.

LISTING 12.10   finalConfirm.jsp

```
<%@ include file="/jsp/cust/AutoLogin.jsp" %>
<%@ page import="com.bfg.product.Product" %>
<%@ page import="java.util.Iterator" %>
<%@ page import="com.bfg.cart.CartItem" %>
<jsp:useBean id="orderaddr" class="com.bfg.customer.Address" scope="session"/>
<jsp:useBean id="ordercredit" class="com.bfg.customer.CreditCard" scope="session"/>
<HEAD>
<TITLE>Final Confirmation</TITLE>
</HEAD>
<BODY>

<%@ include file="/jsp/includes/bfgheader.jsp" %>
<jsp:useBean id="cart" class="com.bfg.cart.Cart" scope="session"/>
<CENTER><H1>Final Confirmation</H1></CENTER>
<FORM METHOD="POST" ACTION="authorizePurchase.jsp">
<table border="0" cellpadding="0" cellspacing="0" style="border-collapse: collapse"
bordercolor="#111111" width="100%">
  <tr>
    <th width="38%" height="23" align="left">Title</th>
    <th width="11%" height="23" align="left">Price</th>
    <th width="28%" height="23" align="center">Quantity</td>
```

LISTING 12.10   Continued

```
    <th width="23%" height="23" align="left">Total</th>
  </tr>
    <%
    Iterator iter = cart.getItems();
    while (iter.hasNext()) {
      CartItem item = (CartItem) iter.next();
      Product prod = item.getProduct();
%>
  <tr>
    <td width="38%" bgcolor="#00FFFF">
    <font style="font-size: 10.0pt; font-family: Times New Roman">
        <A HREF="product/Product.jsp?ISBN=<%= prod.getISBN() %>">
        <%= prod.getTitle() %></A>
    </span><BR><BR></td>
    <td width="11%" bgcolor="#00FFFF">
    <span style="font-size: 10.0pt; font-family: Times New Roman">
    <%= prod.getPriceString() %>
    </span></td>
    <td width="28%" bgcolor="#00FFFF">
    <p align="center"><font size="2">
    <%= item.getQuantity() %>
    </font></td>
    <td width="23%" bgcolor="#00FFFF">
    <span style="font-size: 10.0pt; font-family: Times New Roman">
    <%= item.getLineItemPriceString() %>
    </span></td>
  </tr>
        <% } %>
<TR><TD COLSPAN=4><HR></TD></TR>
<TR><TD> </TD>
<TD> </TD>
<TD ALIGN="center">
<span style="font-size: 10.0pt; font-family: Times New Roman">
    Total
</span></TD>
  <TD>
<span style="font-size: 10.0pt; font-family: Times New Roman">
 <%= cart.getTotalString()%>
</span></TD></TR>
<TR><TD> </TD>
<TD> </TD>
<TD ALIGN="center">
<span style="font-size: 10.0pt; font-family: Times New Roman">
```

LISTING 12.10   Continued

```
      Shipping
  </span></TD>
    <TD>
  <span style="font-size: 10.0pt; font-family: Times New Roman">
   <%= cart.getShippingString(orderaddr)%>
  </span></TD></TR>
  <TR><TD> </TD>
  <TD> </TD>
  <TD ALIGN="center">
  <span style="font-size: 10.0pt; font-family: Times New Roman">
      Tax
  </span></TD>
    <TD>
  <span style="font-size: 10.0pt; font-family: Times New Roman">
   <%= cart.getTaxString(orderaddr)%>
  </span></TD></TR>
  <TR><TD> </TD>
  <TD> </TD>
  <TD ALIGN="center">
  <span style="font-size: 10.0pt; font-family: Times New Roman">
      Order Total
  </span></TD>
    <TD>
  <span style="font-size: 10.0pt; font-family: Times New Roman">
   <%= cart.getGrandTotalString(orderaddr)%>
  </span></TD></TR>
</TABLE>
<P>
The order will be shipped to:<BR>
<%= orderaddr.getFirstName() %> <%= orderaddr.getLastName() %><BR>
<%= orderaddr.getStreet1() %><BR>
<%= orderaddr.getStreet2() %><BR>
<%= orderaddr.getCity() %>, <%= orderaddr.getState() %> <%= orderaddr.getPostal
➥Code() %><P>
And charged to the following credit card:<BR>
<%= ordercredit.getCardOwner() %><BR>
<%= ordercredit.getObscuredNumber() %><P>
<INPUT TYPE=SUBMIT NAME="confirm" VALUE="Confirm Order"><P>
</FORM>

<%@ include file="/jsp/includes/bfgfooter.jsp" %>

</BODY>
```

The Last Mile

As you might imagine, business logic can be the most troublesome part of software development because it needs to conform to the (sometimes illogical) needs of your customer rather than to some pure computer science concept.

When developing business logic, try to place as much of the ruleset into some kind of database or other easily changeable form rather than in the code. In the example of promotions, this was done by reading the promotions from a table.

If a given piece of business-related functionality isn't available at the time that you are writing dependent codes, stub it out with a testing switch so that you can proceed, and make sure that the code flags an error if you try to go live before the actual code is in place.

With this code in place, you've run 25 miles of the marathon. All that needs to be done now is to actually validate the charge (which will again be stubbed out), record the order, and send an order confirmation.

This is what you'll do in the next chapter. You'll also look at order history, order fulfillment, and a general wrap-up of the application and where it could go from there.

13

Completing the Application

The site is almost complete, but there are a number of details still yet to implement to make it a fully functioning application.

In this chapter, you'll learn how to handle important integrations such as credit card authorization. In addition, you'll learn the difference between well-commented code and overcommented code, and you'll learn what needs to be done to make a site truly turn-key.

Charging the Credit Card

Until now, you've done everything you need to do for the site except actually let a customer pay for a purchase. Some might consider this to be a minor oversight, but it's funny how the folks in accounting get a bit upset if they don't see revenue flowing in. So, to keep them happy, you should probably implement credit card authorization.

As has already happened several times, reconsidering the original design in light of what has been learned during development leads to some redesign. For one thing, the original schema for the table to record orders is needlessly redundant with tables that you already have in the database, and it can be simplified a great deal. You can do this by storing the credit card number, credit card address, and shipping address for the order in the CREDIT_CARD and ADDRESS tables that you already have—almost.

There is no problem as far as the addresses go because those tables use cross-references between the customer and the shipping address. So, writing new addresses into the database without cross-referenced entries will keep the entries from showing up in the customer's address book. Otherwise, every time an order is saved, a duplicate copy of the shipping and billing addresses would show up in the address book.

Things are a bit more complicated for credit cards. Assuming that you want to use the existing `createCreditCard` to write a new record for the credit card associated with the order, you'll run into trouble. Because the relationship between credit cards and customers is identified using a key on the credit card that points to the customer ID, you would end up with duplicate credit cards in the wallet if the code just wrote out an exact copy of the credit card record when it stored the order information.

One solution to the credit card duplication is to go back and implement credit cards the same as addresses—with a cross-reference for the card already in the wallet. This is more work than most people would like to tackle in already running code, if it can be avoided. Thankfully, when you created the CREDIT_CARD table, you didn't make CUSTOMER_KEY a NOT NULL field. This means that if you write out the credit card records for the orders with a NULL in that position, those numbers will never be seen in a wallet but can be referenced by `CARD_ID` from the ORDERS table.

Remember, the reason you need to record all this information is that you need to keep a snapshot of the billing and shipping addresses and the credit card information as they were on the day the order was taken, even if they are changed in the address book or wallet later. Listing 13.1 shows the revised ORDERS table.

LISTING 13.1   Revised Schema for ORDERS

```
create table ORDERS (
      ORDER_ID           int not null auto_increment,
      EMAIL_ADDRESS char(50),
      ADDRESS_KEY   int references ADDRESS,
      CARD_KEY           int references CREDIT_CARD,
      ORDER_DATE       date,
      ORDER_SUBTOTAL   float,
      ORDER_TAX        float,
      ORDER_SHIPPING   float,
      ORDER_TOTAL      float,
      primary key(ORDER_ID));
```

All the explicit address and credit card fields have been replaced with references to the appropriate tables. The only things explicitly recorded are the various totals and taxes.

With the new schema in place, you can write an order bean to represent the database schema in Java (see Listing 13.2).

LISTING 13.2   Order.java

```
package com.bfg.product;

import java.util.Vector;
import java.util.HashMap;
import java.util.Iterator;
import java.text.NumberFormat;
import java.sql.*;
import org.apache.log4j.Category;
import org.apache.turbine.services.db.TurbineDB;
import org.apache.turbine.util.db.pool.DBConnection;
import com.bfg.product.Product;
import java.util.ResourceBundle;
import com.bfg.customer.*;
import com.bfg.product.*;
import com.bfg.exceptions.*;
import com.bfg.cart.*;
import javax.naming.NamingException;
import javax.naming.Context;
import javax.naming.InitialContext;
import javax.naming.NamingEnumeration;
import javax.naming.directory.InitialDirContext;
import javax.mail.internet.InternetAddress;
import javax.mail.internet.MimeMessage;
import javax.mail.internet.AddressException;
import javax.mail.Message;
import javax.mail.Session;
import javax.mail.MessagingException;
import javax.mail.Transport;
import javax.servlet.http.*;
import com.braju.format.*;

public class Order {
    private static ResourceBundle sql_bundle =
      ResourceBundle.getBundle("com.bfg.product.SQLQueries");

    private static ResourceBundle email_bundle =
      ResourceBundle.getBundle("com.bfg.emailProperties");
```

LISTING 13.2   Continued

```
static Category cat = Category.getInstance(Order.class);

protected Vector items = new Vector();

public Vector getItems() {
  return items;
}

public void setItems(Vector it) {
  items = it;
}

protected Customer customer;

public Customer getCustomer() {
  return customer;
}

public void setCustomer(Customer c) {
  customer = c;
}

protected Address orderaddr;

public Address getAddress() {
  return orderaddr;
}

public void setAddress(Address addr) {
  orderaddr = addr;
}

protected CreditCard ordercard;

public CreditCard getCreditCard() {
  return ordercard;
}

public void setCreditCard(CreditCard cc) {
  ordercard = cc;
```

LISTING 13.2   Continued

```java
  }

  protected int orderNumber;

  public int getOrderNumber() {
    return orderNumber;
  }

  public void setOrderNumber(int n) {
    orderNumber = n;
  }

  protected Date orderDate;

  public Date getOrderDate() {
    return orderDate;
  }

  public void setOrderDate(Date d) {
    orderDate = d;
  }

  protected double orderSubtotal;

  public double getOrderSubtotal() {
    return orderSubtotal;
  }

  public String getOrderSubtotalString() {
    NumberFormat nf = NumberFormat.getCurrencyInstance();
    return nf.format(getOrderSubtotal());
  }

  public void setOrderSubtotal(double t) {
    orderSubtotal = t;
  }

  protected double orderTax;

  public double getOrderTax () {
    return orderTax;
```

LISTING 13.2   Continued

```java
    }

    public String getOrderTaxString() {
      NumberFormat nf = NumberFormat.getCurrencyInstance();
      return nf.format(getOrderTax());
    }

    public void setOrderTax (double v) {
      orderTax = v;
    }

    protected double orderShipping;

    public double getOrderShipping () {
      return orderShipping;
    }

    public String getOrderShippingString() {
      NumberFormat nf = NumberFormat.getCurrencyInstance();
      return nf.format(getOrderShipping());
    }

    public void setOrderShipping (double v) {
      orderShipping = v;
    }

    protected double orderTotal;

    public double getOrderTotal () {
      return orderTotal;
    }

    public String getOrderTotalString() {
      NumberFormat nf = NumberFormat.getCurrencyInstance();
      return nf.format(getOrderTotal());
    }

    public void setOrderTotal (double v) {
      orderTotal = v;
    }
    public Order() {
```

LISTING 13.2   Continued

```
    super();
}

public Order(Customer cust, Address ad, CreditCard cc, Cart cart) {
  super();
  setAddress(ad);
  setCreditCard(cc);
  setCustomer(cust);
  Iterator item_it = cart.getItems();
  while (item_it.hasNext()) {
      CartItem item = (CartItem) item_it.next();
      items.add(item);
  }
  setOrderSubtotal(cart.getTotal());
  setOrderTotal(cart.getGrandTotal(ad));
  setOrderShipping(cart.getShipping(ad));
  setOrderTax(cart.getTax(ad));
}
public void recordOrder()
  throws Exception {
  DBConnection dbConn = null;
  try
      {
          dbConn = TurbineDB.getConnection();
          if (dbConn == null) {
              cat.error("Can't get database connection");
              throw new Exception();
          }
          Address ad = (Address) getAddress().clone();
          CreditCard cc = (CreditCard) getCreditCard().clone();
          cc.setAddress((Address) cc.getAddress().clone());

          ad.createAddress();
          cc.getAddress().createAddress();
          cc.setCustomer(null);
          cc.createCreditCard();

          PreparedStatement pstmt =
              dbConn.prepareStatement(sql_bundle.getString("createOrder"));
          pstmt.setString(1, getCustomer().getEmail());
          pstmt.setInt(2, ad.getAddressID());
```

LISTING 13.2   Continued

```java
            pstmt.setInt(3, cc.getCardID());
            pstmt.setDouble(4, getOrderSubtotal());
            pstmt.setDouble(5, getOrderTax());
            pstmt.setDouble(6, getOrderShipping());
            pstmt.setDouble(7, getOrderTotal());
            pstmt.executeUpdate();
            pstmt.close();
            pstmt =
                dbConn.prepareStatement(sql_bundle.getString("getOrderID"));
            ResultSet rs = pstmt.executeQuery();
            if (rs.next()) {
                setOrderNumber(rs.getInt(1));
            } else {
                cat.error("Couldn't find record for new Order");
                throw new Exception();
            }
            rs.close();
            pstmt.close();
            Iterator items = getItems().iterator();
            pstmt =
                dbConn.prepareStatement(sql_bundle.getString("addOrderItem"));
            while (items.hasNext()) {
                CartItem item = (CartItem) items.next();
                pstmt.setInt(1, getOrderNumber());
                pstmt.setString(2, item.getProduct().getISBN());
                pstmt.setString(3, item.getProduct().getTitle());
                pstmt.setInt(4, item.getQuantity());
                pstmt.setDouble(5, item.getProduct().getPrice());
                pstmt.setDouble(6, item.getLineItemPrice());
                pstmt.executeUpdate();
            }
            pstmt.close();
            setOrderDate(new java.sql.Date(new java.util.Date().getTime()));
        }
    catch (Exception e)
            {
                cat.error("Error during createOrder", e);
                throw new CustomerActivityException();
            }
    finally
        {
```

LISTING 13.2   Continued

```
            try
                {
                    TurbineDB.releaseConnection(dbConn);
                }
            catch (Exception e)
                {
                    cat.error("Error during release connection", e);
                }
        }
    }
    public static Order findOrder(int orderNumber)
      throws Exception {
      Order order = null;
      DBConnection dbConn = null;
      try
        {
            dbConn = TurbineDB.getConnection();
            if (dbConn == null) {
                cat.error("Can't get database connection");
                throw new Exception();
            }
            PreparedStatement pstmt =
                dbConn.prepareStatement(sql_bundle.getString("findOrder"));
            pstmt.setInt(1, orderNumber);
            ResultSet rs = pstmt.executeQuery();
            if (!rs.next()) {
                rs.close();
                pstmt.close();
                return null;
            }
            order = new Order();
            order.setOrderNumber(rs.getInt("ORDER_ID"));
            order.setAddress(Address.findAddress(rs.getInt("ADDRESS_KEY")));

order.setCreditCard(CreditCard.findCreditCard(rs.getInt("CARD_KEY")));
            order.setOrderDate(rs.getDate("ORDER_DATE"));
            order.setOrderSubtotal(rs.getDouble("ORDER_SUBTOTAL"));
            order.setOrderTax(rs.getDouble("ORDER_TAX"));
            order.setOrderShipping(rs.getDouble("ORDER_SHIPPING"));
            order.setOrderTotal(rs.getDouble("ORDER_TOTAL"));
```

LISTING 13.2   Continued

```
order.setCustomer(Customer.findCustomer(rs.getString("EMAIL_ADDRESS")));
            rs.close();
            pstmt.close();
            pstmt =
                dbConn.prepareStatement(sql_bundle.getString("getOrderItems"));
            pstmt.setInt(1, orderNumber);
            rs = pstmt.executeQuery();
            while (rs.next()) {
                CartItem item = new CartItem();
                Product product = new Product();
                item.setProduct(product);
                item.setQuantity(rs.getInt("QUANTITY"));
                product.setISBN(rs.getString("PRODUCT_ISBN"));
                product.setTitle(rs.getString("PRODUCT_TITLE"));
                product.setPrice(rs.getDouble("UNIT_PRICE"));
                double totalPrice = rs.getDouble("TOTAL_PRICE");
                if (totalPrice == 0F) {
                    item.setPromotionItem(true);
                }
                order.getItems().add(item);
            }
            rs.close();
            pstmt.close();
        }
    catch (Exception e)
        {
            cat.error("Error during createOrder", e);
            throw new CustomerActivityException();
        }
    finally
        {
            try
                {
                    TurbineDB.releaseConnection(dbConn);
                }
            catch (Exception e)
                {
                    cat.error("Error during release connection", e);
                }
        }
```

LISTING 13.2   Continued

```
      return order;
    }
    public void emailReceipt(String email)
      throws NamingException, AddressException, MessagingException {
      Context initCtx = new InitialContext();
      Context envCtx = (Context) initCtx.lookup("java:comp/env");
      Session session = (Session) envCtx.lookup("mail/session");

      Message message = new MimeMessage(session);
      message.setFrom(new InternetAddress(email_bundle.getString("fromAddr")));
      InternetAddress to[] = new InternetAddress[1];
      to[0] = new InternetAddress(email);
      message.setRecipients(Message.RecipientType.TO, to);
      message.setSubject("Receipt for order " + getOrderNumber());
      StringBuffer contents = new StringBuffer();
      contents.append("Thank you for shopping at Books for Geeks.\n\n");
      contents.append("Here is the receipt for your order " + getOrderNumber() +
                      " placed on " + getOrderDate() + "\n\n");
      contents.append("CODE        TITLE                          QUANT  PRICE
TOTAL\n");

contents.append("=================================================================\n
");
      Iterator items = getItems().iterator();
      while (items.hasNext()) {
          CartItem it = (CartItem) items.next();
          Parameters p = new Parameters();
          p.add(it.getProduct().getISBN());
          p.add(it.getProduct().getTitle());
          p.add(it.getQuantity());
          p.add(it.getProduct().getPrice());
          p.add(it.getLineItemPrice());
          contents.append(Format.sprintf("%-10.10s  %-30.30s  %2d     $%5.2f
$%5.2f\n", p));
      }
      message.setContent(contents.toString(), "text/plain");
      Transport.send(message);
    }

}
```

Two bundles are needed here: the SQL bundle for your various queries and the e-mail bundle last used for the lost password code so that order confirmations can be sent.

Two versions of the constructor are provided: one used internally here and a helper version that takes a customer, address, credit card, and cart and then copies all the values to local properties.

There are a few things to note about the recordOrder method (which writes the order to the database). First, the code starts by cloning the addresses and credit card information. This is because you want it to pass them to the create methods to put new ones in the database; you wouldn't want the method to somehow damage the existing ones in the wallet and address book as a side effect.

After recordOrder writes the main ORDERS record, it records all the individual items in ORDER_ITEM. Remember, the whole purpose of this exercise is to preserve order details from changes in the underlying product or customer information, such as a change of address or product price. The ORDERS table records the exact order information as it was entered on the day the order was placed.

findOrder is the mirror of recordOrder. The only thing of note here is that you want to properly preserve the promotion flags. This is done by checking the line item price of the items to see if they are 0. If so, the code sets the promotion flag. This makes them render correctly when displayed in order history.

After the site has recorded the order, you'll want it to e-mail out a receipt. This code works much the same as the lost password code until you get into the body of the message.

One of the things that I miss most about C when I work in Java is sprintf. It's so handy for getting lines of text lined up, especially when doing things like plain-text receipts. Along with atoi, it's the thing I spend the most time coding around. Luckily, there are now public sprintf clones available so that I don't have to do without its capabilities. In this case, I'm using a version written by a programmer named Henrik Bengtsson, which can be obtained from http://www.braju.com/. Because it comes as a ZIP file, you must unzip it to a directory and then JAR it back up in a .jar file; then you can put it in your \TOMCAT\LIB directory and take advantage of it.

One caution regarding this library: Unlike some freeware products, Bengtsson has released the sprintf code for free use only for noncommercial applications. If you were going to deploy a real e-commerce site using it, you would have to contact him to arrange licensing. Typically, for a small library like this, the cost runs less than $100, but you should double-check before you become too dependant on it.

It works almost the same as the C version, except that instead of passing the arguments as a variable argument list to sprintf itself, you build a parameter list with the arguments and hand it in as a single argument. Bengtsson's Web site gives some good examples of how to use the products, but it is pretty clear cut, as emailReceipt shows.

You might recall that recordOrder requires Address and CreditCard to support the clone operation.

To use the clone operation with an object, the class must implement the Cloneable interface. Normally, you simply add implements Cloneable to the class definition, but, unfortunately, the clone method is protected by default, so you need to wrap it in a public method if you want other classes to be able to take advantage of it. Listing 13.3 shows how to do it for the Address class.

LISTING 13.3   Additions to Address.java

```
public class Address implements Cloneable {
.
.
.
    public Object clone() throws java.lang.CloneNotSupportedException {
      return super.clone();
    }
```

We also need to implement clone for the CreditCard class. In addition, you need to make a small change in createCreditCard to allow the customer to be null (for the credit cards written by the order). If you don't, you will get an exception when the method tries to do getCustomer.getCustomerId(). Listing 13.4 shows the changes.

LISTING 13.4   Additions to CreditCard.java

```
public class CreditCard implements Cloneable {
.
.
.
                if (getCustomer() == null) {
                    pstmt.setNull(1, java.sql.Types.INTEGER);
                } else {
                    pstmt.setInt(1, getCustomer().getCustomerId());
                }
.
.
.
    public Object clone() throws java.lang.CloneNotSupportedException {
      return super.clone();
    }
```

A few things need to be added to the cart (see Listing 13.5). One is a stub credit card authorization method, which, for your purposes, will always return `true`. You also need a method to clear the cart after the order is recorded.

LISTING 13.5   Additions to Cart.java

```
import com.bfg.customer.CreditCard;
.

.

.

    public boolean authorizeCharge(CreditCard cc) {
      return true;
    }

    public void clear() {
      contents.clear();
    }
```

Finally, you need the new SQL statements added to the SQLQueries properties file (see Listing 13.6).

LISTING 13.6   New SQLQueries Entries

```
createOrder=INSERT INTO ORDERS (EMAIL_ADDRESS, ADDRESS_KEY, CARD_KEY, ORDER_SUBTO
➥TAL, \
                                ORDER_TAX, ORDER_SHIPPING, ORDER_TOTAL, ORDER_DATE)
VALUES \
                                (?, ?, ?, ?, ?, ?, ?, NOW());
getOrderID=SELECT LAST_INSERT_ID()
addOrderItem=INSERT INTO ORDER_ITEM (ORDER_ID, PRODUCT_ISBN, PRODUCT_TITLE, \
                                QUANTITY, UNIT_PRICE, TOTAL_PRICE) VALUES \
                                (?, ?, ?, ?, ?, ?)
findOrder=SELECT * FROM ORDERS WHERE ORDER_ID=?
getOrderItems=SELECT * FROM ORDER_ITEM WHERE ORDER_ID=?
```

About Credit Cards

Credit card processing is an arcane subject that could easily consume a chapter all by itself. Thankfully for those of us who have to implement credit card handling, it's a lot simpler than it used to be. Until recently, interfacing to a credit card authorization system involved dealing with C-based libraries that had to be coerced to communicate with Java. Now most major players in the authorization business offer native Java interfaces to their systems.

Let's start by talking about the players that take part in a credit card transaction:

- **The merchant**—That's you or your client, the entity (company or individual) that is selling something.

- **The gateway provider**—This is the company providing software and infra-structure to allow you to process charges.

- **The processor**—This is a large company that handles the actual charge against the credit card and transfer of the funds into the merchant's bank.

- **The bank**—This is the place where the money eventually ends up.

When you, as a merchant, want to offer credit card services, you need to set up a business relationship with a processor. At the time of this writing, there were basi-cally four in the United States: First Data, Nova, Visanet, and Paymentech. They all essentially work the same. However, unless you're doing a huge (tens of thousands of transactions a month) volume, they are too expensive to work with directly. So, you should approach a gateway provider, one that aggregates charges for a number of merchants and thus provides larger chunks of business to the processor.

Of course, nothing comes for free. The gateway provider will take another slice of the transaction, in addition to the 2 to 5 percent that the processor takes. It's worth shopping around. I've seen quotes between $200 and $25,000 a month for the same service from different providers.

Another thing to look at when choosing a provider is the quality and simplicity of its API. If a provider doesn't have a native Java API, just walk away from the table. If it does, ask for a test account and try it out.

In your example, a very simple stubbed authorization routine has been done. Listing 13.7 shows a real piece of code from a live e-commerce site interfacing to the API used by Plug & Pay Technologies.

LISTING 13.7   An Example of Interfacing to a Credit Card Provider

```
    public static Properties authorizeCharge(String cardHolder, String cardNumber,
String cardExp,
                                       String cardAddress1,String cardAddress2,
String cardCity,
                                       String cardState, String cardZip,
                                       float amount) {

    DecimalFormat df = new DecimalFormat("###0.00");

    Properties pairs = new Properties();
```

LISTING 13.7   Continued

```
pnpapi pnp = new pnpapi();

String cert_dir = sql_bundle.getString("cert_dir");
String publisher_name = sql_bundle.getString("publisher_name");
String publisher_email = sql_bundle.getString("publisher_email");
boolean debug = sql_bundle.getString("mode").equals("debug");
pairs.put("cert_dir", cert_dir);
pairs.put("publisher-name", publisher_name);
pairs.put("mode","auth");
if (debug) {
    pairs.put("card-name", "pnptest");
} else {
    pairs.put("card-name", cardHolder);
}
pairs.put("card-number", cardNumber);
pairs.put("card-address1", cardAddress1);
pairs.put("card-address2", cardAddress2);
pairs.put("card-city", cardCity);
pairs.put("card-state", cardState);
pairs.put("card-zip", cardZip);
pairs.put("card-country","US");
pairs.put("card-amount", df.format(amount));
pairs.put("card-exp", cardExp);
pairs.put("publisher-email", publisher_email);

Properties results = new Properties();
results = pnp.doTransaction(pairs);

Iterator vals = results.keySet().iterator();

return results;
}
```

Listing 13.8 shows the method in action in a JSP page:

LISTING 13.8   Using authorizeCharge

```
Properties authorization =
            PlugAndPay.authorizeCharge(cardHolder, cardNumber,
            cardExpires, cardAddress1, cardAddress2, cardCity,
```

LISTING 13.8   Continued

```
                    cardState, cardZip, charge_total);

if (!authorization.getProperty("success").equals("yes")) {
    response.sendRedirect("/jsp/declined.jsp");
} else {
    values.put(x.getElement("transaction_id"),
                authorization.getProperty("orderID"));
    values.put(x.getElement("transaction_date"),
                authorization.getProperty("auth_date"));
    values.put(x.getElement("transaction_id"),
                authorization.getProperty("orderID"));
    values.put(x.getElement("charge_amount"),
                authorization.getProperty("card-amount"));
```

Essentially, all it does is marshal up the information needed for the authorization, hand it to the API, and then demarshal the results afterward.

You usually have the choice of how detailed and specific you want the authorization to be, from a simple card validation all the way up to full address and phone number checks. Remember that the more you check, the more likely that simple, harmless typos will cause the order to fail. On the other hand, the more you check, the less likely someone will run a bogus charge. The amount of caution that you want to take in a "high-turnback" environment—such as the adult entertainment industry—is a lot greater than you'd need for an insurance premium application.

You can do other things with most APIs, such as issue credits and get reports. Obviously, you want to make sure that these can't be called spuriously or maliciously.

It's worth writing your code in a somewhat modular fashion so that changing credit card authorization companies doesn't require a complete rewrite of your code. When working on some of my projects, we changed companies three times during development.

Completing the Order

With the beans in place to record orders and authorize credit cards, you can write the JSP to run the credit card and complete the order (see Listing 13.9).

LISTING 13.9   authorizePurchase.jsp

```jsp
<%@ include file="/jsp/cust/AutoLogin.jsp" %>
<%@ page import="com.bfg.product.Product" %>
<%@ page import="com.bfg.product.Order" %>
<%@ page import="java.util.Iterator" %>
<%@ page import="com.bfg.cart.CartItem" %>
<jsp:useBean id="orderaddr" class="com.bfg.customer.Address" scope="session"/>
<jsp:useBean id="ordercredit" class="com.bfg.customer.CreditCard" scope="session"/>
<jsp:useBean id="cart" class="com.bfg.cart.Cart" scope="session"/>
<jsp:useBean id="customer" class="com.bfg.customer.Customer" scope="session"/>

<%
if (!cart.authorizeCharge(ordercredit)) {
    response.sendRedirect("authorizationFailed.jsp");
    return;
}
Order order = new Order(customer, orderaddr, ordercredit, cart);
order.recordOrder();
order.emailReceipt(customer.getEmail());
cart.clear();
pageContext.setAttribute("orderaddr", null, PageContext.SESSION_SCOPE);
pageContext.setAttribute("ordercredit", null, PageContext.SESSION_SCOPE);

%>
<HEAD>
<TITLE>Order Receipt</TITLE>
</HEAD>
<BODY>

<%@ include file="/jsp/includes/bfgheader.jsp" %>
<CENTER><H1>Order Receipt</H1></CENTER>

Thank you for your order, your credit card has been charged
<%= order.getOrderTotalString() %>.  Your order number is
<%= order.getOrderNumber() %>.  Please write down this order number in case you
need to refer to the order at a future date. You will also be receiving a copy of
your
receipt via e-Mail.

<%@ include file="/jsp/includes/bfgfooter.jsp" %>
```

After the normal heading items, the page runs the authorization call to see if a successful result is returned. If not, it redirects to a "We Had a Problem with Your Order" page (which is so much more polite than "You're a deadbeat, get lost").

Assuming that your customer has money in the bank, a new order object is created from all of its component elements and is recorded. Then you can have the page send the nice customer a receipt via e-mail.

Finally, you need to have the page clear out the cart contents and make sure that the order information isn't left in the session, where it might possibly end up bleeding through somewhere that it shouldn't.

This last step might seem overcautious, but I've seen real-life examples of platform failures that caused one person's order information to leak into another session. It's just good common sense to purge the cart as soon as it is no longer needed.

If you go to the site and give final confirmation to an order now, you'll see the screen shown in Figure 13.1.

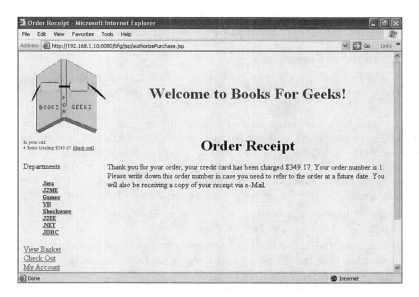

FIGURE 13.1   The order receipt page.

Confirmation will also result in the following e-mail being sent:

```
Return-Path: <turner@blackbear.com>
Received: from JAMES (james [192.168.1.10])
      by linux.blackbear.com (8.11.6/8.11.6) with ESMTP id fAJ4n0H19225
      for <turner@blackbear.com>; Sun, 18 Nov 2001 23:49:01 -0500
```

```
Date: Sun, 18 Nov 2001 23:49:01 -0500
Message-ID: <4544380.1006145340846.JavaMail.james@JAMES>
From: turner@blackbear.com
To: turner@blackbear.com
Subject: Receipt for order 8
Mime-Version: 1.0
Content-Type: text/plain
Content-Transfer-Encoding: 7bit
Status:
Thank you for shopping at Books for Geeks.

Here is the receipt for your order 8 placed on 2001-11-18

CODE          TITLE                          QUANT  PRICE  TOTAL
================================================================
672320959     Java 2 Micro Edition (J2ME) Ap   4    $49.99 $199.96
PALMCASE      Genuine Nagahyde PDA Carrying     1    $25.00 $ 0.00
672321173     Oracle and Java Development       5    $39.99 $199.95
```

FAILING TO HANDLE FAILURE

In almost all cases, all you really need to do as far as exception handling goes in JSP is make sure that you redirect to a friendly failure page rather than spitting Java backtraces all over the page.

You just wrote some code that is the exception to that rule, and you didn't really write it correctly. Consider the following scenario. `authorizeCharge` is called on the cart, and it succeeds. At this point, the customer's card has successfully been charged for the transaction. Now, the next thing the code does is call the `recordOrder` method. What happens if that method throws an exception before the order is recorded in the database (for any number of reasons, including bugs in the code, a database crash, a power failure, and so on)?

That's right—the customer has been charged for an order, but this hasn't been recorded in the database. This is going to lead to a very unhappy customer.

In a perfect world, the code should record the order first with a rollback segment set and then should try to authorize the charge. If it fails, it should roll back the order. But if you want the method to record information such as the credit card authorization number in the order record, this is difficult to do in this order.

Alternatively, you can put a catch around the order record and void the credit card transaction if the recording fails.

Of course, this won't save you from a situation in which the power goes out or the hardware fails before the credit can be issued. In a worst-case scenario, a good gateway provider will have an independent interface that you can use to look at all the charges that have been processed in a given period and match them up against what you have in the database.

Order History

You're down to the last piece of functionality—displaying order history. This is the code on the MyAccount page that will let a customer see his past orders and drill down to a detailed view. To start, you need to add a method to Customer.java (shown in Listing 13.10) to get back a vector of orders for display. Luckily, you already wrote the findOrder code when you created Order.java, so you are already a step ahead.

LISTING 13.10   Addition to Customer.java

```java
import com.bfg.product.Order;
.
.
.
    public Vector getOrderHistory() {
      Vector orders = new Vector();
      DBConnection dbConn = null;
      try
          {
              dbConn = TurbineDB.getConnection();
              if (dbConn == null) {
                  cat.error("Can't get database connection");
              }
              PreparedStatement pstmt =
                  dbConn.prepareStatement(sql_bundle.getString("orderHistory"));
              pstmt.setString(1, getEmail());
              ResultSet rs = pstmt.executeQuery();
              while (rs.next()) {
                  orders.add(Order.findOrder(rs.getInt("ORDER_ID")));
              }
              rs.close();
              pstmt.close();
          }
      catch (Exception e)
          {
              cat.error("Error during getOrderHistory", e);
          }
      finally
          {
              try
                  {
                      TurbineDB.releaseConnection(dbConn);
```

LISTING 13.10   Continued

```
                }
          catch (Exception e)
                {
                     cat.error("Error during release connection", e);
                }
          }
     return orders;
   }
```

Here's the query needed for this method.

`orderHistory=SELECT ORDER_ID FROM ORDERS WHERE EMAIL_ADDRESS=?`

At this point, something that you put into a SQL query string days ago comes back to bite you. The `findCreditCard` query string does a SQL `join` against the CUSTOMER table, even though it doesn't use any fields from it. This means that the order credit cards that you wrote a `null` into for the customer won't be returned from `findCreditCard` when the order is loaded back in. Ah, well, it takes just a moment's work to modify the property file:

`creditQuery=SELECT * FROM CREDIT_CARD WHERE CARD_ID=?`

Now you can add the code to the bottom of MyAccount.jsp to display theprevious orders (see Listing 13.11).

LISTING 13.11   Additions to MyAccount.jsp

```
<%@ page import="com.bfg.product.Order" %>
<%@ page import="java.util.Vector" %>
.
.
.
<center><h2>Order History</h2></center>
<% Vector history = customer.getOrderHistory();

if (history.size() > 0) { %>
<TABLE WIDTH="100%">
  <TR><TH ALIGN="LEFT">Order</TH><TH ALIGN="LEFT">Date</TH>
    <TH ALIGN="LEFT">Amount</TH></TR>
<%
```

LISTING 13.11   Continued

```
Iterator it = history.iterator();
while (it.hasNext()) {
    Order or = (Order) it.next();
%>
        <TR><TD><A HREF="viewOrder.jsp?order=<%= or.getOrderNumber() %>">
            <%= or.getOrderNumber() %> </A></TD>
          <TD><%= or.getOrderDate() %></TD>
          <TD><%= or.getOrderTotalString() %></TD></TR>
<% } %>
</TABLE>
<% } %>
```

There's not much to this piece. It gets a list of orders and displays a summary in table form with a link to viewOrder.jsp. The results are shown in Figure 13.2.

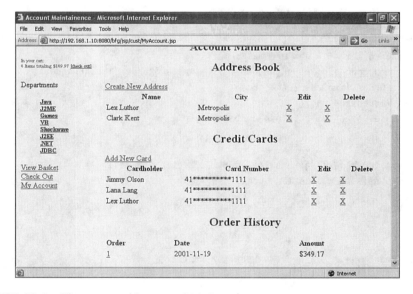

FIGURE 13.2   The new and improved MyAccount page.

Speaking of viewOrder.jsp, Listing 13.12 shows what needs to go into that page.

LISTING 13.12   ViewOrder.jsp

```jsp
<%@ include file="/jsp/cust/AutoLogin.jsp" %>
<%@ page import="com.bfg.customer.Customer" %>
<%@ page import="com.bfg.customer.Address" %>
<%@ page import="com.bfg.customer.CreditCard" %>
<%@ page import="com.bfg.product.Order" %>
<%@ page import="com.bfg.product.Product" %>
<%@ page import="com.bfg.cart.CartItem" %>
<%@ page import="java.util.Iterator" %>
<%@ page import="java.util.Vector" %>
<%@ page import="java.text.NumberFormat" %>
<%@ page import="java.text.DecimalFormat" %>
<jsp:useBean id="customer" class="com.bfg.customer.Customer" scope="session"/>
<% if (customer.getEmail() == null) {
    response.sendRedirect("Login.jsp");
    return;
}
Order or = null;
try {
    NumberFormat nf = new DecimalFormat();
    int ordernum = nf.parse(request.getParameter("order")).intValue();
    or = Order.findOrder(ordernum);
} catch (Exception ex) {
    response.sendRedirect("general_error.jsp");
    return;
}
if (!or.getCustomer().getEmail().equals(customer.getEmail())) {
    response.sendRedirect("noaccess.jsp");
    return;
}
%>
<head>
<title>Order <%= or.getOrderNumber() %></title>
</head>

<%@ include file="/jsp/includes/bfgheader.jsp" %>
<h2 align="center">Order <%= or.getOrderNumber() %></h2>
<table border="0" cellpadding="0" cellspacing="0" style="border-collapse: collapse"
bordercolor="#111111" width="100%">
  <tr>
    <th width="38%" height="23" align="left">Title</th>
    <th width="11%" height="23" align="left">Price</th>
```

LISTING 13.12   Continued

```
    <th width="28%" height="23" align="center">Quantity</td>
    <th width="23%" height="23" align="left">Total</th>
  </tr>
    <%
    Iterator iter = or.getItems().iterator();
    while (iter.hasNext()) {
      CartItem item = (CartItem) iter.next();
      Product prod = item.getProduct();
%>
  <tr>
    <td width="38%" bgcolor="#00FFFF">
    <font style="font-size: 10.0pt; font-family: Times New Roman">
        <A HREF="product/Product.jsp?ISBN=<%= prod.getISBN() %>">
        <%= prod.getTitle() %></A>
    </span><BR><BR></td>
    <td width="11%" bgcolor="#00FFFF">
    <span style="font-size: 10.0pt; font-family: Times New Roman">
    <%= prod.getPriceString() %>
    </span></td>
    <td width="28%" bgcolor="#00FFFF">
    <p align="center"><font size="2">
    <%= item.getQuantity() %>
    </font></td>
    <td width="23%" bgcolor="#00FFFF">
    <span style="font-size: 10.0pt; font-family: Times New Roman">
    <%= item.getLineItemPriceString() %>
    </span></td>
  </tr>
      <% } %>
<TR><TD COLSPAN=4><HR></TD></TR>
<TR><TD> </TD></TR>
<TD> </TD>
<TD ALIGN="center">
<span style="font-size: 10.0pt; font-family: Times New Roman">
    SubTotal
</span></TD>
  <TD>
<span style="font-size: 10.0pt; font-family: Times New Roman">
 <%= or.getOrderSubtotalString()%>
</span></TD></TR>
<TR><TD> </TD>
```

LISTING 13.12   Continued

```
<TD> </TD>
<TD ALIGN="center">
<span style="font-size: 10.0pt; font-family: Times New Roman">
    Shipping
</span></TD>
  <TD>
<span style="font-size: 10.0pt; font-family: Times New Roman">
 <%= or.getOrderShippingString()%>
</span></TD></TR>
<TR><TD> </TD>
<TD> </TD>
<TD ALIGN="center">
<span style="font-size: 10.0pt; font-family: Times New Roman">
    Tax
</span></TD>
  <TD>
<span style="font-size: 10.0pt; font-family: Times New Roman">
 <%= or.getOrderTaxString()%>
</span></TD></TR>
<TR><TD> </TD>
<TD> </TD>
<TD ALIGN="center">
<span style="font-size: 10.0pt; font-family: Times New Roman">
    Total
</span></TD>
  <TD>
<span style="font-size: 10.0pt; font-family: Times New Roman">
 <%= or.getOrderTotalString()%>
</span></TD></TR>
</TABLE>
<P>
<B>Shipped to:</B><BR>
<%= or.getAddress().getFirstName() %>
<%= or.getAddress().getLastName() %><BR>
<%= or.getAddress().getStreet1() %><BR>
<%= or.getAddress().getStreet2() %><BR>
<%= or.getAddress().getCity() %>, <%= or.getAddress().getState() %>
<%= or.getAddress().getPostalCode() %><BR>
<%@ include file="/jsp/includes/bfgfooter.jsp" %>
```

When you are sure that they have logged in, the code needs to try to parse the order number and look it up. Did I mention how much I miss `atoi` in Java? Again, be really, really careful not to let the page display an order unless it belongs to the logged-in user.

From this point down, the code is essentially identical to any other place where the contents of the cart are displayed. In fact, with a few edits, it was basically cut and pasted from the shoppingcart.jsp code (in Listing 10.8). This demonstrates a benefit of using the `CartItem` and `Product` classes commonly for both the cart and the order; it means that you can use a lot of the same methods on both.

Now, when you click on an order from the MyAccount page, you get the order detail page shown in Figure 13.3.

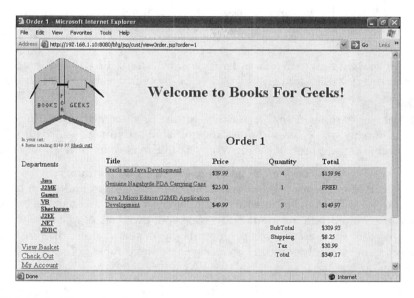

FIGURE 13.3   The order detail page.

In Retrospect

Most developers I've encountered believe that you really end up developing a site twice—the first time to understand the problem and the second time to get everything right.

As I said at the outset, I didn't pretty up the development process to make myself look good. As a result, there are a number of things that I'd go back and re-factor if I were developing this for a production site.

It's not a matter of anything being wrong with the code; it's just that some areas could be improved. These are things that might not be clear at the outset, especially in the area of code reuse, because it is hard to tell what functionalities will be frequently used throughout the code and what will be "one-shot" logic that is needed only once.

There's also a lot of redundant code. For example, lists of products and quantities are displayed throughout the JSP. It would be best to try to find common code and winnow it out, to reduce the overall complexity of the application.

Next Steps for the Site

In addition to second thoughts about what you did code, there are a number of interesting things that you might need to implement depending on how the rest of your business operates. Before moving away from the application, let's talk about a few of these things.

For example, right now, when an order is recorded, that's the end of the story. For all you know, magic fairies come in the middle of the night, read the database, and stuff FedEx packages.

In the real world, someone has to actually put the product in the mail. In a large enough company, you'll have to integrate your application with an existing fulfillment system that was probably designed to handle mail-order or telephone sales.

This is when the large commercial Java application server platforms such as WebLogics, WebSphere, or iPlanet can be helpful. They come bundled (or can be bundled to include) integration with existing enterprise systems such as SAP. In other words, rather than having to hand-code your own classes to communicate with third-party applications, you can use the prewritten modules that are already available in commercial servers. This can save you the trouble of trying to do an integration on your own.

In addition to the code to talk to the fulfillment system, you also might need to add some kind of marker on the order to indicate whether it has been sent out for shipping yet.

Another nicety would be to do real-time stock checking. Right now, the application assumes an infinite amount of each product in stock. In reality, companies run out of things, have to back-order them, and so on. Again, you'd have to integrate with the existing stock-management system to make this work.

Depending on how modern the shipping department is, you might be able to have the order updated to include a UPS or FedEx tracking number after it has been sent. Again, some integration with existing legacy systems will be involved.

Even if none of the above is applicable to your business, you'll want to have some reporting in place so that you can ask questions such as, "How many copies of *Java for Marketers* have I sold in the last month?" Because you're using a standard SQL database, you might want to use a tool such as Crystal Reports (a Windows-based SQL query and reporting product) instead of writing your own reporting. Otherwise, it's straightforward to write these kinds of things. Remember that you'll want to put another layer of security over anything that displays confidential information, lest your competitors start reading your sales figure.

Dotting the I's and Crossing the T's

With all the coding out of the way, the temptation is there to just dust off your hands and go find the nearest bar. But, as is often said, the devil is in the details, a lot of finishing touches should be put on an application before it's really ready to deploy.

To begin, a JavaDoc hasn't been written for anything or commented in the code. How much commenting you want to put into your code is a bit of a philosophical topic. Just about everyone agrees that this is bad commenting style:

```
// Definition of addOneToNumber

public int addOneToNumber (int num) // Takes one argument, number
   // Add one to number and return it
   return (num + 1);
}
```

I call this "Dick and Jane" commenting (after the "See Dick run, run Dick run" books.) I think it's fair to assume that the person reading your code has an IQ above the freezing temperature of water and can read and understand Java code.

So what do you comment, then? Anything tricky or complicated—anything that gave you problems and made you work at it for a bit. The purpose of comments is to save time for the person reading the code after the fact.

You should also drop a line or two of comments before a major section of a method describing what it's intended to do. But, by and large, if you name your variables and methods well and avoid playing games with overly obfuscated coding, you shouldn't need more than one or two comments per method.

Listing 13.13 shows one of the methods from this chapter with comments:

LISTING 13.13   An Example of Commenting

```
    public static Order findOrder(int orderNumber)
      throws Exception {
      Order order = null;
      DBConnection dbConn = null;
      try
          {
              dbConn = TurbineDB.getConnection();
              if (dbConn == null) {
                  cat.error("Can't get database connection");
                  throw new Exception();
              }
              PreparedStatement pstmt =
                  dbConn.prepareStatement(sql_bundle.getString("findOrder"));
              pstmt.setInt(1, orderNumber);
              ResultSet rs = pstmt.executeQuery();

              // If no such order found, return null

              if (!rs.next()) {
                  rs.close();
                  pstmt.close();
                  return null;
              }

              // Create a new order to hold the one we found

              order = new Order();
              order.setOrderNumber(rs.getInt("ORDER_ID"));
              order.setAddress(Address.findAddress(rs.getInt("ADDRESS_KEY")));

order.setCreditCard(CreditCard.findCreditCard(rs.getInt("CARD_KEY")));
              order.setOrderDate(rs.getDate("ORDER_DATE"));
              order.setOrderSubtotal(rs.getDouble("ORDER_SUBTOTAL"));
              order.setOrderTax(rs.getDouble("ORDER_TAX"));
              order.setOrderShipping(rs.getDouble("ORDER_SHIPPING"));
              order.setOrderTotal(rs.getDouble("ORDER_TOTAL"));

order.setCustomer(Customer.findCustomer(rs.getString("EMAIL_ADDRESS")));
              rs.close();
              pstmt.close();

              // Now read in the items associated with the order

              pstmt =
```

LISTING 13.13   Continued

```
                dbConn.prepareStatement(sql_bundle.getString("getOrderItems"));
            pstmt.setInt(1, orderNumber);
            rs = pstmt.executeQuery();
            while (rs.next()) {
                CartItem item = new CartItem();
                Product product = new Product();
                item.setProduct(product);
                item.setQuantity(rs.getInt("QUANTITY"));
                product.setISBN(rs.getString("PRODUCT_ISBN"));
                product.setTitle(rs.getString("PRODUCT_TITLE"));
                product.setPrice(rs.getDouble("UNIT_PRICE"));
                double totalPrice = rs.getDouble("TOTAL_PRICE");
                // If price is zero, must be a promotion item
                if (totalPrice == 0F) {
                    item.setPromotionItem(true);
                }
                order.getItems().add(item);
            }
            rs.close();
            pstmt.close();
        }
    catch (Exception e)
            {
                cat.error("Error during createOrder", e);
                throw new CustomerActivityException();
            }
    finally
        {
            try
                {
                    TurbineDB.releaseConnection(dbConn);
                }
            catch (Exception e)
                {
                    cat.error("Error during release connection", e);
                }
        }
    return order;
}
```

If you count, you'll see three total comments for the entire method. Nothing else really needs to be explained; any competent Java programmer should be able to look at this method and understand it easily.

Javadoc, on the other hand, is a necessity, even if it can be difficult to write. Javadoc is your protection as a developer from having your code altered by other developers. It defines your API and allows other developers to look at the Javadoc to find the interfaces rather than mucking around in your code.

The problem with Javadoc is that it's meant to be formatted and viewed as an HTML document—it is actually rather ugly as it lies on the page in your code. Personally, I believe in the "less is more" school for Javadoc formatting. Even though you can put any kind of HTML in your Javadoc (including pictures of your babies and links to the stuff you're selling on eBay), the more of this kind of thing you put in, the less useful the Javadoc will be when read raw. Listing 13.14 shows one of the shorter source files fully Javadoced.

NOTE

An exhaustive treatise on Javadoc can be found at `http://java.sun.com/j2se/javadoc/`.

LISTING 13.14   Promotions.java with Javadoc

```
/**
 * Promotion is used to implement the Gift With Purchase promotion
 * used by the Books for Geeks Web Site.  It looks for items in the
 * cart which match the target condition, either by specific product
 * or by category.  If the target condition is met, a gift is placed
 * in the cart with the promotionItem flag set, which causes it not to
 * be charged for.
 *
 * @author      James M. Turner
 * @version     %I%,%G%
 */

package com.bfg.cart;

import java.util.Vector;
import java.util.HashMap;
import java.util.Iterator;
import java.text.NumberFormat;
import com.bfg.product.Product;
import com.bfg.product.Category;
```

LISTING 13.14 Continued

```
import org.apache.turbine.services.db.TurbineDB;
import org.apache.turbine.util.db.pool.DBConnection;
import org.apache.turbine.util.TurbineConfig;
import com.bfg.exceptions.ProductActivityException;
import java.sql.*;
import java.util.ResourceBundle;

public class Promotion  {
    private static ResourceBundle sql_bundle =
      ResourceBundle.getBundle("com.bfg.cart.SQLQueries");

    static org.apache.log4j.Category cat =
org.apache.log4j.Category.getInstance(Promotion.class);

    static Vector promotions = new Vector();

    static boolean loaded = false;

    protected String promoName;

    protected Product targetItem;

    protected Category targetCategory;

    protected Product giftItem;

    protected int quantityRequired;

    protected boolean categoryPromotion = false;

    /**
     * Returns the human-readable name of the promotion
     *
     * @return          The name of the promotion.
     */

    public String getPromoName() {
      return promoName;
    }

    /**
```

LISTING 13.14   Continued

```
 * Returns true if this promotion applies to a category rather
 * than an individual product.
 *
 * @return          <code>true</code> if the promotion is applied
 *                  to a category, <code>false</code> if it is
 *                  applied to a single product.
 */

public boolean isCategoryPromotion() {
  return categoryPromotion;
}

/**
 * Returns the product which must be purchased in order to receive
 * the free gift. Only used by promotions which do not have
 * <code>isCategoryPromotion</code> set to true.
 *
 * @return          The product which satisfies the requirement
 *                  for this promotion.
 */

public Product getTargetItem() {
  return targetItem;
}

/**
 * Returns the category which must be purchased in order to receive
 * the free gift. Only used by promotions which have
 * <code>isCategoryPromotion</code> set to true.
 *
 * @return          The category which satisfies the requirement
 *                  for this promotion.
 */

public Category getTargetCategory() {
  return targetCategory;
}

/**
 * Returns the product which is received if the conditions for the
 * promotion are met.
```

LISTING 13.14   Continued

```
 *
 * @return          The product which will be received
 *                  as a gift for this promotion.
 */

public Product getGiftItem() {
  return giftItem;
}

/**
 * Returns the number of the target item that must be purchased in
 * order to receive the gift.  Note that for category promotions,
 * this is the number in aggregate from all items that are in the category.
 *
 * @return          The number of target items required to
 *                  receive the gift.
 */

public int getQuantityRequired() {
  return quantityRequired;
}


/**
 * Returns the list of promotions currently available.  If the
 * promotion list has previously been loaded from the database, it
 * returns a cached copy, otherwise it calls
 * <code>loadPromotions</code> to get the promotions from the
 * database and stores them to the cache.
 *
 * @return          The promotions to be used on the site.
 */

public static Vector getPromotions() {
  if (loaded) {
      return promotions;
  } else {
      loadPromotions();
      loaded = true;
      return promotions;
  }
```

LISTING 13.14   Continued

```
    }

    /**
     * Connects to the database and retrieves the list of
     * promotions. If a promotion is no longer valid because the
     * product or category it references no longer exists, the
     * promotion is ignored.
     *
     */

    public static void loadPromotions() {
      DBConnection dbConn = null;
      try
          {
              dbConn = TurbineDB.getConnection();
              if (dbConn == null) {
                  cat.error("Can't get database connection");
                  return;
              }
              PreparedStatement pstmt =
                  dbConn.prepareStatement(sql_bundle.getString("loadPromotions"));
              ResultSet rs = pstmt.executeQuery();
              while (rs.next()) {
                  Promotion promo = new Promotion();
                  promo.giftItem = Product.findProduct(rs.getString("GIFT_ID"));
                  promo.promoName = rs.getString("PROMO_NAME");
                  promo.categoryPromotion =
                      (rs.getString("PROD_OR_CAT").equals("C"));
                  if (promo.categoryPromotion) {
                      promo.targetCategory =
Category.findCategoryById(rs.getInt("CATEGORY_ID"));
                      if (promo.targetCategory == null) continue;
                  } else {
                      promo.targetItem = Product.findProduct(rs.getString("PROD
➥UCT_ISBN"));
                      if (promo.targetItem == null) continue;
                  }
                  promo.quantityRequired = rs.getInt("DISCOUNT_QUANT");
                  promotions.add(promo);
              }
              rs.close();
```

LISTING 13.14 Continued

```
            pstmt.close();
        }
    catch (Exception e)
        {
            cat.error("Error during loadPromotions", e);
        }
    finally
        {
            try
                {
                    TurbineDB.releaseConnection(dbConn);
                }
            catch (Exception e)
                {
                    cat.error("Error during releaseConnection", e);
                }
        }
}


/**
 * Run all of the current promotions over the shopping cart.
 * Before running the promotions, it removes any existing
 * promotional items from the cart so that each run is a fresh one.
 *
 * @param cart    The shopping cart to calculate promotions for.
 */

public static void runPromotions(Cart cart) {
  cart.removePromotionItems();

  Iterator promos = getPromotions().iterator();

  while (promos.hasNext()) {
      Promotion promo = (Promotion) promos.next();
      promo.runPromotion(cart);
  }
}


/**
 * Run this promotion over the shopping cart.  If the condition is
 * met, add a promotional item to the cart.
```

LISTING 13.14   Continued

```
     *
     * @param cart     The shopping cart to calculate promotions for.
     */

    public void runPromotion(Cart cart) {
      Iterator items = cart.getItems();

      int quant = 0;
      while (items.hasNext()) {
          CartItem item = (CartItem) items.next();
          if (isCategoryPromotion()) {
              if (targetCategory.getProducts().contains(item.getProduct())) {
                  quant += item.getQuantity();
              }
          } else {
              if (item.getProduct().equals(targetItem)) {
                  quant += item.getQuantity();
              }
          }
      }
      if (quant >= quantityRequired) {
          cart.addPromotionItem(giftItem, 1);
      }
    }
}
```

When run through the Javadoc engine with ant javadoc, you end up with the beautifully formatted HTML shown in Figure 13.4.

As you can see, Javadoc will definitely bulk up your source code, especially if you have a lot of instance variables. I've seen source files that were 75% Javadoc when everything was done.

When to write your comments and Javadoc is another matter of debate. Personally, I do it toward the end of the project. My code goes through a lot of flux as I'm writing it, and it would be a tremendous waste to comment and document code that got ripped out a day later.

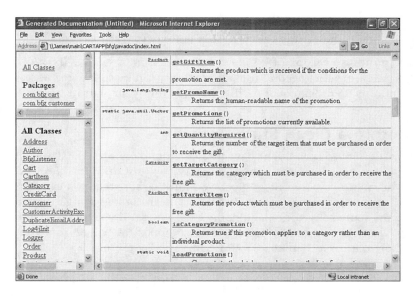

FIGURE 13.4   Javadoc.

On the other hand, the end of a project is usually when things are getting nuts, with bugs coming in from the client faster than you can fix them, along with a push to move the engineering staff to the next project. It requires a degree of discipline to stick with it and put all the commenting in under this kind of pressure.

However, I find that when my brain has become truly muddled, doing some mind-less documentation (and writing Javadoc is about as mindless as it gets) can be a welcome relief.

Making It Turn-Key

As you're cleaning things up, you also should make sure that the application starts up automatically if the server reboots. This is a relatively straightforward operation under UNIX: You just create a series of files in /etc/init.d and link them to the appro-priate /etc/rc.d directories; and things will just start up when init is run. Testing them is a different matter because the only real test is to reboot the machine. Don't assume that things will work without doing this test. For example, the Tomcat startup.sh requires JAVA_HOME to be set. If that is set in your environment, it will work fine when you invoke the `init.d` script from the shell. However, it will fail if it's not in the script or if it is set by root's environment.

Under Windows, things are quite a bit trickier. All the details have been hidden under the hood, and getting things to start automatically takes some effort.

If you're running a version of Windows that understands services (NT, 2000, or XP), most of the things that need to run automatically can be configured as services. If you're running 95 or 98, you'll need to put files into your Startup taskbar folder.

Resetting to a Clean State

As you've developed, you might have messed around with the database schema countless times, renamed and moved property files, discarded JSP files, and so on. Before you walk away from the project, you must be sure that you can start it up from a clean state on a pristine machine. This means provisioning a fresh machine, copying the source directories, and doing a make dist. If you did everything right, the application should be ready to go. If you dropped the ball on something, this is a better time to learn it than at 3:05 A.M. some Sunday morning.

Summary, and on to the Advanced Stuff

As you've learned in this chapter, even when the application is mostly done, still a bit of work can be left to do.

Credit card authorization requires integrating into a third-party application—luckily, this is an easy process because most authorization companies have simple Java-based interfaces. You might also need to integrate into existing accounting, shipping, or inventory systems. You also need to consider database integrity issues during critical "two-phase" operations, such as charging credit cards and then recording an order.

Finishing an application also involves making sure that the code is commented as appropriate and that Javadoc has been written for any externally visible methods.

Break Out the Champagne

You're done! You've got a fully functional e-commerce site up and running and ready to sell books to the masses. Hopefully this walk-through has shown you some tricks and techniques that will help you, whether you're doing a shopping cart site or a company intranet.

In the next few chapters, we'll look at some of the more advanced things that you can do with Tomcat. We'll look at the Struts framework, designed to implement the MVC design paradigm. If you're into design patterns, this is the kind of platform that you'll enjoy deploying on. We'll also look at Enterprise Java beans.

Getting data back and forth and sharing it between applications is more and more critical every day. We'll look at XML, and how you can use Xerces to get XML in and out of Java with a minimum of pain.

LDAP is the other hot data sharing mechanism, and JNDI is how Java likes to talk to it. We'll look at some sample JNDI code, and I'll take you through the often tricky task of adding, modifying and querying an LDAP server.

Finally, we'll spend some time talking about performance considerations with Tomcat. We'll look at the issue of load balancing and failover, and how to integrate Apache with Tomcat to allow Apache to serve your static content, and handle SSL traffic for greater security.

PART IV

Advanced JSP Topics

IN THIS PART

14

Integrating XML into e-Commerce Web Sites

Very few applications live in a vacuum anymore. A large part of software development now involves integration, and a significant part of integration involves getting applications to share data.

XML has emerged as the leading contender for a universal format for data exchange. In this chapter, you'll learn how to use Java to read and write XML data using some of the most popular libraries.

The Benefits of XML

XML has revolutionized data interchange. Whereas complicated fixed-length record files used to be coded to trade information back and forth between applications and companies, many applications now accept XML files that are both more readable by humans and less prone to error.

Fixed-length and delimited file formats might be more compact, but XML offers several advantages. First, when combined with a DTD, an XML document is self-descriptive and self-verifying. That is, the fields give you information about their content, and the DTD describes the valid ordering of the elements so that you can make sure that the document is correctly structured. A file of fixed-length fields doesn't give you any useful information unless you already understand the format that the file was created with.

Furthermore, XML is now widely supported by many tools, from browsers to editors to Java class libraries. This means that, rather than keep reinventing the wheel, you can concentrate on the processing rather than the formatting of the data.

XML is being used in other ways as well, such as with XSL to create content. In this chapter, however, you'll focus on using XML to import and export data from applications. A knowledge of basic XML and DTD format will help a great deal in getting through this material.

The Xerces XML Package

Again, Apache has an XML solution ready for use. Called Xerces, it contains the basic classes you'll need to parse XML. It's a widely used package and, in fact, is the one used inside Tomcat itself.

To install Xerces, you only need to download a Xerces distribution from `http://xml.apache.org/dist/xerces-j/`. As of this writing, the 2.0 release was still in beta, so the examples in this chapter use release 1.4.4.

The distributions come as ZIP files. Unpack the file in a temporary directory, look for it in the top-level directory called xerces.jar, and copy it to your TOMCAT/lib directory. You've now installed XML support. The next step is to do something with it.

A DTD for Products

First, you'll look at reading data from XML files using Xerces. Reading in the product list for the BFG site serves as a good example. To see how this works, you'll begin by writing a DTD to represent products in your shopping cart application so that you can add new books to the database from an XML file (see Listing 14.1).

LISTING 14.1   Product.dtd

```
<?xml version='1.0' encoding='UTF-8' ?>

<!ELEMENT File (Product)*>

<!ELEMENT Product (Title, Authors, Price, Pubdate, Description, Categories)>

<!ATTLIST Product  ISBN    CDATA    #REQUIRED >

<!ELEMENT Title (#PCDATA)>

<!ELEMENT Authors (Author)+>

<!ELEMENT Author (#PCDATA)>

<!ELEMENT Price (#PCDATA)>
```

LISTING 14.1   Continued

```
<!ELEMENT Pubdate (#PCDATA)>


<!ELEMENT Description (#PCDATA)>


<!ELEMENT Categories (Category)+>


<!ELEMENT Category (#PCDATA)>
```

This DTD defines a fairly straightforward XML document format—a series of products with a number of attributes, including multiple authors and categories.

Using this DTD, you can construct a set of test product data, shown in Listing 14.2.

LISTING 14.2   Products.xml

```
<?xml version = "1.0" encoding = "UTF-8"?>
<!DOCTYPE File SYSTEM "Product.dtd">

<File>
 <Product ISBN="0672322366">
  <Title>
   Sams Teach Yourself Visual Basic.NET Web Programming in 21 Days
  </Title>
  <Authors>
   <Author>Peter Aiken</Author>
   <Author>Phil Syme</Author>
  </Authors>
  <Price>39.99</Price>
  <Pubdate>12/18/2001</Pubdate>
  <Description>
Learn how to how to use Visual Basic.NET for Internet programming with
the hands-on techniques and clear explanations used throughout this
practical book.

Visual Basic.NET will integrate state-of-the-art programming language
features, including inheritance, polymorphism, and garbage
collection. The book will explain these key concepts in a simple and
practical way. Web Forms and Web Controls usher in an elegant way to
make dynamic Web pages. The book will cover these topics with how-to
code examples and projects. One of the newest developments in Internet
programming is the use of XML and the SOAP communication
```

LISTING 14.2   Continued

```
protocol. .NET Web Services harness these two technologies and will
be covered in later sections of the book.
  </Description>
  <Categories>
   <Category>.NET</Category>
   <Category>VB</Category>
  </Categories>
 </Product>
 <Product ISBN="0672322854">
  <Title>Real-time Interactive 3D Games</Title>
  <Authors>
   <Author>Allen Partridge</Author>
  </Authors>
  <Price>59.99</Price>
  <Pubdate>11/26/2001</Pubdate>
  <Description>
Delve deeply into 3D character and environment design for interactive
games. Real-Time Interactive 3D Games: Creating 3D Game in Macromedia
Director 8.5/Shockwave Studio will teach developers how to create
attention-grabbing real-time 3D games with Director 8.5/Shockwave
Studio. The book is broken up into three parts: The first part
demonstrates good character and environment design for interactive
games. The second part presents a substantial set of tutorials on the
use of 3D lingo to program games. The final part teaches developers
how to build strategy and surprise into their games to give the player
the best experience possible. This structure mirrors the best game
development practices and gives readers the skills to go out and
develop games on their own. Along the way, Partridge shares some of
his own experiences in game development
  </Description>
  <Categories>
   <Category>Games</Category>
   <Category>Shockwave</Category>
  </Categories>
 </Product>
</File>
```

Writing a SAX Parser

Two modes are supported for XML parsing in Xerces. You can use SAX or DOM. SAX implements event-driven parsing. DOM loads the entire XML document into memory and hands you a pointer to an object hierarchy that represents it.

You'll write a SAX parser first. To parse this XML file, you need to write a class that extends the org.xml.sax.helpers.DefaultHandler class. This class provides a default set of handlers that are called whenever an event occurs during the parsing of the file. Events include finding the start of the document, encountering a start or end element tag, or reading character data.

You can leave most of these event handlers as is because they implement functionality that you don't need to parse a simple data file; a few you will override in your class, to be able to decipher the contents of the XML file, as you can see in Listing 14.3.

LISTING 14.3   SAXProductImporter.java

```java
package com.bfg.xml;

import org.xml.sax.Attributes;
import org.xml.sax.SAXException;
import org.xml.sax.SAXParseException;
import org.xml.sax.XMLReader;
import org.xml.sax.helpers.DefaultHandler;
import java.sql.*;
import java.util.HashMap;
import java.util.Vector;
import java.util.Iterator;
import java.text.NumberFormat;
import java.text.DecimalFormat;
import java.text.SimpleDateFormat;
import java.util.ResourceBundle;

public class SAXProductImporter extends DefaultHandler {
    private static final String
    DEFAULT_PARSER_NAME = "org.apache.xerces.parsers.SAXParser";

    private static ResourceBundle sql_bundle =
      ResourceBundle.getBundle("com.bfg.xml.SQLQueries");

    public static void loadProducts(String uri) {
      SAXProductImporter myclass = new SAXProductImporter();
```

LISTING 14.3   Continued

```
        try {
            XMLReader parser = (XMLReader)Class.forName(DEFAULT_PARSER_NAME).newIn
➥stance();
            parser.setContentHandler(myclass);
            parser.setErrorHandler(myclass);
          parser.setFeature("http://xml.org/sax/features/validation", true);
          parser.parse(uri);

        } catch (org.xml.sax.SAXParseException spe) {
            if (spe.getException() != null)
                spe.getException().printStackTrace(System.err);
          else
                spe.printStackTrace(System.err);
          myclass.rollbackAndQuit();
        } catch (org.xml.sax.SAXException se) {
            if (se.getException() != null)
                se.getException().printStackTrace(System.err);
            else
                se.printStackTrace(System.err);
          myclass.rollbackAndQuit();
        } catch (Exception e) {
            e.printStackTrace(System.err);
          myclass.rollbackAndQuit();
        }
    }
    public void error(SAXParseException se) {
      if (se.getException() != null)
          se.getException().printStackTrace(System.err);
      else
          se.printStackTrace(System.err);
      rollbackAndQuit();
    }

    Connection conn = null;

    HashMap authors = new HashMap();
    HashMap categories = new HashMap();
    int max_author = 0;
    int max_cat = 0;

    public void startDocument() {
```

LISTING 14.3 Continued

```
    try {
        Class.forName("org.gjt.mm.mysql.Driver").newInstance();
        conn =
            DriverManager.getConnection("jdbc:mysql://localhost/BFG");
        Statement st = conn.createStatement();

        ResultSet rs = st.executeQuery("SELECT * FROM CATEGORY");
        while (rs.next()) {
            categories.put(rs.getString("CATEGORY_NAME"),
                        new Integer(rs.getInt("CATEGORY_ID")));
            if (rs.getInt("CATEGORY_ID") > max_cat) {
                max_cat = rs.getInt("CATEGORY_ID");
            }
        }
        rs.close();

        rs = st.executeQuery("SELECT * FROM AUTHOR");
        while (rs.next()) {
            authors.put(rs.getString("AUTHOR_NAME"),
                        new Integer(rs.getInt("AUTHOR_ID")));
            if (rs.getInt("AUTHOR_ID") > max_author) {
                max_author = rs.getInt("AUTHOR_ID");
            }
        }
        rs.close();
        st.executeUpdate("SET AUTOCOMMIT=0");
        st.close();
    } catch (Exception ex) {
        ex.printStackTrace(System.err);
        rollbackAndQuit();
    }
}
public void rollbackAndQuit() {
    try {
        if (conn != null) {
            Statement st = conn.createStatement();
            st.executeUpdate("ROLLBACK");
            st.close();
            conn.close();
        }
    } catch (Exception ex) {}
```

LISTING 14.3   Continued

```java
    System.out.println("Aborting import, rolling back and quitting");
    System.exit(1);
  }
  public void endDocument() {
   try {
       Statement st = conn.createStatement();
       st.executeUpdate("COMMIT");
       st.close();
       conn.close();
   } catch (java.sql.SQLException ex) {
       ex.printStackTrace(System.err);
   }
  }

  public String prod_ISBN = null;
  public String prod_title = null;
  public Vector prod_authors = new Vector();
  public Vector prod_categories = new Vector();
  public Date prod_pubdate = null;
  public double prod_price = 0D;
  public String prod_description = null;

  public StringBuffer chars = new StringBuffer();
  public void startElement(String uri, String local, String raw, Attributes
attrs) {
     chars.setLength(0);
     if (local.equals("Product")) {
         prod_ISBN = attrs.getValue("ISBN");
         prod_authors.clear();
         prod_categories.clear();
         prod_pubdate = null;
         prod_description = null;
         prod_title = null;
     }
  }

  public void endElement(String uri, String local, String raw) {
    if (local.equals("Description")) {
        prod_description = chars.toString();
    }
    if (local.equals("Title")) {
```

LISTING 14.3   Continued

```
        prod_title = chars.toString();
    }
    if (local.equals("Category")) {
        prod_categories.add(chars.toString());
    }
    if (local.equals("Author")) {
        prod_authors.add(chars.toString());
    }
    if (local.equals("Price")) {
        try {
            NumberFormat nf = new DecimalFormat();
            prod_price = nf.parse(chars.toString()).doubleValue();
        } catch (Exception ex) {
            System.out.println("Invalid value for price: " +
                                    chars);
            rollbackAndQuit();
        }
    }
    if (local.equals("Pubdate")) {
        try {
            SimpleDateFormat nf = new SimpleDateFormat("MM/dd/yy");
            prod_pubdate = new Date(nf.parse(chars.toString()).getTime());
        } catch (Exception ex) {
            System.out.println("Invalid value for date: " +
                                    chars);
            rollbackAndQuit();
        }
    }
    if (local.equals("Product")) {
        createProduct();
    }
}

public void characters(char ch[], int start, int length) {
  chars.append(ch, start, length);
}

public void createProduct() {
  try {
      PreparedStatement pstmt =
          conn.prepareStatement(sql_bundle.getString("deleteProd"));
```

LISTING 14.3   Continued

```
pstmt.setString(1, prod_ISBN);
pstmt.executeUpdate();
pstmt.close();
pstmt =
    conn.prepareStatement(sql_bundle.getString("deleteProdXref"));
pstmt.setString(1, prod_ISBN);
pstmt.executeUpdate();
pstmt.close();
pstmt =
    conn.prepareStatement(sql_bundle.getString("deleteCatXref"));
pstmt.setString(1, prod_ISBN);
pstmt.executeUpdate();
pstmt.close();
pstmt =
    conn.prepareStatement(sql_bundle.getString("insertProd"));
pstmt.setString(1, prod_ISBN);
pstmt.setString(2, prod_title);
pstmt.setDouble(3, prod_price);
pstmt.setDate(4, prod_pubdate);
pstmt.setString(5, prod_description);
pstmt.executeUpdate();
Iterator author_it = prod_authors.iterator();
while (author_it.hasNext()) {
    String author = (String) author_it.next();
    int author_id;
    if (authors.get(author) != null) {
        author_id = ((Integer)authors.get(author)).intValue();
    } else {
        pstmt =
            conn.prepareStatement(sql_bundle.getString("insertAuthor"));
        author_id = ++max_author;
        pstmt.setInt(1, author_id);
        pstmt.setString(2, author);
        pstmt.executeUpdate();
        pstmt.close();
        authors.put(author, new Integer(author_id));
    }
    pstmt =
        conn.prepareStatement(sql_bundle.getString("insertAuthorXref"));
    pstmt.setString(1, prod_ISBN);
    pstmt.setInt(2, author_id);
```

LISTING 14.3   Continued

```
                pstmt.executeUpdate();
        }
        Iterator cat_it = prod_categories.iterator();
        while (cat_it.hasNext()) {
            String cat = (String) cat_it.next();
            int cat_id;
            if (categories.get(cat) != null) {
                cat_id = ((Integer)categories.get(cat)).intValue();
            } else {
                pstmt =
                    conn.prepareStatement(sql_bundle.getString("insertCate
➥gory"));
                cat_id = ++max_cat;
                pstmt.setInt(1, cat_id);
                pstmt.setString(2, cat);
                pstmt.executeUpdate();
                pstmt.close();
                categories.put(cat, new Integer(cat_id));
            }
            pstmt =
                conn.prepareStatement(sql_bundle.getString("insertCatXref"));
            pstmt.setString(1, prod_ISBN);
            pstmt.setInt(2, cat_id);
            pstmt.executeUpdate();
        }
    } catch (java.sql.SQLException ex) {
        ex.printStackTrace(System.err);
        rollbackAndQuit();
    }
}


public static void main(String argv[]) {

    if (argv.length == 0) {
        System.exit(1);
    }

    loadProducts(argv[0]);
}


}
```

The LoadProducts method is the standard accessor that you're providing to this class. It begins by instantiating a copy of the SAX parser and sets the content and error handlers to the class you've created. These handlers are called whenever an element is encountered in the XML document or when errors or other events, such as the start of the document, occur.

You can think about the handlers by imagining that the SAX parser is responsible for breaking apart the structure of the document but doesn't know how to do anything with the contents. The handlers that you write are called by SAX to interpret the data as the parse encounters it.

You might want to configure a few features of the parser. Specifically, you'll want to validate against the DTD that you specified; the default for SAX parsers is not to validate the structure. In other words, unless validation is set to on, the DTD declaration of the XML file is ignored and any validly structured XML document is reported as successfully parsed, even if it doesn't match the DTD. After the feature is set, call the parser, wrapping the call in a catch to handle any fatal exceptions from the parse or your handler. All the rest of the functionality occurs as callbacks to the overriding methods you'll supply.

If the XML file doesn't validate against the DTD, the error method is called. You want the code to print the error message so that you can find the syntax error; then you want the code to abort the processing and roll back the database.

When you first start processing a document, the startDocument method opens a database connection and get the current list of categories and authors. It also gets the highest value currently being used for the author and category IDs so that the importer can use them to create new ones, if needed. Because no database locking is occurring in this code, you can run only one of these imports at any given time; otherwise, the same ID numbers would be used for different data.

rollbackAndQuit is a helper that rolls back the database and exits the program. Unfortunately, MySQL supports rollback for only certain types of databases, so this might not work 100% of the time. If you were going to take advantage of rollback functionality, you'd need to download the correct version of the MySQL binary.

When the SAX parser encounters the end of the document, endDocument commits the changes made and closes the connection.

When the parser sees an element start, it calls startElement, which checks to see if it's a product tag. If so, it clears all the values from any previous products encountered during this run.

On an end tag, endElement is called, which takes any character data that has been collected since the start tag and writes it to a holding variable. If it's an end product, the new product is created from the data collected. The result of this is that as each subelement of a product is encountered, it is stored into a holding variable. When the product end tag is found, all those variables are used to create the new product.

When the parser encounters character data, `characters` is called, which appends the data to a buffer. The buffer will be assigned to a tag when the tag ends. Note that because you can have multiple calls to this method for what seems to be a "single" piece of text, you must append all the data together to get the whole string. Some care must be exercised because any whitespace in the document (even the newline after a tag) is considered character data and will call this method. You want to make sure that you process characters only where they are meaningful.

`createProduct` deletes the product if it already exists, along with any cross-references from the product to authors or categories. Then it inserts the product, creates any new authors or categories as needed, and creates the cross-references.

As usual, with the JDBC code you've written, you will need your bundle of SQL queries to make it work (see Listing 14.4).

LISTING 14.4   SQLQueries.properties

```
deleteProd=DELETE FROM PRODUCT WHERE ISBN=?

deleteProdXref=DELETE FROM PRODUCT_AUTHOR_XREF WHERE PRODUCT_ISBN=?

deleteCatXref=DELETE FROM CATEGORY_PRODUCT_XREF WHERE PRODUCT_ISBN=?

insertProd=INSERT INTO PRODUCT (ISBN, TITLE, PRICE, PUB_DATE, DESCRIPTION) \
                VALUES (?, ?, ?, ?, ?)

insertAuthor=INSERT INTO AUTHOR (AUTHOR_ID, AUTHOR_NAME) \
                VALUES (?, ?)

insertCategory=INSERT INTO CATEGORY (CATEGORY_ID, CATEGORY_NAME) \
                VALUES (?, ?)

insertAuthorXref=INSERT INTO PRODUCT_AUTHOR_XREF (PRODUCT_ISBN, AUTHOR_ID) \
                VALUES (?, ?)

insertCatXref=INSERT INTO CATEGORY_PRODUCT_XREF (PRODUCT_ISBN, CATEGORY_ID) \
                VALUES (?, ?)
```

You can then add a bit of code to your build.xml Ant script (see Listing 14.5) to run the program.

LISTING 14.5   Additions to the Ant Script

```
<target name="testxml" depends="dist">
  <java classname="com.bfg.xml.SAXProductImporter" fork="yes">
    <classpath>
    <pathelement path="${java.class.path}"/>
      <fileset dir="c:\tomcat\lib">
        <include name="**/*.jar"/>
      </fileset>
      <fileset dir="c:\tomcat\webapps\bfg\WEB-INF\lib">
        <include name="**/*.jar"/>
      </fileset>
    </classpath>
    <arg value="xml/Products.xml"/>
  </java>
</target>
```

When you run it, everything works as expected.

```
C:\CARTAPP\bfg>ant testxml
Buildfile: build.xml

init:

compile:

dist:

testxml:

BUILD SUCCESSFUL

Total time: 2 seconds
```

Writing a DOM Parser

There's no question that it's easier to write DOM-based code because you can access the entire document structure as a memory object rather than having to collect information as it passes by during a serial parse of the document. You can use the same DTD and XML, but the parser is totally different when written as a DOM implementation, as you can see in Listing 14.6.

LISTING 14.6   DOMProductImporter.java

```java
package com.bfg.xml;

import org.apache.xerces.dom.TextImpl;
import org.xml.sax.SAXParseException;
import org.apache.xerces.parsers.DOMParser;

import org.w3c.dom.Attr;
import org.w3c.dom.Document;
import org.w3c.dom.NamedNodeMap;
import org.w3c.dom.Node;
import org.w3c.dom.Element;
import org.w3c.dom.NodeList;

import java.sql.*;
import java.util.HashMap;
import java.util.Vector;
import java.util.Iterator;
import java.text.NumberFormat;
import java.text.DecimalFormat;
import java.text.SimpleDateFormat;
import java.util.ResourceBundle;

public class DOMProductImporter  {

    private static final String
    DEFAULT_PARSER_NAME = "org.apache.xerces.parsers.DOMParser";
    private static ResourceBundle sql_bundle =
      ResourceBundle.getBundle("com.bfg.xml.SQLQueries");

    public static void loadProducts(String uri) {
      DOMProductImporter myclass = new DOMProductImporter();
        try {
            DOMParser parser =
            (DOMParser)Class.forName(DEFAULT_PARSER_NAME).newInstance();

          parser.setFeature("http://xml.org/sax/features/validation", true);

          parser.parse(uri);
            myclass.readDocument(parser.getDocument());

        } catch (org.xml.sax.SAXParseException spe) {
```

LISTING 14.6   Continued

```
            if (spe.getException() != null)
                spe.getException().printStackTrace(System.err);
        else
                spe.printStackTrace(System.err);
        myclass.rollbackAndQuit();
    } catch (org.xml.sax.SAXException se) {
        if (se.getException() != null)
            se.getException().printStackTrace(System.err);
        else
            se.printStackTrace(System.err);
    myclass.rollbackAndQuit();
    } catch (Exception e) {
        e.printStackTrace(System.err);
    myclass.rollbackAndQuit();
    }
}

Connection conn = null;

HashMap authors = new HashMap();
HashMap categories = new HashMap();
int max_author = 0;
int max_cat = 0;

public void rollbackAndQuit() {
  try {
      if (conn != null) {
          Statement st = conn.createStatement();
          st.executeUpdate("ROLLBACK");
          st.close();
          conn.close();
      }
  } catch (Exception ex) {}
  System.out.println("Aborting import, rolling back and quitting");
  System.exit(1);
}

public void readDocument(Document doc) {
  try {
      Class.forName("org.gjt.mm.mysql.Driver").newInstance();
      conn =
```

LISTING 14.6 Continued

```
                DriverManager.getConnection("jdbc:mysql://localhost/BFG");
        Statement st = conn.createStatement();

        ResultSet rs = st.executeQuery("SELECT * FROM CATEGORY");
        while (rs.next()) {
            categories.put(rs.getString("CATEGORY_NAME"),
                        new Integer(rs.getInt("CATEGORY_ID")));
            if (rs.getInt("CATEGORY_ID") > max_cat) {
                max_cat = rs.getInt("CATEGORY_ID");
            }
        }
        rs.close();

        rs = st.executeQuery("SELECT * FROM AUTHOR");
        while (rs.next()) {
            authors.put(rs.getString("AUTHOR_NAME"),
                    new Integer(rs.getInt("AUTHOR_ID")));
            if (rs.getInt("AUTHOR_ID") > max_author) {
                max_author = rs.getInt("AUTHOR_ID");
            }
        }
        rs.close();
        st.executeUpdate("SET AUTOCOMMIT=0");
        st.close();

        NodeList products = doc.getDocumentElement().getChildNodes();
        if (products != null) {
            int len = products.getLength();
            for (int i = 0; i < len; i++) {
                Node n = products.item(i);
                if (n.getNodeName().equals("Product")) {
                    readProduct((Element)n);
                }
            }
        }
    } catch (Exception ex) {
        ex.printStackTrace(System.err);
        rollbackAndQuit();
    }
}

public void readProduct(Element node) {
```

LISTING 14.6   Continued

```java
String ISBN = node.getAttribute("ISBN");
Vector prod_authors = null;
Vector prod_categories = null;
Date pubdate = null;
String title = null;
double price = 0D;
String description = null;

NodeList children = node.getChildNodes();
if (children != null) {
    int len = children.getLength();
    for (int i = 0; i < len; i++) {
        Node n = children.item(i);
        if (n.getNodeName().equals("Authors"))
            prod_authors = readVector((Element) n, "Author");

        if (n.getNodeName().equals("Categories"))
            prod_categories = readVector((Element) n, "Category");

        if (n.getNodeName().equals("Title"))
            title = readString((Element) n);

        if (n.getNodeName().equals("Description"))
            description = readString((Element) n);

        if (n.getNodeName().equals("Pubdate"))
            pubdate = readDate((Element) n);

        if (n.getNodeName().equals("Price"))
            price = readDouble((Element) n);
    }
}
createProduct(ISBN, prod_authors, prod_categories, pubdate, title, price,
description);
}

public Vector readVector(Element node, String type) {
    Vector results = new Vector();
    NodeList children = node.getChildNodes();
    if (children != null) {
        int len = children.getLength();
```

LISTING 14.6   Continued

```
        for (int i = 0; i < len; i++) {
            Node n = children.item(i);
            if (n.getNodeName().equals(type)) {
                results.add(readString((Element)n));
            }
        }
    }
    return results;
}

public Date readDate(Element node) {
    String dateString = readString(node);
    try {
        SimpleDateFormat nf = new SimpleDateFormat("MM/dd/yy");
        return new Date(nf.parse(dateString).getTime());
    } catch (Exception ex) {
        System.out.println("Invalid value for date: " +
                            dateString);
        rollbackAndQuit();
    }
    return null;
}

public double readDouble(Element node) {
    String doubleString = readString(node);
    try {
        NumberFormat nf = new DecimalFormat();
        return nf.parse(doubleString).doubleValue();
    } catch (Exception ex) {
        System.out.println("Invalid value for double: " +
                            doubleString);
        rollbackAndQuit();
    }
    return 0;
}


public String readString(Element node) {
    StringBuffer sb = new StringBuffer();
    NodeList children = node.getChildNodes();
    if (children != null) {
```

LISTING 14.6   Continued

```
            int len = children.getLength();
            for (int i = 0; i < len; i++) {
                Node n = children.item(i);
                switch (n.getNodeType()) {
                case Node.CDATA_SECTION_NODE: {
                    sb.append(n.getNodeValue());
                    break;
                }
                case Node.TEXT_NODE: {
                    if (n instanceof TextImpl) {
                        if (!(((TextImpl)n).isIgnorableWhitespace())) {
                            sb.append(n.getNodeValue());
                        }
                    } else {
                        sb.append(n.getNodeValue());
                    }
                }
                }
            }
        }
    return sb.toString();
    }

    public void createProduct(String ISBN, Vector prod_authors, Vector prod_cate
➥gories,
                                Date pubdate, String title, double price, String
description) {
        try {
            PreparedStatement pstmt =
                conn.prepareStatement(sql_bundle.getString("deleteProd"));
            pstmt.setString(1, ISBN);
            pstmt.executeUpdate();
            pstmt.close();
            pstmt =
                conn.prepareStatement(sql_bundle.getString("deleteProdXref"));
            pstmt.setString(1, ISBN);
            pstmt.executeUpdate();
            pstmt.close();
            pstmt =
                conn.prepareStatement(sql_bundle.getString("deleteCatXref"));
            pstmt.setString(1, ISBN);
```

LISTING 14.6   Continued

```
    pstmt.executeUpdate();
    pstmt.close();
    pstmt =
        conn.prepareStatement(sql_bundle.getString("insertProd"));
    pstmt.setString(1, ISBN);
    pstmt.setString(2, title);
    pstmt.setDouble(3, price);
    pstmt.setDate(4, pubdate);
    pstmt.setString(5, description);
    pstmt.executeUpdate();
    Iterator author_it = prod_authors.iterator();
    while (author_it.hasNext()) {
        String author = (String) author_it.next();
        int author_id;
        if (authors.get(author) != null) {
            author_id = ((Integer)authors.get(author)).intValue();
        } else {
            pstmt =
                conn.prepareStatement(sql_bundle.getString("insertAuthor"));
            author_id = ++max_author;
            pstmt.setInt(1, author_id);
            pstmt.setString(2, author);
            pstmt.executeUpdate();
            pstmt.close();
            authors.put(author, new Integer(author_id));
        }
        pstmt =
            conn.prepareStatement(sql_bundle.getString("insertAuthorXref"));
        pstmt.setString(1, ISBN);
        pstmt.setInt(2, author_id);
        pstmt.executeUpdate();
    }
    Iterator cat_it = prod_categories.iterator();
    while (cat_it.hasNext()) {
        String cat = (String) cat_it.next();
        int cat_id;
        if (categories.get(cat) != null) {
            cat_id = ((Integer)categories.get(cat)).intValue();
        } else {
            pstmt =
                conn.prepareStatement(sql_bundle.getString("insertCate
```

LISTING 14.6   Continued

```
➡gory"));
                        cat_id = ++max_cat;
                        pstmt.setInt(1, cat_id);
                        pstmt.setString(2, cat);
                        pstmt.executeUpdate();
                        pstmt.close();
                        categories.put(cat, new Integer(cat_id));
                    }
                    pstmt =
                        conn.prepareStatement(sql_bundle.getString("insertCatXref"));
                    pstmt.setString(1, ISBN);
                    pstmt.setInt(2, cat_id);
                    pstmt.executeUpdate();
                }
            } catch (java.sql.SQLException ex) {
                ex.printStackTrace(System.err);
                rollbackAndQuit();
            }
        }

    public static void main(String argv[]) {

        if (argv.length == 0) {
            System.exit(1);
        }

        loadProducts(argv[0]);
    }


}
```

The top of the class is very similar to the SAX version. Some different packages have been imported and a different parser is being used, but so far the code looks remarkably the same. The first big difference occurs when you actually have the code parse the document. With a SAX parser, all the processing happens as a side effect because of the callbacks. With DOM, running the parser produces a document object that is at the top of an XML hierarchy that you need to have your importer walk.

readDocument does the same initializations as when you were using SAX (reading in the category and author list from the database). But then it gets a list of the child nodes of the document root—the File element. The children of the file element must be Product elements, according to the DTD.

The code then iterates over the `Product` elements, calling `readProduct` on them in turn. `readProduct` gets the ISBN attribute and then iterates over its child nodes, looking for the various values that it needs to build a product. After all the values are read from the subelements, it calls `createProduct`.

`readVector` is put into service to read in two different elements: the author and category lists. It makes sure that the children are what it expects them to be (the type), although the DTD should validate against anything but the right values. After all the values are read using `readString`, it returns the vector.

`readDate` and `readDouble` just parse the result of doing a `readString`. `readString` assembles the characters in an element, ignoring any unnecessary whitespace.

`createProduct` is almost identical to the version used with SAX. The only difference between them is that DOM hands the data in as arguments rather than using global variables.

You will likely find this version much cleaner and easier to read than the SAX version. This purity comes at a price, however. The program currently reads in a few products, but imagine that you want to have it read in several million records instead. By its nature, DOM would want to read the entire thing into memory and build one huge structure to maintain it.

As you might imagine, this can put a serious crimp on your swap space and performance because hundreds of megabytes or even gigabytes of RAM are used trying to manage it.

On the other hand, SAX throws away the XML as soon as it's processed, which means that the SAX version could handle a billion records as easily as a dozen. Whether MySQL could handle a billion records is another matter, of course.

So, choosing between SAX and DOM is a matter of deciding whether it's more important to keep the memory usage down or have the ability to traverse the entire structure at will. One advantage of using DOM is that you can modify and output the XML again, as demonstrated in the next section.

Generating XML

At the beginning of this chapter, you learned about using XML as a medium for doing data interchange. Suppose you want to send a vendor an XML file with order data in it. You could just write a method that creates the XML manually using prints, but this is dangerous because you might forget to include an end tag or you might make some other simple syntactic XML mistake. You can use DOM to generate a file on the fly from database data and be assured that it will be formatted as proper XML. Again, you need to start by defining a DTD for the XML file that's going to hold your orders (see Listing 14.7)

LISTING 14.7   Order.dtd

```
<?xml version='1.0' encoding='UTF-8' ?>

<!ELEMENT File (Order)*>

<!ELEMENT Order (email_address, address, credit_card, order_date, order_subtotal,
                 order_tax, order_shipping, order_total, items)>

<!ATTLIST Order  order_id    CDATA      #REQUIRED >

<!ELEMENT email_address (#PCDATA)>

<!ELEMENT order_date (#PCDATA)>

<!ELEMENT order_subtotal (#PCDATA)>

<!ELEMENT order_tax (#PCDATA)>

<!ELEMENT order_shipping (#PCDATA)>

<!ELEMENT order_total (#PCDATA)>

<!ELEMENT address (address_id, first_name, last_name, street_1, street_2, city,
state, postal_code)>

<!ATTLIST address address_id CDATA #REQUIRED>

<!ELEMENT first_name (#PCDATA)>

<!ELEMENT last_name (#PCDATA)>

<!ELEMENT street_1 (#PCDATA)>

<!ELEMENT street_2 (#PCDATA)>

<!ELEMENT city (#PCDATA)>

<!ELEMENT state (#PCDATA)>

<!ELEMENT postal_code (#PCDATA)>

<!ELEMENT credit_card (address, card_type, card_number, card_ownername, card_exp-
```

LISTING 14.7   Continued

```
month,
                        card_expyear)

<!ATTLIST credit_card card_id CDATA #REQUIRED>

<!ELEMENT card_type (#PCDATA)>

<!ELEMENT card_number (#PCDATA)>

<!ELEMENT card_ownername (#PCDATA)>

<!ELEMENT card_expmonth (#PCDATA)>

<!ELEMENT card_expyear (#PCDATA)>

<!ELEMENT items (item)*>

<!ELEMENT item (product_isbn, product_title, quantity, unit_price, total_price)>

<!ELEMENT product_isbn (#PCDATA)>

<!ELEMENT product_title (#PCDATA)>

<!ELEMENT quantity (#PCDATA)>

<!ELEMENT unit_price (#PCDATA)>

<!ELEMENT total_price (#PCDATA)>
```

Notice that the address element inside the credit card element is reused rather than duplicating fields.

Now you can write your exporter (see Listing 14.8). You need a number of new imports to make this work, including all the SQL, most of the BFG classes, and some new XML ones.

LISTING 14.8   DOMOrderExporter.java

```
package com.bfg.xml;

import org.apache.xerces.dom.TextImpl;
import org.xml.sax.SAXParseException;
```

LISTING 14.8   Continued

```
import org.apache.xerces.parsers.DOMParser;
import org.apache.turbine.services.db.TurbineDB;
import org.apache.turbine.util.db.pool.DBConnection;
import org.apache.turbine.util.TurbineConfig;
import org.w3c.dom.Document;
import org.w3c.dom.Node;
import org.w3c.dom.Element;
import org.w3c.dom.DOMImplementation;
import org.w3c.dom.DocumentType;
import java.io.*;
import java.sql.*;
import java.util.HashMap;
import java.util.Vector;
import java.util.Iterator;
import java.text.NumberFormat;
import java.text.DecimalFormat;
import java.text.SimpleDateFormat;
import java.util.ResourceBundle;
import org.apache.xml.serialize.Serializer;
import org.apache.xml.serialize.XMLSerializer;
import org.apache.xml.serialize.OutputFormat;
import com.bfg.product.Order;
import com.bfg.customer.Address;
import com.bfg.customer.CreditCard;
import com.bfg.cart.CartItem;
import org.apache.xerces.dom.DocumentTypeImpl;
import org.apache.xerces.dom.DOMImplementationImpl;
import org.apache.xerces.dom.DocumentImpl;

public class DOMOrderExporter  {
    private static final String
    DEFAULT_PARSER_NAME = "org.apache.xerces.parsers.DOMParser";

    private static ResourceBundle sql_bundle =
      ResourceBundle.getBundle("com.bfg.xml.SQLQueries");

    public static void printOrders() {
      DOMOrderExporter myclass = new DOMOrderExporter();
        try {
            DOMParser parser =
```

LISTING 14.8   Continued

```
                (DOMParser)Class.forName(DEFAULT_PARSER_NAME).newInstance();

        parser.setFeature("http://xml.org/sax/features/validation", true);
        DOMImplementation domImpl = new DOMImplementationImpl();
        DocumentType docType = null;
           docType = domImpl.createDocumentType( "File", null, "Order.dtd" );

        Document document = new DocumentImpl(docType);
        Element root = document.createElement("File");
        document.appendChild(root);
        Iterator orders = Order.getAllOrders().iterator();
        while(orders.hasNext()) {
            Order order = (Order) orders.next();
            myclass.generateOrder(order, document, root);
        }

            OutputFormat    format  = new OutputFormat( document );
        format.setIndent(3);
           FileWriter  stringOut = new FileWriter("orders.xml");
           XMLSerializer    serial = new XMLSerializer( stringOut, format );
           serial.asDOMSerializer();
           serial.serialize( document.getDocumentElement() );
       } catch (org.xml.sax.SAXException se) {
           if (se.getException() != null)
               se.getException().printStackTrace(System.err);
           else
               se.printStackTrace(System.err);
       } catch (Exception e) {
           e.printStackTrace(System.err);
       }
    }

    public void addElement(Document document, Node node, String name, String value)
{
    Node tmp = document.createElement(name);
    tmp.appendChild(document.createTextNode(value));
    node.appendChild(tmp);
    }

    public void generateOrder(Order order, Document document, Element root) {
      Element order_el = document.createElement("order");
```

LISTING 14.8   Continued

```
    order_el.setAttribute("order_id", String.valueOf(order.getOrderNumber())));
    root.appendChild(order_el);
    addElement(document, order_el, "email_address",
order.getCustomer().getEmail());
    Node addr = generateAddress(order.getAddress(), document);
    order_el.appendChild(addr);
    Element credit_card = document.createElement("credit_card");
    CreditCard card = order.getCreditCard();
    credit_card.appendChild(generateAddress(card.getAddress(), document));
    credit_card.setAttribute("card_id", String.valueOf(card.getCardID()));
    addElement(document, credit_card, "card_type", card.getCardType());
    addElement(document, credit_card, "card_ownername", card.getCardOwner());
    addElement(document, credit_card, "card_number", card.getCardNumber());
    addElement(document, credit_card, "card_expmonth", String.valueOf(card.get
➥ExpMonth())));
    addElement(document, credit_card, "card_expyear", String.valueOf(card.getEx
➥pYear())));
    addElement(document, order_el, "order_date",
order.getOrderDate().toString());
    addElement(document, order_el, "order_subtotal",
String.valueOf(order.getOrderSubtotal()));
    addElement(document, order_el, "order_shipping",
String.valueOf(order.getOrderShipping()));
    addElement(document, order_el, "order_tax", String.valueOf(order.getOrder
➥Tax())));
    addElement(document, order_el, "order_total", String.valueOf(order.getOrder
➥Total())));
    Element items_el = document.createElement("items");
    order_el.appendChild(items_el);
    Iterator items = order.getItems().iterator();
    while (items.hasNext()) {
        CartItem item = (CartItem) items.next();
        Element item_el = document.createElement("item");
        items_el.appendChild(item_el);
        addElement(document, item_el, "product_isbn",
item.getProduct().getISBN());
        addElement(document, item_el, "product_title", item.getProduct().getTi
➥tle());
        addElement(document, item_el, "quantity", String.valueOf(item.getQuan
➥tity())));
        addElement(document, item_el, "unit_price", String.valueOf(item.getProd
```

LISTING 14.8   Continued

```
➥uct().getPrice()));
        addElement(document, item_el, "total_price", String.valueOf(item.get
➥LineItemPrice()));
    }
}

public Node generateAddress(Address addr, Document document) {
  Element tmp = document.createElement("address");
  tmp.setAttribute("address_id", String.valueOf(addr.getAddressID()));
  addElement(document, tmp, "first_name", addr.getFirstName());
  addElement(document, tmp, "last_name", addr.getLastName());
  addElement(document, tmp, "street_1", addr.getStreet1());
  addElement(document, tmp, "street_2", addr.getStreet2());
  addElement(document, tmp, "city", addr.getCity());
  addElement(document, tmp, "state", addr.getState());
  addElement(document, tmp, "postal_code", addr.getPostalCode());
  return tmp;
}

public static void main(String argv[]) {

  TurbineConfig tc = new TurbineConfig("./",
                                       "TurbineResources.properties");
  tc.init();

    if (argv.length == 0) {
        System.exit(1);
    }

  printOrders();
}
```

Even though content is being generated instead of being parsed, you still use the same DOM parser class.

To start fresh, create a DomImplementationImpl. When you have it, use it to create a document type so that you can get the right doctype tag at the top of the file that will reference your DTD. Then use the document type to request a DocumentImpl, which will serve as the top of your XML hierarchy.

Just as you had to walk through the tree of nodes when you were unpacking the XML object, now you have to build the tree, starting with the top-level `File` element. Adding an element to the document consists of two steps. First you create a new element against the document. Then you append it to the node of which you want it to be a child.

After the root node is set up, the method needs to iterate over the orders and create a child `Order` node for each one. When that's done, it uses the XMLSerializer to write the XML to orders.xml.

You are going to spend a lot of time writing code to add nodes with text content, which normally takes three steps. `addElement` is a helper function to simplify things. `generateOrder` does the actual work of producing the XML for each order.

Generating each order is just a matter of creating the appropriate element and subelements to hold all the values. Because the method needs to write out two addresses, break it into a separate function, `generateAddress`.

Because you're going to be using classes that depend on connection pooling from Turbine, you can't take a shortcut as was done with the importers when a direct database connection was opened. You need to initialize Turbine.

You also need to add something to `Order` to get all the orders (see Listing 14.9).

LISTING 14.9   Additions to Order.java

```java
public static Vector getAllOrders() {
  Vector orders = new Vector();
  DBConnection dbConn = null;
  try
    {
        dbConn = TurbineDB.getConnection();
        if (dbConn == null) {
            cat.error("Can't get database connection");
        }
        PreparedStatement pstmt =
            dbConn.prepareStatement(sql_bundle.getString("allOrders"));
        ResultSet rs = pstmt.executeQuery();
        while (rs.next()) {
            orders.add(Order.findOrder(rs.getInt("ORDER_ID")));
        }
        rs.close();
        pstmt.close();
    }
  catch (Exception e)
    {
        cat.error("Error during getOrderHistory", e);
    }
```

LISTING 14.9   Continued

```
    finally
        {
            try
                {
                    TurbineDB.releaseConnection(dbConn);
                }
            catch (Exception e)
                {
                    cat.error("Error during release connection", e);
                }
        }
    return orders;
    }
```

The allOrders query is very simple:

```
allOrders=SELECT ORDER_ID FROM ORDERS
```

Now you can modify your build.xml to run this class instead. When you do an ant testxml, you'll get a perfectly formatted XML document with your orders (or, in this case, order). Listing 14.10 shows the output.

LISTING 14.10   An XML Order

```
<?xml version="1.0" encoding="UTF-8"?>
<!DOCTYPE File SYSTEM "Order.dtd">
<File>
   <order order_id="1">
      <email_address>turner@blackbear.com</email_address>
      <address address_id="27">
         <first_name>Jimmy&apos;s</first_name>
         <last_name>Mom</last_name>
         <street_1>The Old Farm</street_1>
         <street_2/>
         <city>Hicksville</city>
         <state>OH</state>
         <postal_code>44546</postal_code>
      </address>
      <order_date>2001-11-19</order_date>
      <order_subtotal>309.93</order_subtotal>
      <order_shipping>8.25</order_shipping>
      <order_tax>30.993</order_tax>
      <order_total>349.173</order_total>
      <items>
```

LISTING 14.10   Continued

```
        <item>
            <product_isbn>672321173</product_isbn>
            <product_title>Oracle and Java Development</product_title>
            <quantity>4</quantity>
            <unit_price>39.99</unit_price>
            <total_price>159.96</total_price>
        </item>
        <item>
            <product_isbn>PALMCASE</product_isbn>
            <product_title>Genuine Nagahyde PDA Carrying Case</product_title>
            <quantity>1</quantity>
            <unit_price>25.0</unit_price>
            <total_price>0.0</total_price>
        </item>
        <item>
            <product_isbn>672320959</product_isbn>
            <product_title>Java 2 Micro Edition (J2ME) Application
Development</product_title>
            <quantity>3</quantity>
            <unit_price>49.99</unit_price>
            <total_price>149.97</total_price>
        </item>
      </items>
    </order>
</File>
```

Summary

The Xerces parser offers a way to easily read and write XML data from Java. You have your choice of two different methods of parsing: You can use SAX, which is an event-driven parser that uses callbacks to event handlers that you provide, or you can use DOM, which loads the entire XML document into an object-oriented tree of nodes that your code can walk to discover content.

You can also use DOM to create a brand-new hierarchy and then generate XML output based on it. This has the advantage of always generating syntactically correct XML.

More packages are being written each day to use XML in some way. In fact, it is nearly impossible to develop a major application anymore without needing to read or write XML. As a result, learning to use the Java XML tools is now a critical skill.

15

Using LDAP with JNDI

The Lightweight Directory Access Protocol (LDAP) is one of those standards that, like XML, has taken the industry by storm. It seems like every product or platform that needs to perform user authentication or directory management has integrated LDAP support in some form—and it's a near certainty that the code you write will need to do so, too.

In this chapter, you'll learn how the LDAP protocol can be interfaced with Tomcat using the Java Naming and Directory Interface (JNDI).

The World of LDAP

Databases are great for storing data that needs to be cross-referenced and easily searched. But the problem with databases is that they require a lot of overhead, in terms of both hardware to run them and software to access them.

The other problem with databases is that everyone who develops one ends up using a slightly different schema, even if they're storing the same data. This makes it difficult to write general-purpose applications that don't need to have specific information about each installation's database layout provided to them.

One solution to this problem is to use a directory-oriented storage mechanism rather than a database. In a directory, the same fields are always used for the same types of data.

LDAP grew out of the old X.500 directory standard that was a part of the ISO oligarchy. Like most things ISO, X.500 was complicated, specialized to certain types of networking, and generally not what the masses were looking for.

LDAP is intended to provide an open, convenient way for organizations to manage directory-style information in a way that all of their applications can share. It's part of the overall push to let enterprises share data rather than create islands of data around each application. A directory literally can be used like a phone directory—to store contact information about individuals—but it also can store data such as salary details, information about nonhuman entities such as corporate divisions or servers, or even information about trading card collections.

In the scope of your sample application, you might want to store your customer information using an LDAP directory if you have a direct-mailing application that could take its input from an LDAP source. That way, you could do a direct-mail advertising campaign to your customer base without having to convert from a proprietary database format.

As with most of the technologies in this book, a thorough tutorial on LDAP would take an entire other book. The basics can be covered in a few pages, however.

The LDAP Schema

Like SQL, the heart of LDAP is a schema (or set of schemas). An LDAP schema defines what kind of data will be stored and how it's organized. For example, you might have a schema object called a `person` that stores information such as last name and title.

What makes LDAP powerful is that every entry in an LDAP database has a uniquely identified type or set of types. Because the schemas are globally registered, and because every datum is associated with one or more universally unique type identifiers, you know that if an object has the `person` object class, you'll be able to ask for the `givenName` attribute to get the first name. Moreover, because each datum reports its type(s), and because you can get schema definitions from the LDAP server, you'll always know exactly what type of information an LDAP entity holds.

In LDAP, each object is uniquely identified by a distinguished name (DN). The DN allows you to make a reference to the object that identifies only that particular piece of data. A DN consists of a series of attributes that uniquely identify the object. They're a bit like a domain name, in that the most general piece of information is rightmost in the DN.

For example, you might want an object that represents your company as a whole (which typically would serve as the root object for all the objects dealing with your company). A common scheme for this is to use the o (organization) attribute, with your domain name as the value. So `o=bfg.com` is the DN that uniquely identifies your company.

If you want to talk about the marketing division, you could use the ou attribute (organizational unit)—thus ou=marketing,o=bfg.com. As mentioned before, the most specific piece of information is placed leftmost.

Now say that you want to talk about Bob Jones, who works in marketing. You would use the uid (user ID) field along with a unique identifier—for example:

uid=bjones, o=bfg.com

Note that you don't need to specify ou=marketing in the DN because the uid and o attributes are enough to uniquely distinguish Bob, unless different departments have overlapping user IDs (a large corporation might). In that case, the DN would be this:

uid=bjones, ou=marketing, o=bfg.com

Another DN for a computer might be this:

uid=deepthought, ou=webservers, ou=hardware, o=bfg.com

This DN specifies a server named deepthought, which is a Web server. All the computers are further placed under the hardware OU and finally are organized under the bfg.com organization.

The leftmost element in a DN is called the relative distinguished name (RDN). That is because that element distinguishes among different entities that live below the object specified by the remainder of the DN.

In LDAP, each object can both store data and be the parent of objects that also store data. So, an organization object can both store information about the organization and have children (the employees, or organizational units, or products sold). In the Windows world, the Windows Registry works in the same manner.

Objects have two properties associated with them. They have object classes that they are members of, and they have attributes of those object classes.

The object classes define what attributes are available to an object through the LDAP schema. Object classes have a hierarchy; if you create an object of type OrganizationalPerson, which is a derivative class of person, you'll get all the attributes available to person as well. However, if you do a search and specify objectClass=Person, you won't get these objects, which is something to look out for.

Attributes are individual properties associated with the class. For example, Person has attributes such as sn (surname) and givenName.

Getting LDAP'ed

LDAP is available both as an open-source implementation and as a commercial product, such as the iPlanet Directory Server. The standard open-source implementation is OpenLDAP, which is available in source form and in RPMs for Linux. If you have a Linux distribution, you probably have a copy of LDAP on your RPMs CD; adding it is as easy as doing `rpm --install`. If you don't have OpenLDAP, you can get it from www.openldap.org.

For Windows, you need to get a ported version. We'll be using one available from http://www.fivesight.com/downloads/openldap.asp.

After downloading it and extracting LDAP into C:\TMP, you should copy the openl-dap directory (which might be named something like openldap-2.0.11) to C:\ and rename it as OPENLDAP. You need to make some configuration changes to the slapd.conf file (see Listing 15.1).

LISTING 15.1   slapd.conf

```
# $OpenLDAP: pkg/ldap/servers/slapd/slapd.conf,v 1.8.8.6 2001/04/20 23:32:43 kurt
Exp $
#
# See slapd.conf(5) for details on configuration options.
# This file should NOT be world readable.
#
include         /openldap/schema/core.schema
include         /openldap/schema/cosine.schema
include         /openldap/schema/inetorgperson.schema


# Define global ACLs to disable default read access.

# Do not enable referrals until AFTER you have a working directory
# service AND an understanding of referrals.
#referral    ldap://root.openldap.org

pidfile             /temp/slapd.pid
argsfile        /temp/slapd.args

# Load dynamic backend modules:
# modulepath  %MODULEDIR%
# moduleload  back_ldap.la
# moduleload  back_ldbm.la
# moduleload  back_passwd.la
# moduleload  back_shell.la


#####################################################################
# ldbm database definitions
```

LISTING 15.1 Continued

```
######################################################################

database        ldbm
suffix                  "dc=bfg,dc=com"
rootdn                  "cn=chiefgeek,dc=bfg,dc=com"
rootpw                  GeekGuru
directory       /openldap/data/bfg
```

Here the sample file has been removed, the bfg database has been added, and some absolute directory paths have been set so that you don't have to mess around with environment variables.

The bfg entry basically says that you're creating an LDAP database uniquely identified as dc=bfg,dc=com (which also can be read as bfg.com, the same as saying o=bfg.com). The DN of the entity with privileges to modify the database is set using the rootdn tag and can be read as "common name chiefgeek from bfg.com." You also have to specify the password. The root DN is the "master DN" for an LDAP database, the one allowed to make changes to anything inside the database.

Finally, you tell OpenLDAP where to find the files to store the data for bfg. OpenLDAP will create the files, but you need to create the directory.

Now you're ready to import your initial dataset for the bfg database. You can do that by creating an LDIF file, which is a text representation of an LDAP database, and then using a tool called slapadd to dump the data into LDAP. The bfg.ldif file is shown in Listing 15.2. Most of the fields are self-explanatory, but a few need deciphering.

LISTING 15.2 bfg.ldif

```
dn: dc=bfg, dc=com
objectclass: top

dn: cn=chiefgeek,dc=bfg, dc=com
cn:chiefgeek
sn:Geek
userPassword: GeekGuru
objectclass: top
objectclass: person

dn: o=bfg,dc=bfg,dc=com
o: bfg
objectclass: top
objectclass: organization
```

LISTING 15.2   Continued

```
description: Books For Geeks, Inc.
telephoneNumber: 1-603-555-1212
street: 1 Geek Way
l: Nashua
st: NH
postalCode: 03031

dn: ou=admin,dc=bfg, dc=com
ou: admin
description: Administrative
objectclass: top
objectclass:  organizationalUnit

dn: ou=sales,dc=bfg, dc=com
ou: sales
description: Sales
objectclass: top
objectclass: organizationalUnit

dn: ou=editorial,dc=bfg, dc=com
ou: editorial
description: Editorial
objectclass: top
objectclass: organizationalUnit

dn: uid=bjones,dc=bfg, dc=com
objectclass: top
objectclass: inetOrgPerson
uid: bjones
cn:Bob Jones
o: bfg
ou: admin
employeeNumber: 1
givenName: Bob
sn: Jones
userPassword: thegeek
telephoneNumber: x1234
title: Chief Geek
```

In this code, you start by defining the root of the LDAP hierarchy. In most cases, that's the domain name of the company. An entry for the rootdn is defined as well, even through it's not required.

Next you define an entry for the company and then one for each of the organizational units inside the company. Notice that an object can have more than one `objectclass` entry; it inherits the attributes of each class. You also can have multiple attributes with the same name. For example, the `cn` (common name) field might have both `Bob Jones` and another entry of `Robert Jones`.

Finally, you have an entry for the president of the company.

The entries are required to go in this order because you can't reference an entity as an attribute (for example, bfg as an o organization attribute) until it has been defined.

To use slapadd, you need to place a copy of your slapd.conf file in the sysconf subdirectory of C:\OPENLDAP. You need to run slapadd *before* you start OpenLDAP. After you've imported the data (see Figure 15.1), you can start OpenLDAP. You can do that by running slapd.exe from the OPENLDAP directory, or you can use the command `slapd install` if you're running a services-friendly version of Windows such as 2000, NT, or XP Pro. Then install OpenLDAP as a service.

FIGURE 15.1   Running slapadd.

Some search tools come with OpenLDAP, but they are a pain to use. Instead, grab an LDAP browser such as the LDAP Browser/Editor available from `http://www.iit.edu/~gawojar/ldap`. After starting it up, add your new bfg database to its connection list (see Figure 15.2) and connect (see Figure 15.3); you are presented with your LDAP data as you entered it (see Figure 15.4).

ALTERNATIVES TO OPENLDAP

Most of the time, open-source tools are not only cheaper but they also have at least as many features as their commercial counterparts. Occasionally, as with OpenLDAP, you've got an implementation for which you're getting what you (don't) pay for.

OpenLDAP is reliable but primitive to work with. If you have the money, you might want to invest in one of the commercial products instead.

Sun offers an LDAP server as part of the iPlanet suite. Because iPlanet has a trial version, you can try it out first and decide whether you want to spend the money for a full license. Novel, among others, also makes an LDAP server.

FIGURE 15.2   Configuring LBE.

FIGURE 15.3   Connecting with LBE.

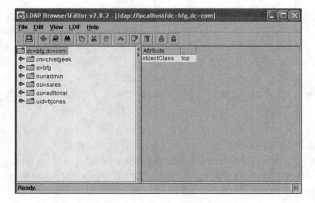

FIGURE 15.4   Viewing the BFG LDAP data.

JNDI

Now you're ready to talk to LDAP from Java. To do this, you use the Java Naming and Directory Interface (JNDI). JNDI can be used for a lot more than just interfacing to LDAP. For example, you can use JNDI to talk to DNS. But for now, our discussion will be restricted to JNDI as it pertains to LDAP.

JNDI itself doesn't know anything about LDAP. Instead, it provides a general interface that lets a programmer talk to a number of different resources (such as NIS, LDAP, or DNS) using the same API. What all these have in common is the notion that a name can be looked up in some kind of directory to return information about that name. For example, in DNS, a name maps to an IP address. In LDAP, a name (represented as a DN or an RDN) maps to an LDAP object with attributes and possibly child objects.

Directory services such as LDAP register themselves with JNDI as providers. When you request an initial context from JNDI, you specify which service you want to use.

A context is a relative reference into a JNDI tree. For example, in LDAP, the initial context that JNDI returns is the root of the LDAP database (in this case, o=bfg.com). From there, you can use an RDN to find a child of the current object without needing to refer to the entire DN.

It is also possible to talk directly to LDAP without using JNDI, using tools such as the Novel LDAP Class Libraries. Although there is nothing wrong with this approach, most developers have chosen to use the JNDI interface instead.

In almost all cases when interfacing to an LDAP server, you want to be able to do four things to an LDAP server: search it, get an entry, modify an entry, and add an entry. You can do these four things very easily by using the JNDI API directly (see Listing 15.3).

LISTING 15.3   Employee.java

```java
package com.bfg.employee;

import java.util.Hashtable;
import javax.naming.*;
import javax.naming.directory.*;
import java.util.Vector;
import java.util.HashMap;
import java.sql.*;
import java.util.Iterator;
import org.apache.turbine.services.db.TurbineDB;
import org.apache.turbine.util.db.pool.DBConnection;
import org.apache.log4j.Category;
```

LISTING 15.3   Continued

```
import java.util.ResourceBundle;

public class Employee implements java.lang.Comparable {

    static Category cat = Category.getInstance(Employee.class);
    protected String pFirstName;

    public String getFirstName() {
      return pFirstName;
    }

    public void setFirstName(String firstName) {
     pFirstName = firstName;
    }

    protected String pLastName;

    public String getLastName () {
      return pLastName;
    }

    public void setLastName (String lastName) {
     pLastName = lastName;
    }

    protected String pUserID;

    public String getUserID () {
      return pUserID;
    }

    public void setUserID (String userID) {
     pUserID = userID;
    }

    protected String pPassword;

    public String getPassword () {
      return pPassword;
    }

    public void setPassword (String password) {
```

LISTING 15.3 Continued

```
    pPassword = password;
  }

  protected String pOrganization;

  public String getOrganization () {
    return pOrganization;
  }

  public void setOrganization (String org) {
    pOrganization = org;
  }

  protected String pOrgUnit;

  public String getOrgUnit() {
    return pOrgUnit;
  }

  public void setOrgUnit(String ou) {
    pOrgUnit = ou;
  }

  protected String pEmployeeNumber;

  public String getEmployeeNumber () {
    return pEmployeeNumber;
  }

  public void setEmployeeNumber (String empno) {
    pEmployeeNumber = empno;
  }

  protected String pTelephone;

  public String getTelephoneNumber() {
    return pTelephone;
  }

  public void setTelephoneNumber(String telno) {
    pTelephone = telno;
```

LISTING 15.3   Continued

```java
    }

    protected String pTitle;

    public String getTitle() {
      return pTitle;
    }

    public void setTitle(String title) {
      pTitle = title;
    }
    public static Employee findEmployee(String userID) {
      Vector employees = runEmployeeSearch("(uid=" + userID + ")");
      if (employees.size() > 0) {
          return((Employee) employees.elementAt(0));
      } else {
          return null;
      }
    }

    public void createEmployee() throws NamingException {
      Hashtable env = new Hashtable();
      env.put(Context.INITIAL_CONTEXT_FACTORY,
              "com.sun.jndi.ldap.LdapCtxFactory");
      env.put(Context.PROVIDER_URL,
              "ldap://localhost:389/");
      env.put(Context.SECURITY_AUTHENTICATION, "simple");
      env.put(Context.SECURITY_PRINCIPAL, "cn=chiefgeek,dc=bfg,dc=com");
      env.put(Context.SECURITY_CREDENTIALS, "GeekGuru");

      DirContext ctx = new InitialDirContext(env);
      Attributes myAttrs;
      String uid = getFirstName().substring(0,1) + getLastName();
      uid = uid.toLowerCase();
      myAttrs = new BasicAttributes(true);
      Attribute oc = new BasicAttribute("objectclass");
      oc.add("top");
      oc.add("inetOrgPerson");
      myAttrs.put(oc);
      myAttrs.put("uid", uid);
      myAttrs.put("cn", getFirstName() + " " + getLastName());
      myAttrs.put("givenname", getFirstName());
```

LISTING 15.3   Continued

```
    myAttrs.put("sn", getLastName());
    myAttrs.put("o", getOrganization());
    myAttrs.put("ou", getOrgUnit());
    myAttrs.put("userPassword", getPassword());
    myAttrs.put("telephoneNumber", getTelephoneNumber());
    myAttrs.put("employeeNumber", getEmployeeNumber());
    myAttrs.put("title", getTitle());
    boolean success = false;
    int count = 0;
    String uidnum = uid;
    while (!success) {
        try {
            ctx.createSubcontext("uid=" + uidnum + ",dc=bfg,dc=com", myAttrs);
            success = true;
        } catch (NameAlreadyBoundException e) {
            count++;
            uidnum = uid + count;
            myAttrs.put("uid", uidnum);
        }
    }
    ctx.close();
    setUserID(uidnum);
}

public void modifyEmployee() throws NamingException {
  Hashtable env = new Hashtable();
  env.put(Context.INITIAL_CONTEXT_FACTORY,
          "com.sun.jndi.ldap.LdapCtxFactory");
  env.put(Context.PROVIDER_URL,
          "ldap://localhost:389/");
  env.put(Context.SECURITY_AUTHENTICATION, "simple");
  env.put(Context.SECURITY_PRINCIPAL, "cn=chiefgeek,dc=bfg,dc=com");
  env.put(Context.SECURITY_CREDENTIALS, "GeekGuru");

  DirContext ctx = new InitialDirContext(env);

  Attributes myAttrs;
  myAttrs = new BasicAttributes(true);
  myAttrs = new BasicAttributes(true);
  Attribute oc = new BasicAttribute("objectclass");
  oc.add("top");
```

LISTING 15.3   Continued

```
      oc.add("inetOrgPerson");
      myAttrs.put(oc);
      myAttrs.put("uid", getUserID());
      myAttrs.put("cn", getFirstName() + " " + getLastName());
      myAttrs.put("givenname", getFirstName());
      myAttrs.put("sn", getLastName());
      myAttrs.put("o", getOrganization());
      myAttrs.put("ou", getOrgUnit());
      myAttrs.put("userPassword", getPassword());
      myAttrs.put("telephoneNumber", getTelephoneNumber());
      myAttrs.put("employeeNumber", getEmployeeNumber());
      myAttrs.put("title", getTitle());

      ctx.modifyAttributes("uid=" + getUserID() +",dc=bfg,dc=com",
                           DirContext.REPLACE_ATTRIBUTE,
                           myAttrs);
    ctx.close();
  }

  public boolean equals(Employee e) {
    return (getUserID() != null) && (e.getUserID() != null)
        && getUserID().equals(e.getUserID());
  }
  public static Vector getAllEmployees() {
    return runEmployeeSearch("(objectclass=inetOrgPerson)");
  }
  public static Vector runEmployeeSearch(String search) {
    Vector employees = new Vector();
    try {
        Hashtable env = new Hashtable();
        env.put(Context.INITIAL_CONTEXT_FACTORY,
                "com.sun.jndi.ldap.LdapCtxFactory");
        env.put(Context.PROVIDER_URL,
                "ldap://localhost:389/");
        env.put(Context.SECURITY_AUTHENTICATION, "simple");
        env.put(Context.SECURITY_PRINCIPAL, "cn=chiefgeek,dc=bfg,dc=com");
        env.put(Context.SECURITY_CREDENTIALS, "GeekGuru");

        DirContext ctx = new InitialDirContext(env);
        SearchControls constraints = new SearchControls();
```

LISTING 15.3   Continued

```
            constraints.setSearchScope(SearchControls.SUBTREE_SCOPE);

        NamingEnumeration results =
            ctx.search("dc=bfg, dc=com", search, constraints);
        while (results != null && results.hasMore()) {
            Employee e = new Employee();
            SearchResult sr = (SearchResult) results.next();
            Attributes attrs = sr.getAttributes();
            e.setFirstName((String)attrs.get("givenname").get());
            e.setLastName((String)attrs.get("sn").get());
            e.setPassword(new String(((byte[])attrs.get("userPassword").get())));
            e.setUserID((String)attrs.get("uid").get());
            e.setOrganization((String) attrs.get("o").get());
            e.setOrgUnit((String) attrs.get("ou").get());
            e.setTelephoneNumber((String) attrs.get("telephoneNumber").get());
            e.setTitle((String) attrs.get("title").get());
            e.setEmployeeNumber((String) attrs.get("employeeNumber").get());
            employees.add(e);
        }
        ctx.close();
    } catch (NamingException ex) {
        System.err.println("Problem getting attribute:" + ex);
        ex.printStackTrace();
    }
    return employees;
}

public int compareTo(Object o) {
  Employee e = (Employee) o;
  int  comp = getLastName().compareTo(e.getLastName());
  if (comp != 0) {
      return comp;
  }

  return getFirstName().compareTo(e.getFirstName());
}

}
```

It's always nice to implement `Comparable` for object classes such as `employees` that you might want to sort in lists. This means that you can use the built-in Java sorting functionality on them.

You need to provide object properties for any attributes that you want to store and retrieve, just as you would for an object that is sourced from a database.

You're going to write a generalized method to find one or more employees based on an LDAP filter, so here you only have to call the search method with the appropriate filter and then see if you get an employee record.

With record creation, you get into the interesting stuff. You begin by instantiating a JNDI context that points to your LDAP server. You need to provide authentication because you're adding information; this requires nonanonymous privileges (you'll also need this when reading data back out because you want the password, which is normally concealed).

In LDAP, you can control what operations can be done by anyone (similar, for example, to doing an anonymous FTP) and what operations require authentication. By default, insertion of records can't be done without providing authentication.

After you've established a context, you need to generate a user ID. You don't want to have the person creating the account specify the ID because the user ID is the unique part of the DN for an employee; you can't have two jsmith entries if there is a John Smith and a James Smith, so you'll need to have the code check for that. Make the user ID the first letter of the first name and the entire last name.

Go through and set all the attributes for the new object. If an attribute has two values, such as `objectclass`, create another attribute object, put the values in it, and then add that object to the main attribute object.

With all the attributes in place, the code enters a loop. It tries to create a new subcontext of the JNDI context (which, for LDAP contexts, means that it creates a new LDAP record). If it gets a `NameAlreadyBound` exception, this means that that DN is already in use. In that case, the code appends a 1 to the end of the user ID (jsmith1, for example) and loops around to try again. If the DN is still in use, it tries 2, 3, and so forth until one succeeds.

When you get a good insertion, set the uid record of this employee to the value that worked, and then return.

Modifying an existing user uses essentially the same code, except that it calls `modifyAttributes` instead of `createSubcontext`. The `REPLACE_ATTRIBUTE` flag indicates that you should overwrite an attribute of the same name rather than adding to it.

The `getAllEmployees` method also uses the `search` method, which directly follows it. It requests all objects of type `inetOrgPerson`, which is the object class that you used to define the employees.

The employee search method is handed an LDAP search string and sets the search constraints to search the entire LDAP tree (you also can request one-level or root-only searches).

When matches are found, all the attributes are copied out of the LDAP record into the appropriate properties in the object.

The `compareTo` method just tries comparing the last names and then compares the first names if the last names are equals.

Testing LDAP Reading

After building and compiling the `Employee` bean, you can test it with some stand-alone JSP pages. To begin, see if you can read employee records out of the database (see Listing 15.4).

The test program takes an employee user ID as an argument and then uses the `findEmployee` method to look it up in LDAP. If an employee is found and returned, the code displays various pieces of information about that person (see Figure 15.5); otherwise it prints an error message.

LISTING 15.4   testLdapRead.jsp

```
<%@ page import="com.bfg.employee.Employee" %>

<HEAD><TITLE>Look for employee test</TITLE></HEAD><BODY>
<%
Employee emp = Employee.findEmployee(request.getParameter("uid"));
if (emp != null) {
%>

Found employee <%= emp.getFirstName() %> <%= emp.getLastName() %>!<P>
First Name: <%= emp.getFirstName() %><BR>
Last Name: <%= emp.getLastName() %><BR>
Password: <%= emp.getPassword() %><BR>
Title: <%= emp.getTitle() %><BR>
Employee Num: <%= emp.getEmployeeNumber() %><BR>
Telephone: <%= emp.getTelephoneNumber() %><P>
<% } else { %>
Employee not found!
<% } %>
</BODY>
```

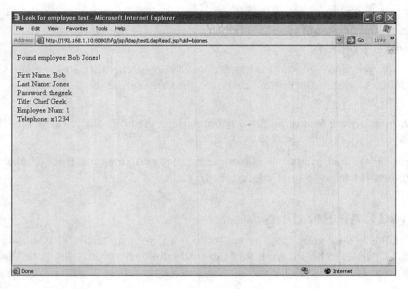

FIGURE 15.5 Running testLdapRead.jsp.

Testing LDAP Creation

Now you can try a JSP to test LDAP record creation (see Listing 15.5). Model this page after the form-submission pages that you've written to this point. A couple of refinements have been added to make the code a bit more straightforward, mainly in the form of notNull and bn (blanks from nulls) helper functions defined at the top. When the page is first requested (or if all the values aren't filled out), it displays a form with all the employee fields (see Figure 15.6). When all the fields are filled out correctly, it uses LDAP to create the record and to display the uid that was assigned (see Figure 15.7).

You have to explicitly set orgUnit to "" if it's null because you're going to use it later in an equals test and you don't want to get a null pointer exception. A future enhancement would be to get a list of valid ou values from LDAP and use those values to create the pull-down rather than hardwiring in this information.

LISTING 15.5 testLdapCreate.jsp

```
<%@ page import="com.bfg.employee.Employee" %>
<jsp:useBean id="emp" class="com.bfg.employee.Employee" scope="request"/>
<jsp:setProperty name="emp" property="*"/>

<HEAD><TITLE>Create new employee</TITLE></HEAD><BODY>
<%!
private boolean notNull(String str) {
```

LISTING 15.5   Continued

```
    return ((str != null) && (str.length() > 0));
}

private String bn (String val) {
    if (val == null) return "";
    return val;
}
%>
<%
if (emp.getOrgUnit() == null) {
    emp.setOrgUnit("");
}

if (request.getParameter("SUBMITTED") != null) {
    if (notNull(emp.getLastName()) &&
      notNull(emp.getFirstName()) &&
      notNull(emp.getTitle()) &&
      notNull(emp.getEmployeeNumber()) &&
      notNull(emp.getOrgUnit()) &&
      notNull(emp.getTelephoneNumber()) &&
      notNull(emp.getPassword())) {
      emp.setOrganization("bfg");
      emp.createEmployee();
      out.write("Created employee " + emp.getUserID() + "!</BODY>");
      return;
    }
}
%>
<H1><CENTER>Create New Employee</CENTER></H1>
<FORM ACTION="testLdapCreate.jsp" METHOD="POST">
<INPUT TYPE="HIDDEN" NAME="SUBMITTED" VALUE="YES">
<TABLE WIDTH="75%" BORDER=1>
  <TR><TD>Last Name: </TD>
  <TD><INPUT TYPE="TEXT" NAME="lastName"
            VALUE="<%= bn(emp.getLastName()) %>"></TD></TR>
  <TR><TD>First Name: </TD>
  <TD><INPUT TYPE="TEXT" NAME="firstName"
            VALUE="<%= bn(emp.getFirstName()) %>"></TD></TR>
  <TR><TD>Title: </TD>
  <TD><INPUT TYPE="TEXT" NAME="title"
            VALUE="<%= bn(emp.getTitle()) %>"></TD></TR>
  <TR><TD>Emp Num: </TD>
  <TD><INPUT TYPE="TEXT" NAME="employeeNumber"
            VALUE="<%= bn(emp.getEmployeeNumber()) %>"></TD></TR>
```

LISTING 15.5   Continued

```
<TR><TD>Division: </TD>
<TD><SELECT NAME="orgUnit">
  <OPTION VALUE="">Please Select
  <OPTION VALUE="admin"
    <%= emp.getOrgUnit().equals("admin")?"SELECTED":"" %>>
    Administrative
  <OPTION VALUE="sales"
    <%= emp.getOrgUnit().equals("sales")?"SELECTED":"" %>>
    Sales
  <OPTION VALUE="editorial"
    <%= emp.getOrgUnit().equals("editorial")?"SELECTED":"" %>>
    Editorial
  </SELECT>
</TD>
<TR><TD>Telephone Number: </TD>
<TD><INPUT TYPE="TEXT" NAME="telephoneNumber"
           VALUE="<%= bn(emp.getTelephoneNumber()) %>"></TD></TR>
<TR><TD>Password</TD>
<TD><INPUT TYPE="TEXT" NAME="password"
           VALUE="<%= bn(emp.getPassword()) %>"></TD></TR></TABLE>
<CENTER><INPUT TYPE=SUBMIT VALUE="Create User"></CENTER>
</BODY>
```

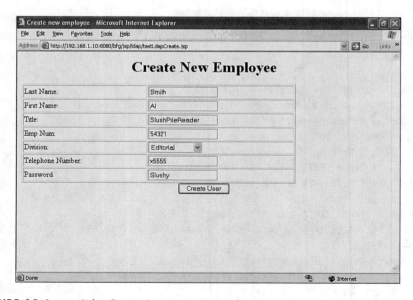

FIGURE 15.6   testLdapCreate.jsp requesting values.

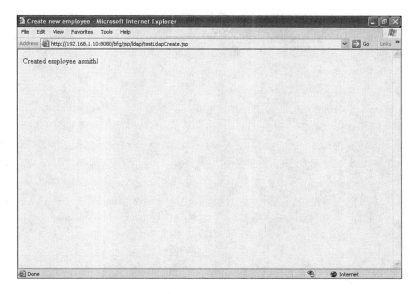

FIGURE 15.7   testLdapCreate.jsp creating a user.

After you run it, you can bring up the LDAP browser and confirm for yourself that the entry has been dropped into the LDAP database (see Figure 15.8).

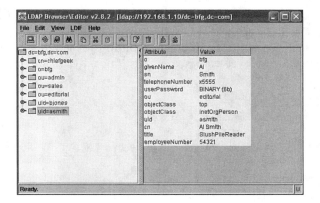

FIGURE 15.8   The new employee record appears.

If you run this repeatedly on the same last name and first initial, you can see that the uid remains unique via the addition of a number to the end of the uid (see Figure 15.9). Now you know where JSMITH34234 comes from on all those AOL accounts.

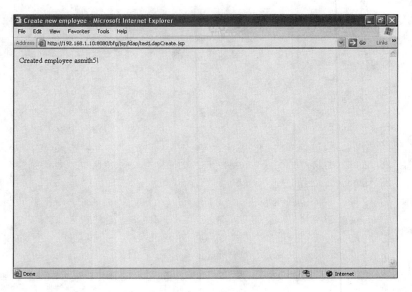

FIGURE 15.9   Adding more of the same name.

Trying Out LDAP Modification

Writing a JSP to modify employee information is very similar to creating employee records (see Listing 15.6), although it saves a bit of time by having the form submit back to itself. On this page, the uid to modify is handed in as an argument (presumably from another page with a pull-down or fill-in-the-blank input field). The page checks to see if the employee requested exists; if not, it generates an error.

LISTING 15.6   testLdapModify.jsp

```
<%@ page import="com.bfg.employee.Employee" %>

<HEAD><TITLE>Modify employee</TITLE></HEAD><BODY>
<%!
private boolean notNull(String str) {
    return ((str != null) && (str.length() > 0));
}

private String bn (String val) {
    if (val == null) return "";
    return val;
}
```

LISTING 15.6   Continued

```
%>

<%
Employee emp = Employee.findEmployee(request.getParameter("uid"));
if (emp == null) {
    out.write("Employee Not Found!</BODY>");
    return;
}

if (request.getParameter("SUBMITTED") != null) {
    JspRuntimeLibrary.introspect(emp, request);
    if (notNull(emp.getLastName()) &&
      notNull(emp.getFirstName()) &&
      notNull(emp.getTitle()) &&
      notNull(emp.getEmployeeNumber()) &&
      notNull(emp.getOrgUnit()) &&
      notNull(emp.getTelephoneNumber()) &&
      notNull(emp.getPassword())) {
        emp.setOrganization("bfg");
        emp.modifyEmployee();
        out.write("Modified employee " + emp.getUserID() + "!</BODY>");
        return;
    }
}

if (emp.getOrgUnit() == null) {
    emp.setOrgUnit("");
}
%>
<H1><CENTER>Modify Employee</CENTER></H1>
<FORM ACTION="testLdapModify.jsp" METHOD="POST">
<INPUT TYPE="HIDDEN" NAME="SUBMITTED" VALUE="YES">
<INPUT TYPE="HIDDEN" NAME="uid" VALUE="<%= emp.getUserID() %>">
<TABLE WIDTH="75%" BORDER=1>
  <TR><TD>Last Name: </TD>
  <TD><INPUT TYPE="TEXT" NAME="lastName"
              VALUE="<%= bn(emp.getLastName()) %>"></TD></TR>
  <TR><TD>First Name: </TD>
  <TD><INPUT TYPE="TEXT" NAME="firstName"
              VALUE="<%= bn(emp.getFirstName()) %>"></TD></TR>
```

LISTING 15.6   Continued

```
<TR><TD>Title: </TD>
<TD><INPUT TYPE="TEXT" NAME="title"
            VALUE="<%= bn(emp.getTitle()) %>"></TD></TR>
<TR><TD>Emp Num: </TD>
<TD><INPUT TYPE="TEXT" NAME="employeeNumber"
            VALUE="<%= bn(emp.getEmployeeNumber()) %>"></TD></TR>
<TR><TD>Division: </TD>
<TD><SELECT NAME="orgUnit">
  <OPTION VALUE="">Please Select
  <OPTION VALUE="admin"
    <%= emp.getOrgUnit().equals("admin")?"SELECTED":"" %>>
    Administrative
  <OPTION VALUE="sales"
    <%= emp.getOrgUnit().equals("sales")?"SELECTED":"" %>>
    Sales
  <OPTION VALUE="editorial"
    <%= emp.getOrgUnit().equals("editorial")?"SELECTED":"" %>>
    Editorial
  </SELECT>
</TD>
<TR><TD>Telephone Number: </TD>
<TD><INPUT TYPE="TEXT" NAME="telephoneNumber"
            VALUE="<%= bn(emp.getTelephoneNumber()) %>"></TD></TR>
<TR><TD>Password</TD>
<TD><INPUT TYPE="TEXT" NAME="password"p
            VALUE="<%= bn(emp.getPassword()) %>"></TD></TR></TABLE>
<CENTER><INPUT TYPE=SUBMIT VALUE="Modify User"></CENTER>
</BODY>
if (request.getParameter("SUBMITTED") != null) {
    JspRuntimeLibrary.introspect(emp, request);
    if (notNull(emp.getLastName()) &&
      notNull(emp.getFirstName()) &&
      notNull(emp.getTitle()) &&
      notNull(emp.getEmployeeNumber()) &&
      notNull(emp.getOrgUnit()) &&
      notNull(emp.getTelephoneNumber()) &&
      notNull(emp.getPassword())) {
      emp.setOrganization("bfg");
      emp.modifyEmployee();
      out.write("Modified employee " + emp.getUserID() + "!</BODY>");
```

LISTING 15.6   Continued

```
    return;
    }
}

if (emp.getOrgUnit() == null) {
    emp.setOrgUnit("");
}
%>
<H1><CENTER>Modify Employee</CENTER></H1>
<FORM ACTION="testLdapModify.jsp" METHOD="POST">
<INPUT TYPE="HIDDEN" NAME="SUBMITTED" VALUE="YES">
<INPUT TYPE="HIDDEN" NAME="uid" VALUE="<%= emp.getUserID() %>">
<TABLE WIDTH="75%" BORDER=1>
  <TR><TD>Last Name: </TD>
  <TD><INPUT TYPE="TEXT" NAME="lastName"
              VALUE="<%= bn(emp.getLastName()) %>"></TD></TR>
  <TR><TD>First Name: </TD>
  <TD><INPUT TYPE="TEXT" NAME="firstName"
              VALUE="<%= bn(emp.getFirstName()) %>"></TD></TR>
  <TR><TD>Title: </TD>
  <TD><INPUT TYPE="TEXT" NAME="title"
              VALUE="<%= bn(emp.getTitle()) %>"></TD></TR>
  <TR><TD>Emp Num: </TD>
  <TD><INPUT TYPE="TEXT" NAME="employeeNumber"
              VALUE="<%= bn(emp.getEmployeeNumber()) %>"></TD></TR>
  <TR><TD>Division: </TD>
  <TD><SELECT NAME="orgUnit">
    <OPTION VALUE="">Please Select
    <OPTION VALUE="admin"
      <%= emp.getOrgUnit().equals("admin")?"SELECTED":"" %>>
      Administrative
    <OPTION VALUE="sales"
      <%= emp.getOrgUnit().equals("sales")?"SELECTED":"" %>>
      Sales
    <OPTION VALUE="editorial"
      <%= emp.getOrgUnit().equals("editorial")?"SELECTED":"" %>>
      Editorial
    </SELECT>
  </TD>
  <TR><TD>Telephone Number: </TD>
```

LISTING 15.6   Continued

```
<TD><INPUT TYPE="TEXT" NAME="telephoneNumber"
            VALUE="<%= bn(emp.getTelephoneNumber()) %>"></TD></TR>
<TR><TD>Password</TD>
<TD><INPUT TYPE="TEXT" NAME="password"p
            VALUE="<%= bn(emp.getPassword()) %>"></TD></TR></TABLE>
<CENTER><INPUT TYPE=SUBMIT VALUE="Modify User"></CENTER>
</BODY>
```

If the employee does exist and the form has already been submitted, the code fills in all the values from the form in the emp employee record. The conventional way to conditionally set all the placeholder variables to their bean counterparts is to place a jsp:setProperty inside a conditional piece of Java code—for example:

```
if (request.getParameter("SUBMITTED") != null) { %>
<jsp:setProperty name="emp" property="*"> <%
```

A slightly less awkward-looking method is to use the JspRuntimeLibrary.introspect call. This is exactly what happens when you do a setProperty. I discovered this method by looking at the Java code that resulted from doing a setProperty in a JSP.

JspRuntimeLibrary is found in the org.apache.jasper.runtime package, and I'm not sure how safe I would feel using it in code that I wanted to be 100% portable: That package might not be available in all implementation.

If you haven't submitted the form yet, or if the form isn't totally valid, you display the current values for the user (see Figure 15.10). You also can see that Al, like many new users, has used his wife's name as his password and is likely to get a call from the IT department if it runs a cracking program against the password file and learns this. Easily guessed passwords such as a spouse's name or birth dates are easy targets for hackers.

> **NOTE**
>
> If you are a system administrator, something that I highly recommend you do regularly is to run a cracking program. I've found guess rates as high as 40% running the password-guessing crack program against my /etc/shadow password file on a UNIX system.

For a moment, imagine that on Al's first day, the chief editor and all the rest of the editorial staff accept an offer en masse to relocate to Books for Nerds. Suddenly Al finds himself upgraded from slush pile reader (the slush pile, by the way, is the stack of unsolicited manuscripts that appear in a publisher's mailbox) to chief editor. So, the appropriate change is made by the Human Resources department using the form that you just created and is applied to his record. The results are shown in Figure 15.11.

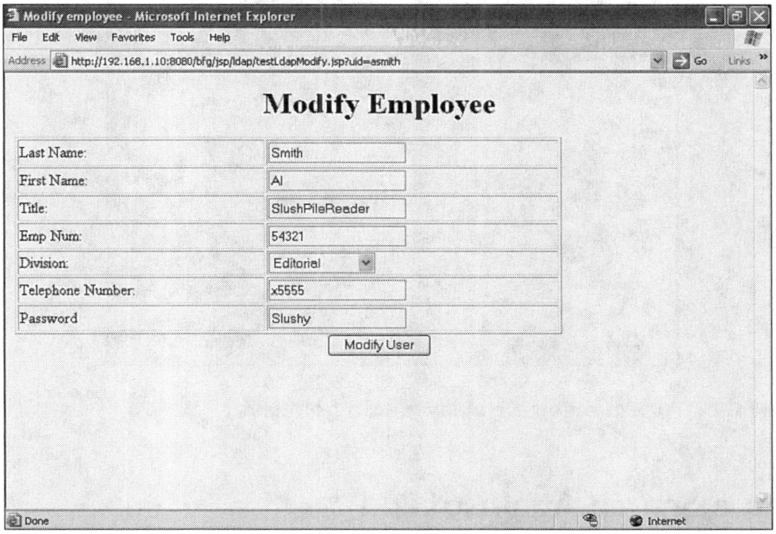

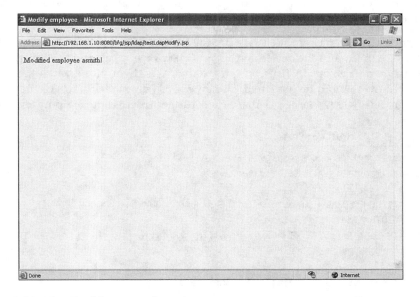

FIGURE 15.10   The employee modification screen.

FIGURE 15.11   The big promotion.

Unable to believe his luck, Al checks via his LDAP browser (Al is an unusually technically savvy slush pile reader) and finds that, in fact, his record has been changed.
(See Figure 15.12.)

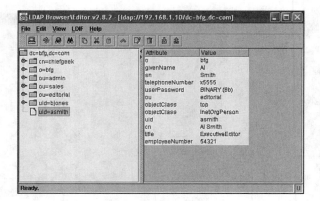

FIGURE 15.12   The promoted employee seen from LBE.

Running a Search Against LDAP

With a large piece of the company gone, it hardly seems worthwhile, but IT decides to continue on with its LDAP project and writes a page to list the company phone directory (not the wisest thing to do, perhaps, given that someone seems to be using it to recruit the company's personnel, but what the heck!).

The phone list page is simplicity itself (see Listing 15.7). It gets an `iterator` over the vector of employees returned from the `getAllEmployees` call and then displays a table (shown in Figure 15.13). You can see that Al is there, along with a large number of his relatives whom he has hired, all named Al. These are artifacts of the development process, when a large number of records got inserted during unit testing.

LISTING 15.7   testLdapSearch.jsp

```
<%@ page import="com.bfg.employee.Employee" %>
<%@ page import="java.util.Iterator" %>

<HEAD><TITLE>Employee Directory</TITLE></HEAD><BODY>
<TABLE WIDTH="75%" BORDER=1>
  <TR><TH>Last Name</TH><TH>First Name</TH><TH>Title</TH><TH>Ext</TH></TR>
<%

Iterator employees = Employee.getAllEmployees().iterator();
while (employees.hasNext()) {
    Employee e = (Employee) employees.next();
%>
    <TR><TD><%= e.getLastName() %></TD>
```

LISTING 15.7   Continued

```
      <TD><%= e.getFirstName() %></TD>
      <TD><%= e.getTitle() %></TD>
      <TD><%= e.getTelephoneNumber() %></TD></TR>
<%
}
%>
</TABLE>
</BODY>
```

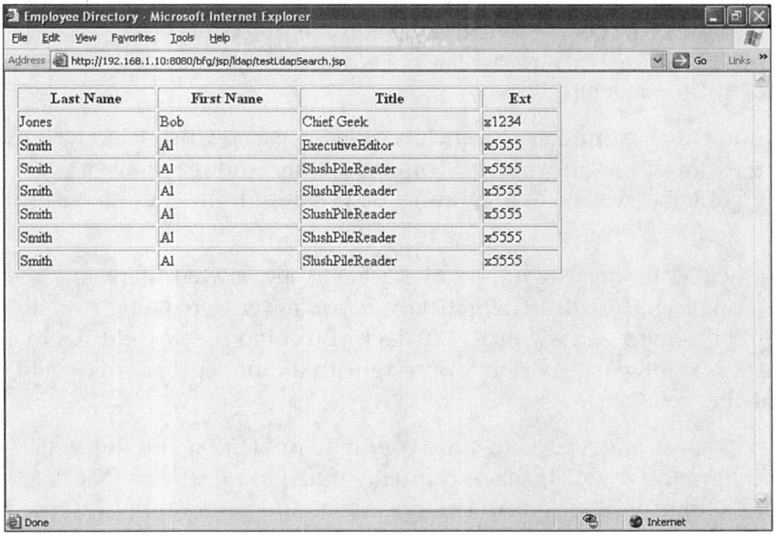

FIGURE 15.13   The employee listing.

Creating Your Own Schemas

The "stock" LDAP schemas are quite extensive. When you add in the registered schemas created by individual organizations, just about every piece of information that you could possibly imagine can be represented with a schema.

Still, the day might come when you find that you have to record the tail length of a user's pet llama or the number of goldfish that someone can eat in a minute, or, on a more practical note, something important to your business, such as health insurance identification numbers. This is when you'll want to extend the LDAP schema universe.

To understand the process, let's look at two schema entries from the core LDAP set.

```
attributetype ( 2.5.4.13 NAME 'description'
     EQUALITY caseIgnoreMatch
     SUBSTR caseIgnoreSubstringsMatch
     SYNTAX 1.3.6.1.4.1.1466.115.121.1.15{1024} )
objectclass ( 2.5.6.6 NAME 'person' SUP top STRUCTURAL
     MUST ( sn $ cn )
     MAY ( userPassword $ telephoneNumber $ seeAlso $ description ) )
```

The first line defines an attribute type called description. It has a unique attribute ID number of 2.5.4.13, is compared to itself with no case sensitivity, looks for substrings also without case sensitivity, and is an object of type 1.3.6.1.4.1.1466.115.121.1.15 (which is a string, believe it or not) with a maximum length of 1024 characters.

The second entry defines an object class called person, which is derived from the top object, must have a surname and a common name, and may have a password, a telephone number, a "see also" entry, and a description. It has a unique ID number of 2.5.6.6.

The unique ID numbers are important because they're what the data placed in the database is associated with. Theoretically, if you never were going to want outside groups to be able to access your LDAP data, you could use any old IDs to create your new entries, as long as they didn't overlap with a number that you would be using from existing schemas.

In reality, it's not much good to store your data in LDAP if you don't plan to share it, at least internally. A SQL database is usually much more efficient for data that won't be shared among applications or organizations. And you don't want your data to conflict with a schema that you might decide to include in your LDAP implementation at a later date. Thus, it's worth getting your own prefix so that you can assign your own LDAP ID numbers without conflicting with anyone else's.

Technically, the number that you're applying for is an object identification number (OID), and you get it from the Internet Assigned Number Authority (IANA). These are the same folks who do things such as track assigned port numbers.

As far as IANA is concerned, you're actually applying for a private enterprise number, which is the prefix that you use to extend an Simple Network Monitoring Protocol (SNMP) Management Information Base (MIB). A MIB is a description of what remote monitoring can be done to a specific piece of hardware or software attached to a network, using the SNMP protocol. It turns out that these numbers use the same numbering system, so applying for one is the same as applying for the other. You can find the form at http://www.iana.org/cgi-bin/enterprise.pl. It takes about a week to get the number back.

When you've received your prefix, you can use it to create a new schema file for the data that you want to collect, and then you can configure your slapd.conf file to make that schema available.

Summary

LDAP is a standardized way to share directory-style information between applications in your organization, or between organizations. LDAP uses distinguished names (DNs) to uniquely identify each object in an LDAP database and uses a schema to describe what types of objects are allowed to reside in that database.

Each object has one or more object classes, which determine the attributes that are available to the object. Objects can be both storers of data and parents to subobjects.

LDAP can be accessed in Java using JNDI. To access an LDAP database, you get an initial context to the root of the LDAP database and then use searches to find the specific object that you want to reference.

In the next chapter, you'll see an example of how to use Struts, an application framework based on the MVC pattern.

16

The Struts Application Framework

Programmers who started doing Web sites back when CGI coding was the hot technology are accustomed to developing sites in a certain way. For example, a form will be presented on one page, a second page is loaded to process the data when the customer hits Submit, and so on.

JSP allows you to refine this somewhat. For example, in this book you have frequently used the same page to both display and process a form. But there's an entirely new way to organize Web sites using the MVC pattern. In this chapter, you'll get a quick introduction to Struts.

The MVC Pattern

Until now, you've been using what the programming hotshots call "model 1" designs. In a model 1 site, the JSP provides both the display and the flow control of the site, and it hooks up to the business logic as well.

Model 1 sites have a couple of problems, especially when you start dealing with large, complex applications. For one thing, the JSP starts to get pretty unwieldy because you have to place more flow control into it.

In addition, you end up with a lot of cases in which you begin to process a JSP, realize that you need to move on to the next step, and have to do a redirect in the middle of the file.

You also find yourself with hard-coded URLs throughout your JSP and have a huge task on your hands every time you want to update a filename or move a directory.

A solution exists in the form of "model 2" platforms. Model 2 is also known as MVC (Model-View-Controller), a design pattern that originated with the SmallTalk language.

Here's a simple example that highlights the difference in approaches. Let's say that you want to let a user click a button on a page that will take them to a signup form, where they then can fill in their information. Then when they submit the page, it writes it to the database and takes them back to the main page.

In a model 1 approach, the link would be an HREF that takes the user to a different page that has the form on it. The user fills in the form and hits Apply, and the submit goes to yet another page that processes the data, redisplays the form (with errors highlighted, if there's a problem), and otherwise writes the data to the database and goes to the main page via an explicit redirect.

In the MVC approach, the URL specified in the HREF on the main page doesn't actually refer to a hard-coded page. Instead, it is a functional reference that tells the MVC controller which actions to take when it is requested. In this case, the controller determines that it's he signup form that needs to be displayed.

When the user submits the form, the MVC controller first sends it off to be validated. If the validation fails, the controller returns to the same form with the errors displayed. If the validation succeeds, the controller passes it on for processing and then returns the user to the main page again.

The difference is that, in a MVC design, all the control rests in the hands of the controller (appropriately, don't you think?). The JSP pages have no knowledge of where actions lead.

A First Look at Struts

It's very easy to provide a complicated description of how MVC works. I'm going to try to provide a simple, if slightly incomplete version, using Struts as an example.

Struts is an Apache model 2 implementation. Describing Struts is a bit of a chicken-and-egg problem because you're really developing three pieces of the application at once. But it might be easier to understand by looking at it first from the perspective of a finished site.

NOTE

Struts was written by Craig McClanahan of Sun Microsystems. I'm grateful to Craig for suggestions that he made regarding this chapter. Assume that all mistakes are mine and that all golden nuggets are his.

A user loads myAccount.jsp, a normal JSP with some custom tag libraries loaded to support Struts. When the user clicks on a link or submits a form, instead of being sent directly going to another JSP, the data is copied from the request into an `ActionForm` object with properties that mirror the data that is being sent from the page—this is the "model" part of MVC.

WHAT ARE TAGLIBS?

A taglib allows a developer to embed functionality into a JSP document using a format that looks more like HTML. You've already seen taglibs in use, in the form of the `<jsp:useBean>` tag.

Tomcat allows developers to write their own taglibs, and the Struts developers have taken advantage of this fact to extend JSP to handle specific functionality that Struts wants to provide to JSP pages.

Next, control is passed to an `Action` object, which runs any business logic needed to complete the user's request and determines what page the user needs to go to next. `Action` returns an object to the Controller (Struts), which uses an XML file to determine what JSP to dispatch to based on the status returned from `Action`.

Finally, the new JSP displays any results (the "view"), and sets up for the next user request.

Setting Up Struts

Installing Struts is actually fairly easy. You need to have the Xerces XML parser available to Tomcat; Chapter 14, "Integrating XML in E-Commerce Sites," describes how to do this.

As of this writing, the current release of Struts is 1.0. Download the ZIP file from the FTP server at apache.org, and unpack it into \STRUTS. Now copy the webapps\struts-blank.war file to \TOMCAT\webapps\struts-bfg.war.

Stop and start the Tomcat server, and you'll see that there is now a struts-bfg subdirectory under webapps. You've just created a Struts-compliant Web app that you'll use to rebuild the MyAccount functionality of the BFG site using Struts.

The struts-config.xml File

You can think of struts-config.xml as the traffic cop that controls the entire flow of an application under Struts. It lives in the WEB-INF subdirectory of your newly created struts-bfg directory under Tomcat. Listing 16.1 shows one modified for your application.

LISTING 16.1   struts-config.xml

```xml
<?xml version="1.0" encoding="ISO-8859-1" ?>

<!DOCTYPE struts-config PUBLIC
        "-//Apache Software Foundation//DTD Struts Configuration 1.0//EN"
        "http://jakarta.apache.org/struts/dtds/struts-config_1_0.dtd">

<!--
    BFG Struts Configuration File
-->


<struts-config>
  <!-- ========== Form Bean Definitions ===================================== -->
  <form-beans>
    <form-bean  name="creditcardForm" type="com.bfg.struts.creditcardForm"/>
    <form-bean  name="addressForm" type="com.bfg.struts.addressForm"/>
    <form-bean  name="accountForm" type="com.bfg.struts.accountForm"/>

  </form-beans>

  <!-- ========== Global Forward Definitions ============================= -->
  <global-forwards>

    <forward  name="myaccount"   path="/myAccount.jsp"/>

  </global-forwards>

  <!-- ========== Action Mapping Definitions ============================= -->
  <action-mappings>

    <action     path="/CreditCard"
                type="com.bfg.struts.cardAction"
                name="creditcardForm"
                scope="request">
      <forward  name="CCaddress"   path="/CCAddress.jsp"/>
    </action>
    <action     path="/CreditCardAddr"
                type="com.bfg.struts.cardAddrAction"
                name="addressForm"
                scope="request">
    </action>
```

LISTING 16.1   Continued

```
    <action     path="/Address"
                type="com.bfg.struts.addressAction"
                name="addressForm"
            input="/Address.jsp"
                scope="request">
        <forward  name="address"   path="/Address.jsp"/>
    </action>
    <action     path="/myAccount"
                type="com.bfg.struts.accountAction"
                name="accountForm"
                scope="request">
        <forward  name="address"    path="/Address.jsp"/>
        <forward  name="creditcard"   path="/CreditCard.jsp"/>
    </action>

 </action-mappings>


</struts-config>
```

The `form-beans` section provides a mapping between a text name for the form bean and the class that implements it. In general, you need a form bean for each page that submits data, but there are exceptions. The form bean has placeholder variables to store the results of submitting the form, and it has validation logic to ensure that the form is filled out correctly. Form beans extend the class `ActionForm`.

Forward directives map strings that will be handled back from `Action` objects to the JSP to which they should be directed. The `global-forwards` section defines strings that any `Action` can use; forwards defined in a specific action definition can be used only for that action.

Now you get into the meat of the file—the action mappings. Each entry starts with a path entry. This corresponds to the URL that you would put in a form `ACTION` tag. Struts does some magic behind the scenes, adding .do to the URL to get it processed here. The .do is removed before matching against the actions. The mapping for the .do is set up in the `web.xml` descriptor for the Web application; the one provided by Struts in its WAR file has it already defined.

The type refers to the class of the object (which is derived from the `Action` class) that will handle the processing of the action and direct the controller to forward to the appropriate next page. `Action` classes contain the business logic of the bean.

The name tells Struts what ActionForm to use to store the data coming off the JSP. Remember that you defined the mapping between these names and the actual classes in the first section of the file. ActionForms act a bit like a jsp:setProperty tag, using self-reflection to extract the properties from the request and set the ActionForm's properties using them. The advantage of using an ActionForm (the model) rather than setting the bean used for the business logic directly is that if you have to back out or reset the values due to validation, for example, you don't affect the underlying state of the business bean.

The scope specifies how long the actionForm will persist. This allows you to have the data available through several Action steps. Remember, the scope refers to the processing of the submit, not the display of the previous page; if you specify a request, you'll have access to the data all the way through the JSP display of the view.

You finish by defining the valid forwarding tags for this action step (in addition to any global ones) and what JSP this forwarding should take you to.

In this file, you're defining four distinct actions: going from the first page of the credit card form to the credit card address (credit cards are broken into two pages for this example), moving from the credit card address to the main page again, moving from an address book edit to the main page, and moving from the main page to an address or credit card edit.

If an action does form validation and might need to return to the form to display errors, the input entry defines the page to which the step should return.

You'll get a better idea of how this all fits together by looking at the code in action. Start with a rewrite of the MyAccount page from the original application (see Listing 16.2). You should put the JSP files into a new directory called strutsjsp. This will prevent them from interfering with the regular application.

LISTING 16.2   myAccount.jsp

```
<%@ page language="java" %>
<%@ page import="com.bfg.customer.Address" %>
<%@ page import="com.bfg.customer.CreditCard" %>
<%@ taglib uri="/WEB-INF/struts-html.tld"
        prefix="html" %>
<%@ taglib uri="/WEB-INF/struts-logic.tld"
        prefix="logic" %>
<%@ taglib uri="/WEB-INF/struts-bean.tld"
        prefix="bean" %>
<%@ include file="/jsp/cust/AutoLogin.jsp" %>
<jsp:useBean id="customer" class="com.bfg.customer.Customer" scope="session"/>
```

LISTING 16.2 Continued

```
<% if (customer.getEmail() == null) {
    response.sendRedirect("Login.jsp");
    return;
}
%>
<html:html>
<head>
<title>
  <bean:message key="myaccount.title"/>
</title>
<%@ include file="/jsp/includes/bfgheader.jsp" %>

<h2 align="center"><bean:message key="myaccount.title"/></h2>
<center><h2><bean:message key="myaccount.addrbook"/></h2></center>
  <html:form action="/myAccount">
  <html:hidden property="action" value="newaddr"/>
  <html:submit>
    <bean:message key="myaccount.createaddr"/>
  </html:submit>
  </html:form>
<TABLE WIDTH="100%">
<logic:iterate id="entry" name="customer" property="addressBook"
type="java.util.Map.Entry">
    <% Address addr = (Address) entry.getValue(); %>
  <TR><TD><%= addr.getFirstName() %> <%= addr.getLastName() %></TD>
<TD><%= addr.getCity() %></TD>
<TD>
      <html:form action="/myAccount">
  <html:hidden property="action" value="editaddr"/>
  <INPUT TYPE="HIDDEN" NAME="addressIndex" value="<%= addr.getAddressID() %>">
    <html:submit>
      <bean:message key="myaccount.edit"/>
    </html:submit>
  </html:form>
</TD>
<TD>
      <html:form action="/myAccount">
  <html:hidden property="action" value="deleteaddr"/>
  <INPUT TYPE="HIDDEN" NAME="addressIndex" value="<%= addr.getAddressID() %>">
    <html:submit>
      <bean:message key="myaccount.delete"/>
```

LISTING 16.2   Continued

```
    </html:submit>
   </html:form>
  </TD>
 </TR>
</logic:iterate>
</TABLE>
<center><h2><bean:message key="myaccount.wallet"/></h2></center>
  <html:form action="/myAccount">
  <html:hidden property="action" value="newcard"/>
  <html:submit>
    <bean:message key="myaccount.createcard"/>
  </html:submit>
  </html:form>
<TABLE WIDTH="100%">
<logic:iterate id="entry" name="customer" property="wallet"
type="java.util.Map.Entry">
    <% CreditCard card = (CreditCard) entry.getValue(); %>
  <TR><TD><%= card.getCardOwner() %> <%= card.getObscuredNumber() %></TD>
<TD>
      <html:form action="/myAccount">
  <html:hidden property="action" value="editcard"/>
  <INPUT TYPE="HIDDEN" NAME="cardIndex" value="<%= card.getCardID() %>">
    <html:submit>
      <bean:message key="myaccount.edit"/>
    </html:submit>
   </html:form>
</TD>
<TD>
      <html:form action="/myAccount">
  <html:hidden property="action" value="deletecard"/>
  <INPUT TYPE="HIDDEN" NAME="cardIndex" value="<%= card.getCardID() %>">
    <html:submit>
      <bean:message key="myaccount.delete"/>
    </html:submit>
   </html:form>
  </TD>
 </TR>
</logic:iterate>
</TABLE>
</html:html>
```

The JSP starts normally enough, except for some directives to make the Struts taglibs available. The `<html:html>` is the first new thing. You're using HTML creation constructs from the Struts library rather than doing them yourself. Some, such as the HTML tag here, are fairly straightforward: It outputs a HTML tag.

The `bean:message` tag lets you drop a value from a resource file (adjusted for the appropriate locale) into JSP. This allows you to automatically internationalize your content by supplying locale-specific property files. You define your message property file using an `ApplicationResource` tag in your web.xml file, as you'll see later in the chapter when you edit it.

The `html:form` tag sets up this form to be handled by Struts, adding a .do to the end of the action, among other things. Remember that Struts maps all files ending in .do to be handled via the Struts controller.

You will also use special tags for the form fields. In the case of the Create button for the address book, you'll use a hidden field in the `Action` to decide where to go next.

The `logic:iterate` tag is a useful one, repeating the JSP between the start and end of the tag, once for each entry in the `Collection` specified in the property of the named object. In this case, it is iterating over the `addressBook HashMap` of the customer object. The `id` property of the `iterate` tag specifies the name of a Java variable to hold each value. In turn, the type field specifies the name of the class that each entry will be cast to, so the collection had better actually hold values of this type to avoid throwing an exception.

Even with the best tag library, I find that sometimes I need to code something using straight JSP. In this case, there's no good way with Struts to create a hidden form field with a computed value. Craig points out that you could create a custom taglib to do it, but for a one-shot deal like this, it is easier to code it as JSP.

The wallet and individual credit cards are displayed using similar code.

The ActionForm

When one of the Submit buttons is hit, the controller looks up the name of the requested `ACTION` in the struts-config.xml file. In this case, it finds that the page requested /myAccount and therefore needs to store any form data into `accountForm` (see Listing 16.3) through introspection. `accountForm` just holds the values in normal bean property fashion.

LISTING 16.3   accountForm.java

```java
package com.bfg.struts;

import javax.servlet.http.HttpServletRequest;
import javax.servlet.http.HttpServletResponse;
import org.apache.struts.action.ActionForm;
import org.apache.struts.action.ActionMapping;

public class accountForm extends ActionForm {
  protected String action;
  protected String cardIndex;
  protected int addressIndex;

  public void setAction(String text) {
    action = text;
  }
  public String getAction() {
    return action;
  }

  public void setCardIndex(String text) {
    cardIndex = text;
  }
  public String getCardIndex() {
    return cardIndex;
  }

  public void setAddressIndex(int val) {
    addressIndex = val;
  }
  public int getAddressIndex() {
    return addressIndex;
  }
}
```

After storing the values, Struts checks to see if a validator method has been defined for the ActionForm. In this case, there isn't, which is the same as having a successful validation. The config file also specified the class of the bean that implements the business logic, which must extend Action and implement the method perform.

Because ActionForm and Action sound so similar, it's worth repeating the distinction. The ActionForm has the placeholders for any submitted data and validates the data. The Action defines the business logic and determines what the ultimate destination of the action is.

The Action

Because there's no validation, control always is handed over to the accountAction class, shown in Listing 16.4.

LISTING 16.4   accountAction.java

```java
package com.bfg.struts;

import javax.servlet.http.HttpServletRequest;
import javax.servlet.http.HttpServletResponse;
import javax.servlet.ServletException;
import org.apache.struts.action.ActionForm;
import org.apache.struts.action.Action;
import org.apache.struts.action.ActionMapping;
import org.apache.struts.action.ActionForward;
import org.apache.struts.util.PropertyUtils;
import com.bfg.customer.Address;
import com.bfg.customer.Customer;
import com.bfg.customer.CreditCard;
import java.io.*;

public class accountAction extends Action {
    public ActionForward perform(ActionMapping mapping,
                                 ActionForm form,
                                 HttpServletRequest request,
                                 HttpServletResponse response)
        throws IOException, ServletException {
        accountForm af = (accountForm) form;
        Customer cust = ((Customer)request.getSession().getAttribute("customer"));
        if (af.getAction().equals("newaddr")) {
            request.setAttribute("addressForm", new addressForm());
            return mapping.findForward("address");
        }

        if (af.getAction().equals("newcard")) {
            request.setAttribute("creditCardForm", new creditcardForm());
            return mapping.findForward("creditcard");
```

LISTING 16.4   Continued

```
        }
        if (af.getAction().equals("editaddr")) {
            try {
                Address addr =
                    (Address) cust.getAddressBook().get(new Integer(af.getAddressIn
➥dex()));
                if (addr == null) {
                    return mapping.findForward("myaccount");
                }

                addressForm ad_form = new addressForm();
                PropertyUtils.copyProperties(ad_form, addr);
                request.setAttribute("addressForm", ad_form);
                return mapping.findForward("address");
            } catch (Exception ex) {
                ex.printStackTrace();
            }
        }

        if (af.getAction().equals("editcard")) {
            try {
                CreditCard card =
                    (CreditCard) cust.getWallet().get(new Integer(af.get
➥CardIndex()));
                if (card == null) {
                    return mapping.findForward("myaccount");
                }

                creditcardForm cc_form = new creditcardForm();
                PropertyUtils.copyProperties(cc_form, card);
                request.setAttribute("creditcardForm", cc_form);
                return mapping.findForward("creditcard");
            } catch (Exception ex) {
                ex.printStackTrace();
            }
        }
        if (af.getAction().equals("deleteaddr")) {
            try {
                Address addr =
                    (Address) cust.getAddressBook().get(new Integer(af.getAddressIn
➥dex()));
```

LISTING 16.4   Continued

```
            if (addr == null) {
                return mapping.findForward("myaccount");
            }

            cust.getAddressBook().remove(new Integer(addr.getAddressID()));
            cust.deleteAddress(addr);
            addr.deleteAddress();
            return mapping.findForward("myaccount");
        } catch (Exception ex) {
            ex.printStackTrace();
        }
    }
    if (af.getAction().equals("deletecard")) {
        try {
            CreditCard card =
                (CreditCard) cust.getWallet().get(new Integer(af.get
➥CardIndex()));
            if (card == null) {
                return mapping.findForward("myaccount");
            }

            cust.getWallet().remove(new Integer(card.getCardID()));
            card.deleteCreditCard();
            return mapping.findForward("myaccount");
        } catch (Exception ex) {
            ex.printStackTrace();
        }
    }
    return mapping.findForward("myaccount");
    }

}
```

You first cast the `ActionForm` argument into the appropriate subclass so that you can access the properties. An `Action` must accept a generic `ActionForm` as an argument to match the calling signature from Struts, but you need to get the properties specific to the accountForm, so you need to cast it.

If the action requested was a new address, create a new `addressForm` object (which has placeholders for all the address properties) and return a forwarding request to go to the address entry form. You do the same thing for a new credit card request. You really don't need to create a new blank form because this will be done automatically by Struts; the ActionForms are associated with the JSP pages by the structs-conf.xml file.

If the user requested to edit an existing card, the code needs to get the address out of the address book. If it isn't found (somehow the user requested one that he doesn't own), you just have Struts throw him back to the myAccount page. Otherwise, the method creates a new addressForm and uses the copyProperties method to move all the properties from the address object to the model held in the addressForm bean. (Luckily, you were careful to use the same property names throughout.) Then the method returns a forwarding request to the address edit form. Again, the same logic holds for the credit card editing code. If the method needs to delete an address or credit card, it does so and returns to the myAccount page.

The Address Editing Page

When the address page (see Listing 16.5) is brought up, it displays the fields for the address. One of the nice features of using the Struts html:text tag is that it automatically handles filling in previous values and even does null to empty string conversion. Struts will also do type conversion on the way out, turning a text field into an int, for example.

LISTING 16.5   Address.jsp

```
<%@ page language="java" %>
<%@ taglib uri="/WEB-INF/struts-html.tld"
        prefix="html" %>
<%@ taglib uri="/WEB-INF/struts-bean.tld"
        prefix="bean" %>
<%@ include file="/jsp/cust/AutoLogin.jsp" %>
<%
{
    Customer customer =
    (Customer) pageContext.getAttribute("customer", PageContext.SESSION_SCOPE);
    if (( customer == null) || (customer.getEmail() == null)) {
      response.sendRedirect("Login.jsp");
      return;
    }
}
%>
<html:html>
<head>
<title>
```

LISTING 16.5   Continued

```
  <bean:message key="myaddr.title"/>
</title>
<%@ include file="/jsp/includes/bfgheader.jsp" %>

<h2 align="center"><bean:message key="myaddr.title"/></h2>
<html:errors/>
<html:form action="/Address">
<html:hidden property="addressID"/>
<bean:message key="myaddr.field.firstname"/> <html:text property="firstName"/><BR>
<bean:message key="myaddr.field.lastname"/>  <html:text property="lastName"/><BR>
<bean:message key="myaddr.field.street1"/> <html:text property="street1"/><BR>
<bean:message key="myaddr.field.street2"/> <html:text property="street2"/><BR>
<bean:message key="myaddr.field.city"/> <html:text property="city"/>
<bean:message key="myaddr.field.state"/> <html:text property="state"/>
<bean:message key="myaddr.field.postal"/> <html:text property="postalCode"/><BR>
<html:submit/>
</html:form>
</html:html>
```

The `html:errors` tag lets you display the validation errors (which you'll define in the `addressForm ActionForm`) in a JSP file.

If the customer is doing an edit, the `addressForm` will have already been created and validated with appropriate data in the `accountAction`, so this form will act as if the customer has already submitted the values and come back from validation.

The `addressForm` (see Listing 16.6) that holds the model for the address starts out with the properties for the address but then has one additional method.

LISTING 16.6   addressForm.java

```
package com.bfg.struts;

import javax.servlet.http.HttpServletRequest;
import javax.servlet.http.HttpServletResponse;
import org.apache.struts.action.ActionForm;
import org.apache.struts.action.ActionError;
import org.apache.struts.action.ActionErrors;
import org.apache.struts.action.ActionMapping;

public class addressForm extends ActionForm {
```

LISTING 16.6   Continued

```
protected int addressID = -1;
protected String firstName;
protected String lastName;
protected String street1;
protected String street2;
protected String city;
protected String state;
protected String postalCode;

public int getAddressID() {
  return addressID;
}

public void setAddressID(int id) {
  addressID = id;
}

public String getFirstName() {
  return firstName;
}

public void setFirstName(String name) {
  firstName = name;
}

public String getLastName() {
  return lastName;
}

public void setLastName(String name) {
  lastName = name;
}

public String getStreet1 () {
  return street1;
}

public void setStreet1(String street) {
  street1 = street;
```

LISTING 16.6   Continued

```
        }

        public String getStreet2 () {
          return street2;
        }

        public void setStreet2(String street) {
          street2 = street;
        }

        public String getCity () {
          return city;
        }

        public void setCity(String c) {
          city = c;
        }

        public String getState () {
          return state;
        }

        public void setState(String st) {
          state = st;
        }

        public String getPostalCode () {
          return postalCode;
        }

        public void setPostalCode(String pc) {
          postalCode = pc;
        }

        public ActionErrors validate(ActionMapping mapping,
                                     HttpServletRequest request) {

            ActionErrors errors = new ActionErrors();
          if ((lastName == null) ||
             (lastName.length() == 0)) {
```

LISTING 16.6   Continued

```
                errors.add("lastName",
                        new ActionError("error.lastname.required"));
        }
        if ((firstName == null) ||
            (firstName.length() == 0)) {
            errors.add("firstName",
                        new ActionError("error.firstname.required"));
        }
        if ((street1 == null) ||
            (street1.length() == 0)) {
            errors.add("street1",
                        new ActionError("error.street1.required"));
        }
        if ((city == null) ||
            (city.length() == 0)) {
            errors.add("city",
                        new ActionError("error.city.required"));
        }
        if ((state == null) ||
            (state.length() == 0)) {
            errors.add("state",
                        new ActionError("error.state.required"));
        }
        if ((postalCode == null) ||
            (postalCode.length() == 0)) {
            errors.add("postalCode",
                        new ActionError("error.postal.required"));
        }
        return errors;
    }

}
```

The validate method is called between when the form is submitted and when the
Action object is invoked. If the validation fails (because of one or more errors being
returned), the Action never even sees the form submission. This is another way that
Struts isolates the business logic from form handling. ActionError instantiation
automatically looks up the string against the ApplicationResource, meaning that all
error messages can be internationalized.

If the validation succeeds, the controller hands off to the business logic, as implemented in the Action (see Listing 16.7). Because the addressForm initializes the ID to -1, the code can tell whether it's creating or editing a record. It either creates a new Address object by copying the properties out of the form into the object and then calls createAddress, or it finds the old address in the address book, copies the properties, and calls updateAddress. In either case, flow returns to the myAccount page afterward.

LISTING 16.7   addressAction.java

```
package com.bfg.struts;

import javax.servlet.http.HttpServletRequest;
import javax.servlet.http.HttpServletResponse;
import javax.servlet.ServletException;
import org.apache.struts.action.ActionForm;
import org.apache.struts.action.Action;
import org.apache.struts.action.ActionMapping;
import org.apache.struts.action.ActionForward;
import org.apache.struts.util.PropertyUtils;
import com.bfg.customer.Address;
import com.bfg.customer.Customer;
import java.text.NumberFormat;
import java.io.*;

public class addressAction extends Action {
    public ActionForward perform(ActionMapping mapping,
                                 ActionForm form,
                                 HttpServletRequest request,
                                 HttpServletResponse response)
    throws IOException, ServletException {
    addressForm af = (addressForm) form;
    Customer cust = ((Customer)request.getSession().getAttribute("customer"));
    try {
        if (af.getAddressID() == -1) {
            Address addr = new Address();
            PropertyUtils.copyProperties(addr, af);
            addr.createAddress();
            cust.addAddress(addr);
            return mapping.findForward("myaccount");
        } else {
            Address addr = Address.findAddress(af.getAddressID());
            PropertyUtils.copyProperties(addr, af);
```

LISTING 16.7   Continued

```
                    addr.updateAddress();
                    cust.getAddressBook().put(new Integer(addr.getAddressID()),
                                            addr);
                    return mapping.findForward("myaccount");
                }
        } catch (Exception ex) {
            ex.printStackTrace();
        }
        return mapping.findForward("address");
    }

}
```

Two-Step Forms

The credit card code shows how you can implement a form that is filled out in two steps. The first page (see Listing 16.8) looks much like the Address.jsp code, letting the user fill out or edit the credit card information.

LISTING 16.8   CreditCard.jsp

```
<%@ page language="java" %>
<%@ taglib uri="/WEB-INF/struts-html.tld"
        prefix="html" %>
<%@ taglib uri="/WEB-INF/struts-bean.tld"
        prefix="bean" %>
<%@ include file="/jsp/cust/AutoLogin.jsp" %>
<%
{
    Customer customer =
    (Customer) pageContext.getAttribute("customer", PageContext.SESSION_SCOPE);
    if (( customer == null) || (customer.getEmail() == null)) {
      response.sendRedirect("Login.jsp");
      return;
    }
}
%>
<html:html>
<head>
<title>
```

LISTING 16.8   Continued

```
  <bean:message key="mycard.title"/>
</title>
<%@ include file="/jsp/includes/bfgheader.jsp" %>

<h2 align="center"><bean:message key="mycard.title"/></h2>
<html:errors/>
<html:form action="/CreditCard">
<html:hidden property="cardID"/>
<bean:message key="mycard.field.cardOwner"/> <html:text property="cardOwner"/><BR>
<bean:message key="mycard.field.cardType"/>
<html:select property="cardType">
<html:option value="">SELECT</html:option>
<html:option value="VISA">Visa</html:option>
<html:option value="MC">MasterCard</html:option>
<html:option value="AMEX">American Express</html:option>
<html:option value="DISC">Discover</html:option>
</html:select><BR>
<bean:message key="mycard.field.cardNumber"/>
<html:text property="cardNumber"/><BR>
<bean:message key="mycard.field.expires"/>
<html:select property="expMonth">
  <html:option value="0">SELECT</html:option>
  <html:option value="1">Jan</html:option>
  <html:option value="2">Feb</html:option>
  <html:option value="3">Mar</html:option>
  <html:option value="4">Apr</html:option>
  <html:option value="5">May</html:option>
  <html:option value="6">Jun</html:option>
  <html:option value="7">Jul</html:option>
  <html:option value="8">Aug</html:option>
  <html:option value="9">Sep</html:option>
  <html:option value="10">Oct</html:option>
  <html:option value="11">Nov</html:option>
  <html:option value="12">Dec</html:option>
</html:select> /
<html:select property="expYear">
  <html:option value="0">SELECT</html:option>
  <html:option value="2002">02</html:option>
  <html:option value="2003">03</html:option>
  <html:option value="2004">04</html:option>
```

LISTING 16.8 Continued

```
  <html:option value="2005">05</html:option>
  <html:option value="2006">06</html:option>
  <html:option value="2007">07</html:option>
  <html:option value="2008">08</html:option>
  <html:option value="2009">09</html:option>
  <html:option value="2010">10</html:option>
  <html:option value="2011">11</html:option>
  <html:option value="2012">12<P></html:option>
</html:select><BR>
<html:submit/>
</html:form>
</html:html>
```

When you do a select using the Struts taglib, you use the html:option tag for the values. Again, the taglib automatically causes the right one to be preselected if the page already has values.

There are no surprises with the credit card validation code in the bean form for this page (see Listing 16.9). I've left out the card number checksum validations to keep things compact, but in the real site, you would put them in along with date checks.

LISTING 16.9 creditcardForm.java

```
package com.bfg.struts;

import javax.servlet.http.HttpServletRequest;
import javax.servlet.http.HttpServletResponse;
import org.apache.struts.action.ActionForm;
import org.apache.struts.action.ActionError;
import org.apache.struts.action.ActionErrors;
import org.apache.struts.action.ActionMapping;

public class creditcardForm extends ActionForm {
    protected int cardID = -1;
    protected String cardOwner;
    protected String cardType = "";
    protected String cardNumber;
    protected int expMonth = 0;
    protected int expYear = 0;

    public int getCardID() {
```

LISTING 16.9   Continued

```
    return cardID;
  }

  public void setCardID(int id) {
    cardID = id;
  }

  public String getCardOwner() {
    return cardOwner;
  }

  public void setCardOwner(String name) {
    cardOwner = name;
  }

  public String getCardType() {
    return cardType;
  }

  public void setCardType(String name) {
    cardType = name;
  }

  public String getCardNumber () {
    return cardNumber;
  }

  public void setCardNumber(String name) {
    cardNumber = name;
  }

  public int getExpMonth () {
    return expMonth;
  }

  public void setExpMonth(int month) {
    expMonth = month;
  }

  public int getExpYear () {
```

LISTING 16.9   Continued

```
    return expYear;
}

public void setExpYear(int year) {
  expYear = year;
}

public ActionErrors validate(ActionMapping mapping,
                              HttpServletRequest request) {

    ActionErrors errors = new ActionErrors();
  if ((cardNumber == null) ||
      (cardNumber.length() == 0)) {
        errors.add("cardNumber",
                  new ActionError("error.cardnumber.required"));
  }
  if ((cardOwner == null) ||
      (cardOwner.length() == 0)) {
        errors.add("cardOwner",
                  new ActionError("error.cardowner.required"));
  }
  if ((cardType == null) ||
      (cardType.length() == 0)) {
        errors.add("cardType",
                  new ActionError("error.cardtype.required"));
  }
  if (expMonth == 0) {
        errors.add("expMonth",
                  new ActionError("error.expmonth.required"));
  }
  if (expYear == 0) {
        errors.add("expYear",
                  new ActionError("error.expyear.required"));
  }
  return errors;
}
}
```

If the card passes, the next step is to gather the address. So, the action (see Listing 16.10) stores the credit card information in a session property for the moment. You could also have done this by specifying that the creditcardForm object should be session scoped in the XML configuration file—it's pretty much a matter of style.

Then the method either gets a new Address object or gets the old one from the credit card that's being edited so that the address form can be filled in with it.

LISTING 16.10   cardAction.java

```
package com.bfg.struts;

import javax.servlet.http.HttpServletRequest;
import javax.servlet.http.HttpServletResponse;
import javax.servlet.ServletException;
import org.apache.struts.action.ActionForm;
import org.apache.struts.action.Action;
import org.apache.struts.action.ActionMapping;
import org.apache.struts.action.ActionForward;
import org.apache.struts.util.PropertyUtils;
import com.bfg.customer.Address;
import com.bfg.customer.CreditCard;
import com.bfg.customer.Customer;
import java.text.NumberFormat;
import java.io.*;

public class cardAction extends Action {
    public ActionForward perform(ActionMapping mapping,
                            ActionForm form,
                            HttpServletRequest request,
                            HttpServletResponse response)
    throws IOException, ServletException {
    creditcardForm ccf = (creditcardForm) form;
    Customer cust = ((Customer)request.getSession().getAttribute("customer"));
    request.getSession().setAttribute("cardData", ccf);
    if (ccf.getCardID() == -1) {
        request.setAttribute("addressForm", new addressForm());
        return mapping.findForward("CCaddress");
    } else {
        try {
            CreditCard card =
                (CreditCard) cust.getWallet().get(new Integer(ccf.getCardID()));
            if (card == null) {
```

LISTING 16.10   Continued

```
                return mapping.findForward("myaccount");
            }
            addressForm ad_form = new addressForm();
            PropertyUtils.copyProperties(ad_form, card.getAddress());
            request.setAttribute("addressForm", ad_form);
            return mapping.findForward("CCaddress");
        } catch (Exception ex) {
            ex.printStackTrace();
        }
    }
    return mapping.findForward("myaccount");
    }
}
```

With a little cleverness, you could have made the address JSP code serve two purposes: to handle both the normal address case and the credit card case. For the moment, you can use a separate JSP (see Listing 16.11) for the credit card address, which is a copy of Address.jsp with the following differences show in bold.

LISTING 16.11   CCAddress.jsp

```
<%@ page language="java" %>
<%@ taglib uri="/WEB-INF/struts-html.tld"
        prefix="html" %>
<%@ taglib uri="/WEB-INF/struts-bean.tld"
        prefix="bean" %>
<%@ include file="/jsp/cust/AutoLogin.jsp" %>
<%
{
    Customer customer =
    (Customer) pageContext.getAttribute("customer", PageContext.SESSION_SCOPE);
    if (( customer == null) || (customer.getEmail() == null)) {
      response.sendRedirect("Login.jsp");
      return;
    }
}
%>
<html:html>
<head>
<title>
  <bean:message key="myccaddr.title"/>
```

LISTING 16.11   Continued

```
</title>
<%@ include file="/jsp/includes/bfgheader.jsp" %>

<h2 align="center"><bean:message key="myccaddr.title"/></h2>
<html:errors/>
<html:form action="/CreditCardAddr">
<bean:message key="myaddr.field.firstname"/> <html:text property="firstName"/><BR>
<bean:message key="myaddr.field.lastname"/>  <html:text property="lastName"/><BR>
<bean:message key="myaddr.field.street1"/> <html:text property="street1"/><BR>
<bean:message key="myaddr.field.street2"/> <html:text property="street2"/><BR>
<bean:message key="myaddr.field.city"/> <html:text property="city"/>
<bean:message key="myaddr.field.state"/> <html:text property="state"/>
<bean:message key="myaddr.field.postal"/> <html:text property="postalCode"/><BR>
<html:submit/>
</html:form>
</html:html>
```

Because the code uses the same addressForm object, the validations come for free. If they succeed, the controller hands off to cardAddrAction (see Listing 16.12), which gathers together the saved credit card information and the newly gathered address. It then either creates or updates the credit card record.

LISTING 16.12   cardAddrAction.java

```
package com.bfg.struts;

import javax.servlet.http.HttpServletRequest;
import javax.servlet.http.HttpServletResponse;
import javax.servlet.ServletException;
import org.apache.struts.action.ActionForm;
import org.apache.struts.action.Action;
import org.apache.struts.action.ActionMapping;
import org.apache.struts.action.ActionForward;
import org.apache.struts.util.PropertyUtils;
import com.bfg.customer.Address;
import com.bfg.customer.Customer;
import com.bfg.customer.CreditCard;
import java.text.NumberFormat;
import java.io.*;

public class cardAddrAction extends Action {
```

LISTING 16.12   Continued

```
public ActionForward perform(ActionMapping mapping,
                             ActionForm form,
                             HttpServletRequest request,
                             HttpServletResponse response)
    throws IOException, ServletException {
    addressForm af = (addressForm) form;
    creditcardForm ccf =
        (creditcardForm) request.getSession().getAttribute("cardData");

    if (ccf == null) {
        return mapping.findForward("myaccount");
    }

    request.getSession().setAttribute("cardData", null);
    Customer cust = ((Customer)request.getSession().getAttribute("customer"));
    try {
        if (ccf.getCardID() == -1) {
            Address addr = new Address();
            PropertyUtils.copyProperties(addr, af);
            addr.createAddress();
            CreditCard card = new CreditCard();
            PropertyUtils.copyProperties(card, ccf);
            card.setAddress(addr);
            card.setCustomer(cust);
            card.createCreditCard();
            cust.getWallet().put(new Integer(card.getCardID()),
                                 card);
            return mapping.findForward("myaccount");
        } else {
            CreditCard card =
                (CreditCard) cust.getWallet().get(new Integer(ccf.getCardID()));
            if (card == null) {
                return mapping.findForward("myaccount");
            }
            PropertyUtils.copyProperties(card, ccf);
            card.updateCreditCard();
            PropertyUtils.copyProperties(card.getAddress(), af);
            card.getAddress().updateAddress();
            return mapping.findForward("myaccount");
        }
```

LISTING 16.12   Continued

```
      } catch (Exception ex) {
         ex.printStackTrace();
      }
      return mapping.findForward("CCaddress");
   }


}
```

You need to make sure that the code nulls out the saved credit card data so that the application doesn't leave it around for someone else due to some weird session leak.

Listing 16.13 shows the `ApplicationResources` file that you've been using to get your strings.

LISTING 16.13   ApplicationResources.properties

```
myaccount.title=BFG Account Maintainance Page
myaccount.addrbook=Address Book
myaccount.createaddr=Create New Address
myaccount.wallet=Credit Cards
myaccount.createcard=Create New Credit Card
myaccount.edit=EDIT
myaccount.delete=DELETE
myaddr.title=BFG Address Book Maintainance Page
myaddr.field.firstname=First Name:
myaddr.field.lastname=Last Name:
myaddr.field.street1=Street Addr 1:
myaddr.field.street2=Street Addr 2:
myaddr.field.city=City:
myaddr.field.state=State:
myaddr.field.postal=Postal Code:
mycard.title=BFG Credit Card Maintainance Page:
myccaddr.title=BFG Credit Card Address Page
mycard.field.cardOwner=Card Owner Name:
mycard.field.cardType=Card Type:
mycard.field.cardNumber=Card Number:
mycard.field.expires=Card Expires:
error.lastname.required=Last Name Required<BR>
error.firstname.required=First Name Required<BR>
error.street1.required=Street Address Required<BR>
error.city.required=City Required<BR>
```

LISTING 16.13 Continued

```
error.state.required=State Required<BR>
error.postal.required=Postal Code Required<BR>
error.cardnumber.requied=Card Number Required<BR>
error.cardowner.required=Card Owner Required<BR>
error.cardtype.required=Card Type Required<BR>
error.expmonth.required=Card Expiration Month Required<BR>
error.expyear.required=Card Expiration Year Required<BR>
```

Configuring the Web Application Descriptor

Now you need to edit the web.xml (see Listing 16.14) deployment file in the struts-bfg Web application directory to customize it for the application.

LISTING 16.14 web.xml

```xml
<?xml version="1.0" encoding="ISO-8859-1"?>

<!DOCTYPE web-app
  PUBLIC "-//Sun Microsystems, Inc.//DTD Web Application 2.2//EN"
  "http://java.sun.com/j2ee/dtds/web-app_2_2.dtd">

<web-app>


  <servlet>
    <servlet-name>log4j-init</servlet-name>
    <servlet-class>com.bfg.services.Log4jInit</servlet-class>

    <init-param>
      <param-name>log4j-init-file</param-name>
      <param-value>WEB-INF/log4j.properties</param-value>
    </init-param>

    <load-on-startup>1</load-on-startup>
  </servlet>
  <!-- Standard Action Servlet Configuration (with debugging) -->
  <servlet>
    <servlet-name>action</servlet-name>
    <servlet-class>org.apache.struts.action.ActionServlet</servlet-class>
    <init-param>
```

LISTING 16.14   Continued

```
    <param-name>application</param-name>
    <param-value>com.bfg.struts.ApplicationResources</param-value>
  </init-param>
  <init-param>
    <param-name>config</param-name>
    <param-value>/WEB-INF/struts-config.xml</param-value>
  </init-param>
  <init-param>
    <param-name>debug</param-name>
    <param-value>2</param-value>
  </init-param>
  <init-param>
    <param-name>detail</param-name>
    <param-value>2</param-value>
  </init-param>
  <init-param>
    <param-name>validate</param-name>
    <param-value>true</param-value>
  </init-param>
  <load-on-startup>2</load-on-startup>
</servlet>
<!-- Standard Action Servlet Mapping -->
<servlet-mapping>
  <servlet-name>action</servlet-name>
  <url-pattern>*.do</url-pattern>
</servlet-mapping>


<!-- The Usual Welcome File List -->
<welcome-file-list>
  <welcome-file>index.jsp</welcome-file>
</welcome-file-list>
<!-- Struts Tag Library Descriptors -->
<taglib>
  <taglib-uri>/WEB-INF/struts-bean.tld</taglib-uri>
  <taglib-location>/WEB-INF/struts-bean.tld</taglib-location>
</taglib>

<taglib>
  <taglib-uri>/WEB-INF/struts-html.tld</taglib-uri>
  <taglib-location>/WEB-INF/struts-html.tld</taglib-location>
```

LISTING 16.14   Continued

```
  </taglib>

  <taglib>
    <taglib-uri>/WEB-INF/struts-logic.tld</taglib-uri>
    <taglib-location>/WEB-INF/struts-logic.tld</taglib-location>
  </taglib>

</web-app>
```

The top of the file is mostly the same as the one for the main BFG site—setting up the Log4j logger.

The remainder of web.xml configures Struts. The only part that you care about is the ApplicationResources entry. As you should recall, it defines the property file used to store language-independent strings for all your prompts and Web content.

The servlet-mapping piece is the part that sets up the mapping that any file ending in .do will be handed off to the Struts ActionServlet for handling.

The taglib sections define the tag libraries that Struts needs to do its job and are available to developers under JSP.

To deploy the code, add some code to your build.xml (see Listing 16.15) for a new target called diststrut that deploys to the bfgstrut application. It should copy both the normal JSP files and your special Struts because the new JSP pages need some of the normal ones, such as autoLogin.

LISTING 16.15   Additions to build.xml

```
  <property name="stappdir" value="${tomcatdir}/webapps/struts-bfg"/>
  .
  .
  .
  <target name="diststrut" depends="compile">
    <mkdir dir="${stappdir}/WEB-INF/lib"/>
    <mkdir dir="${stappdir}/logs"/>
    <jar jarfile="${stappdir}/WEB-INF/lib/${jarfile}">
      <fileset dir="src" includes="**/*.class"/>
      <fileset dir="props" includes="**/*.properties"/>
     </jar>
    <copy todir="${stappdir}/WEB-INF">
      <fileset dir="." includes="struts/web.xml"/>
      <fileset dir="." includes="TurbineResources.properties"/>
```

LISTING 16.15   Continued

```
        <fileset dir="props" includes="log4j.properties"/>
    </copy>
    <copy todir="${stappdir}">
        <fileset dir="struts-jsp"/>
    </copy>
    <mkdir dir="${stappdir}/jsp"/>
    <copy todir="${appdir}/jsp">
        <fileset dir="jsp"/>
    </copy>
</target>
```

After doing an ant `diststrut` and restarting the server, go to `http://local-host:8080/struts-bfg/myAccount.jsp` and you'll get a display of your account, which is much the same as with the model 1 version that you wrote originally (see Figure 16.1).

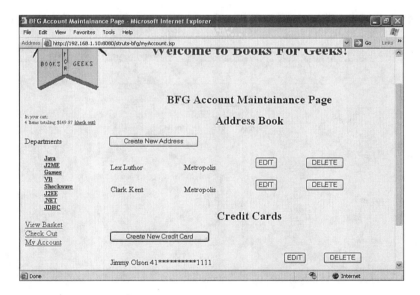

FIGURE 16.1   The Struts version of MyAccount.

When you edit a credit card, you can see the new multi-page credit card editing in operation. This code was fairly easy to write using Struts; it would have been much more involved if it had been done using model 1 (see Figures 16.2 and 16.3).

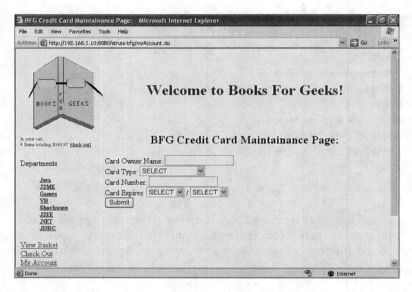

FIGURE 16.2   The first page of a multipage credit card form.

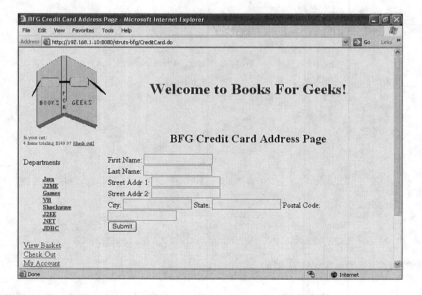

FIGURE 16.3   The second page of a multipage credit card form.

Summary

Struts is an application framework based on the Model-View-Controller design pattern. In a Struts application, a controller decides what actions to take and where to pass control based on the results of validating form data through an `ActionForm` and applying business logic found in the `Action`.

In addition, Struts offers a customer tag library that allows many common JSP tasks, such as iterating over a collection to be replaced with a single tag.

There's no question that in some places it's appropriate and desirable to use an MVC design, such as the one that Struts offers. It gives you centralized control of your URLs, helps separate your business logic from the JSP display code, and promotes code reuse.

On the other hand, it can be extremely difficult to code. You have to think about three different pieces at the same time (the JSP, the `ActionForm`, and the `Action`), and making changes on the fly is much more difficult. You also start to lose the overall sense of the application structure because many things (such as deciding which page to go to next) begin to happen as side effects behind the scenes.

It is often good advice to reserve MVC-based sites for applications large enough to warrant them. Using MVC design for a small or even medium-size problem could be a little bit like using a jack hammer to drive finishing nails. You'll end up spending more time configuring and setting up objects than actually implementing business logic.

17

Enterprise JavaBeans

When used appropriately, Enterprise JavaBeans (EJB) provides a powerful way to centralize all the business logic and database access of many enterprise applications into a single tightly controlled bundle residing under a single platform. By using EJB, you can ensure that a change in business rules needs to be replicated only on the EJB server instead of over a half dozen applications, but only on the EJB server.

That being said, EJBs add an entire layer of complexity to an application. It's important to understand when and when not to use them, lest you end up using a sledgehammer to drive finishing nails.

The Pros and Cons of EJB

There is a case to be made for using EJBs in certain situations. It's important to identify those cases so that you can make a valid assessment regarding whether your project is a good candidate for an EJB deployment.

For example, do you have an absolute requirement for distributed computing? One of EJB's major selling points is that it allows you to keep all your business logic and database access in a central location. This means that you can greatly reduce the possibility that two applications will implement the same business logic in two different ways. It also means that you have only a single location to change when you need to update business logic.

However, don't be faked out by salespeople or your local head-in-the-clouds architect. "Someday wanting to be able to run distributed" is not a valid argument for incurring the pain of EJBs.

Another selling point of EJB is transaction processing (TP). If TP is a critical part of your application, you should consider EJB for that feature alone. One strength of an EJB is that it has strong support for rolling back your application (as opposed to your database) on exceptions.

Also, if you need to be able to manage concurrent operations (for example, multiple application servers that all need to stay in sync with each other), EJB will give you that benefit. This makes issues such as seamless failover (see Chapter 18, "Security, Load Balancing, Failover, and Other Considerations") much easier to implement.

On the other hand, I personally don't like coding EJB. I think that EJB has been vastly oversold in the marketplace and has led to some multimillion-dollar projects being made out of nice, clean half-million–dollar ones. I once was involved in a massive 40-engineer project centered on an EJB deployment that was generally acknowledged by most of the developers to be at least twice as complex as it needed to be because of the EJB overhead.

Now, if the project had actually required EJBs, it would have been worth the trouble. However, the only reason that this project was being developed using EJB technology was because of the customer's vague belief that it might want to some day leverage EJB functionality. In addition, EJB allowed us to justify using the very EJB-centric platform vendor that we had partnered with. In short, we were using EJB for political rather than technical reasons.

And I'm not alone. Industry gurus The Gartner Group issued a report in 2001 on EJB platforms. The report stated that companies have overspent by $1 billion on EJB platforms since 1998 and are expected to waste another $2 billion by 2003.

I especially love a quote from one of Gartner's VPs: "The application server vendors are encouraging customers to purchase higher-end technology that they just don't need. It's like buying gourmet food to feed kids at summer camp. It's just not necessary."

Why am I so down on EJBs? In short, because they're *hard to code with*. As you'll see when you begin to develop using EJB, you end up having to write the code twice, once for the client and once for the server. EJBs make you jump through incredible hoops to get anything done, increase the complexity of your code tremendously, and usually require deployment platforms that chew up your money and require equally massive hardware to run.

EJB in 30 Seconds

EJB is a complicated beast; it would require an entire book to cover it in detail. In this chapter, complex issues such as transaction control won't be covered. Instead, here is a very quick overview of how EJB works for distributed processing.

To begin, you need an EJB server. This is the centralized beast that actually does all the work. In the examples, you'll be using the open source JBoss platform. On this server, you'll put two of the three pieces of your application: the remote interface and the enterprise bean. The third piece (the home interface) will live on the client and will be used to communicate with the server.

The remote interface is just an interface that describes the distributed class and what messages it legally can handle. The bean is the actual code that does the work. It needs to match the remote interface as far as the signature of each of the methods is concerned.

On the client side, you will use the home interface. The home interface is just an interface that describes the available methods that you can use to create or find instances of the class.

To use the distributed class, you should use JNDI to get a handle on the remote EJB server, request an instance of your home interface, and then use the interface to invoke a remote call on the EJB server.

Stateless, Stateful, and Entity Beans

EJB allows for several types of beans: stateless, stateful, and entity. As you progress from stateless to entity, the beans offer more functionality, but at the cost of more required coding.

Stateless Beans

The easiest bean type, and the one you'll look at first, is a stateless session bean. Session beans are usually likened to verbs in English; they are used for actions, such as adding something to the database or computing a value.

Stateless session beans are throwaway objects. They are maintained in a pool on the EJB server. They keep no state between calls, and they operate strictly on the data passed in via the call.

Stateful Beans

Stateful session beans are allowed to maintain state between calls. By the name, you would think that a stateful bean would be associated directly with a client and that the relationship would be maintained between calls. In fact, you'd be right.

Entity Beans

The third kind of bean is an entity bean. An entity bean is very stateful; it represents something permanent, such as a database. When you make a request to an entity bean, you can be actually doing selects, inserts, and updates against a database. This property is called persistence.

Two types of entity beans also exist. A bean-managed persistence (BMP) entity bean has code that explicitly tells how to read and write data from the database. It's similar to the code you've written that reads and writes orders from MySQL.

The other type of persistent entity bean uses container-managed persistence (CMP). In CMP, a mapping is set up between database columns and bean properties, and the EJB server automatically figures out how to map operations onto the database.

Setting Up JBoss

As with most things open source, setting up JBoss is relatively simple. To begin, you need to download and install a copy of the JBoss ZIP file from www.jboss.org. These examples use version 2.4.3. Be sure to get the base version, not the version with Tomcat (you've already got Tomcat and you don't need another copy, especially a version 3 copy).

Unpack JBoss into C:\jboss, which will result in it actually going into C:\jboss\Jboss-2.4.3. If you change directories to C:\jboss\Jboss-2.4.3\bin\ and type run.bat, JBoss will start up. That's it, as far as setup for JBoss goes. You can also start it by double-clicking run.bat from a file browser. For reference, a first-time iPlanet setup takes about six hours.

Before you can compile or run EJB code under Tomcat, you need to move a bunch of .jar files into the lib directory under Tomcat. These can be found in the \jboss\Jboss-2.4.3\client subdirectory. Move everything that isn't already present in the tomcat\lib directory except the jndi.jar file—there's already one in Tomcat, and copying another copy causes a sealing exception.

COMMERCIAL EJB IMPLEMENTATION

When you talk about commercial players in the EJB market, you have basically four choices: iPlanet, Oracle, WebLogic, and WebSphere.

iPlanet has an interesting history. It started life as Netscape's Web suite. Netscape was then bought by AOL and partnered with Sun on what was then called iPlanet. Finally, AOL dumped iPlanet, leaving it in Sun's hands. In spite of the musical chairs, iPlanet is a robust, if complicated, set of tools that includes an LDAP implementation and an EJB platform. But with a 4% market share, it has to be considered an also-ran.

In another attempt to avoid being typecast as a database-only vendor, Oracle has its own J2EE/EJB implementation. Unfortunately, as with iPlanet, Oracle has failed to gain any significant visibility in the market.

WebLogic from BEA is the dominant player, with a whopping 52% market share. As with all the commercial offerings, it isn't cheap or lightweight to host, but it has generally good reviews from the user community.

WebSphere is IBM's entry into the EJB race. With 14% of the market, this is the only serious competition to BEA, and it is also thought of well by developers.

Note that the market share figures used here are from a fall 2001 report from the Meta Group.

Creating a Stateless Session Bean

Now you can move on to actually creating your first EJB. To begin, create a new subdirectory called ejb in your com/bfg source hierarchy. You're going to move the logic that computes sales tax into a bean called Cart. Start by writing the remote interface (see Listing 17.1), which extends EJBObject. There's not much to it really— it just declares the calling parameters for the computeTax call and specifies that it throws RemoteException, as all EJB beans must.

By convention, if a bean implements a functionality called Foo, the remote interface is called Foo, the home interface is called FooHome, and the enterprise bean is called FooBean.

LISTING 17.1   Cart.java

```
package com.bfg.ejb.cart;

import javax.ejb.EJBObject;
import java.rmi.RemoteException;

public interface Cart extends EJBObject
{
    public double computeTax(double amount, String state) throws RemoteException;
}
```

Next, you will write the home bean (see Listing 17.2), which extends EJBHome. Again, it's just a stub that doesn't even define the methods for the class; it just tells how to create a remote interface object.

LISTING 17.2   CartHome.java

```
package com.bfg.ejb.cart;

import java.io.Serializable;
```

LISTING 17.2   Continued

```java
import java.rmi.RemoteException;
import javax.ejb.CreateException;
import javax.ejb.EJBHome;

public interface CartHome extends EJBHome
{
    Cart create() throws RemoteException, CreateException;
}
```

Finally, you write the bean itself (see Listing 17.3), which extends SessionBean. In
addition to the computeTax method, which implements the actual logic, you need to
implement a bunch of empty methods to handle EJB functionality that you don't
care about in this example.

LISTING 17.3   CartBean.java

```java
package com.bfg.ejb.cart;

import java.rmi.RemoteException;
import javax.ejb.SessionBean;
import javax.ejb.SessionContext;

public class CartBean implements SessionBean
{
    public double computeTax(double amount, String state)
    {
        if ((state != null) &&
            (state.compareTo("MA") < 0)) {
            return amount * 0.05D;
        } else {
            return amount * 0.10D;
        }
    }

    public void ejbCreate()
    {}

    public void ejbPostCreate()
    {}

    public void ejbRemove()
```

LISTING 17.3   Continued

```
  {}

  public void ejbActivate()
  {}

  public void ejbPassivate()
  {}

  public void setSessionContext(SessionContext sc)
  {}
}
```

To deploy the EJB, you need to package it appropriately for JBoss. This means building a custom .jar file with some special configuration files, which are written in XML. The first of these is the ejb-jar.xml file (see Listing 17.4), which describes the bean.

LISTING 17.4   ejb-jar.xml

```
<?xml version="1.0" encoding="UTF-8"?>

<ejb-jar>
    <description>BFG EJB Overkill Example</description>
    <display-name>BFG Overkill</display-name>
    <enterprise-beans>
      <session>
        <ejb-name>Cart</ejb-name>
        <home>com.bfg.ejb.cart.CartHome</home>
        <remote>com.bfg.ejb.cart.Cart</remote>
        <ejb-class>com.bfg.ejb.cart.CartBean</ejb-class>
        <session-type>Stateless</session-type>
        <transaction-type>Bean</transaction-type>
      </session>
    </enterprise-beans>
</ejb-jar>
```

As you can see, in this simple case, the ejb-jar.xml file simply defines the name of the bean and the description text. It also declares which classes to use for the home, remote, and bean; and states that it's stateless.

You also should create a jboss.xml file (see Listing 17.5), which sets up the JNDI mapping between the bean and its JNDI name.

LISTING 17.5   jboss.xml

```
<?xml version="1.0" encoding="UTF-8"?>
<jboss>
  <enterprise-beans>
    <session>
      <ejb-name>Cart</ejb-name>
      <jndi-name>bfg/Cart</jndi-name>
    </session>
  </enterprise-beans>
</jboss>
```

To deploy an application, you need to set up a .jar with the following structure:

```
C:\CARTAPP\bfg>jar tf bfgejb.jar
META-INF/
META-INF/ejb-jar.xml
META-INF/jboss.xml
com/
com/bfg/
com/bfg/ejb/
com/bfg/ejb/cart/
com/bfg/ejb/cart/CartHome.class
com/bfg/ejb/cart/Cart.class
com/bfg/ejb/cart/CartBean.class
META-INF/MANIFEST.MF
```

This is copied into the jboss deploy directory, where it is automatically incorporated into the EJB environment. Listing 17.6 shows the Ant scripting to do it.

LISTING 17.6   Ant Scripting for JBoss

```
  <property name="jbossdir" value="/jboss/Jboss-2.4.3/"/>
  .
  .
  .
  <target name="makejboss" depends="compile">
    <jar jarfile="bfgejb.jar">
      <fileset dir="ejb" includes="**/*"/>
      <fileset dir="src" includes="com/bfg/ejb/**/*.class"/>
```

LISTING 17.6   Continued

```
    </jar>
  </target>

  <target name="deployjboss" depends="makejboss">
    <copy todir="${jbossdir}/deploy">
      <fileset dir="." includes="bfgejb.jar"/>
    </copy>
  </target>
```

The makejboss target bundles up the ejb subdirectory (which has a single subdirectory called META-INF) and the ejb-specific classes into a .jar. The deployjboss target places it in the right directory under the JBoss hierarchy to be deployed.

When you do a deployjboss, the .jar file is copied into JBoss's deployment directory. JBoss automatically takes note of the new file, unpacks it, and makes it available for use. Listing 17.7 shows the results of a deployment.

LISTING 17.7   Deploying bdgejb.jar

```
[AutoDeployer] Auto deploy of file:/C:/jboss/JBoss-2.4.3/deploy/bfgejb.jar
[J2EE Deployer Default] Deploy J2EE application: file:/C:/jboss/JBoss-
2.4.3/deploy/bfgejb.jar
[J2eeDeployer] Create application bfgejb.jar
[J2eeDeployer] install EJB module bfgejb.jar
[Container factory] Deploying:file:/C:/jboss/JBoss-
2.4.3/tmp/deploy/Default/bfgejb.jar
[Verifier] Verifying file:/C:/jboss/JBoss-
2.4.3/tmp/deploy/Default/bfgejb.jar/ejb1001.jar
[Container factory] Deploying Cart
[ContainerManagement] Initializing
[ContainerManagement] Initialized
[ContainerManagement] Starting
[ContainerManagement] Started
[Container factory] Deployed application: file:/C:/jboss/JBoss-2.4.3/tmp/deploy/
Default/bfgejb.jar
 [J2EE Deployer Default] J2EE application: file:/C:/jboss/JBoss-
2.4.3/deploy/bfgejb.jar is deployed.
```

Now you can write a Tomcat JSP page to test your new bean, shown in Listing 17.8.

LISTING 17.8   TestTax.jsp

```
<%@ page import="javax.naming.*" %>
<%@ page import="javax.naming.directory.*" %>
<%@ page import="java.util.Hashtable" %>
<%@ page import="com.bfg.ejb.cart.CartHome" %>
<%@ page import="com.bfg.ejb.cart.Cart" %>
<%@ page import="javax.rmi.PortableRemoteObject" %>

<%
Hashtable env = new Hashtable();
env.put(Context.INITIAL_CONTEXT_FACTORY,
     "org.jnp.interfaces.NamingContextFactory");
env.put(Context.PROVIDER_URL,
     "jnp://localhost:1099");
env.put(Context.URL_PKG_PREFIXES, "org.jboss.naming:org.jnp.interfaces");

DirContext ctx = new InitialDirContext(env);
Object ref = ctx.lookup("bfg/Cart");

CartHome home = (CartHome) PortableRemoteObject.narrow(ref, CartHome.class);
Cart cart = home.create();
%>
    Tax on $5.00 in MA is <%= cart.computeTax(5.00D, "MA") %><BR>
    Tax on $5.00 in CA is <%= cart.computeTax(5.00D, "CA") %><BR>
```

First, the code needs to get a handle on the context for your bean so that it can request a copy. This sets up a connection to an EJB server running on your local machine.

Now you can get a reference to your bean by using the name that you set up with the jboss.xml file.

From the reference, you can get a copy of your Home object. You then use the Home object to get a copy of the remote interface.

Finally, you can use the stub to invoke the methods remotely, resulting in the correct results (see Figure 17.1).

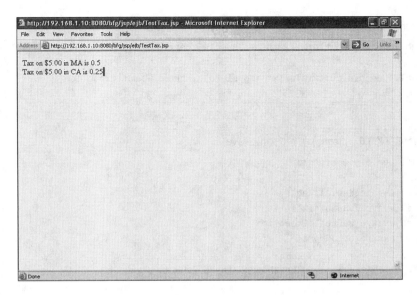

FIGURE 17.1   Computing tax the hard way.

Being Stateful

Suppose that you'd like a bean that is a little less flighty than a stateless session bean. You can create a stateful bean instead. For example, extend your cart bean to carry a total of items that you've added to your cart and then compute the tax and the total.

To begin, create a new set of classes based on the name StatefulCart (shown in Listings 17.9, 17.10, and 17.11).

LISTING 17.9   StatefulCart.java

```
package com.bfg.ejb.cart;

import javax.ejb.EJBObject;
import java.rmi.RemoteException;

public interface StatefulCart extends EJBObject
{
    public void clearTotal() throws RemoteException;

    public void addItem(double price, int quantity) throws RemoteException;
```

LISTING 17.9   Continued

```
public double getTotal() throws RemoteException;

public double computeTax(String state)   throws RemoteException;
}
```

LISTING 17.10   StatefulCartHome.java

```
package com.bfg.ejb.cart;

import java.io.Serializable;
import java.rmi.RemoteException;
import javax.ejb.CreateException;
import javax.ejb.EJBHome;

public interface StatefulCartHome extends EJBHome
{
    StatefulCart create() throws RemoteException, CreateException;
}
```

LISTING 17.11   StatefulCartBean.java

```
package com.bfg.ejb.cart;

import java.rmi.RemoteException;
import javax.ejb.SessionBean;
import javax.ejb.SessionContext;

public class StatefulCartBean implements SessionBean
{
    double total = 0D;

    public void clearTotal() {
      total = 0D;
    }

    public void addItem(double price, int quantity) {
      total += price * quantity;
    }

    public double getTotal() {
```

LISTING 17.11   Continued

```
    return total;
  }

  public double computeTax(String state)
  {
      if ((state != null) &&
          (state.compareTo("MA") < 0)) {
          return total * 0.05D;
      } else {
          return total * 0.10D;
      }
  }

  public void ejbCreate()
  {}

  public void ejbPostCreate()
  {}

  public void ejbRemove()
  {}

  public void ejbActivate()
  {}

  public void ejbPassivate()
  {}

  public void setSessionContext(SessionContext sc)
  {}
}
```

As you can see, this has simply taken the old cart bean and added a state variable to hold the total; it also used new methods to get, add to, and clear the total. The compute tax method has changed to take only the state as an argument.

Now add the new bean to the ejb-jar.xml and jboss.xml files (see Listings 17.12 and 17.13).

LISTING 17.12   Additions to ejb-jar.xml

```xml
<session>
  <ejb-name>StatefulCart</ejb-name>
  <home>com.bfg.ejb.cart.StatefulCartHome</home>
  <remote>com.bfg.ejb.cart.StatefulCart</remote>
  <ejb-class>com.bfg.ejb.cart.StatefulCartBean</ejb-class>
  <session-type>Stateful</session-type>
  <transaction-type>Bean</transaction-type>
</session>
```

LISTING 17.13   Additions to jboss.xml

```xml
<session>
  <ejb-name>StatefulCart</ejb-name>
  <jndi-name>bfg/StatefulCart</jndi-name>
</session>
```

Finally, write some JSP to test it (see listing 17.14).

LISTING 17.14   TestStatefulTax.jsp

```jsp
<%@ page import="javax.naming.*" %>
<%@ page import="javax.naming.directory.*" %>
<%@ page import="java.util.Hashtable" %>
<%@ page import="com.bfg.ejb.cart.StatefulCartHome" %>
<%@ page import="com.bfg.ejb.cart.StatefulCart" %>
<%@ page import="javax.rmi.PortableRemoteObject" %>

<%
Hashtable env = new Hashtable();
env.put(Context.INITIAL_CONTEXT_FACTORY,
     "org.jnp.interfaces.NamingContextFactory");
env.put(Context.PROVIDER_URL,
     "jnp://localhost:1099");
env.put(Context.URL_PKG_PREFIXES, "org.jboss.naming:org.jnp.interfaces");

DirContext ctx = new InitialDirContext(env);

Object ref = ctx.lookup("bfg/StatefulCart");

StatefulCartHome home =
```

LISTING 17.14 Continued

```
      (StatefulCartHome) PortableRemoteObject.narrow(ref, StatefulCartHome.class);

StatefulCart cart = home.create();

cart.clearTotal();
cart.addItem(4.95D, 2);
cart.addItem(2.00D, 4);

%>

      Total before tax is <%= cart.getTotal() %><BR>
      Tax on $5.00 in MA is <%= cart.computeTax("MA") %><BR>
      Tax on $5.00 in CA is <%= cart.computeTax("CA") %><BR>
```

Because you're using a stateful bean, the total persists between the calls to addItem and you get the right result, as shown in Figure 17.2.

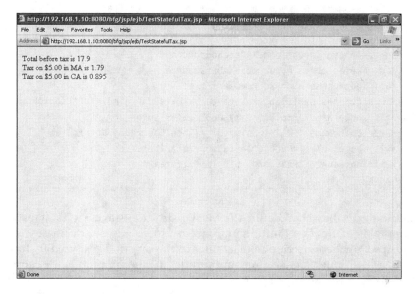

FIGURE 17.2 The stateful cart comes through.

Talking to MySQL with Entity Beans

If all EJB let you do was talk to transient objects, it wouldn't have much use. Of course, EJB lets you do a lot more—including talking to databases.

You'll see now how to use container-managed persistence (CMP) to get at your data for customers and addresses using the JAWS CMP feature of JBoss.

JAWS is the JBoss implementation of container-managed persistence. Each vendor has its own technologies under development for CMP (it's still a new concept, and the standards are in a state of flux).

Setting up JAWS is just a matter of editing a few configuration files. The configuration files that you will need to alter are in the conf\default subdirectory of JBoss. The first, called jboss.jcml, is used to define the data sources (among other things). Find the section marked JDBC and change it to read as follows in Listing 17.15.

LISTING 17.15   Changes to jboss.jcml

```
  <mbean code="org.jboss.jdbc.JdbcProvider"
name="DefaultDomain:service=JdbcProvider">
    <attribute name="Drivers">org.gjt.mm.mysql.Driver</attribute>
  </mbean>

  <mbean code="org.jboss.jdbc.XADataSourceLoader"
      name="DefaultDomain:service=XADataSource,name=mySQLDB">
      <attribute name="DataSourceClass">
          org.jboss.pool.jdbc.xa.wrapper.XADataSourceImpl</attribute>
      <attribute name="PoolName">mySQLDS</attribute>
      <attribute name="URL">jdbc:mysql://localhost/BFG</attribute>
      <attribute name="JDBCUser">bfguser</attribute>
      <attribute name="Password">bfg</attribute>
    </mbean>
```

The additions to jboss.jcml define the MySQL driver as the default database driver and supply the connection information needed to get to your database instance. They also set up a connection pool, similar to the one that you used in Turbine. You can also set up values such as timeouts and the maximum number of connections, but just go with the defaults for now.

You also need to edit standardjaws.xml and change the datasource and type-mapping entries. The top of the file will then look like this:

```
<?xml version="1.0" encoding="UTF-8"?>
<jaws>
```

```
<datasource>java:/mySQLDS</datasource>
<type-mapping>mySQL</type-mapping>
<debug>false</debug>
```

If you restart JBoss, you should see signs that things were done right. Look for the
following entries in the console output:

```
 .
 .
 .
[JdbcProvider] Initializing
[JdbcProvider] Loaded JDBC-driver:org.gjt.mm.mysql.Driver
[JdbcProvider] Initialized
 .
 .
 .
[XADataSourceLoader] Starting
[mySQLDS] XA Connection pool mySQLDS bound to java:/mySQLDS
[XADataSourceLoader] Started
```

You should also copy the mm.mysql.jar file from the Tomcat lib subdirectory to the
jboss lib/ext subdirectory so that JBoss will know how to communicate with MySQL.

With JAWS configuration out of the way, it's on to actually writing classes that use it.
To begin, define two sets of bean classes for addresses and customers that look
mostly like the ones that you created before. Now, however, you're including many
set and get methods, just as if the beans were normal beans running under JSP
(shown in Listings 17.16 and 17.17).

LISTING 17.16   Customer.java

```java
package com.bfg.ejb.customer;

import javax.ejb.EJBObject;
import java.rmi.RemoteException;

public interface Customer extends EJBObject
{
    public String getEmail() throws RemoteException;

    public void setEmail(String em) throws RemoteException;

    public String getPassword() throws RemoteException;
```

LISTING 17.16   Continued

```java
    public void setPassword(String pw) throws RemoteException;

    public int getCustomerId() throws RemoteException;

    public void setCustomerId(int id) throws RemoteException;

}
```

Remember, this defines the methods that can be used against an instance of the
Customer class returned from the Home object.

LISTING 17.17   Address.java

```java
package com.bfg.ejb.customer;

import javax.ejb.EJBObject;
import java.rmi.RemoteException;

public interface Address extends EJBObject
{
    public String getFirstName() throws RemoteException;

    public void setFirstName(String val) throws RemoteException;

    public String getLastName() throws RemoteException;

    public void setLastName(String val) throws RemoteException;

    public String getStreet1() throws RemoteException;

    public void setStreet1(String val) throws RemoteException;

    public String getStreet2() throws RemoteException;

    public void setStreet2(String val) throws RemoteException;

    public String getCity() throws RemoteException;

    public void setCity(String val) throws RemoteException;
```

LISTING 17.17   Continued

```java
    public String getState() throws RemoteException;

    public void setState(String val) throws RemoteException;

    public String getPostalCode() throws RemoteException;

    public void setPostalCode(String val) throws RemoteException;

    public Integer getAddressId() throws RemoteException;

    public void setAddressId(Integer val) throws RemoteException;

}
```

Address is similar to Customer, except that there are more methods to code. They all have to throw RemoteException because EJB throws it if something goes wrong during invocation on the EJB server.

LISTING 17.18   CustomerHome.java

```java
package com.bfg.ejb.customer;

import javax.ejb.EJBHome;
import javax.ejb.CreateException;
import javax.ejb.FinderException;
import java.rmi.RemoteException;
import java.util.Collection;

public interface CustomerHome extends EJBHome {

    public Customer create(String Email, String Password)
      throws RemoteException, CreateException;

    public Customer findByPrimaryKey (String Email)
      throws RemoteException, FinderException;

    public Collection findAll()
      throws RemoteException, FinderException;

}
```

The Home class (see Listing 17.19) defines the operations that can be used to create or retrieve a copy of the class. In addition to the `create` method that you saw for session beans, entity beans must at least define `findByPrimaryKey`, which is used to return an instance of the object that matches the unique primary key for the database. You may also define `findAll`, which returns all instances in a collection.

LISTING 17.19   AddressHome.java

```java
package com.bfg.ejb.customer;

import javax.ejb.EJBHome;
import javax.ejb.CreateException;
import javax.ejb.FinderException;
import java.rmi.RemoteException;
import java.util.Collection;

public interface AddressHome extends EJBHome {

    public Address create(String firstName, String lastName,
                          String street1, String street2,
                          String city, String state,
                          String postalCode)
      throws RemoteException, CreateException;

    public Address findByPrimaryKey (Integer id)
      throws RemoteException, FinderException;

    public Collection findByAddressBookOwner (Integer id)
      throws RemoteException, FinderException;

    public Collection findAll()
      throws RemoteException, FinderException;
}
```

The Home class for addresses (see Listing 17.19) also has `findByPrimaryKey` and `findAll`, but it adds `findByAddressBookOwner`, which takes a customer ID as an argument and returns all the addresses in the customer's address book. This requires a little special handling, as you will soon see.

LISTING 17.20   CustomerBean.java

```java
package com.bfg.ejb.customer;

import javax.ejb.EntityBean;
import javax.ejb.EntityContext;
import java.rmi.RemoteException;

public class CustomerBean implements EntityBean
{
    EntityContext ctx;

    public int id;

    public String email;

    public String password;

    public String ejbCreate (String Email, String Password) {
      email = Email;
      password = Password;
      return null;
    }

    public void ejbPostCreate(String Email, String Password) { }
    public String getEmail () {
      return email;
    }

    public void setEmail (String Email) {
      email = Email;
    }

    public String getPassword() {
      return password;
    }

    public void setPassword(String Password) {
      password = Password;
    }

    public int getCustomerId() {
      return id;
```

LISTING 17.20   Continued

```
    }

    public void setCustomerId(int Id) {
      id = Id;
    }

    public void setEntityContext(EntityContext ctx) { this.ctx = ctx; }

    public void unsetEntityContext() { ctx = null; }

    public void ejbActivate() { }

    public void ejbPassivate() { }

    public void ejbLoad() { }

    public void ejbStore() { }

    public void ejbRemove() { }
}
```

Entity beans such as `CustomerBean.java` (see Listing 17.20) need to store their context, so you need to have it stored in the bean's local properties. You'll also notice that the properties variables for the state (`email` and `password`) need to be public, which is the opposite of what you would do in a normal bean.

Because the creation is actually handled by JAWS, you just need to set the state variables. JAWS takes care of the database for you. Normal `get` and `set` methods are used for the instance variables.

Again, because you're coding an entity bean, you need it to be able to store and flush its context. This is boilerplate code.

AddressBean.java is so identical to CustomerBean.java that it's not worth including; it's the same, except that it has different instance variables. The only thing to note is that the `create` always returns the type of the primary key, so it returns an `Integer` in this case rather than a `String`.

LISTING 17.21   Additions to ejb-jar.xml

```
<entity>
    <ejb-name>Customer</ejb-name>
    <home>com.bfg.ejb.customer.CustomerHome</home>
    <remote>com.bfg.ejb.customer.Customer</remote>
    <persistence-type>Container</persistence-type>
  <ejb-class>com.bfg.ejb.customer.CustomerBean</ejb-class>
    <prim-key-class>java.lang.String</prim-key-class>
    <reentrant>False</reentrant>
    <cmp-field><field-name>id</field-name></cmp-field>
    <cmp-field><field-name>email</field-name></cmp-field>
    <cmp-field><field-name>password</field-name></cmp-field>
    <primkey-field>email</primkey-field>
</entity>
```

Now you do all the configurations to make this work. First, you add the entities to your ejb-jar.xml. Start by creating an entity entry for Customer, which defines the home, remote, and ejb-class classes, just as you did for a session bean (see Listing 17.21).

Next, you define this entity as using container persistence rather than bean persistence, which tells JBoss to use JAWS with this entity.

You have to declare the type of the primary key. It must match the value returned by the create method and also must match what you declare to be the type of the variable used to hold the primary key in the object.

The reentrant field refers to whether the bean can call itself (in other words, if it can loop back during a call and make another call to the same bean).

Now you have to declare all the container-managed fields. Note that you declare the variable name, not the accessor. It should now be clear why they had to be public. Finally, declare the field that acts as the primary key.

The address entity is declared in the same manner (see Listing 17.22).

LISTING 17.22   Adding Address to ejb-jar.xml

```
    <entity>
      <ejb-name>Address</ejb-name>
      <home>com.bfg.ejb.customer.AddressHome</home>
      <remote>com.bfg.ejb.customer.Address</remote>
      <ejb-class>com.bfg.ejb.customer.AddressBean</ejb-class>
      <persistence-type>Container</persistence-type>
```

LISTING 17.22   Continued

```
        <prim-key-class>java.lang.Integer</prim-key-class>
        <reentrant>False</reentrant>
        <cmp-field>
          <field-name>addressid</field-name>
        </cmp-field>
        <cmp-field>
          <field-name>firstname</field-name>
        </cmp-field>
        <cmp-field>
          <field-name>lastname</field-name>
        </cmp-field>
        <cmp-field>
          <field-name>street1</field-name>
        </cmp-field>
        <cmp-field>
          <field-name>street2</field-name>
        </cmp-field>
        <cmp-field>
          <field-name>city</field-name>
        </cmp-field>
        <cmp-field>
          <field-name>state</field-name>
        </cmp-field>
        <cmp-field>
          <field-name>postalcode</field-name>
        </cmp-field>
        <primkey-field>addressid</primkey-field>
      </entity>

  </enterprise-beans>
```

This section (shown in Listing 17.23) follows the end of the enterprise bean section and is used to assign security and transaction control to the methods of the beans defined previously. Entity beans are required to declare the transaction control for certain methods—for yours, you can just require transaction control for all the methods. In a more advanced application, transaction control could be used to make sure that all parts of an operation are complete for the transaction to be recorded.

LISTING 17.23   More Additions to ejb-jar.xml

```
<assembly-descriptor>
  <container-transaction>
    <method>
      <ejb-name>Customer</ejb-name>
      <method-name>*</method-name>
    </method>
    <method>
      <ejb-name>Address</ejb-name>
      <method-name>*</method-name>
    </method>
    <trans-attribute>Required</trans-attribute>
  </container-transaction>
</assembly-descriptor>
```

Next, you have to set up the JNDI mappings in jboss.xml (see Listing 17.24).

LISTING 17.24   Additions to jboss.xml

```
<entity>
  <ejb-name>Customer</ejb-name>
  <jndi-name>bfg/Customer</jndi-name>
</entity>
<entity>
  <ejb-name>Address</ejb-name>
  <jndi-name>bfg/Address</jndi-name>
</entity>
```

The additions to jboss.xml look the same as the other entries you made, except that you use an entity tag rather than a session tag.

Finally (on the JBoss side), you need to tell JAWS how to map between the database tables and the variables in the classes. This is done with a new file called jaws.xml, which is also bundled in the .jar file under the META-INF directory (see Listing 17.25).

LISTING 17.25   jaws.xml

```
<jaws>
    <enterprise-beans>
                    <ejb-name>Customer</ejb-name>
                    <table-name>CUSTOMER</table-name>
            <entity>
```

LISTING 17.25   Continued

```
                    <create-table>false</create-table>
                    <cmp-field>
                            <field-name>id</field-name>
                            <column-name>CUSTOMER_ID</column-name>
                    </cmp-field>
                    <cmp-field>
                            <field-name>email</field-name>
                            <column-name>EMAIL_ADDRESS</column-name>
                    </cmp-field>
                    <cmp-field>
                            <field-name>password</field-name>
                            <column-name>PASSWORD</column-name>
                    </cmp-field>
            </entity>
            <entity>
                    <ejb-name>Address</ejb-name>
                    <table-name>ADDRESS</table-name>
                    <create-table>false</create-table>
                    <cmp-field>
                            <field-name>addressid</field-name>
                            <column-name>ADDRESS_ID</column-name>
                    </cmp-field>
                    <cmp-field>
                            <field-name>firstname</field-name>
                            <column-name>FIRST_NAME</column-name>
                    </cmp-field>
                    <cmp-field>
                            <field-name>lastname</field-name>
                            <column-name>LAST_NAME</column-name>
                    </cmp-field>
                    <cmp-field>
                            <field-name>street1</field-name>
                            <column-name>STREET_1</column-name>
                    </cmp-field>
                    <cmp-field>
                            <field-name>street2</field-name>
                            <column-name>STREET_2</column-name>
                    </cmp-field>
                    <cmp-field>
                            <field-name>city</field-name>
```

LISTING 17.25   Continued

```
                              <column-name>CITY</column-name>
                 </cmp-field>
                 <cmp-field>
                         <field-name>state</field-name>
                         <column-name>STATE</column-name>
                 </cmp-field>
                 <cmp-field>
                         <field-name>postalcode</field-name>
                         <column-name>POSTAL_CODE</column-name>
                 </cmp-field>
                   <finder>
                      <name>findByAddressBookOwner</name>
                   <query>,ADDRESS_BOOK
                   WHERE ADDRESS_BOOK.CUSTOMER_KEY={0} AND
                   ADDRESS_BOOK.ADDRESS_KEY=ADDRESS.ADDRESS_ID
                   </query>
                   <order></order>
                 </finder>
            </entity>
      </enterprise-beans>
      <debug>True</debug>
</jaws>
```

Each entity begins with a matchup against the ejb-name that you declared in ejb-tar.xml. Then you need to tell JAWS which table the query will be run against.

If the table doesn't exist in the database and the create-table parameter is set to true, JAWS automatically creates it, which is not something that you want in this case.

The cmp-field entries map between individual fields and the variable that hold them in the class.

The entries for Address are the same until the very end.

Because you're defining a customer findBy that joins against another table, you need to tell JAWS what SQL statements to use. You can figure out what to put in the query field by imagining that JAWS will place the text SELECT <TABLE>.* FROM <TABLE> directly in front of the SQL that you place there. That's why it starts with a ","—because you need to separate the second table from the first.

The debug directive causes the SQL statements generated by JAWS to appear in the JBoss log, which is useful when you are first developing your code and you want to make sure that the SQL statements generated by JAWS are correct.

OH, NO! CAN'T CREATE!

Unfortunately, you can't use the JBoss/JAWS `create` methods for your nice new EJB classes. Why? JAWS doesn't know how to deal with serial or auto-increment fields. That means that when you do the insert, JAWS includes the ID value, which will be 0, in the insert. This means that you'll always be inserting 0 into the table.

According to the JBoss support forum, lots of workarounds exist, but most of them are uglier than doing it without EJB at all—and some are downright unlikely to be bulletproof at all.

Until the JBoss folks work this out, it will seriously limit the practical use of the JAWS interface for CMP implementations. You can always go ahead and do a BMP implementation instead, but it's a lot more work.

To test the example, cook up another JSP file that puts your new classes through their paces (see Listing 17.25).

LISTING 17.26   TestCustomer.jsp

```
<%@ page import="javax.naming.*" %>
<%@ page import="javax.naming.directory.*" %>
<%@ page import="java.util.Hashtable" %>
<%@ page import="java.util.Collection" %>
<%@ page import="java.util.Iterator" %>
<%@ page import="com.bfg.ejb.customer.CustomerHome" %>
<%@ page import="com.bfg.ejb.customer.Customer" %>
<%@ page import="com.bfg.ejb.customer.AddressHome" %>
<%@ page import="com.bfg.ejb.customer.Address" %>
<%@ page import="javax.rmi.PortableRemoteObject" %>

<%
Hashtable env = new Hashtable();
env.put(Context.INITIAL_CONTEXT_FACTORY,
      "org.jnp.interfaces.NamingContextFactory");
env.put(Context.PROVIDER_URL,
      "jnp://localhost:1099");
env.put(Context.URL_PKG_PREFIXES, "org.jboss.naming:org.jnp.interfaces");

DirContext ctx = new InitialDirContext(env);
Object custref = ctx.lookup("bfg/Customer");

Object addrref = ctx.lookup("bfg/Address");

CustomerHome custhome =
```

LISTING 17.26 Continued

```
        (CustomerHome) PortableRemoteObject.narrow(custref, CustomerHome.class);

AddressHome addrhome =
        (AddressHome) PortableRemoteObject.narrow(addrref, AddressHome.class);
Customer cust = custhome.findByPrimaryKey("turner@blackbear.com");

Address addr = addrhome.findByPrimaryKey(new Integer(1));

%>
Found Customer!<BR>
ID = <%= cust.getCustomerId() %><BR>
email = <%= cust.getEmail() %><P>

Found Address!<BR>
<%= addr.getFirstName() %> <%= addr.getLastName() %> <BR>
<%= addr.getStreet1() %><BR>
<%= addr.getStreet2() %><BR>
<%= addr.getCity() %> <%= addr.getState() %> <%= addr.getPostalCode() %><P>
<TABLE><TR><TD>ID</TD></TR>
<%
Collection coll = custhome.findAll();
Iterator it = coll.iterator();

while (it.hasNext()) {
    cust = (Customer) it.next();
%>
<TR><TD><%= cust.getCustomerId() %></TR><TD><%= cust.getEmail() %></TD></TR>
<% } %>

</TABLE>
<%
coll = addrhome.findByAddressBookOwner(new Integer(cust.getCustomerId()));

it = coll.iterator();
while (it.hasNext()) {
    addr = (Address) it.next();
%><HR>
Wallet Entry <%= addr.getAddressId() %><BR>
<%= addr.getFirstName() %> <%= addr.getLastName() %> <BR>
<%= addr.getStreet1() %><BR>
<%= addr.getStreet2() %><BR>
<%= addr.getCity() %> <%= addr.getState() %> <%= addr.getPostalCode() %><P>
<% } %>
```

Even though you're using only one EJB server, you need to look up two different contexts because you're using two different entity beans.

First try looking up customers and addresses by their primary keys. That worked, so use the `findAll` method on the customer bean to get a list of all your customers in a table. Finally, get the address book for the last customer and display the addresses. The results can be seen in Figure 17.3.

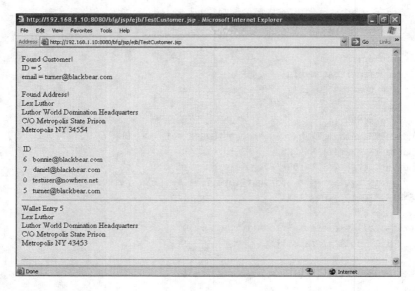

FIGURE 17.3   Entity beans on parade.

A Final Goodbye to EJB

Well, that was a quick look at a little bit of what EJB can do. As is, the chapter barely scratched the surface of everything you need to know to fully implement applications using EJB.

In summary, EJBs allow you to develop applications with centralized business logic that implement transaction processing, and they allow for synchronization between multiple applications.

An EJB has three components: the home interface, the remote interface, and the bean. Beans can be stateless, stateful, or persistent (entity) beans.

JBoss is an open source implementation of EJB that can be easily integrated with Tomcat.

18

Security, Load Balancing, Failover, and Other Considerations

Getting your site up and running, code-wise, is usually only 3/4 of the battle. Just because you can make it jump through hoops on your local workstation doesn't mean that it's going to make the grade when you deploy it on your big Sun 9999 MegaServer at your hosting facility.

This chapter is about all the other tasks that you end up having to think about when you deploy a Web site: security, performance, and reliability.

Some of this is better left to an expert. If you're going to need to use public-key infrastructure (PKI) security beyond the level of simple Secure Socket Layer (SSL) encryption, you are better off hiring a PKI guru. Similarly, if you deploy using Oracle, hiring an Oracle guru to tune your database is a reasonable investment.

However, as in most things in the industry, it pays to at least know enough to be dangerous about all of these topics.

Security, Part 1

Security is visited twice in this chapter. On your first visit, physical, network, and administrative security will be covered.

You're Paranoid, but Are You Paranoid Enough?

The first truism of security is that you match your level of paranoia to the degree of risk. If you're deploying a server that's going to live inside a secure intranet and store the company softball schedule, you can basically do whatever you please. The risk of intrusion is low, and the value of the data is minimal.

On the other hand, if you're deploying an e-commerce site on the open Internet that takes people's credit card information, you should assume that every 16-year-old with a computer has made it a personal mission to break into your site and pilfer your data.

THE WORST-CASE SCENARIO: A CAUTIONARY TALE

Admittedly, playboy.com is a high-profile target. But, that should have made the site all the more wary. Imagine, if you will, how Hugh and company must have felt when scores of their users received the following e-mail:

"...since the summer of 1998, a shady hacker group known as ingreslock 1524 has maintained full access to the Playboy Enterprises Inc. (PEI) corporate network.

Even when the PEI Web sites were defaced by BoW/H4G1S and were 'secured,' we retained our full access (no, installing SSH doesn't make you secure).

We did have some very big plans to use the hundreds of thousands of customer details (names, addresses, order history, and credit card information) harvested to automatically purchase hundreds of different products from different online companies (Amazon, Barnes and Noble, QVC, Yahoo!, and even Playboy) to be sent to each Playboy customer, thus resulting in over $10 million worth of fraud claims being made to credit card and, in turn, insurance companies globally.

In case you think this is some kind of hoax, we have included your personal details below.

Name: [DELETED]

Credit Card Number & Expiry: [DELETED]

Your details are currently circulating the underworld of anarchists and credit card fraudsters, so we highly recommend that you contact your bank before much fraud is committed. We have also distributed over a million e-mail addresses to marketing and 'spam' organizations, so you will certainly have a lot of fun deleting unwanted e-mail into the future!

Online companies can learn many lessons from this compromise:

1. Do not use the same root or administrative (Oracle, Webserv, etc.) user passwords across different hosts on the same network.

2. Never assume that by installing the latest security patches and installing SSH that you are secure.

3. Do not use insecure authentication methods, including nis, nis+ or .rhosts.

4. Do not protect your passwords with des in your shadow files; use md5.

End users can learn an important lesson from this compromise:

1. Do not trust companies with your details online.

It has been emotional. We'd like to thank the Playboy systems team for providing us with an interesting and challenging target. I'm sure that a big security company will make easy money auditing their systems and hopefully deploying a more secure network—although we'll be back to test it again."

Because the customers were actually sent their real credit card information, it was clear that playboy.com had been compromised, which was a huge embarrassment for the company and a potentially costly one.

The first thing that I recommend is that you go out and get a good book on firewalls and security. You should keep in mind a few rules of thumb, in addition to the helpful ones that were mentioned in the sidebar by the Playboy hackers:

- An open port is an invitation to trouble. Never run a service or enable an `inetd` entry (the UNIX program that controls what network services are accessible) unless you absolutely need to.

- Your spouse's name is not a secure password. Neither is a business-related term. Two good easy-to-remember but hard-to-crack strategies are using two unrelated English words separated by a nonalpha character, such as grape*allenwrench, and using the first letters of a phrase, such as tatvotsse, which stands for "These are the voyages of the Star Ship Enterprise."

- Using a two-tiered network topography with an external firewall box forwarding packets to a DMZ *can* make things more secure, but only if set up right. If it is set up wrong, it can actually make things less secure. To be set up right, the firewall box should run an absolute minimum number of programs and should forward requests through secure filtering programs (such as smail for SMTP traffic) rather than use port forwarding.

- Using biometric- or "dongle"–based security devices such as a SecurID card or a fingerprint scanner might be appropriate if the risk factor is high enough. As an example, a SecurID card generates a new six-digit number that is synchronized to a similar number generator running on the server. Unless the two numbers match, you can't log in. This means that you need to have physical possession of the card to gain access. A more advanced version requires you to key in a four-digit PIN as well, meaning that even stealing the card won't gain you access. The downside is that these types of solutions are expensive, especially when there are a large number of users to validate.

- Always set security options as high as you can without impairing the operation of your server. For example, if myserver talks to mydatabase as its JDBC source, but no one else needs to talk to mydatabase, mydatabase should allow incoming database requests only from myserver. Also, if there is a need to allow users to use SSH to log into the server, restrict it to specific incoming IP addresses, if possible, and turn off the SSH packet-forwarding feature. In general, try to make access as specific as possible.

Physical Security

Network security is only the first step in securing your application. You also have to consider that, given physical access to the server and enough time, nearly any security scheme can be defeated.

If you have the option to use an encrypted file system with your operating system (Linux has several available, and later versions of Windows also have one) and it won't be a performance hit, use it. This will give you some edge because it prevents the hackers from mounting your hard drive as a secondary drive on another system and rummaging through it. Unfortunately, to be truly secure, the operating system needs to prompt you for the encryption password when the machine boots, which makes it impossible to do an unattended reboot.

But, the best defense against this kind of attack is to keep the server where busy little fingers can't get at it. The chance that your site might be attacked by hackers is a good reason to host off-site with a service that offers good security. Remember, even if your site is physically secure, it might not be protected from internal misdoings by your fellow employees. According to some studies, most security breaches come from current or former employees.

Where Were You When the Lights Went Out? (Offsite Hosting)

The best-designed Web site in the world is reduced to an inert hunk of scrap when a flow of electrons is removed. Choosing a place to host your site can be as important to your overall success as choosing the right people to implement it. Here are a few things to look for:

- Redundant power with a backup generator, 100% UPS
- Multiple data lines (T3 or better) from different vendors with no single physical point of failure
- Twenty-four-hour staffing with knowledgeable people in the first tier of support
- Good physical security
- Good fire suppression

WHAT ARE SUPPORT TIERS?

You've experienced support tiers if you've ever called technical support for a product. Is the first person you talk to the person who developed the product?

No, the first person you talk to is a minimum-wage, call-center employee who takes down your information and, if you're lucky, gives you a canned answer.

If the problem is beyond the employee's ability, the problem is escalated to a second tier, usually to support engineers with some idea of which end of an Ethernet cable is which.

The third tier is usually developers or network engineers. It can be very hard to get a call escalated to this level because those folks get paid real money. From many companies' perspectives, they usually have better things to do than fix your problem.

In the world of Internet Web site hosting, the first tier in a 24-hour support center are junior engineers, who can handle very basic system administration and can pick up the phone to call a more senior person when they get in trouble.

As someone who has been third-tier support, I can tell you that those 3:24 A.M. phone calls from the support center were not a high point of my life. It can also take more than two to three hours to get escalated to third tier, which will seem like eternity if your Web site is dark.

Administrative Security

Because of the danger of attacks from within, the final link in the security chain is administrative security. Don't give anyone access to the boxes who doesn't need it, and if someone has a temporary need, turn off the access afterward. Restrict root and Administrator access, and use journaled superuser access tools such as sudo rather than giving someone the root password. Don't let any one person have sole knowledge of important security information (for one thing, that person might get hit by a bus.)

As mentioned before, this is one of those topics for which it's worth your while to bring in an expert to point out the chinks in the armor.

Integrating with Apache

Theoretically, you could deploy your application entirely on Tomcat. In fact, for low volume sites, this is entirely appropriate. For one of several reasons, however, you might want to layer Tomcat under Apache. These reasons are as follows:

- To offload the mundane serving of static pages and images to the more efficient Apache server

- Because you want to host sites under several virtual hostnames

- Because you want to use SSL

Integrating Apache and Tomcat is fairly simple, *if you follow the rules*. First, you will need a copy of Apache for your architecture. If you're running Linux, you might already have it installed; otherwise, you can grab an RPM from one of the many sources on the Web (including www.apache.org) and install it according to the instructions provided with the software. After it's installed, you need to edit /etc/httpd/conf/httpd.conf and set the basic information about your server name and such. You can then start it up with the command /etc/init.d/httpd start. You can make it start every time you boot by copying that file to your rc.6 (or whatever the appropriate run level is for your Linux installation).

For Win32, you download either the .msi or the .exe files from the Apache Web site (www.apache.org) and install the appropriate file. The install will prompt you for your network domain, server name, and administrator's e-mail address. It will also ask if it should be made available to all users or only to you. Usually, you would select all users.

After it is installed, you'll have a Web server running on port 80 with a basic blank Web site. Now you're ready to integrate with Tomcat.

To do this, you will need the mod_webapp module, which is downloadable from http://jakarta.apache.org/builds/jakarta-tomcat-4.0/release/v4.0/bin/.

You should select the appropriate version for your operating system and extract the mod_webapp.so module. Under Windows, it goes into \Program Files\Apache Group\Apache\modules (assuming that this is where you installed it). Under Linux, it goes in /etc/httpd/modules. For Windows, you also have to put libapr.dll in the same directory.

Now bring up an editor on httpd.conf, which is in either...\Apache\conf for Windows or /etc/httpd/conf for Linux. Look for the end of the section of LoadModule directives and add the following:

```
LoadModule webapp_module      modules/mod_webapp.so
```

Then find the end of the section of AddModule directives and add the following:

```
AddModule mod_webapp.c
```

If the AddModule directives are above the LoadModule directives in your httpd.conf, put the LoadModule line in with the rest of the LoadModule directives and insert the AddModule directly under it. The AddModule directive must come second.

Now restart Apache (either /etc/init.d/httpd restart in Linux or using the option off the Apache program group in Windows). You shouldn't get an error message of any kind. If you do, double-check the location of the modules and the directives that you added.

Now check your Tomcat server.xml configuration file and make sure that this section is uncommented:

```
<!-- Define an Apache-Connector Service -->
  <Service name="Tomcat-Apache">

    <Connector className="org.apache.catalina.connector.warp.WarpConnector"
     port="8008" minProcessors="5" maxProcessors="75"
     enableLookups="true"
     acceptCount="10" debug="0"/>
```

```
<!-- Replace "localhost" with what your Apache "ServerName" is set to -->
<Engine className="org.apache.catalina.connector.warp.WarpEngine"
 name="Apache" defaultHost="localhost" debug="0" appBase="webapps">

  <!-- Global logger unless overridden at lower levels -->
  <Logger className="org.apache.catalina.logger.FileLogger"
          prefix="apache_log." suffix=".txt"
          timestamp="true"/>

  <!-- Because this Realm is here, an instance will be shared globally -->
  <Realm className="org.apache.catalina.realm.MemoryRealm" />

  </Engine>

</Service>
```

You need to replace localhost with whatever your actual hostname is, which is the same thing that Apache was configured with for the server name. If you're just testing locally, localhost will do for both.

Restart Tomcat—it must be running to start Apache when the following change is made.

Now go back to your httpd.conf file. You're going to configure your Books for Geeks site to be served via Apache. To do this, you should add the following to the end of the httpd.conf file:

```
WebAppConnection conn      warp  localhost:8008
WebAppDeploy    bfg  conn  /bfg/
```

This tells Apache to pass anything coming in with a URL starting with /bfg to the Tomcat server listening on port 8008. This is the warp connector port, not the normal port that Tomcat uses when serving pages to the Web.

Unfortunately, things are reported to still be a little shaky for this feature, at least on the Windows side (it works fine under Linux). Specifically, there have been reports of communication failures between the two sides (Apache and Tomcat) under loaded conditions.

Load Balancing

Round-Robin DNS

One popular choice for load balancing is round-robin DNS. In a round-robin competition, each player has a match against every other competitor. Similarly, with this method of load balancing, you set up your DNS server to deliver more than one possible IP address for the same domain name. Each time a DNS server is queried, it hands out the next IP on the list and then cycles back again to the first entry. Because a local machine asks for the address only once, it goes back to the same machine on each subsequent request.

Round-robin DNS has the advantage that it's cheap and easy to set up. The problem with it, however, is that it doesn't deal well with situations in which one server is getting overloaded or dies. Normally, this isn't an issue because if requests are being distributed in a roughly even fashion, the load should be about even, too.

Another big problem with round-robin DNS is that if you need to remove a server from the pool, it can take 20 minutes to 24 hours for the change to occur, depending on the Time To Live value of your DNS statement of authority record.

Smart Switches

The next step up the ladder when trying to balance a load is to use a smart switch in front of a number of servers. The quintessential example is a Cisco LocalDirector.

A smart switch can direct traffic using heuristics designed to truly load-balance, making sure that all your servers receive an equal load. In addition, the switch can hide the internal IP addresses of your servers, making it appear that all the traffic is going to one single machine. This makes it easier to change your internal network topology as you need to.

A smart switch can also automatically drop a dead machine out of the pool, minimizing downtime.

The Quick-and-Dirty Solution

To avoid the problem of DNS propagation delays that was mentioned in the section on round-robin DNS, you can use a script that does explicit redirection instead.

You can do a quick-and-dirty redirector that allows you to add or drop servers instantly with a single file edit. Listing 18.1 shows what it looks like.

LISTING 18.1 RandomRedirect.jsp

```
<%
int numSites = 5;
int thisTime = (new java.util.Random()).nextInt(numSites);
String[] Sites = {"www.newsoftheweird.com", "www.dilbert.com",
                "www.userfriendly.org", "www.luckedcompany.com",
                "www.boston.com/globe/living/comics"};

response.sendRedirect("http://" + Sites[thisTime]);
%>
```

In this example, you redirect randomly to one of five Web sites. Now imagine that instead of those five sites, it was www1.bfg.com, www2.bfg.com, and so on. And, instead of being called RandomRedirect.jsp, it was called index.jsp and was located in the root HTML directory of www.bfg.com. What would happen when someone asked for www.bfg.com?

That's right, the user would be randomly redirected to one of the five servers—poor man's load balancing. If a site goes down, you just change the list of sites, and no one gets sent to it.

The downside to this method is that, after the initial page display, all the subsequent pages show up as www1 (or whatever) in the URL status bar. And if someone bookmarks a page, that user will always return to that same server. Still, this method offers an alternative to the expense of smart switches.

Load Balancing and Session Persistence

If you use a method of load balancing that doesn't ensure that all requests for a given session go to the same server, you might run into problems with session persistence. For example, suppose that you have two machines (www1 and www2). A customer comes to the site, and a session object is created for the shopping cart on www1 (the machine that the customer is assigned to by the load-balancing mechanism used). If the customer doesn't continue to use www1 for the remainder of the session, he'll lose the state of the shopping cart.

Luckily, all of these methods listed don't have a problem with this pitfall. Round-robin DNS makes the selection of an IP address only once for a given client, so the client consistently uses the same IP until the machine reboots or the DNS expires. Most smart switches can direct all requests from the same client to the same server. And if you explicitly redirect to a server, it will always go to the same machine, by design.

Writing Applications for Multimachine Service

When you write a Web application for multiple-machine deployment, the main thing that you need to keep in mind is that you cache database state at your own risk. Although it's okay to cache certain values, such as product catalogs, which are read-only and change infrequently, it's not okay to cache customer information that can change from minute to minute.

The high-end Java platforms provide support to keep multiple servers in sync. Unfortunately, Tomcat does not. This just means that you need to keep the issue in the back of your mind at all times during development.

Frankly, you should already be thinking about it because many of the problems of concurrency that can plague a multiple machine architecture also crop up when thinking about multiple simultaneous sessions.

The Failover Fallacy

One of the complaints that fans of expensive EJB platforms like to level against Tomcat is that it doesn't provide failover support.

By failover, they're referring to the capability to seamlessly move a session from one server to another if the first server goes belly up. Any server can offer the other kind of failover, which is dropping a dead server out of a server pool, if you use a smart switch.

Just how important is session failover? For most sites, not very. For example, suppose that you have a fairly unstable site, which results in a Web server crashing once a week (anything more frequent than that, and your site has no business being live). Further say that you have five servers and get around 100,000 users a day—a pretty busy site—and a typical user's session lasts 10 minutes.

That's approximately 700,000 users a week. During any one time, you could expect (with even distribution), 1/144th of your daily users would be in a current session (1,440 minutes in a day, 10 minutes in a session).

Furthermore, your traffic is divided among five servers, so that's really 1/720th of your daily traffic, or about 138 users. So, out of 700,000 user sessions, you would lose state on 138, or .019%, of all sessions. This is a 99.981% uptime, a little off the gold standard of "three nines," but pretty close.

And what happens to those users who got dumped? Did their houses get repossessed? Did they have their tax returns audited? No, they lost their current session state and got put back into a fresh, new session.

It's possible that a very few of them might have been at the critical point between authorizing the credit card and recording the order, but those chances are slim indeed—and even a platform with session failover won't save you from that in all cases.

And implementing failover support is no small feat. Usually, all of your objects have to be serializable. You don't get the functionality "out of the box"; you have to design your entire application to take advantage of it.

So, unless you have an absolute mandate from someone of 100% uptime requirements, get a cup of cocoa and stop worrying about failover.

Database Tuning

Sometimes you can get a quick-and-easy payoff in performance with a little database tuning. For example, consider a 1,000-row table with the following schema:

```
CREATE TABLE DEADBEATS (
     DEBTOR     CHAR(40),
     OWES       FLOAT,
     LENDER     CHAR(40));
```

If you run a query asking for the count of matches between deadbeats who are also lenders, you can see that it takes quite some time:

```
mysql> select COUNT(*) FROM DEADBEATS LEFT JOIN DEADBEATS DB ON DEADBEATS.DEBTOR
=DB.LENDER;
+----------+
| COUNT(*) |
+----------+
|   100000 |
+----------+
1 row in set (8.62 sec)
```

Putting an index on the DEBTOR column speeds things up a bit:

```
mysql> CREATE INDEX DEBTOR_INDEX ON DEADBEATS(DEBTOR);
Query OK, 1000 rows affected (0.01 sec)
Records: 1000  Duplicates: 0  Warnings: 0

mysql> select COUNT(*) FROM DEADBEATS LEFT JOIN DEADBEATS DB ON DEADBEATS.DEBTOR
=DB.LENDER;
+----------+
| COUNT(*) |
+----------+
|   100000 |
+----------+
1 row in set (7.73 sec)
```

An index on the LENDOR column makes it go 30 times faster!

```
mysql> CREATE INDEX LENDOR_INDEX ON DEADBEATS(LENDER);
Query OK, 1000 rows affected (0.01 sec)
Records: 1000  Duplicates: 0  Warnings: 0

mysql> select COUNT(*) FROM DEADBEATS LEFT JOIN DEADBEATS DB ON DEADBEATS.DEBTOR
=DB.LENDER;
+----------+
| COUNT(*) |
+----------+
|   100000 |
+----------+
1 row in set (0.28 sec)
```

Why isn't every column of every table indexed? Because when you put an index on a table, it needs to be updated on every insert or update. Too many indexes can make these operations expensive, so you can end up borrowing from Paul to pay Peter.

In addition to creating indexes, a good DBA can help you rewrite queries to be more efficient, optimize your database-configuration parameters, and recommend hardware upgrade (especially memory or disk) that can help. You should also look to the specific documentation for your database. It should have a section (or, in the case of Oracle, entire manuals) on how to tune for best performance.

Security, Part 2 (SSL)

You've already seen that you need to provide various types of security for the server itself. You also need to provide security for transactions between the customer and your site.

If you're doing e-commerce, you will really want to use SSL for at least the parts of the transaction in which you're passing private information back and forth. Setting up SSL under Apache is technically easy but administratively challenging.

HOW DOES SSL WORK?

To begin, you need to understand a little bit about PKI (that's public key infrastructure) and cryptography.

Modern cryptography is based on using a *key* to encrypt *plain text* into *cyphertext*. This is done using complex mathematical formulas and long keys. The key length is important because, if the key is too short, you could break the code by brute trial and error. (The hacker could just say, "Let me see, there are five possible keys, did one work? Did two work? ...")

A 140-bit key has 2^{140} possible values, which is a 1.4 followed by 42 zeros. Needless to say, that would take a while to break by exhaustive trial. But, for this example, let's assume that your key is a number between 1 and 10.

If the two of us could meet in advance and agree on a key to use, I could just send you the *cyphertext* and you would know that key 3 would give you the *plain text*. Unfortunately, it would be unreasonable to have one-to-one business relationships between every Web site and every possible customer, each with a secret key.

If I went to your Web site, you could assign me a key and then we could use that key for the rest of the conversation. Alas, so could any eavesdropper who tapped the line. We need some way to agree on a key that no one else can overhear.

For this, we can use *public key cryptography*. In this system, there are two keys: a public one and a private one. If I give you my public key, you (or anyone else) can encrypt a message using it. But—and this is the important bit—no one can decrypt it except the owner of the private key.

Conversely, if I encrypt a message with my private key, anyone can decrypt it with my public key and get the *plain text*, but only I could have sent it. This is called a digital signature.

So, when your browser connects to `secure.bfg.com` using SSL, the first thing that happens is that the Web site sends its certificate to the browser. The certificate is the public key encrypted with the CA's private key. The browser checks to see whether the CA is on its list of registered CAs, which means that the browser has a copy of the CA's public key.

If the CA is not on the list, an obnoxious warning message about an unknown CA comes up. Otherwise, the browser uses the public key to decrypt the signed certificate. Inside is the public key for the Web server. The browser generates a one-time key, encrypts it with the server's public key, and then sends it back. Only the server can decrypt the one-time key because only the server has the private key.

Now both the server and the browser have a one-time key that they can use to talk to each other, and no one else could have overheard the conversation.

If you ever want to hear someone really laugh hard, tell a Web site developer that you need to have SSL up by the end of the day. The reason he'll be laughing so hard is that the physical paperwork side of SSL takes at least three days, if you're lucky. Take a walk through the process, and you'll see why.

First, you need choose a certificate authority (CA). This is the person who will certify that you are you and not some 15-year-old (I am tired of picking on 16-year-olds) operating out of her mom's kitchen.

DO YOU NEED A CA?

You can run Apache in SSL mode without getting the certificate signed by a CA. But anyone cruising to your site will get a nasty warning message on his browser that reads something like this:

"Information that you exchange with this site cannot be viewed or changed by others. However, there is a problem with the site's security certificate."

> Needless to say, this will not be inspiring confidence in people to use their credit cards on your site.
>
> This is also why you want to make sure that the certificate authority that you pick is well recognized by the browsers in use in the community. Because certificate authorities can't be added easily to older versions of browsers, the older ones might not recognize newer CAs.

It used to be that, as far as certificate authorities went, you had your choice of Verisign or Verisign. And it wasn't cheap—you were looking at about a $300 minimum cost.

Service still isn't cheap from Verisign; 40-bit encryption (which is a joke, from a security standpoint) costs $350, and 128-bit encryption costs nearly $900. That is quite an investment.

Luckily, there's now competition in the marketplace, and you can find CAs such as Equifax that offer 128-bit certificates for as little as $175.

The CAs have step-by-step instructions for each type of Web server. Here are the steps in the process of applying and installing a certificate for Books for Geeks in Linux.

Before starting this, though, you might be asking, "Why Linux?" For several reasons. First, configuring SSL under Windows is a complicated process requiring a C compiler and an installation of Perl. Second, it requires you to run Apache, which I've already mentioned doesn't integrate reliably with Tomcat under Windows. Finally, many industry insiders (including The Gartner Group) no longer consider Windows to be a secure platform for deploying Web applications, due to the numerous exploitable holes that have been found in the operating system. Windows makes a nice environment for developing your application, but when it comes time to deploy it, you will probably need to move to Linux.

1. Make sure that OpenSSL has been installed. You're going to install this certificate on a Linux server, so you can install OpenSSL using rpmfind.

2. Go to /etc/httpd/conf/ssl.key.

3. Generate a server certificate with this command:

```
[root@bfg ssl.key]# openssl genrsa -des3 -out server.key 1024
Generating RSA private key, 1024 bit long modulus
............++++++
.............++++++
e is 65537 (0x10001)
Enter PEM pass phrase:
Verifying password - Enter PEM pass phrase:
```

NOTE

Do *not* forget the password you enter. If you do, you're going to be really out of luck because you'll lose all ability to control your certificate.

4. In a safe location, back up the server.key file that is produced.

5. Issue the following command, which will generate a certificate request that you'll send to the CA. The input that you provide is shown in italics.

```
[root@linux ssl.key]# openssl req -new -key server.key -out server.csr
Using configuration from /usr/share/ssl/openssl.cnf
Enter PEM pass phrase: [password]
You are about to be asked to enter information that will be incorporated
into your certificate request.
What you are about to enter is what is called a Distinguished Name or a
DN.
There are quite a few fields but you can leave some blank
For some fields there will be a default value,
If you enter '.', the field will be left blank.
-----
Country Name (2 letter code) [AU]:US
State or Province Name (full name) [Some-State]:New Hampshire
Locality Name (eg, city) []:Salem
Organization Name (eg, company) [Internet Widgits Pty Ltd]:Books For
Geeks, Inc.
Organizational Unit Name (eg, section) []:
Common Name (eg, your name or your server's hostname) []:secure.bfg.com
Email Address []:chiefgeek@bfg.com

Please enter the following 'extra' attributes
to be sent with your certificate request
A challenge password []:
An optional company name []:
```

6. Usually, the CA will have some way to upload the CSR (certificate request) to its Web site. Normally, it's just a copy and paste into a form. Upload it, and fill out the rest of the information, including who you are, how you're going to pay, and so on.

7. Now the fun begins. You need to fax the CA proof of who you are, which usually involves either having a Dun and Bradstreet DUNS number or sending your articles of incorporation, business license, and so on. In a large corporation, it can take a day or two just to get this paperwork sent.

> **NOTE**
>
> You can get a DUNS number for free from Dun and Bradstreet's Web site; it takes around a week.

8. Now you wait. Eventually (in a day or two, at best, or in a week, at worst), you'll be sent a certificate in the mail with instructions on how to unpack it.

9. Now go into Apache's httpd.conf, enable SSL, enter the name of your certificate, and you're ready to roll. You can now surf to `https://secure.bfg.com/` with peace of mind.

By the way, if you want your Web server to start up automatically under Linux and you used a password when setting up your server key, you're going to have to enter the password manually every time the server reboots, which can be a little inconvenient at 4 A.M. You can modify the `httpd` script in init.d as follows to make the process automatic:

```
start() {
        echo -n $"Starting $prog: "
        daemon "$httpd `moduleargs` $OPTIONS < /etc/httpd/ssl.pass"
        RETVAL=$?
        echo
        [ $RETVAL = 0 ] && touch /var/lock/subsys/httpd
        return $RETVAL
}
```

Of course, now you're storing your certificate password in plain text on the system. Life is full of trade-offs.

The End of the Book

Well, here you are, 18 chapters later, with a better understanding of what goes into integrating JSP and JDBC into a working Web site.

By now, you should understand that security is a critical consideration when deploying a Web site. You need to consider several types of security: physical, network, and administrative.

Hosting off-site reduces several of your security concerns and also might increase your reliability because of factors such as redundant power and network connections. You can spread the load between more than one server by using load balancing, and you can reduce the load by tuning your database properly and using Apache for mundane HTTP requests.

You should use SSL to encrypt secure traffic between the server and the client. This is difficult to do under Windows, and because Windows has security issues outside of SSL, you almost always want to deploy these types of solutions under Windows. Running SSL requires a certificate. Getting the certificate from a CA is the major delay in bringing up SSL on a site.

A few points are worth repeating before you dash off to implement the Great American Web Site:

- There is no replacement for having a good idea of what you want to do before you start trying to do it.

- You can spend so much time planning that you never get around to actually doing.

- Don't be afraid to rework or refactor in light of lessons learned.

- Keep up with the latest technologies, but don't feel that you have to use them just because they're trendy.

- Before writing a major piece of code, ask yourself whether anyone else has already done it and, if so, whether it can be reused or purchased?

All of the technologies used in this book are evolving—some had active betas ongoing as the book went to press. Keep up with the latest advances—new features can make the hard stuff easy but can also make what was easy hard.

Good luck, and good coding!

PART V

Appendixes

IN THIS PART

A

Getting and Installing JDK, Ant, and Tomcat

Installation procedures are never a pleasant experience. Thankfully, the software you need to make Tomcat work is fairly simple to install. The major differences are between Windows installs and Linux installs, with a few additional complications among the various versions of Windows.

Installing JDK Under Windows

The Java Developer Kit (JDK) is also sometimes known as the Java SDK (for Software Development Kit). In short, the JDK is the Java base—everything else you'll do is built on it. The JDK contains the Java compiler, the runtime interpreter, the libraries, and other assorted items needed to compile and run Java.

The JDK shouldn't be confused with the JRE, the Java Runtime Environment, which allows a user to run Java code that already has been compiled, but not to actually compile new code.

Getting the Binary Distribution

Begin at Sun's Web site, `http://java.sun.com/j2se/1.3/download-windows.html`. This will bring you to the Java for Windows page. Find and click the Download button for the Java 2 SDK.

This will take you to a licensing page. Read through the license agreement. If you agree, click Accept at the bottom of the page. This will take you to a page where you can select a site to download the distribution.

Choose whichever one fits your fancy (or seems to run the fastest), and save the file j2sdk-1_3_1_01-win.exe to a location that you'll be able to find later—the desktop or the My Documents folder are good choices.

Unpacking the JDK Distribution

When the file download is complete, you might be given the option to open it, depending on the browser you've used. If so, open the file. Otherwise, use a file explorer to view the directory where you've saved the file, and double-click it.

When the installer starts running, click Next on the first screen and the license agreement, which will bring you to the screen labeled Choose Destination Location.

You can pick any location you like, but the default (which is C:\jdk1.3.1_01) is fine.

Next, you're asked to choose the components to install. Select everything but Java Sources; if you have enough disk space, you can select it as well.

Clicking Next causes the installer to run, unpacking the application as requested.

Configuring JAVA_HOME and PATH

To complete the installation, you need to configure two environment variables: JAVA_HOME and PATH. This is done differently depending on whether you're running Windows 95 or 98 or Windows NT, 2000, or XP.

Windows 95 or 98

From the Windows taskbar, click Start, Run. Then type in **notepad c:\autoexec.bat**.

Add the following lines to the bottom of the file:

```
SET PATH=%PATH%;C:\JDK1.3.1_01\BIN
SET JAVA_HOME=C:\JDK1.3.1_01
```

Save the file and reboot.

Windows NT, 2000, or XP

Open the control panel and double-click System.

Click the Advanced Tab and then the button marked Environment Variables. Then click the button marked New under the System Variables section. When the New Variable window opens, type in **JAVA_HOME** for the variable name and **C:\JDK1.3.1_01** for the value (assuming that this is where you installed the JDK).

Click the PATH variable in the scrolling window under System Variables, and then click Edit. Go to the end of the variable value box and add ;C:\JDK1.3.1_01\bin.

Save the changes to your environment variables by selecting the OK button, and close the Control Panel.

Testing the Windows JDK Installation

To test the installation, open a command window (Start, Program Files, Accessories, Command Prompt), and type **java** at the command line. You should see this:

```
C:\Documents and Settings\james>java
Usage: java [-options] class [args...]
          (to execute a class)
   or  java -jar [-options] jarfile [args...]
          (to execute a jar file)

where options include:
    -hotspot      to select the "hotspot" VM
    -server       to select the "server" VM
    -classic      to select the "classic" VM
                  If present, the option to select the VM must be first.
                  The default VM is -hotspot.

    -cp -classpath <directories and zip/jar files separated by ;>
                  set search path for application classes and resources
    -D<name>=<value>
                  set a system property
    -verbose[:class|gc|jni]
                  enable verbose output
    -version      print product version and exit
    -showversion  print product version and continue
    -? -help      print this help message
    -X            print help on non-standard options
```

If you don't see this output (specifically, if you see a message about not finding the command), type **echo %PATH%**. You should see your JDK directory somewhere in the string that is printed. If you don't, recheck the steps to set the PATH variable.

Installing JDK Under Linux

Installing the JDK under Linux requires similar steps, but because Linux is such a different creature, you'll do them in very different ways than Windows requires.

Getting the Binary Distribution

Point your browser to http://java.sun.com/j2se/1.3/download-linux.html and click Continue under Red Hat RPM Shell.

Accept the license agreement, and choose a server to download from. Save the file in the /tmp/ directory.

Installing the Distribution

As root, cd to /tmp and type **./j2sdk-1_3_1_01-linux-i386-rpm.bin**. Agree to the license by entering **yes**. This creates a file called jdk-1.3.1_01.i386.rpm in /tmp. Install it using rpm:

```
[root@linux tmp]# rpm —install jdk-1.3.1_01.i386.rpm
```

This unpacks the distribution as /usr/java/jdk1.3.1_01.

Setting JAVA_HOME and PATH

Create the file /etc/profile.d/jdk.sh as root with the following content:

```
PATH="$PATH:/usr/java/jdk1.3.1_01/bin"
JAVA_HOME=/usr/java/jdk1.3.1_01/
export JAVA_HOME PATH
```

As root, issue the following command:

```
chmod a+x /etc/profile.d/jdk.sh
```

Testing the Linux JDK Installation

Log out and log back in again; then type **java**. You should see the following:

```
[turner@linux turner]$ java
Usage: java [-options] class [args...]
           (to execute a class)
   or  java -jar [-options] jarfile [args...]
           (to execute a jar file)


where options include:
    -client       to select the "client" VM
    -hotspot      is a synonym for the "hotspot" VM   [deprecated]
    -server       to select the "server" VM
    -classic      to select the "classic" VM
                  If present, the option to select the VM must be first.
                  The default VM is -client.

    -cp -classpath <directories and zip/jar files separated by :>
                  set search path for application classes and resources
    -D<name>=<value>
                  set a system property
    -verbose[:class|gc|jni]
                  enable verbose output
    -version      print product version and exit
    -showversion  print product version and continue
```

```
-? -help        print this help message
-X              print help on non-standard options
```

If you don't get this output, do echo $PATH and make sure that the /usr/java/jdk1.3.1/bin directory is part of your path. If it is not, you should recheck the step in which you set up PATH.

Installing Ant Under Windows

Ant allows you to write a build script once and use it to rebuild and redeploy your distribution whenever you need to. Ant is especially well suited to Java and contains a number of specialized features intended specifically for the Java developer.

Downloading the Distribution

Point your browser to http://jakarta.apache.org/builds/jakarta-ant/release/v1.4.1/bin/ and select the binary zip file. Save the file to a known location.

Unpacking the Distribution

Open the saved file using a zip unarchiver and extract all the files, preferably to C:\ (which will create a directory C:\jakarta-ant-1.4.1). Be sure to click Use Folder Names in the Extract dialog box, if it's offered.

Adding Ant to the Windows Path

Refer to the instructions appropriate for your operating system in the previous section "Installing JDK Under Windows." Using the same procedure that you used to add JDK to the PATH environment variable, add the following:

```
;C:\jakarta-ant-1.4.1\bin
```

Reboot if you are running Windows 95 or 98.

Testing Ant

Open a command window by choosing Start, Program Files, Accessories. At the command prompt, type **ant**. You should see the following:

```
C:\Documents and Settings\james>ant
Buildfile: build.xml does not exist!
Build failed
```

This tells you that Ant is in place and that it couldn't find a build.xml file, which is the file that Ant uses to determine what actions need to take place to build or deploy an application.

Installing Ant Under Linux

Unlike the JDK deployment, Ant is unpacked using `tar` rather than installed using rpm.

Downloading the Distribution

Point your browser to `http://jakarta.apache.org/builds/jakarta-ant/release/v1.4.1/bin/` and select the binary tar.gz file. Save the file to /tmp.

Unpacking the Distribution

As root, `cd` to /usr/local (or another location where you want to deploy packages such as Ant) and then run this command:

```
[root@linux local]# gunzip -c /tmp/jakarta-ant-1.4.1-bin.tar.gz | tar xf -
```

This creates the directory /usr/local/jakarta-ant-1.4.1.

Adding Ant to PATH

Create the file /etc/profile.d/ant.sh as root with the following content:

```
PATH="$PATH:/usr/local/jakarta-ant-1.4.1/bin"
ANT_HOME=/usr/local/jakarta-ant-1.4.1/

export PATH ANT_HOME
```

Testing Ant

Log out and then log back in. Type **ant** at a shell prompt. You should see the following:

```
[turner@linux turner]$ ant
Buildfile: build.xml does not exist!
Build failed
```

Again, as with Windows, this tells you that the binary for Ant is in place but that it didn't find a `build.xml` file in the current directory (which is what you would expect).

Installing Tomcat Under Windows

With JDK and Ant in place, you can install the last piece of the basic JSP architecture—the JSP server itself. In this case, you'll be installing Apache Tomcat.

Downloading the Distribution

Point your browser to `http://jakarta.apache.org/builds/jakarta-tomcat-4.0/release/v4.0.1/bin/` and select the binary zip file. Save the file to a known location.

Unpacking the Distribution

Open the saved file using a zip unarchiver and extract all the files, preferably to C:\ (which will create a directory C:\jakarta-tomcat-4.0.1). Be sure to click Use Folder Names in the Extract dialog box, if it's offered.

Testing Tomcat

Click Program, Run, and enter **c:\jakarta-tomcat-4.0.1\bin\startup.bat**

You should see a window with content similar to this, indicating that Tomcat is up and running:

```
Starting service Tomcat-Standalone
Apache Tomcat/4.0.1
Starting service Tomcat-Apache
Apache Tomcat/4.0.1
```

If you open a browser and point it to `http://localhost:8080/`, you should see the Web page shown in Figure A.1.

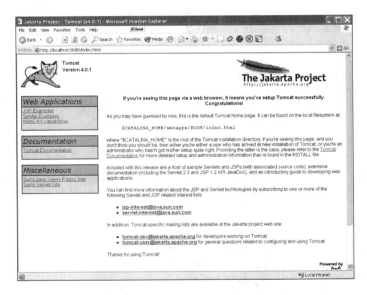

FIGURE A.1 The Tomcat startup window.

Assuming that your JDK is installed correctly and that you have JAVA_HOME set, there's essentially no way that Tomcat will fail to start up. If it doesn't start, though, recheck your JDK install.

Installing Tomcat Under Linux

As with the other packages, installing Tomcat is essentially the same under Linux as under Windows.

Downloading the Distribution

Point your browser tohttp://jakarta.apache.org/builds/jakarta-tomcat-4.0/release/v4.0.1/rpms/ and select the noarch rpm file and the webapps rpm file.

Save the files to /tmp.

Unpacking the Distribution

cd to /tmp and, as root, run the following:

```
# rpm — install tomcat4-4.0.1-1.noarch.rpm


Don't forget to setup vars in /etc/tomcat4/conf/tomcat4.conf to
adapt the RPM to your JDK for example.
As supplied we assume you're using IBM JDK 1.3.0

For security purposes, tomcat is no more activated by
default so don't forget to use chkconfig under root :
/sbin/chkconfig —add tomcat4

# /sbin/chkconfig — add tomcat4
# rpm —install tomcat4-webapps-4.0.1-1.noarch.rpm
```

This installs Tomcat to /etc/tomcat4 and /var/tomcat4.

Editing the /etc/tomcat4/tomcat.conf File

As root, edit /etc/tomcat4/conf/tomcat.conf and set the value for JAVA_HOME as appropriate (the location where you unpacked the JDK).

Testing Tomcat

As root, try /etc/init.d/tomcat4 start. Open a browser and point it to http://localhost:8180/. You should see the Web page shown in Figure A.1.

As with Windows, it's almost impossible to mess up this install. Check your PATH variable if it doesn't seem to work.

B

Getting and Installing MySQL and JDBC for MySQL

Unlike its more expensive cousins, such as Oracle, MySQL is relatively simple to install on either Linux or Windows. This appendix takes you through the installation process and also discusses some details of MySQL post-install configuration.

Installing MySQL on Windows

Installing MySQL is a uniform process across all versions of Windows. The only difference is that, under later releases (Windows NT, Windows 2000, and Windows XP), it can be installed as a service so that it's always available.

Getting the Binary Distribution

Point your browser to http://www.mysql.com/downloads/mysql-3.23.html. Click the Windows download link.

Next you'll choose a site from which to download; try to pick one at least in the same country as your computer (although I suppose you could try downloading it from Chile, if that kind of thing appeals to you).

Save the ZIP file to somewhere you can find it; the My Documents folder or the desktop generally work best.

Unpacking the MySQL Distribution

When the file is finished downloading, open it from the directory where it was saved and extract the zip file to a temporary directory, such as C:\TEMP\MYSQL.

Running the MySQL Installer

If you unpacked to C:\TEMP\MYSQL, you'll find a file called SETUP.EXE in that directory. Run it. Accept the default options for all the installation questions, including installing it into C:\MYSQL, and let it install.

Completing the First-Time MySQL Setup

Click Start and type in the following:

```
C:\mysql\bin\winmysqladmin.exe
```

The MySQL admin window comes up briefly and then disappears. On the taskbar, you'll see a stoplight with a little green light on it, indicating that MySQL is running.

Differences Between MySQL Under Windows 95 and 98 and Windows 2000, XP, and NT

Under the Windows 2000, XP, and NT operating systems, MySQL is installed as a service, which means that you do not need to explicitly start it after you boot. Under Windows 95 and 98, you need to run winmysqladmin to start MySQL after each reboot.

Adding MySQL Binaries to the Path

Follow the directions in Appendix A, "Getting and Installing JDK, Ant, and Tomcat," for adding JDK to the path. Choose the appropriate operating system and add **;C:\MYSQL\BIN** to the end of the PATH variable.

Creating a Test Database

Open a command prompt window and type the following (user commands are in bold):

```
C:\Documents and Settings\james>mysqladmin create TestDB

C:\Documents and Settings\james>mysql TestDB
Welcome to the MySQL monitor.  Commands end with ; or \g.
Your MySQL connection id is 5 to server version: 3.23.45-nt

Type 'help;' or '\h' for help. Type '\c' to clear the buffer.

mysql> create table TestTable (
    -> String1  CHAR(40),
    -> String2  CHAR(40));
Query OK, 0 rows affected (0.04 sec)
```

```
mysql> insert into TestTable values ('Foo', 'Bar');
Query OK, 1 row affected (0.00 sec)

mysql> select * from TestTable;
+---------+---------+
| String1 | String2 |
+---------+---------+
| Foo     | Bar     |
+---------+---------+
1 row in set (0.00 sec)

mysql> quit
Bye


C:\Documents and Settings\james>
```

Installing MySQL Under Linux

Installing under Linux is as simple as installing under Windows. The only difference is that you use the Linux RPM package manager instead of an installation binary.

Downloading the Binary Distribution

Point your browser to:

http://www.mysql.com/downloads/mysql-3.23.html.

If you are running a Redhat Linux release or another release that supports the RPM file format, click the each of the five Linux Red Hat RPM download links. Save them to /tmp.

If you are not running a RPM-compatible version of Linux, download the tar.gz file for your hardware architecture to /tmp.

Installing the Linux MySQL Distribution

If you downloaded the RPM version of the distribution, cd to /tmp and, as root, do an rpm --install on each of the files to install them—for example:

```
rpm --install MySQL-client-3.23.45-1.i386.rpm
```

There is no need to make any changes to the path because MySQL is installed into /usr/bin.

The mysql-server RPM installs an entry in /etc/init.d called mysqld to make MySQL start upon booting. Copy this entry into the appropriate rc.d directory.

Start MySQL by issuing this command (as root):

```
/etc/init.d/mysqld start
```

Installing the Linux MySQL Distribution (tar.gz Version)

If you downloaded the tar.gz version, , follow the following procedure:

```
shell> groupadd mysql
shell> useradd -g mysql mysql
shell> cd /usr/local
shell> gunzip < /tmp/mysql-3.23.47-pc-linux-gnu-i686.tar.gz | tar xvf -
shell> ln -s mysql-3.23.47-pc-linux-gnu-i686 mysql
shell> cd mysql
shell> scripts/mysql_install_db
shell> chown -R root  /usr/local/mysql
shell> chown -R mysql /usr/local/mysql/data
shell> chgrp -R mysql /usr/local/mysql
shell> chown -R root /usr/local/mysql/bin
shell> bin/safe_mysqld --user=mysql &
```

Depending on the version of MySQL you downloaded, the string mysql-3.23.47-pc-linux-gnu-i686 may be slightly different. Note that if you want MySQL to start automatically, you'll need to create an init.d entry to run the bin/sage_mysqld binary.

Creating a Test Database

Open a command prompt window and type the following (user commands are in bold):

```
$ mysqladmin create TestDB

$ mysql TestDB
Welcome to the MySQL monitor.  Commands end with ; or \g.
Your MySQL connection id is 5 to server version: 3.23.45-nt

Type 'help;' or '\h' for help. Type '\c' to clear the buffer.

mysql> create table TestTable (
    -> String1  CHAR(40),
    -> String2  CHAR(40));
Query OK, 0 rows affected (0.04 sec)

mysql> insert into TestTable values ('Foo', 'Bar');
Query OK, 1 row affected (0.00 sec)
```

```
mysql> select * from TestTable;
+---------+---------+
| String1 | String2 |
+---------+---------+
| Foo     | Bar     |
+---------+---------+
1 row in set (0.00 sec)

mysql> quit
Bye


$
```

Permissions and Security Under MySQL

First, if this database will hold any sensitive information, you need a password to access the root account. Otherwise, anyone can change and grant permissions on every database and table inside MySQL without a password.

To do this, issue the following commands from the console:

```
mysqladmin -uroot password <password>
```

Here, <password> is the password that you want to assign to the root user.

Access can be controlled on a site, database, or table basis to a combination of specific users, hosts, and users at hosts.

Users are not explicitly created, but are created using grant statements. For example, now that you have a database called TestDB, create a user called DbUser who has permission to read, but not write from the tables in that database. Notice that, with a password in place, you need to enter it to gain access for root.

```
[turner@linux tmp]$ mysql -uroot -p TestDB
Enter password:
Reading table information for completion of table and column names
You can turn off this feature to get a quicker startup with -A

Welcome to the MySQL monitor.  Commands end with ; or \g.
Your MySQL connection id is 542 to server version: 3.23.41

Type 'help;' or '\h' for help. Type '\c' to clear the buffer.
```

These next lines are read as: "Grant select privileges on all tables in the TestDB database to DbUser1 if that user is connecting from the local host and uses the password pw1."

```
mysql> grant select on TestDB.* to DbUser1@localhost identified by 'pw1';
Query OK, 0 rows affected (0.00 sec)
```

The next lines basically say, "Grant insert privileges on the specific table TestTable in the database TestDB to DbUser2 on localhost identified by pw2."

```
mysql> grant insert on TestDB.TestTable to DbUser2@localhost identified by 'pw2'
;
Query OK, 0 rows affected (0.01 sec)
```

The following lines are read as: "Grant insert, update, and select on all database tables in TestDB to DbUser3."

```
mysql> grant insert,update,select on TestDB.* to DbUser3@localhost identified by
 'pw3';
Query OK, 0 rows affected (0.00 sec)
```

Finally, these next lines can be read as: "Grant all privileges on all TestDB tables (including table creations and destruction) to DbRoot.

```
mysql> grant all on TestDB.* to DbRoot@localhost identified by 'pw4';
Query OK, 0 rows affected (0.00 sec)

mysql> quit
Bye
```

Start by testing DbUser1. As expected, the user can read from tables but can't insert into them.

```
[turner@linux tmp]$ mysql -uDbUser1 -p TestDB
Enter password:

Type 'help;' or '\h' for help. Type '\c' to clear the buffer.

mysql> select * from TestTable;
+---------+---------+
| String1 | String2 |
+---------+---------+
| Foo     | Bar     |
+---------+---------+
1 row in set (0.00 sec)

mysql> insert into TestTable values ('Foo1', 'Bar1');
ERROR 1142: insert command denied to user: 'DbUser1@localhost' for table 'Test-
Table'
```

```
mysql> quit
Bye
```

DbUser2 has a unique situation. This user can insert records into one specific table but can't read them back.

```
[turner@linux tmp]$ mysql -uDbUser2 -p TestDB
Enter password:

Type 'help;' or '\h' for help. Type '\c' to clear the buffer.

mysql> insert into TestTable values ('Foo1', 'Bar1');
Query OK, 1 row affected (0.00 sec)
mysql> select * from TestTable;
ERROR 1142: select command denied to user: 'DbUser2@localhost' for table 'Test-
Table'
mysql> quit
Bye
```

DbUser3 has a somewhat more normal existence. This user can read, write, and update any table in the database but can't create a new one.

```
[turner@linux tmp]$ mysql -uDbUser3 -p TestDB
Enter password:

Type 'help;' or '\h' for help. Type '\c' to clear the buffer.

mysql> select * from TestTable;
+---------+---------+
| String1 | String2 |
+---------+---------+
| Foo     | Bar     |
| Foo1    | Bar1    |
+---------+---------+
2 rows in set (0.00 sec)

mysql> insert into TestTable values  ('Foo2', 'Bar2');
Query OK, 1 row affected (0.00 sec)

mysql> create table TestTable2 (
    -> String3 CHAR(50));
ERROR 1142: create command denied to user: 'DbUser3@localhost' for table 'TestTa
ble2'
mysql> quit
Bye
```

Only DbRoot can do everything, but even this user's power is limited to the TestDB database. If DbRoot tried to wield power elsewhere, she'd be turned back.

```
[turner@linux tmp]$ mysql -uDbRoot -p TestDB
Enter password:
Reading table information for completion of table and column names
You can turn off this feature to get a quicker startup with -A

Welcome to the MySQL monitor.  Commands end with ; or \g.
Your MySQL connection id is 546 to server version: 3.23.41

Type 'help;' or '\h' for help. Type '\c' to clear the buffer.

mysql> create table TestTable2 (
    -> String3 CHAR(50));
Query OK, 0 rows affected  (0.00 sec)

mysql> quit
Bye
```

In addition to using the user@localhost format, you can use user@foo.bar.com to allow a user to come in from a specific site (via either JDBC or the mysql client). This is commonly used in two-tier and three-tier application architectures, in which the database server and the applications server are placed on separate physical machines. This is often done because the performance tuning needed to make a database server run efficiently is often not the same as the tuning needed to run a Web server well. This also allows multiple Web servers to be operated against a common database.

Other format variants include these:

- user@"%.bar.com", to allow a user to come in from any machine in the bar.com domain
- user@"%", to allow a user to come in on any machine

It is very important to restrict permissions properly. If you're creating a user who only will use JDBC connections from a specific machine, put that machine restriction in the grant statement.

You can see what privileges a user has by using the show grants command, as shown here:

```
mysql> show grants for DbUser3@localhost;
+------------------------------------------------------------------------------
-----+
```

```
| Grants for DbUser3@localhost
|
+-------------------------------------------------------------------------------
-----+
| GRANT USAGE ON *.* TO 'DbUser3'@'localhost' IDENTIFIED BY PASSWORD
'78a36c1c267f0583' |
| GRANT SELECT, INSERT, UPDATE ON TestDB.* TO 'DbUser3'@'localhost'
|
+-------------------------------------------------------------------------------
-----+
2 rows in set (0.00 sec)
```

USAGE is simply the ability to connect to the database.

Installing JDBC Support for Tomcat

Set your browser to `http://sourceforge.net/projects/mmmysql/` and download the latest version of the MM.MySQL driver to a convenient location (C:\TEMP\mm for Windows, or /tmp for Linux).

Open a command prompt (Windows) or use the command `cd /tmp` (Linux). Run the following command:

```
C:\TEMP\mm>jar xf mm.mysql-2.0.8-you-must-unjar-me.jar
```

This creates a directory called mm.mysql-2.0.8. You'll find a file called mm.mysql-2.0.8-bin.jar inside it. Copy that file to the lib directory underneath your Tomcat install. You've just installed the MySQL driver.

C

A Books for Geeks Quickstart

The previous two appendixes took you through the process of installing the basic JSP and MySQL environment that you will use in any JSP project. This appendix leads you through the process of installing the components that are unique to the example project used in this book.

A note of caution: Many of the packages used are in alpha or beta release, which means that by the time you go to download and install them, files might have been moved or changed. Check the Web site for errata regarding these issues.

Installing the Books for Geeks Example in Windows

1. Follow the instructions in the previous two appendixes to install JDK, Ant, Tomcat, MySQL, and MM.MySQL for your appropriate operating system.

2. Go to `http://jakarta.apache.org/log4j/jakarta-log4j-1.1.3.zip`, open the archive using WinZip, and extract the archive to C:\temp\log4j. Find the dist/lib subdirectory, and copy log4j.jar to C:\JAKARTA-TOMCAT-4.0.1\LIB.

3. Go to http://jakarta.apache.org/builds/jakarta-turbine/archive/turbine.old/2.1b4/, click `tdk-3.0a4.zip`, and open the archive extract to `C:\TEMP`. Copy `velocity-1.2-dev.jar` and `turbine-2.1b4.jar` from the tdk\share\lib subdirectory to `C:\JAKARTA-TOMCAT-4.0.1\LIB`. Be sure that you do not use the later releases because it doesn't have the `turbine-2.1.jar` file in it.

4. Unzip the CARTAPP zip file into `C:\TEMP`.

5. Open an editor in `C:\TEMP\CARTAPP\bfg\build.xml` and change the definition of tomcatdir to `C:\JAKARTA-TOMCAT-4.0.1\`.

6. Do an ant `dist` in the `C:\TEMP\CARTAPP\bfg` directory.

7. Edit the server.xml file in `C:\JAKARTA-TOMCAT-4.0.1\CONF` by adding the following:

```
<!— BFG Context —>
<Context path="/bfg" docBase="bfg" debug="0"
        reloadable="true">
  <Environment name="maxExemptions" type="java.lang.Integer"
              value="15"/>
  <Parameter name="context.param.name" value="context.param.value"
              override="false"/>
  <Resource name="mail/session" auth="CONTAINER"
            type="javax.mail.Session"/>
  <ResourceParams name="mail/session">
    <parameter>
      <name>mail.smtp.host</name>
      <value>192.168.1.1</value>
    </parameter>
  </ResourceParams>
</Context>
```

8. Change `192.168.1.1` to your SMTP mail server.

9. Stop Tomcat if it's running, and restart it.

10. cd to C:\TEMP\SQL\BFG.

11. Run `DATABASE_CREATE.BAT`.

12. Set your browser to `http://localhost:8080/bfg/jsp`, and you should see the application running. If not, make sure that the basic Tomcat installation is working according to the instructions given in Appendix A, "Getting and Installing JDK, Ant, and Tomcat."

Installing the Books for Geeks Example in Linux

1. Follow the instructions in the previous two appendixes to install JDK, Ant, Tomcat, MySQL, and MM.MySQL for your appropriate operating system.

2. Go to `http://jakarta.apache.org/log4j/jakarta-log4j-1.1.3.zip`, open the archive using WinZip, and extract the archive to /tmp/log4j. Find the dist/lib subdirectory, and copy log4j.jar to /var/tomcat4/lib.

3. Go to `http://jakarta.apache.org/builds/jakarta-turbine/alpha/3.0a4/`, click `tdk-3.0a4.zip`, and open the archive extract to `/tmp`. Copy `velocity-1.2-dev.jar` and `turbine-2.1.jar` from the `share/lib` subdirectory to `/var/tomcat4/lib`. Be sure that you do not use the 3.0a5 release because it doesn't have the turbine-2.1.jar file in it.

4. Unzip the CARTAPP zip file into `/tmp`.

5. Open an editor in `/tmp/CARTAPP/bfg/build.xml` and change the definition of tomcatdir to `/var/tomcat4`.

6. Do an `ant dist` in the `/tmp/CARTAPP/bfg` directory.

7. Edit the `server.xml` file in `/var/tomcat4/conf/`, adding the following:

```
<!— BFG Context —>
<Context path="/bfg" docBase="bfg" debug="0"
         reloadable="true">
  <Environment name="maxExemptions" type="java.lang.Integer"
             value="15"/>
  <Parameter name="context.param.name" value="context.param.value"
             override="false"/>
  <Resource name="mail/session" auth="CONTAINER"
            type="javax.mail.Session"/>
  <ResourceParams name="mail/session">
    <parameter>
      <name>mail.smtp.host</name>
      <value>192.168.1.1</value>
    </parameter>
  </ResourceParams>
</Context>
```

8. Change `192.168.1.1` to your SMTP mail server.

9. Stop Tomcat, if it's running, and restart it (enter the command `/etc/init.d/tomcat4 stop`, wait 30 seconds, and then enter `/etc/init.d/tomcat4 start` as root.)

10. cd to `/tmp/CARTAPP/sql/bfg`.

11. Run `database_create.sh`. If you've set a root password (which you should have) for MySQL, you'll have to type it several times.

12. Set your browser to `http://localhost:8180/bfg/jsp`, and you should see the application running. If not, check to make sure that Tomcat is running properly by going to the base Tomcat index page.

Symbols

A

K-L

Other Related Titles

JMX: Managing J2EE with Java Management Extensions
Juha Lindfors, Marc Fleury, the JBoss Group
0-672-32288-9
$39.99 US

Jini and JavaSpaces Application Development
Robert Flenner
0-672-32258-7
$49.99 US

Wireless Java Programming with Java 2 Micro Edition
Yu Feng, Dr. Jun Zhu
0-672-32135-1
$49.99 US

Developing Java Servlets, Second Edition
James Goodwill
0-672-32107-6
$39.99 US

Java 2 Micro Edition Application Development
Stefan Haustein, Michael Kroll
0-672-32095-9
$49.99 US

EJB: Rapid Enterprise Development
Peter Thaggard
0-672-32178-5
$49.99 US

Java Connector Architecture: Building Custom Connectors and Adaptors
Atul Apte
0-672-32310-9
$49.99 US

JXTA: Java P2P Programming
Daniel Brookshier, N. Borwanker
0-672-32366-4
$39.99 US

Java Web Services Unleashed
Robert Brunner
0-672-32363-X
$49.99 US

JBoss Administration and Development
Scott Stark, Marc Fleury, the JBoss Group
0-672-32347-8
$49.99 US

Java Deployment (JNLP, WebStart, J2EE, J2SE)
Mauro Marinilli
0-672-32182-3
$39.99 US

SAMS
www.samspublishing.com

All prices are subject to change.